ID0849967

Coal and tobacco

Whitehaven in 1642 (above) and in 1738 (below)

'The South East Prospect of Whitehaven in the Year 1642' (detail) is reproduced by courtesy of Carlisle Library. 'The East Prospect of the Town and Harbour of Whitehaven', taken from an engraving by Richard Parr, based on Matthias Read's 'Bird's Eye View of Whitehaven, 1738', is reproduced by courtesy of Whitehaven Museum.

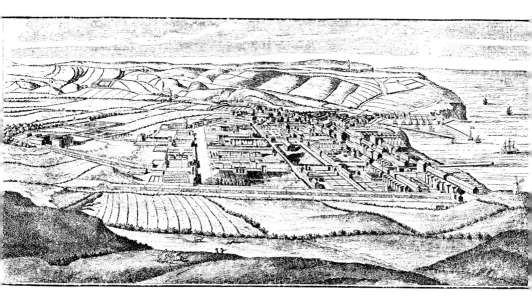

COAL AND TOBACCO

The Lowthers and the Economic Development
of West Cumberland, 1660–1760

J. V. BECKETT

Lecturer in History, University of Nottingham

CAMBRIDGE UNIVERSITY PRESS

Cambridge
London   New York   New Rochelle
Melbourne   Sydney

Published by the Press Syndicate of the University of Cambridge
The Pitt Building, Trumpington Street, Cambridge CB2 1RP
32 East 57th Street, New York, NY 10022, USA
296 Beaconsfield Parade, Middle Park, Melbourne 3206, Australia

First published 1981

Printed in Great Britain by The Anchor Press Ltd
and bound by Wm Brendon & Son Ltd
both of Tiptree, Essex

British Library Cataloguing in Publication Data
Beckett, J V
    Coal and tobacco.
    1. Cumbria, Eng. – Industries – History
    2. Lowther family
    I. Title
    338'.0092'2 HC257.C/ 80–40785

ISBN 0 521 23486 7

TO MY
MOTHER AND FATHER

Contents

Tables

Illustrations

Note on Dates

All dates prior to 2 Sept 1752 are in the Old (Julian) Style, except that the new year is taken to start on 1 January. From 14 September 1752 dates are in the New (Gregorian) Style.

Preface

West Cumberland today is primarily renowned for its nuclear plant at Windscale. Once, however, the ports of Whitehaven and Workington were centres of trade and commerce on a par with Liverpool, Bristol and Glasgow. Coal, the eighteenth-century equivalent of twentieth-century oil, was mined at various points along the Cumberland coastline. Much of it was sent to Ireland, and the prosperity engendered by the trade enabled west Cumberland to thrive. Whitehaven enjoyed a short-lived but lucrative tobacco trade, and the confidence that this inspired led to the planning of new industries and trade routes. But as this book will attempt to show, the region remained overdependent upon its coal industry; too many of the plans never got off the drawing board, and the local economy failed to change sufficiently to accommodate rapid development. Consequently the period covered by this book was one of considerable, but unsustained prosperity for the region.

If coal made economic development possible, one family was supremely responsible for turning potential into reality: the Lowthers. Indeed, this book is largely a study of two men, Sir John Lowther (1642–1706), and his son Sir James (1673–1755), and the area that they did so much to develop in the seventeenth and eighteenth centuries. Their papers are voluminous, yet their careers have never been studied in any detail. I shall hope to repair this omission, but not within the conventional biographical mould. Jointly their active lives spanned the period during which Cumbria, and particularly the west coast area, underwent a rapid rise in economic importance. During the later years of his life, Sir James Lowther came to dominate west Cumberland as few men dominated a comparable area of England under the first two Hanoverians.

Less central to the book, but significant in itself, is the suggestion of an alternative interpretation of Whitehaven's economic history to that provided forty years ago by Percy Ford. In an article entitled 'Tobacco and Coal: A Note on the Economic History of White-haven', *Economica*, ix (1929), Ford argued that 'the early develop-ment of its coal mining industry and trade had been financed in part from the profits of the import and export of tobacco' (p. 192). This book will attempt to show that such a view is untenable. The two trades were almost entirely separate, and merchant capital was only ploughed back into industry – and new industries at that, rather than coal – from the later 1740s. The present book also builds upon, and in places corrects, J. E. Williams' article, 'Whitehaven in the Eighteenth Century', *Economic History Review*, 2nd series, viii (1956). Williams only partly amended Ford's argument. Here the suggestion will be advanced that coal was the staple from which most other developments grew. Tobacco may have been a lucrative adjunct for a number of years, but coal provided the economic foundation upon which the region was built.

This book has been several years in the writing. It began during the two years that I spent as Lord Adams Research Fellow in the University of Newcastle upon Tyne (1974–76), and I should like to thank the trustees of that post whose generous sponsorship enabled me to undertake the majority of the research. It has been completed alongside teaching posts at Wroxton College (the British campus of Fairleigh Dickinson University, New Jersey, U.S.A.) and the Universities of Hull and Nottingham. I should like to thank the Earl of Lonsdale, Lord Crawford of Balcarres, R. F. Dickinson Esq. and Mr and Mrs O. R. Bagot, who made the book possible by allowing me to consult their family papers, the University of Michigan Press for permission to print the table on p. 107, and the Mary Fair fund for a generous grant towards the expenses of publication.

In preparing *Coal and Tobacco* I have sustained many debts to friends and colleagues, and I should like to take this opportunity of thanking them for giving of their time to advise and help me. Although it is invidious to single out individuals, it would be less than grateful were I not to mention several people who have been particularly helpful. Amongst the many archivists and librarians from whose knowledge I have benefited are Mrs Anna Rossiter and Mr Jeremy Godwin of Carlisle Record Office, Mr R. E. Wilkinson and Miss M. Brander of Carlisle Library, and Dr Nicholas Cox of the Public Record Office. Individuals that I should like to thank for help with specific points include Dr Colin Brooks, Professor L. M. Cullen, Dr E. Cruikshanks, Dr P. G. M. Dickson, Mrs A. Eaglesham, Dr E. J. Evans, Mr D. Hay, the late Mr D. S. Hepburn, Professor G. S. Holmes, Mr C. R. Hudleston, Dr C. P. Macgregor, Dr C. B. Phillips, Mr G. Simmons, Dr W. A. Speck and Dr O. Wood. Finally, some special debts of gratitude: to Bruce Jones, for his unfailing help in guiding me through the Lowther papers in Carlisle Record Office; to Dr David Smith, for his advice and help with the statistical analysis; to Dr Joan Thirsk and my former colleague Donald Woodward, for reading and critically commenting on various drafts of the manuscript; and to my wife, for her patience and understanding as this book has taken shape. The faults that remain are my own.

Beeston
Nottingham
December 1979

Introduction

Cumbria today consists of the historic counties of Cumberland and Westmorland, together with the north Lancashire districts of Furness and Cartmel, an area of some one and a half million acres in all. It is a natural region, although this has only been recognized for administrative purposes since the 1974 local government reorganization. At its heart is the central mass of the Lakeland hills, while its limits are defined by the Scottish border to the north, the western slopes of the Pennines to the east, Morecambe Bay to the south and the Irish sea to the west. The Eden valley, running south-east from Carlisle, and the Solway and west Cumberland plains are the most fertile areas, while the lowland part of the Furness peninsula is suitable for stock-rearing. Various minerals have been found in the region: lead and copper in the Pennine hills, copper around Keswick and the Langdales, iron in the south-west of the region, and coal along the west coast.

Before the hills and lakes of Cumbria became a tourist attraction at the end of the eighteenth century, the region had always been isolated from the rest of the country. Traditionally Scottish travellers took the eastern route through England, to avoid both the terrain and the people. Celia Fiennes shuddered in 1698 at 'those inaccessible high rocky barren hills which hangs [sic] over ones head in some places and appear very terrible'. Defoe considered Westmorland 'eminent only for being the wildest, most barren and frightful of any that I have passed over in England, or even in Wales itself'. The 1695 edition of *Camden's Britannia* described the eastern part of the region as 'a lean, hungry, desolate sort of country'.[1] It was wild countryside; the sheriff of Northumberland armed Lord Keeper Guilford and his entourage with 'a dagger, knife, pen-knife and fork' when they set out from Newcastle for Carlisle in the later seventeenth century.[2] Border raiding and conflict with the Scots only came to an end in

I

1745. Overall, Sir Edward Seymour was probably reflecting the views of many of his contemporaries when he told local landowner James Grahme in 1700 that 'a worser country for people and travellers I never met withal'.[3]

When Seymour passed through Cumbria it was sparsely populated; something like 95,000 people lived in Cumberland and Westmorland, or, to put it another way, some 2 per cent of the national population occupied 5 per cent of the country's total acreage. Apart from the growing west Cumberland port of Whitehaven, only three towns were of any note: Carlisle, the county town of Cumberland, with between 2000 and 3000 inhabitants; Kendal with around 2000; and Penrith, 1350. A century later, at the first census of 1801, the two counties had a combined population of 158,000, an overall increase of 66 per cent. As with other areas, the rate of growth was approximately twice as fast in the second half of the century as in the first. Cumberland's overall increase had been the more rapid: roughly 80 per cent by contrast with Westmorland's 36 per cent.* The rates reflected differences in the occupational structures of the two counties. Westmorland in 1801 was still predominantly agricultural, with only four towns of over 1000 inhabitants. In Cumberland, by contrast, extensive mining, new industries and trading connexions, had brought urban growth. Six towns had more than 3000 inhabitants.[4]

Industrial and commercial change was undoubtedly the most striking feature of Cumbrian development in the later seventeenth and eighteenth centuries, the most significant features being coal mining along the west coast (with a related trade to Ireland), iron mining in Furness, and the establishment of trading links with America and the Baltic. Iron and coal had been worked in Cumbria as early as the twelfth and thirteenth centuries. Systematic mineral workings only began, however, in the mid-sixteenth century when the Mines Royal Company worked copper in Newlands, Borrowdale, Caldbeck and Grasmere. Today's Lakeland tourists would be hard pressed to imagine Keswick as an industrial centre, and the beautiful Newlands valley scarred with copper workings, but this activity brought a certain amount of prosperity to the region. In 1574, for

---

* These figures make the data presented in P. Deane and W. A. Cole, *British Economic Growth, 1688–1959*, 2nd edn (Cambridge, 1967), p. 103, seem intrinsically unlikely. Their suggestion of a 10 per cent decline in the two counties between 1701 and 1751 was obtained by using a base figure of 135,000 for 1701. Local evidence indicates that this is too high.

example, wages were paid, and other payments made to 360 local people. Even though the Keswick enterprise did not outlast Elizabeth's reign, its success acted as a stimulant to other industrial concerns. Iron had been produced in Furness during the first half of the sixteenth century, but bloomsmithies were outlawed in 1564, presumably in an attempt to ensure that charcoal would be available for the Mines Royal. After the Mines Royal Company departed, iron forges were established, at Cunsey by 1623, and at Ulpha a couple of years later.[5] Systematic coal mining began in the sixteenth century around Parton and Workington on the west coast. Both the coal and iron industries grew rapidly in the course of the seventeenth century.

Before taking a detailed look at these developments in the century or so after 1660, a cautionary note needs to be sounded. The regional economy as a whole was not transformed. Even if some of the less than flattering descriptions of contemporaries and historians can be ignored, many aspects of the Cumbrian economy remained unchanged. Agricultural improvement, for example, came late, and new techniques were only slowly adopted.

The pattern of landownership in the later seventeenth and eighteenth centuries was characterized by a drift of property towards the region's more prosperous owners. A solid core of gentry families fashioned and directed society. They acted as the effective organs of local government, although only two or three of them would have ranked with the greater gentry elsewhere in England. Generally they were substantial neither in numbers nor wealth. Cumbria, as one traveller noted in 1710, was a region 'depopulated of gentry'. As late as 1754 one of the wealthiest could comment that 'the gentlemen in general have very inconsiderable [estates]'.[6] Eight, or possibly nine, gentry families spent in excess of £10,000 on property in the period 1680–1750, of whom five had a significant interest from non-landed sources. These included an East India nabob and a family of Appleby lawyers. Perhaps the most significant feature of the land market was the role of the Lowthers. The four branches of the family in the region (including the viscounts Lonsdale) spent £142,000 on property during the same period. When the accidents of birth and inheritance brought the estates into the hands of one man, Sir James Lowther of Lowther (created Earl of Lonsdale 1783) in 1756, he was reputed to be one of the wealthiest men in England.

The few peers who owned estates in Cumbria were generally absentee, limiting their local interests to rent collection and borough politics. As a group they sold land to the value of some £85,000 between 1680 and 1750, whilst purchasing only about £70,000 worth. Of this latter sum, £46,000 was spent by the Lonsdales, the region's one indigenous peerage family.[7]

As for the smaller landowners, known locally as yeomen, their position was rather different from that of their contemporaries elsewhere in England. The decline of the lesser owners, so much a feature of the century after 1688 in southern and midland counties, occurred largely post-1815 in the north-west.[8] Travellers and commentators have left a rather one-sided view of this group. Wordsworth was particularly guilty. He painted a romanticized picture of Cumbria, describing a static society characterized by its hardy statesmen who lived close to poverty on land which had 'for more than five hundred years been possessed by men of their name and blood'. Not too much store should be set by this picture, which was uncritically accepted by Macaulay in the nineteenth century and Trevelyan in the twentieth.[9] It ignores what amounted to considerable mobility among the lesser owners. On the Earl of Carlisle's estate in north-east Cumberland, for example, of the 745 fines assessed at the twenty-five manor courts for which records survive between 1727 and 1750, 293 (40 per cent) were purchase fines, an average of nearly twelve at each court.[10] Furthermore, the yeomen were not quite as poor as Wordsworth and others implied. In national terms Cumberland and Westmorland had long been regarded as impoverished; for the purposes of taxation they had been given special rating in 1389, and generations of vigilant MPs had maintained this situation. Evidence for the later seventeenth and eighteenth centuries, however, indicates an increase in prosperity Inventory evidence from Kendal deanery (admittedly one of the wealthiest areas of the region) suggests a rise in yeoman prosperity between the later seventeenth century and the second quarter of the eighteenth.[11] This may explain why so many new schools were opened in the region between 1660 and 1800; 44 in Cumberland and 28 in Westmorland. As a result, the region had a relatively high literacy rate.[12] Quite why the position of the Cumbrian yeomanry should have been different from that of their southern contemporaries is not clear, but it may have been related to the structure of agriculture and the availability of industrial by-employment.

Throughout the eighteenth century most Cumbrians maintained themselves by subsistence agriculture, thereby ensuring that mixed husbandry prevailed in the region. Arable crops were mostly oats and bigg (an inferior variety of barley), which were cultivated for animal and domestic consumption. Wheat and rye are only occasionally found in inventory lists. Cattle were the lynchpin of the economy, with greater and lesser owners alike involved in breeding and rearing. The value of cattle recorded in yeoman inventories was consistently greater than that of sheep. Many local landowners benefited from the Scottish droving trade. Cattle were driven into Cumbria between June and December, sold to local farmers for winter fattening, and then re-sold to graziers further south in the spring. Fairs were held throughout the region, both in small villages such as Orton and Shap, and larger centres including Carlisle, Penrith and Kendal. By the later eighteenth century 10,000 Scottish cattle were sold annually at the September fair held in the village of Brough, a few miles west of Carlisle. The prosperity of the trade may have been linked to the long fall in grain prices between the mid-seventeenth and the mid-eighteenth centuries. This trend, which was reflected in rising per capita real incomes, almost certainly brought about an increase in the consumption of meat and dairy products.[13]

By contrast, the eighteenth century was not a period of great prosperity for sheep rearing since wool prices followed a generally downward trend. This may be one reason for the distinctly secondary place of sheep in the Cumbrian economy. Inventory evidence shows that yeoman flocks rarely exceeded 200, with a later seventeenth-century average of around 50 for both highland and lowland farmers. The larger flocks seem to have been concentrated in southern Lakeland, particularly around Kendal, the main woollen town of the region.

The prosperity of the cattle trade, the continuing hold of customary tenure which ensured that farms remained small, and the inhospitable landscape and climate – inimical to both investment and experiment – combined to delay the introduction of improved husbandry. Nonetheless changes did come; indeed, the potato was introduced in the mid-seventeenth century, rather earlier than elsewhere. Many of the new agricultural practices were pioneered in the region during the 1730s and 1740s by John Nowell, steward of the Earl of Carlisle's rather bleak territory between Carlisle and the

Northumberland border. Nowell introduced progressive leases on the estate, increased the size of farms, and cultivated new root crops on the earl's home farm. Despite Nowell's success, only isolated examples can be found of improvements taking place elsewhere in the region. Little consistent effort was made to enclose or to use lease covenants to improve farming, and the almost universal condemnation of local practices by commentators at the end of the eighteenth century suggests that progress had not been rapid; indeed, it is clear that turnips and artificial grasses, which have often been taken as a sign of progress, were cultivated in only a few of the west Cumberland parishes by the 1790s.[14]

The yeomanry not only benefited from the cattle trade, they were also well situated to capitalize upon the opportunities for by-employment. Cumbria, with its many customaryhold tenants in a pastoral economy, had the type of background favourable to the development of countryside industries.[15] Cloth was woven in all the valleys radiating from Kendal, while in 1686 it was reported from west Cumberland that 'the country is already in the practice of making linen, sacking, coarse woollens, stockings and hats'.[16] 'Yeomen' doubled as blacksmiths, carpenters and tanners; they developed interests in salt panning and shipping, and some in west Cumberland even combined working at the coal-face with farming.[17]

Whatever the relative importance of the cattle trade and by-employments in ensuring continued prosperity, especially among the lesser landowners of the region, it was heavy industry which was the driving force behind economic change. Wordsworth's view of Cumbria, outdated in 1700, was totally misleading by the later eighteenth century. By then, far from being untouched by the gathering momentum of industrial development, parts of the region had been in the van of progress. The introduction of blast furnaces in 1711 gave the Furness iron industry a massive boost, and the area remained one of the principal English charcoal-iron producing centres thereafter. This industry has been described elsewhere, however,[18] and attention here must, perforce, be focussed on the rapid economic development of the west coast region.

Coal mining, linked to a ready-made and expanding market in Ireland, provided the base from which flowed all the other developments in west Cumberland. Exports of coal to Ireland began early in the seventeenth century, and the relationship which developed between Dublin and west Cumberland was remarkably similar, on a smaller scale, to that between London and Tyneside. Demand for coal in London stimulated the north-eastern coal industry in terms of a multiplier effect of secondary and tertiary employment.[19] The pull of the Dublin market performed a similar function in west Cumberland. Opportunities arose from promoting industries which used coal as their fuel (i.e. coal-fuel), such as salt panning, glass making and ore smelting. Whitehaven's geographical position facilitated the development of new trading links. Enterprising ships' masters recognized the profits to be made from trading across the Atlantic rather than simply pursuing the not very profitable coal trade. Some of them turned merchants, and played a vital role in promoting Whitehaven as a tobacco entrepôt. By the 1740s the link with America was threatening to undermine the coal trade. On a less substantial scale, trading connexions were established with the West Indies and the Baltic. Vessels outward bound for the colonies required an export cargo. Sir John Lowther, owner of Whitehaven, made efforts to establish textile manufactures in his new town to meet this demand, while the expansion of the Cumbrian cloth centres in the eighteenth century can perhaps be explained, in part, by such needs. Kendal's population had reached 8000 by 1801, Penrith's 3800 and Carlisle's 10,000.[20] However, much of the cargo was acquired outside the region. Certainly the coastal towns benefited from the industrial and commercial activity. Whitehaven's population increased seven-fold in the seventy-eight years after 1685, while Workington also showed a considerable increase. Furthermore, the tobacco trade had secondary effects. Newly rich merchants turned their wealth into industrial developments and landownership. They became leading figures during the 1740s in ironworks, glassworks, ropewalks, shipbuilding and other activities. Their search for small estates pushed up the price of land in west Cumberland at a time when coal-bearing property near to the west coast was in considerable demand. The resulting price inflation amazed Sir James Lowther. He suggested in 1753 that 'people are mad to give such prices for small parcels of land as they do in Cumberland, they don't give such prices near London, where those that are in the funds want to lay out millions they have there in landed estates'.[21] Once they owned land, the merchants sought a voice in local affairs, some becoming JPs and land tax commissioners, as well as serving in the office of sheriff.

Yet the prosperity generated by the 1740s was short-lived; the second half of the eighteenth century saw the west Cumberland economy grow at a slower pace, with the momentum built up before 1750 tailing off. Many of the developments proved to be superficial. Perhaps most importantly much of the tobacco trade was lost to Glasgow during the 1750s and was never regained. As a result, the merchants' capital resources ran dry; they could not sustain the level of enterprise upon which they had embarked in the heady years of the 1740s, when Whitehaven stood second only to London in the quantity of its tobacco imports. When, for example, Peter How, one of the town's leading merchants, failed in 1763, the casualties of his bankruptcy included a snuffery and an iron forge. Two other merchants had helped him promote the latter.

The superficiality of the developments was also clear from the failure to attract labour to the area. A steady trickle rather than a stream of migrants found their way to west Cumberland. Notably lacking amongst them, however, were the vigorous and entrepreneurially-minded skilled workers who were often crucial for long term development. Whereas, for example, Sheffield's ironmasters usually emerged from the ranks of the secondary metalworkers, and in the west Midlands the greater ironmasters evolved from lesser status, this was not the case in west Cumberland.[22] The craftsmen and middle-rank merchants who became the rising entrepreneurs elsewhere were deterred both by the region's physical isolation and the lack of investment capital. The local gentry simply did not have the resources to invest, and the merchants were only able to do so for a few years.

All of this took place under the watchful eye of the Lowthers, the dominant entrepreneurial family. The economic and social history of west Cumberland in the seventeenth and eighteenth centuries is inextricably interwoven with the history of the Lowthers; to write about the one without the other would be misleading, since they played a part, either major or minor, in more or less every development. They were model eighteenth-century landowning-entrepreneurs, typical of a *genre* which made such an important contribution to early economic growth through their prominence in mining, townbuilding and transport improvement. Sir John Lowther kept every possible iron in the fire, even to the extent of burning his fingers on occasion. His own son was critical of his diffusion of interests; 'his great mistake', according to Sir James writing in 1746, 'was that he would join in any expense to encourage anything but collieries'.[23] For his own part, he was determined to keep his interests to coal mining, although he found himself drawn into new industrial ventures including salt panning, glass manufacture, and, indirectly, the Baltic and colonial trades. As a colliery entrepreneur he was a considerable success, and he also proved to be adept in other roles. When a shipping crisis during the 1730s threatened his hard work in cultivating the Irish market, he helped to plug the gap by acquiring shares in vessels. He used his influence in London to promote his own business affairs, and to aid those of the merchants. His seat in Parliament provided the means of promoting legislation designed to help the north-west, such as harbour and turnpike improvement bills, and of opposing measures likely to be damaging to west Cumberland's interests.

Lowther's active life brought him the personal satisfaction of great wealth and considerable political influence in his native county. Friends and enemies alike were prepared to admit that Lowther, and his father before him, were west Cumberland's most important entrepreneurs. Walter Lutwidge, a local merchant, and a hostile witness by the time he wrote in the 1740s, accepted that in west Cumberland Sir James Lowther was 'without flattery . . . the centre of motion'. In other letters Lutwidge referred to Lowther as 'our great man', thereby consciously imitating the popular epithet for Sir Robert Walpole to describe the relationship between Lowther and the area. In 1751, William Brown, the Tyneside colliery viewer, told Carlisle Spedding, Lowther's Whitehaven colliery steward, that he found 'a secret satisfaction in hearing of the welfare of Sir James who without dispute has been the great instrument of the present flourishing condition of Whitehaven and places adjacent'.[24]

A study of the Lowthers is, in effect, an investigation of their interaction with the local economy. Rapid expansion of the coal industry during the second half of the seventeenth century can be dated from Sir John Lowther's coming of age in 1663; a further acceleration of the pace was linked with Sir James Lowther's decision to widen his horizons in west Cumberland from the early 1720s. An understanding of the interaction is vital for an appreciation of the expansion during the later seventeenth and early eighteenth centuries, and the retardation which followed. Thus, whilst the present book is primarily a study of the entrepreneurial role pioneered by Sir John Lowther and brought to fruition by his son, and whilst each

chapter is basically concerned with the Lowthers' role in developments, the economy of the region is studied to provide a firm frame-
work within which to examine the role of its most important entrepreneurial family. In so doing, the crucial importance of coal, and
the rather less vital role of tobacco, except for a few years in the
1740s, will become apparent.

This approach helps to overcome some of the drawbacks posed by
having to take most of the material from the Lowther papers.
Membership of Parliament (father and son sat in the House of
Commons for most of the period 1664–1755), and London residence,
were not only important for the roles that the Lowthers could play
in advancing west Cumberland's development, but also for the
correspondence generated by their absence. Events in Cumbria can
be pieced together from papers surviving in the family archive,
which has been relatively inaccessible until recent times. However,
the fullness of these papers raises certain methodological problems,
because no substantial body of material has survived for any of the
other entrepreneurs or merchants involved in the region's transformation. After all, the Lowthers were not alone, even if they towered
above their fellows in the scale of enterprise and the size of profits.
Among the coal-owning landowners the Curwen, Christian and
Senhouse families were closely connected with the developments of
these years, while tobacco merchants such as Walter Lutwidge,
Peter How and William Hicks, became significant figures in various
aspects of the region's economic development. Only a few papers
survive for these families, most notably a couple of letter books of
Walter Lutwidge. Even with the customs records these hardly add
up to an effective counterweight to the great bulk of material provided by the major source. Some chapters of this book have had to
be written almost entirely from the Lowther papers; indeed, the
chronological structure is partially determined by the quality of the
records during the lifetimes of Sir John and Sir James Lowther.
Obviously this raises the danger of exaggeration and distortion. No
one would question the Lowthers' prominence in west Cumberland's
development, but it is easy to overemphasize their already central
position because more is known about them than anyone else.* In
addition, the nature of the evidence drawn from their papers may

* Similar problems are found in other regions. See, for example, Barrie Trinder's remarks
  on the hazards of a comparative study of the Shropshire entrepreneurs in *The Industrial
  Revolution in Shropshire* (Chichester, 1973), pp. 196–7.

itself be misleading. To take an example, a good deal of information is provided by the regular correspondence passing between the Lowthers in London and their stewards in Whitehaven. However, it is known that major policy decisions were often postponed until they visited Whitehaven. As a result, it is possible to underestimate the significance of some events, or even to omit them altogether, simply because they receive little or no attention in the correspondence. To complicate the situation, it is known that the steward was deliberately misled on occasion, and consequently transmitted information to London which turned out to be incorrect. The historian can be equally misled when he has only one major archival source. These difficulties have to be recognized from the outset, although they are not insurmountable.

Whatever the shortcomings of the evidence, the important role of the Lowthers will emerge in the chapters of this book. The extent of their success was remarkable. Even beginning with capital backing from an established landed family, the progress which they had made by the 1660s was not sufficient for Sir John Lowther to have any real advantages over the other west Cumberland landowners with coal resources on their estates. Yet by the 1720s potential rivals had been left far behind, and Sir James Lowther was able to make a bid to monopolize the region's coal trade. How such a situation arose, why Sir James failed to capitalize upon his position to the full, and what the reactions were to his efforts in the region, form the background questions to this study.

The Lowthers: Landowning-Entrepreneurs

The landowning-entrepreneur was a vital cog in the machinery of economic development. From the sixteenth century landowners can be found promoting new agricultural products and taking advantage of the growing demand for coal. Indeed, arguably their most important contribution to industrial development came before the main thrust of the industrial revolution, in the form of mineral exploitation. After all, they owned the resources, and they were more likely than any other section of the population to have the capital required for mining. By the later seventeenth century their influence was on the wane. Some landed men continued to operate mining concerns into the nineteenth century, but the majority had pulled out by then, happy to collect the income from a safe lease rather than risk further investment. The gentry of south-west Lancashire, for example, began their retreat in the 1730s, and had virtually abandoned the local coalfield to outside capital by 1800.[1] For some of those owners who chose to remain, mining was merely an appendage, albeit an expensive one, to their estate affairs. But for the west Cumberland entrepreneurs, the Lowthers in particular, it was quite the opposite. Ostensibly the Lowthers were country gentlemen, absentee owners who left their large estate, mansion and home farm, in the care of a land steward for nine months of each year while they looked after the county's business in Parliament. In fact, this was a façade concealing a well-oiled business machine in which agricultural affairs played a distinctly secondary role to the chief enterprise, colliery development. By contrast with those landowners whose fortunes suffered irreparable damage through dabbling in mining ventures, the Lowthers, with single-minded determination, geared their estate management and finances to the task of accumulating a colliery fortune. Such was their success that by 1750 some three-quarters of their Cumberland revenue came from the collieries.

Such a situation would have been difficult to predict when the

Lowthers first set foot in west Cumberland early in the 1630s. The family had been established in north Westmorland for several centuries, but Sir John Lowther of Lowther's purchase of the manor of St Bees in 1630 was almost certainly a speculative venture designed to acquire coal-bearing land which he and his successors could exploit. This former monastic property, which included the tiny hamlet of Whitehaven, is situated on a jutting promontory just at the point where the Cumberland coastline reaches its furthest point west. Lowther paid £2450 for the manor, and shortly afterwards he settled Christopher (1611–44), his second son, at St Bees. When Sir John died in 1637 he bequeathed him the property.[2]

The choice of Christopher Lowther to manage the newly acquired estate was by no means fortuitous. Brought up to trade, Christopher had established a variety of contacts with Ireland, contacts which were to prove extremely valuable to him when he started mining coal, and manufacturing salt for sale in Ireland. Lowther's fortunes looked even brighter when he acquired an estate in north Westmorland through his marriage to Frances, heiress of Christopher Lancaster of Sockbridge, and his social status improved when he was raised to a baronetcy in 1642. Such rapid progress was brought to an untimely end when he died in 1644, at the early age of 33. His wife had predeceased him, and John, his only son and heir, was a one year old minor.[3]

Little is known about the twenty years which followed, but once Sir John Lowther came of age in 1663 he took up his father's mantle with gusto. Not content to watch his Cumberland interests evolve gradually, he began, almost immediately, to develop them along systematic and rigorous lines. He was determined to exploit the coal resources of his estate, to conquer the nascent Irish market, and to build a new community around the small hamlet of Whitehaven. He was responsible over the years that followed for having Whitehaven created a separate port, laying out a new town to a carefully conceived plan, and promoting new industries and trade routes to supplement the staple link with Ireland.

James Lowther carried on, after Sir John's death in 1706, where his father had left off. A younger son, he was already pursuing a successful career in government service when Sir John decided to disinherit Christopher, his spendthrift, alcoholic, eldest son.*[4] Like

* Christopher inherited the baronetcy. He died without issue in 1731, when the title reverted to James.

his brother, James had been educated at Oxford and the Inns of Court; like his father he sat in Parliament. Sir John represented Cumberland from 1664 until 1700; James sat for Carlisle, 1694–1702, Cumberland, 1708–22, 1727–55, and Appleby, 1723–27. With only a six year gap during the first decade of the eighteenth century, and a few months after James was ousted in the 1722 Cumberland election, father and son sat in Parliament for a span of ninety-one years. For the last six of his years in the Commons, Sir James was the longest-serving member of either house.

As Parliamentarians the Lowthers were, in essence, backbenchers (although Sir John was a commissioner in the Admiralty between 1689 and 1694, and Sir James held Ordnance posts between 1696 and 1708).[5] Their main reason for being in Parliament was to further the interests of Cumbria. As Sir James put it in 1746, 'I abhor the thoughts of being so long in Parliament if it was not necessary to serve the poor county where my estate is.'[6] Representation in Parliament was important to many early industrialists,[7] and Lowther's decision to abandon his Ordnance career in 1708 and return to the lower house, was a recognition of this need. It gave him the base from which to support or oppose national legislation likely to have local repercussions, and in addition to sponsor bills specifically relating to Cumbrian affairs. The drawbacks to not being in Parliament became apparent in 1706 when an act was passed to facilitate the establishment of a harbour at Parton, a mile north of Whitehaven. The Lowthers opposed this on the grounds that it was a threat to the prosperity of Whitehaven, but since neither of them was in the house, and Thomas Lamplugh, the bill's sponsor, was then sitting for Cockermouth, they could do little to prevent its passing.

Political acumen was one characteristic shared by father and son; another very important one was a commercial orientation. Sir John Lowther described himself as 'a man of business, with an estate not to be improved and preserved without pains and care'.[8] He successfully passed this ethic on to his son who, as early as 1691, was helping with estate business and by 1700 was regarded as 'an equal assistant'.[9] It was in everyone's interest, according to Sir James Lowther, to be 'punctual and fair dealing' in business; he would 'rather have less concerns regularly carried on than greater matters in confusion'.[10] John Stevenson, a distant cousin and a close business associate during the 1740s, described how Lowther had 'no opinion of anyone that is not punctual in business, a head not turned to it and that do not look strictly and principally into their own affairs'.[11] Such attitudes did not necessarily imply personal control of all that went on. Sir John developed his Cumbrian interests with only infrequent visits to Whitehaven, and his son could see no reason to depart from his example. By the time his elder brother was disinherited, James had already begun to establish business contacts, and was successfully pursuing a career in government service. Thus, as he told his father in 1705, 'I must acknowledge that my own inclination to a life of business in London will in all likelihood occasion my living there for the most part.'[12]

Of course not everyone appreciated the Lowthers' business acumen and claims to fair dealing. Walter Lutwidge was particularly scathing, during the 1740s, about what he regarded as Sir James Lowther's unscrupulous business methods. He believed that Lowther 'thought he could do what he would with me when he had got me into his debt', and complained that 'it would be endless to set forth the injuries I have received from Sir James and his myrmidons, and all because I wont go on giving up my children's bread'. Later still he referred to Lowther as 'an inhuman tyrant'.[13]

Behind this commercial outlook lay a puritanical thriftiness encompassing a belief that they were promoting the interests of west Cumberland not simply to glorify the family name, but also for the general good of the region. Sir James, for example, referred to his father on several occasions as 'a public spirited man'. Sir John Lowther saw his landpurchasing policy as being for 'the general benefit of the whole country [sic]'. Whilst agreeing with the sentiment, Sir James also recognized that 'the malice of the world will say that you did it for the improvement of your estate, though the better sort know at the same time, the great advantage that country [sic] and the revenue reap through it'. Later in life he emphasized the same theme; ''tis a grievous spirit', he wrote in 1743, 'there is in mankind, to be against anybodys laying things together though it is for the benefit of the public as well as the particular family'.[14] In particular, this public concern was expressed in the Lowthers' attitude towards the employment of the poor. Sir James even sponsored a bill in the House of Commons in 1726, 'to hinder the poor people from being starved by people that harass and oppress them'.[15] In 1752 he wrote of how he would 'rejoice at anything going forward in any part of the country [sic] to employ the poor and labouring people'.[16] Such an attitude reflected the views of sixteenth-and seventeenth-century 'projectors', for whom concern about the poor acted as a motive for cultivating new crops and establishing manufactures. Of course, this was only part of the story; the extent of the Lowthers' industrial activities took them into a very different world to that of the woad-growing Sir Anthony Cope in Elizabeth I's reign, even if they shared common philanthropic aims with him.[17]

Parsimony was a characteristic more noticeable of Sir James Lowther than of his father. Sir John was careful rather than overtly mean with money, but he encouraged economy in his son by allowing him £25 a quarter at college: 'the less he spent the more I gave him towards the next'. Thereafter James Lowther became excessively concerned to avoid ostentation and wealth. He developed strong views on luxury and extravagance, writing in 1734, for example, of how, in spite of the country being overburdened with taxes, 'the courtiers are so amazingly profuse in their clothes, equipage, entertainments etc as gives a dismal prospect'.[18] Five years later Sir John Clerk, the Scottish coal owner from Penicuik, found Lowther living in Whitehaven 'in the midst of great riches . . . but in a poor way'.[19] In London, Lowther lived for many years in the Inns of Court, buying his own town house only in 1727. Various descriptions emphasize his meanness. In 1710, Sir Christopher Musgrave, a Westmorland landowner and local MP, could see no reason for the people of Cumberland to owe much allegiance to Lowther, he 'having so great an estate and doing so little good with it'. John Stevenson claimed in the 1740s that Lowther loved money more than anything else, while Walter Lutwidge described him in 1748 as 'a covetous man'. Other stories are less plausible, such as the account of his returning to St George's coffeehouse in London, 'to acquaint the woman who kept it that she had given him a bad halfpenny' having earlier in the day paid her twopence for a dish of coffee.[20]

The Lowthers believed in charitable giving, although Sir James seems to have been rather more adept at theorizing than practising his own preaching. He wrote two 'Advices'[21] on the subject, but only occasionally dispensed charity in Whitehaven, even at times of considerable distress in the town.[22] His various interests in London hospitals (including governorships of St Thomas', St Bartholomew's, St George's, the Foundling Hospital and the London Infirmary) were not matched by appropriate financial contributions.[23] John

Wesley, in a letter to Lowther following a conversation which took place in September 1754, noted 'that you have given some hundreds of pounds to the hospitals, and wish it had been ten thousand'. The letter went on to contrast the financial strings to which Sir James was attached with the irrelevance of riches in the afterlife. 'I fear you are covetous', wrote Wesley, 'that you love the world. And if you do, as sure as the Word of God is true, you are not in a state of salvation. . . . Oh Sir, I beseech you . . . examine yourself, whether you do not love money.'[24] Evidently Lowther concluded that he did not, since the will that he had made a month earlier was not altered.

Finally, this picture of the Lowthers as single-minded, thrifty businessmen with a strong social conscience can be substantiated from a long description of Sir James written in 1742 by John Stevenson. It is worth quoting at length as the only contemporary account of his character which we have:

I think there is nothing (except money) he is more desirous of possessing than the respect, dependence and almost adoration of his friends and relations; and to have it insinuated with seriousness his riches, power and abilities, and the want of such people in their country. He will seem modestly to reject such opinion of him, but no man was ever fonder of hearing it now and then, and will endeavour himself to lead people into the confession of it, and almost always repeating his own wise conduct of his life and affairs and conducting that of others. . . . He loves to talk and to be heard and full of repetitions to have his actions and undertakings applauded, and that they should all be thought to lend to the good of his country, yet these encomiums should be used with moderation and brevity, for he will quickly take the lead himself.[25]

A similar word picture of Sir John Lowther might have described a more modest man, but if Sir James was self-satisfied there can be no doubt that he had at least some justification. By the later years of his life he had the largest rental income of the Cumbrian gentry; his mines were the most productive and profitable on the west coast; he was a successful businessman and financier; a Fellow of the Royal Society; an active member of the Society for the Promotion of Christian Knowledge; and a long-standing member of Parliament with an interest in several seats. When in Cumberland he was automatically elected foreman of the Grand Jury. He had even cheated death, surviving a leg amputation in 1750 at the age of 77.[26] His summer visits to Whitehaven had become occasions of considerable significance. According to the abstract of a letter Lowther wrote in 1734 to Henry Newman, secretary of the SPCK, he was met on the high road by the high sheriff, chief gentlemen, clergymen and principal freeholders living for about thirty miles in length in that part of the country, who accompanied him (to Whitehaven) where he was received by thousands in the high streets, the bells ringing, the great guns firing and the ships putting out their colours.[27]

Admittedly this was an election year, but even allowing for some exaggeration this must have been something of an occasion. Rumours circulated in 1751 that he would receive a peerage. The death of the senior member of the Lowther family, the third viscount Lonsdale, without issue, left it without a title. Many people regarded it as unthinkable that such a wealthy family should remain for long without a peerage, and felt that Lowther should be elevated to the House of Lords. Nonetheless, he claimed to have given no encouragement to such speculation, and no title was forthcoming.[28] He was rather less complacent at being overlooked for Lonsdale's positions of lord-lieutenant and *custos rotulorum* of Cumberland and Westmorland. He was only offered Westmorland, which he turned down in disgust.[29] As early as 1731 he was 'reckoned the richest commoner in England', according to Sir John Clerk, and at his death in 1755 the *Gentleman's Magazine* extended his supposed supremacy to the whole of Great Britain. Even if its estimate that he was 'worth above a million' was probably too high[30] (see appendix 2), he had provided the foundations of the enormous wealth enjoyed by Sir James Lowther of Lowther in the second half of the eighteenth century.

The Lowthers' landed estate was centred on Flatt Hall, their chief seat, which lay about a mile inland from Whitehaven. With the manor of St Bees as their starting point, Sir John and Sir James Lowther spent more than £60,000 acquiring property in Cumbria. By 1701 Sir John had put together an estate of some 5300 acres,[31] but no later surveys exist from which to measure the growth in terms of physical size. In addition to the acquisitions shown in table 1.1, Sir James leased several parcels of land near to Whitehaven, and during the 1740s spent more than £30,000 purchasing the manor of Laleham (and adjoining properties), which straddled the Thames some sixteen miles west of London.

If these purchases are closely analysed the importance of colliery affairs becomes apparent. The Westmorland properties were bought

Table 1.1. *The Lowthers' property purchases in Cumbria, 1660–1755.*

	Number of purchases	Cost £
Sir John Lowther		
Properties proximate to Whitehaven	61	11,426
Properties in Westmorland	15	715
	76	12,141
Sir James Lowther		
Properties proximate to Whitehaven	64	34,432
Properties proximate to Workington and Maryport	13	12,023
Cockermouth burgages	25	2,864
Lease of Seaton colliery	1	1,000
	103	50,319
Total	179	£62,460

Source: See appendix 3.

by Sir John Lowther to consolidate the estate inherited through his father's marriage, while the burgages were Sir James' indulgence, purchased as part of his push to establish a political interest in the parliamentary borough of Cockermouth. These, together with the isolated acquisition at Workington in 1751, had little bearing on the central estate policy. For the rest, however, the pattern is clear; the Lowthers sought to establish a consolidated holding of property first around Whitehaven, and later at Ribton, east of Maryport.

It was by no means unusual for landowners to concentrate on consolidating their property holdings, but for the Lowthers, colliery considerations made such a policy vital. When they cast their eyes upon a tract of land, the questions that they asked concerned the coal beneath it and the mining rights, rather than its potential for agricultural improvement and enclosure. As Sir John put it, 'land alone, remote from trade and manufacture, is a very indifferent business'.[32] Mining on a large scale required a consolidated area of land. Originally mines were drained through soughs driven from the side of a hill, with the water running away along channels. Although the introduction of steam engines in the eighteenth century was a considerable improvement, an owner still needed a large area of land to ensure that he did not have to sink more shafts than were absolutely necessary. It simply was not economic to mine in a small area. The Lowthers were well aware of this; both father and son stressed on a number of occasions the need to 'lay things together',[33] by acquiring manors (which gave them the right to mine under all but the independent freehold properties), and by buying out, wherever possible, the remaining freeholders. Hensingham, the manor immediately east of St Bees, was acquired in the 1690s, and Moresby and Distington, to the north, in 1737. Nearly half of Sir John's purchases, and at least eighteen of Sir James', were of parcels of land near to Whitehaven, all costing less than £100 each. The pattern was similar at Ribton where Sir James bought the manor, together with the neighbouring manor of Dearham, in 1722.

Technological deficiency generally ensured that eighteenth-century mining expanded laterally. Sir John Lowther began mining in a small area of Whitehaven previously exploited during his father's lifetime. In 1666 he was keen to acquire 'all the lands lying near this town' within a one mile radius. By the 1680s his interest had spread to the adjoining manors, as a result of which he widened the radius to four miles in 1688 and to five miles two years later.[34] Although it was not until the 1730s that the Lowthers bought Moresby and Distington, the success of their accumulation policy can be measured from a comment in the 1690s. By then Sir John had 'almost all the valuable collieries in Moresby . . . and has got an absolute command over most of the remaining collieries, it being in his power to open and shut them at his pleasure'. In Distington he had obtained 'the largest interest and has so interwoven himself with the rest that whenever they come to be wrought they likewise must needs fall under his government'.[35] Sir James Lowther continued this policy of pushing out into the adjoining manors. He purchased all of Thomas Lamplugh's colliery interests in Distington in 1714 for £2400, and eleven years later bought out Richard Sanderson, the last remaining substantial freeholder in Moresby. From the later 1720s his expanding mining interests forced him to look even further inland: Weddicar and Stockhow, to the east and south-east of Whitehaven respectively, were purchased in 1726; Scalegill, also to the south-east, in 1730; Wreah, between Weddicar and Hensingham, in 1732; a large estate at Corkickle, just south of Whitehaven, in 1734; Moorside Park in Arlecdon, east of Whitehaven, in 1739; and, finally, Frizington demesne, to the east beyond

Hensingham, in 1750. These purchases, together with the manors of Moresby and Distington and a number of smaller consolidatory acquisitions, cost Lowther over £21,000, and gave him a considerable area of land around the town (figure 1.1).

Such an expansion policy had to be vigorously pursued if it was to be successful. The estate stewards were ordered to make meticulous inspections of any property the Lowthers considered buying, especially in regard to the vendor's title.[36] High prices had to be paid. Sir John Lowther decided in the 1690s that he would have to pay over the odds rather than take the risk of being outbid for property he required for consolidation purposes. 'As for the purchase of Bransty', he told Thomas Tickell, the estate steward, 'though extreme dear I would have you conclude.'[37] Such a policy was hazardous; those with property to sell raised their asking price, producing a vicious circle which it was hard to break. Consequently, while Sir James, like his father, wanted to pay 'reasonable' or 'middling' prices, he found himself drawn on to pay more than he intended. John Spedding, his steward from the 1720s, found it 'amazing' in 1742 'what extravagant prices are given for land sold in this neighbourhood by public cant, forty years purchase is reckoned cheap'. A decade later Lowther believed that higher prices were paid for small parcels of land in west Cumberland than near London.[38]

High prices were one means of inducing local freeholders to part with their property; tactical manoeuvres, ranging from the dubious to the downright dishonest, were others. One expedient was to foreclose mortgages. Sir John Lowther learnt in 1688 that small properties were not easy to acquire, 'but that mortgages may be had, which is a good hint . . . and I am ready to proceed'. Two years later his steward was told that 'you must get up all arrears of rent and all money lent upon bond where it is not in order to a purchase'.[39] Sir James Lowther employed similar techniques, acquiring Stockhow in 1726 and Frizington in 1750 through mortgage foreclosures.[40] A second tactic was to have the steward decry the value of any land particularly coveted by the Lowthers, and play up that of any for which they had no special concern. Thus, in 1723, Sir James informed John Spedding that he was to emphasize in Whitehaven the deplorable state of the coal trade, since this might enable him to 'buy all collieries at reasonable prices'. Two years later Spedding was informed that because 'there can be no thoughts of buying

1.1 Sir James Lowther's major properties around Whitehaven

ground at Parton to any advantage', it was time to talk 'of the high value of it there'.[41] A third technique was to try to secure government patronage in return for a concessionary price. Spedding wrote in 1742 that 'in the disposal of tidewaiters' places I shall consider how far it may have influence in getting in such lands as are convenient for you to buy'. The following year Lowther told his steward that 'if Williamson makes things easy about his estate . . . I will try and get him into the salt office or customs'. John Stamper offered Lowther a property in 1747 'for £1000 and to get him a tidewaiter's place, or for £1200 without the place'.[42] A fourth tactic was to play upon people's weaknesses. In 1740, for example, Spedding found that Attorney Williamson 'wanted money to support a son he has at Oxford, so that I thought it a fit time to attack him, and think . . . got it cheaper than I expected'.[43] Finally, blatant dishonesty was not ruled out. The St Bees School Court of 1742 granted Lowther a lease of royalties in the school lands for 867 years at a rent of £3 10s per annum. Even Spedding had previously thought only in terms of a 31 or 99 year lease, while a commentator of 1824 believed that it ought to have been for a much shorter term and at a rent of £120 or £140 a year. Indeed, the lease was voided in 1827, and the then tenant, the Earl of Lonsdale, ordered to pay compensation. So how did Lowther obtain the lease? Only three governors, including Spedding, attended the 1742 court. Since this was not a quorum, after the meeting Thomas Lutwidge, a Whitehaven merchant, was induced by Lowther to sign 'a note prior to the date of my lease that he agrees to the lease'.[44] Lutwidge was indebted to Lowther at the time.

The corollary to this vigorous purchasing and leasing policy was a desire to dispose of outlying properties of no use for mining purposes. Sir James Lowther informed his steward in 1707 that 'I shall be willing enough to sell parcels of land that lie scattered and are not valuable for anything else but the rent, when I can sell them dear'.[45] He was particularly anxious to dispose of the Westmorland estate, and used it from time to time as a bargaining counter with other landowners. He hoped to exchange it with John Brougham during the 1720s. Brougham purchased the manors of Moresby and Distington in 1722 (at a time when Lowther believed that it would prejudice a legal case in which he was involved if he was to be the purchaser), but his main estates were in Westmorland. Lowther hoped that he might entice Brougham to part with the west coast manors in return for a concessionary price on the Westmorland estate.[46] In the end nothing came of the scheme, and Lowther never disposed of the property.

The Lowthers' policy of estate expansion was clearly defined and positively pursued, yet it may be argued that consolidation in this way was practised by many landowners, with or without mining interests. The importance of colliery affairs comes out more clearly when attention is focussed on how the estate was run. Management was geared towards exploiting the collieries in such a way that the Lowthers (and here Sir James was particularly culpable) begrudged repairing tenants' property, although they spent money improving Flatt Hall. Improved husbandry was practised on the home farm, but no attempt was made to encourage the tenants to use more productive techniques. Finally, land was leased out in small parcels rather than being consolidated by engrossing or enclosure.

An eighteenth-century landowner had a wide variety of tasks above and beyond deciding whether to add to his property or to sell land: he had to look after his home farm and gardens; find tenants to whom he might lease land; ensure that they paid rent and fines punctually and adhered to lease covenants; and, finally, meet estate outgoings, hire and pay labour. On a small estate one man might be able to undertake all of these tasks, but as the property expanded, so it would become necessary to employ help. When, as in the Lowthers' case, the situation was compounded by non-residency, personal control was impossible, and substitutes were required in the form of stewards. It was necessary, as Sir John Lowther expressed it, to devolve 'all great charges . . . upon well chosen servants'.[47] The hundreds of long letters which, in consequence, passed between London and Whitehaven, are a mine from which the historian can quarry information about how the estate was organized and run.

The estate steward had control of all affairs in Whitehaven. His duties included collecting rents, drawing up leases, allocating plots of land to new arrivals in Whitehaven, setting the price of coal, acting as chief election agent, and substituting for the Lowthers in Whitehaven during the winter months. It is a measure of the importance placed on mining that experience in the post of colliery steward was normally regarded as a necessary stepping-stone to the top position. Thus John Gale was understandably annoyed when he was passed over for estate steward following Thomas Tickell's death in 1692.

After ten years in charge of the collieries he might reasonably have expected promotion. He and William Gilpin, the man appointed, were never on good terms because of Gale's ill-feeling. John Spedding and James Spedding both graduated through the hierarchy, as table 1.2 reveals.

Table 1.2. *Estate and colliery stewards.*

Estate stewards	Colliery stewards
Thomas Tickell 1666–92	John Gale 1682–1707
William Gilpin 1693–1722	John Spedding 1707–30
Richard Gilpin ⎫ 1722–30	Carlisle Spedding 1730–55
John Spedding ⎭	James Spedding 1755–58
John Spedding 1730–58	
James Spedding (estate and colliery) 1758–78	

The division of responsibility between Whitehaven and London was determined not only by the communications difficulties, but also the trust that the Lowthers were prepared to place in the particular steward. Overall responsibility remained with the Lowthers, while day-to-day decisions were taken by the steward. As Sir James Lowther put it, in a succinct statement of the position in 1728,

I shall expect that all things that can be done in my absence be regularly carried on that I may have more time to look into those things when I am in the country which require my immediate inspection and particular direction.[48]

Decisions for which the steward felt himself unable to take full responsibility were either referred to London by letter, or deferred until the Lowthers were in Whitehaven. Sir John Lowther was only infrequently in the town. He visited in 1681 (when he moved into Flatt Hall from his previous residential seat in Westmorland), 1682, 1685 and 1687, but thereafter not until his retirement in 1698. He then resided permanently in the town until his death in 1706. Sir James Lowther made bi-annual visits between 1706 and 1726, and annual trips north thereafter, except for a handful of years when ill-health detained him in London. Infrequent visits could badly affect estate matters. Spedding reminded Sir James in 1744, when he was considering missing the summer visit for a second successive year, that it would be 'a great hindrance to your affairs here which it is impossible to carry on with the same success as if you were here'.[49]

The steward was asked to take a number of minor decisions on estate and colliery affairs in addition to offering advice when major decisions were necessary. Sir John Lowther left Thomas Tickell to set the rents of houses in Corkickle 'as you think fit' in 1680, and eight years later to buy or lease Castlerigg tenement 'as you judge most convenient for me'. Fearing the loss of a possible land purchase while letters were in the post, Lowther told Tickell in 1691 to 'give some earnest, or draw articles if I approve, or in small things of £200 or £300 in value, if in Moresby or Hensingham, you may contract absolutely if you cannot gain time to acquaint me'.[50] Sir James developed a similar rapport with his stewards. In 1731 he admitted to John Spedding that 'you know my mind so fully about Seaton and other collieries and purchases that I have little to add'. Just as the steward might refer a problem to London for adjudication, so he might be asked for an opinion regarding a major decision simply because of his residence on the spot. In 1707, for example, Sir James Lowther sent instructions to William Gilpin about future mining policy, but added that 'I mention nothing wherein I would not be glad to be set right if I mistake'.[51]

Finally, the Lowthers put absenteeism to good use by acting as London agents to their own business interests. Sir John Lowther contracted to buy Harras Park, part of St Bees, from his London base in 1681, while Sir James found his residence in the capital to be convenient for concluding the purchase of Moresby and Distington in 1737. In addition, Sir James negotiated for mining equipment, including Newcomen engines, and assiduously supplied his stewards with information about technological breakthroughs which he thought might be employed to advantage at Whitehaven.[52]

Mutual trust between employer and employee was vital in an absentee situation. Frequent correspondence and regular summer visits minimized the risks to absentee landowners faced with leaving their estates in the hands of paid servants, but many eighteenth-century stewards could not resist the temptation to indulge in embezzlement and sharp practice. The development of a double entry book-keeping system in this period may have been a direct response to the problems of venal stewards.[53] The Lowthers were fortunate in their choice of servants as the absence of turnover shown in table 1.2 suggests, although even they had occasional cause for concern. John

Gale's dismissal as colliery steward in 1707 followed allegations of corruption,[54] and the joint responsibility of John Spedding and Richard Gilpin during the 1720s was an uneasy alliance which ended with Gilpin's being driven out by the greater efficiency of Spedding. Generally, however, the Lowthers were able to rely upon their employees, and to place considerable trust in them.

The Gilpins and Speddings are notable for their long tenure of office on the Lowther estate. William Gilpin, a local attorney with a small estate of his own a few miles east of Carlisle, was a man of substance who was expected to carry weight in Whitehaven because of his standing as a country gentleman. Richard, his son, was not of the same calibre, and was dismissed in 1730 for incompetence.[55] In effect, from William Gilpin's retirement in 1722 until 1778, members of the Spedding family were in overall control of the estate. John and Carlisle Spedding were the first and fourth sons of Edward Spedding, one of Sir John Lowther's Westmorland tenants who migrated to west Cumberland in the 1680s. Lowther obtained for him a position in the customhouse. Despite this, Spedding left goods and money totalling only £17 when he died in 1706.[56] From 1700, when John Spedding was first taken on at Whitehaven as a fifteen year old domestic servant, the great attraction of the brothers was their loyalty. 'The improvement of your estate', John Spedding was to tell Sir James Lowther many years later, 'has been the chief concern of my life.' It was an added bonus that Carlisle Spedding, employed in 1710 when plans fell through for him to follow his other two brothers to sea, proved to be one of the most brilliant mining engineers of the eighteenth century. Lowther grew to trust the Speddings; indeed, John Stevenson told John Spedding in 1750 that Lowther had frequently made 'no less than an open declaration . . . of his thankfulness to God for having met with you'.[57]

In part, such trust was cultivated; a sensible landowner protected the interests of his stewards as a means of increasing their dependency. The Lowthers obtained sinecure customs positions and encouraged the private business interests of their stewards. Family contacts were also important: Richard Gilpin was employed in succession to his father; John Spedding's son James worked with Lowther in London for a couple of years during the 1730s; Carlisle Spedding's eldest son, James, succeeded him as colliery steward, while his second son, Thomas, was financed through Trinity College, Dublin. After taking Holy Orders Thomas was presented to a living of which Lowther had the patronage.[58] For their part, the Spedding brothers invited Lowther to stand as godfather to their sons, whom they seem to have named with some forethought; both had sons with the christian name of James, while John Spedding's second son was called Lowther.

Such a close relationship between employer and employee had considerable repercussions for estate affairs. The Lowthers used their stewards as frontmen, buffers between themselves and the local people of Whitehaven. Sir John Lowther instituted the policy with Tickell in the 1680s, and carried it on through the personal authority of Gilpin. This technique reached its apogee in the Spedding brothers, especially John Spedding. Sir James Lowther sent specific instructions to Whitehaven regarding the brothers' dealings with others. Thus, when in the 1720s he considered the possibility of leasing collieries in Ayrshire, the brothers were told that as a means of making Lowther's intentions clear, they should offer their houses for sale as if in preparation for moving to Scotland. It became impossible to consult Lowther without John Spedding being informed. Walter Lutwidge commented in 1747 that 'I know his usefulness to you and that I may as well remove Skiddaw* as remove him out of your favour.' For his part, Lowther was prepared to admit that the confidence he placed in Spedding made it 'notorious in the country that you are my agent in everything'. Not surprisingly, Spedding made many enemies. He referred in 1724 to the 'sort of people I have daily to deal with and how pleased many of them would be to vent their utmost fury upon me'. Lutwidge was doubtless not alone in hoping for his demise; 'if he should trip off', he wrote when Spedding was indisposed in 1748, 'Sir James would be more under his own power'.[59]

Such a situation could make the steward's position appear overpowerful to outsiders. Sir John Clerk of Penicuik visited Whitehaven in 1739, and mistakenly described Lowther as 'an indolent old man [who] knows nothing about coal works but in order to grow rich carried them on by the best advice and seems indeed to be well served'.[60] Had he accepted the proffered invitation to dinner at Flatt, his opinion might have changed; it was only at Lowther's table that local men could bypass Spedding. Thus, Lutwidge, out of favour in 1748 and consequently uninvited, nevertheless found it relevant to

---

* Skiddaw, just north of Keswick in the heart of the Lake District, was thought by many people at that time to be the highest mountain in England. See D. Defoe, *A Tour Through the Whole Island of Great Britain* (1962 edn), ii, p. 274.

find out from others what Lowther was saying of him. He was doubtless relieved to find Sir James was saying 'nothing scurrilous of me
at his table as usual'. Lowther himself kept 'an account of those that
dine with me at Whitehaven which I keep to avoid giving offence
lest I should omit those that are proper to dine with me . . . because
if I should omit to invite any people of note in the town they will take
it ill'. Six or eight people (almost exclusively men) dined with
Lowther on many of the evenings that he was in Whitehaven.
Significantly, merchants, ships' captains and local gentry were the
most frequent guests.[61]

The most positive demonstration of the Lowthers' priorities in estate
matters was in their attitude to the tenantry. No landowner could hide
behind his steward for ever. Innovations and alterations were much
more warmly received by the tenants if they originated with the
owner rather than his paid servant. Careful handling of tenants,
particularly good ones, was essential.[62] Too efficient a steward could
seriously harm his employer's social and political interest. For the
purpose of prestige, and for electoral reasons, owners sometimes
found it expedient to underlet land and retain old tenants of dubious
efficiency. The convention of allowing farms to pass from father to
son, together with the rejection of a rack-renting policy, may have
been inimical to greater efficiency; unlike his steward, however, the
owner had, as his first priority, to balance economics against politics
and expediency.

With their puritanical sense of business efficiency, the Lowthers
could have been expected to take a positive attitude in encouraging
new and improved habits among their tenants. In practice they were
remarkably traditional in their approach to estate matters. Although
they practised the new husbandry techniques on their home farm,
little or no effort was made to encourage the tenants' habits through
restrictive covenants in leases, or to introduce greater efficiency by
enlarging farms. A comparison with their approach to the property
kept 'in hand' brings out the contradictory nature of their attitude
to estate affairs.

Like many landowners the Lowthers were inherently suspicious
of their tenants; indeed, their guiding principle was that tenants 'are
constantly taking all advantages against their landlords'. Sir John
Lowther recognized the value of a good tenant, and tempered strict-
ness with mercy. In 1687, for example, he told Tickell not to put 'R.

Dixon clear off unless there be very good cause, for he will give as much as any, and understands farming very well'. Others were less sympathetically treated, especially when they asked for rent abatements or other financial help. Too severe an approach, however, could simply lead to the tenant taking matters into his own hands.[63] Edward Spedding, father of the stewards, reacted to Lowther's refusal in 1696 to terminate his lease prematurely. Gilpin reported that

he has cut down all the wood, neglects the houses and (that he may do the farm as much mischief as he can) he has taken a piece of ground off Mr Fletcher and sets upon it all the manure that is produced upon yours, and is besides in a great arrear of rent; his design is to force you to turn him off.[64]

If anything, Sir James Lowther was even more determined than his father not to allow tenants to take such liberties. Gilpin was warned to watch for tenants 'endeavouring . . . to run in arrears but you will seize in time'. Many years later Spedding was instructed to 'tell Mr Latus . . . that you cant justify the letting him keep the land any longer when there are so many that will take it as a favour to let them have it and will pay punctually'. As a further means of controlling tenants Lowther favoured short, usually seven to nine year, leases. In 1749 he expressed approval of a lease that Spedding had negotiated 'unless you can get [the prospective tenant] to raise the rent a little or take a shorter lease'.[65]

As to the actual size of farms, the Lowthers' attitude was governed by what they saw as the best interests of the collieries. Many of the miners were part-time, and the Lowthers considered it necessary to provide them with a parcel of land on which they could cultivate a little grain. Some kept horses for use in the collieries, while others had a cow. Consequently Sir John Lowther told Tickell that he 'would not willingly let much to any one man, but have all things near the town parcelled out to gratify many'. Tickell was to 'accommodate every townsman with some parcel of land if possible'.[66] John Spedding advised Sir James Lowther in 1723 that it was 'much in your interest to have colliers take up little pieces of ground for houses and gardens on the sides of the moor about Ribton, Harras and Akebank'. Lowther agreed: 'I shall sell no more of my land but just to fix colliers and leaders with little houses and gardens on the skirts of the moor.' Such a policy brought fragmented holdings, and as Gilpin recognized, made 'improvement impossible'. It ensured that the size of farms near Whitehaven remained small. Significantly, the

1754 estate rental notes only four enclosures, all of properties 'in hand'.[67]

The Lowthers also resented having to make any capital investment in estate buildings. They followed the standard practice in Cumbria of putting property into repair prior to the commencement of a lease, and then expecting the tenant to undertake any necessary repairs other than major structural alterations. As Sir James told Spedding in 1727, he was 'willing to put the house in repair but in all cases shall expect the tenants to do the ordinary repairs during the term'.[68] Occasionally he would let an unrepaired property at a reduced rent if the prospective tenant would agree to undertake the necessary alterations. In 1729, for example, he was unwilling

to let Stockhow mill for rebuilding at 20s a year for twelve years and £7 a year for the residue of 21, but if you think it sufficient I will let it for 40s per annum for the first twelve years and £5 a year for the residue, which is as good for the farmer if he means honestly, but he must be obliged in what manner to build it and to keep it in good repair.[69]

Such practices only worked when plenty of tenants were available. At other times the repairs had to be undertaken, as in 1726 when Spedding agreed a new lease with the tenant of Weddicar, 'only he insists to have a hedge made to divide the high grounds which as he is an industrious man . . . I believe we shall be forced to comply with'.[70]

Finally, the Lowthers generally refrained from interfering with their tenants' husbandry techniques. Sir James, in particular, was certainly acquainted with the new practices. He was 'very glad' when he heard in 1729 that quantities of marl had been found on the west Cumberland estate. Spedding believed that 'such a method of improvement . . . rightly introduced in this country [sic] . . . may be one of the best means of making corn and hay more plentiful amongst us'. By the 1740s Lowther also had the example of his Middlesex estate. He told Spedding in 1746 of the 'very fine wheat, barley, clover and other grass' at Laleham, and three years later again noted the 'very fine corn and clover grass'. Such evidence made him scornful of Cumberland's 'poor yeomen', who toiled 'for a little sorry oats and bigg'.[71] Yet he made no attempt to adjust the terms of leases as a means of persuading his own tenants to make better use of their farms.

The Lowthers' main concern was that a tenant could not plough out the heart of the land, and then terminate the lease prematurely. Covenants designed to provide such a safeguard were inserted in leases, and the wording varied little over time. The earliest surviving lease, from 1686, invoked the tenant not to plough more than one-third of the land, and to lime and manure what he ploughed. The standard covenant in Sir James Lowther's day bound the tenant

not to plough above one-third in any one year and no part above three years together, and those succeeding each other, and then to lie fallow six years, to manure what is ploughed, to keep down the whins, to spend the vestures &c, leave the manure at the end of the term.

Normally the tenant was expected to follow a (or 'the') course of good husbandry, or 'a regular course of husbandry'. The use of lime was usually stipulated in Sir John's leases, but not invariably in his son's.[72] Indeed, from some of his comments, Sir James was apparently not fully apprized of the covenants in his leases. Robert Maxwell, the Scottish agriculturalist, inspected the estate in 1750. He made various suggestions about lease covenants, but these were ignored when Frizington Hall and demesne were let to Daniel Stephenson the following year, on a forty-one year term. Stephenson was only enjoined to follow the course of good husbandry, to till, manure and manage the lands.[73]

An interesting comparison can be drawn between these hostile attitudes to the tenantry and outdated husbandry clauses, and the approach to property in hand. The same rules on spending did not apply to Flatt Hall (now called Whitehaven castle). Sir John Lowther purchased the site, together with the old house that stood there, for £1000 in 1675. Before moving in six years later he designed and built a new south-west wing, an addition which led local antiquarian Thomas Denton to describe the house in 1688 as 'a stately new pile of building lately erected'. Sir John was again his own architect when a new south-east wing was added in 1698. Work began in April, before he set out from London, so that 'I may the better direct the finishing part'. These renovations, completed in June 1699, cost £396. A further £461 was spent in 1702 and 1703 repairing the wall surrounding the Hall. Sir James Lowther was not interested in building a great mansion for himself, although he instigated a number of improvements. Almost all of these took place between 1718 and 1729. Overall expenditure of £2249 is recorded between 1699 and 1729, although the accounts may not be complete.[74]

Surrounding the Hall were gardens. Sir John Lowther had a new orchard laid out in 1688, for which he sent fruit trees from London, and a second garden in 1696. Sir James Lowther showed less personal interest in the gardens, although he gave strict instructions that the fruit trees were to be properly tended and replaced if necessary. His main contribution came in the form of a nursery aquarium which was laid out in 1731 and 1732. This was stocked with carp and tench personally chosen by Lowther, and a further pond was dug in 1733. Lowther's letters to Spedding often included specific instructions relating to their upkeep, although whether they were intended as a commercial fish farm or simply for recreation is not clear.[75]

White Park, adjoining the gardens to the north of Flatt, was the Lowthers' home farm. It was first used as such when Sir John Lowther retired to Whitehaven in 1698, but some of the activities were discontinued in 1709 since it was clear that Sir James would not be a frequent visitor to the town. The Park was again being used as a home farm in the 1740s. Spedding reported in 1747 that workmen were 'improving the wet meadows by trenching and scouring the Pow [a stream which ran through Whitehaven] which may be of great advantage to be brought to bear'. Robert Maxwell was asked to give advice in 1750, and his report included recommendations about the use of root crops and drainage. Lowther paid no heed to the comments relating to lease covenants, although some of Maxwell's ideas were put into practice at White Park. Twenty-eight pounds of Dutch white clover seed was bought for the Park in Dublin in 1747, and a similar amount in 1752. Turnips were sold in 1750. In addition, cattle were reared on the farm both before 1709 and again in the 1740s. The Lowthers took advantage of the droving trade to provide winter pasture for Scottish cattle.[76]

If a suitable tenant could not be found for a farm, it was taken in hand temporarily, usually to be stocked with cattle. Richard Lamplugh had been grazing sheep on Ribton demesne when Sir James Lowther bought it in 1722. Neither he nor his steward had any experience of sheep, and discussions revealed that such activities were likely to be less profitable than cattle. Since legal difficulties prevented the property being leased until 1724, Lowther purchased cattle for rearing in the meantime. A chronic grain shortage developed in west Cumberland by the 1740s, which encouraged the use of unproductive land. Lowther commented in 1748 that 'it is a matter of great consequence to have all the hay ground that can be contrived near Whitehaven'. Rather than leave the land as grass he enclosed four small properties, for which a tenant could not be found, 'for hay'.[77]

The Lowthers' landed income grew with the expansion of their holdings, as table 1.3 illustrates. No obvious explanation exists for the variations in this list, except that much of the increase was accounted for by property acquisitions. The jump in 1738, for example, followed the purchase of the manors of Moresby and Distington the previous year. Rent increases must also have played a part. A few

Table 1.3. *Rental figures for the Lowther estate, 1686–1754.**

Year	Rental £	Year	Rental £	Year	Rental £
1686	679	1732	1,170	1741	2,965
1687	728	1733	1,743	1742	2,983
1690	809	1734	1,938	1743	2,786
1693	821	1735	2,072	1744	2,830
1728	1,502	1736	2,139	1751	3,455
1730	1,032	1737	2,282	1754	3,320
1731	1,797	1738	2,603		

* These figures include fines charged on change of tenant (on customaryhold property) although these were never very substantial; average revenue derived from them amounted to only £32 a year between 1738 and 1754. They were certainly not sufficient to explain the variations in these figures.

Source: Carlisle Record Office, D/Lons/W Rentals.

comments may be made about the rental. The 1690s was a decade of bad harvests nationally (including four successive failures between 1695 and 1698). This pattern was reflected in west Cumberland. Gilpin reported to Sir John Lowther that the St Bees tenants 'are become generally poor, insomuch that for want of stocks their lands grow out of tillage, and (besides the hazard of farmers breaking) I find it will be difficult to keep up the former rents'. Four successive harvest failures were again recorded between 1708 and 1711. Only a few leases came up for renewal, but in one or two cases the rent was reduced. From the later 1720s a gradual upward trend of rents is discernible, which had become quite marked by the 1740s. Part of St Bees demesne, for example, let at £16 a year in 1731, was re-let in 1740 for £20, while Weddicar demesne was leased for £47 in

1732, £50 in 1741 and £60 in 1750. Such a trend was against the national pattern in the 1730s and 1740s, decades often referred to as a period of agricultural depression. The Cumberland picture may well have reflected increasing prosperity for predominantly pastoral areas. Low grain prices in the southern and midland counties possibly led to increased demand for meat, a demand that Cumberland, with its well-established droving trade, was well placed to try to meet.[78]

Apart from their Cumberland estate, the Lowthers also derived an income from the property they owned in Westmorland and Middlesex. During Sir John Lowther's lifetime the Westmorland income was variously calculated at £190 in 1696, £249 in 1701 and £203 in 1705. The manor of Waitby was sold in 1714, but Sir James Lowther still estimated that his Westmorland estate yielded about £200 a year in 1751. The Laleham rental was £1120 when Lowther first began to receive the rents in 1743. Despite the fact that his consolidatory purchases were reckoned to have added a further £119 to the rental, at the time he died it had fallen to £1059, the effect no doubt of the agricultural depression in the corn counties. By adding together the west Cumberland and Laleham figures, and allowing a further £200 for Westmorland, it is possible to suggest that Lowther received a total rental income of £4580 in the last year of his life.[79]

This income was gross; in order to calculate net income, customary and free rents payable by the Lowthers on property that they held in lease, pensions, taxes, and the cost of repairs to property, have to be deducted. Rents, pensions and annuities averaged £109 a year during Sir John Lowther's lifetime. This figure rose in 1706 because of the £200 annuities which Sir James had to pay to his disinherited brother Christopher and his unmarried sister Jane. It was partially offset by a £63 reduction in rents. The annuities ceased when both Sir Christopher and Jane died in 1731. However, Sir James also had to find £30 for tithes, stipends and salaries of incumbents, together with royalties and salt pan rents which, by the 1750s, amounted to £278 a year. Westmorland and Middlesex outgoings totalled £47.[80] Little evidence survives to support the Lowthers' oft-repeated complaint that they were overtaxed. Sir John Lowther paid £10 land tax in 1705, and four years later his son paid £18, yet these were years in which the tax was regarded by many contemporaries as being at its most burdensome. Even in 1744, when the estate was much larger, Sir James paid only £36 on a four shilling rate, just

1·27 per cent of his rental income. The fact that he made no effort to pass on the burden to his tenants indicates that it was not as onerous as the public utterances suggested. Lowther only paid £1 to the window tax in 1715, but when it was reassessed in 1747 he considered boarding up some of the 123 windows in Flatt Hall. A year later he proposed to the Treasury that it should levy the tax according to the size of windows, but when this was rejected, Spedding was ordered to implement plans for blocking up windows. The Lowthers also claimed to be overassessed to local taxes, although in reality Sir James' burden was not excessive. In 1744 he paid £87 land tax, county, highway and poor rates, just 3 per cent of his Cumberland rental for the year.[81] Ten years later, in the last full year of his life, rents, annuities and taxes amounted to little more than 13 per cent of Lowther's gross Cumberland rental. Allowing for some adjustments to take account of missing evidence, such outgoings on all his estates did not exceed 12 per cent of gross income, a figure which would have been approximately 2 per cent higher had the land tax been levied at four, rather than two, shillings in the pound. This figure does not, of course, take into account the expense of property repairs, which are impossible to calculate from the available data.

No landowner with an income of nearly £5000 a year was likely to ignore the benefits to be derived from his estate; yet, in one sense, the Lowthers treated the land they owned in west Cumberland with scant regard. Their land purchase policy was specifically geared to colliery needs, the agricultural potential being of little concern. It is worth noting that, whereas the Lowthers' estate stewards normally served an apprenticeship as colliery manager, most eighteenth-century published manuals directed to estate stewards included little, and sometimes no, mention of mineral interests.[82] Improved husbandry on the home farm, and extensions to Flatt Hall, contrasted sharply with the small farms, unprogressive lease covenants, and a marked reluctance to sink capital in property repairs. The Lowthers were sufficiently committed to industrial development virtually to ignore the agricultural potential of their property, giving it a distinctly secondary role in the allocation of priorities for improvement. The justification for such a policy lay in successful colliery exploitation; had this proved to be unrewarding, the Lowthers were sufficiently versatile to turn their attention to agricultural improvements. But this was never necessary.

Coal: Monopoly and Competition

Although the exploitation of coal resources in England did not reach significant levels until the Tudor period, the growth of output during the sixteenth and seventeenth centuries was a vital prerequisite for the industrial revolution. Professor Nef went so far as to argue that this growth, at a time of crisis in the timber industry during the century prior to the civil war, amounted to an industrial revolution in itself. Be that as it may – and considerable doubt has been expressed about the figures he employed[1] – coal was certainly used for a number of industrial processes in the seventeenth century. These included lime burning, saltmaking, glassmaking and the preparation of alum (used in leather manufacture and as a mordant in dyeing). However, until the eighteenth century something like two-thirds of all production was for domestic consumption. Greater industrial use was hampered by the lack of an effective means of smelting ferrous metals with coal, and the prohibitive cost of transport. Not until Abraham Darby's discoveries began to be widely adopted in the mid-eighteenth century, and Henry Cort's innovations were introduced during the 1780s, did the problems of the iron industry recede. At the same time, canals solved the transport problems. Until the second half of the eighteenth century coal production was geared to small industries and local domestic consumption, except for areas such as Tyneside and west Cumberland where sea transport could be used.

Water transport was the key to a successful coal industry. Possibly half of all English output was transported by water in the eighteenth century. The phenomenal growth of the Newcastle coal trade was almost entirely dependent upon demand from the south of England: London, which may have consumed as much as one-sixth of all English production, the hinterland of the other east and south coast ports, and an inland trade extending as far as Oxfordshire.[2] West

Cumberland also depended on water transport to sell its coal. Like Tyneside, it had a substantial interest in supplying a capital city – in this case Dublin – and its subsidiary ports. Both regions had to face the hazards which went with such market dependence: the fear of being undercut for price by other coalfields; the periodic depressions which were the bugbear of a single-commodity trade; and the problems of intra-area disputes and competition. The major consideration was always to keep the trade going, whatever the circumstances.

In general terms the west Cumberland coal trade depended for its market on Ireland, and for its output on the Lowthers. Admittedly some coal was exported coastwise, and other owners contributed to the overall picture, but these were the major components. The Irish market was never wholly secure, while the Lowthers' ability to supply was occasionally in doubt. In the early 1720s Sir James Lowther had difficulty keeping his production in line with Irish demand. As a result, he looked to extend his interests to other areas of the coalfield, a decision which had considerable repercussions for the whole coal trade.

The Irish market was critical for the west Cumberland coal industry; indeed, Sir James Lowther sold there more than 90 per cent of the coal raised from his collieries. Variations in the seams have made west Cumberland a high-cost working area, so that the intensive working of the eighteenth century indicates the strength of demand from across the Irish sea. Coal exports to Ireland began in 1605, mainly from Parton where the harbour could accommodate up to sixteen vessels at a time. However, the pier was destroyed in a gale shortly before Sir Christopher Lowther began developing Whitehaven in the 1630s, and by the time it was rebuilt sixty years later the trade had passed to Whitehaven and Workington.[3] By the later years of the seventeenth century the west Cumberland ships' masters had come to dominate the Irish market, but their dependence on this one outlet had inherent problems. No one could predict whether or not Irish demand would continue to expand, and at what rate. It was possible that in time the Irish would be able to supply their own needs. Again, the fear was always present that Cumberland would lose its competitiveness by comparison with other English, Welsh and Scottish coalfields enjoying coastal proximity to Ireland. In fact, these problems did not prove to be serious, although contemporaries could never ignore the potential dangers; in 1750 west

Cumberland still provided some 70 or 80 per cent of the coal sold in Ireland.[4]

Each of these possible problems raised its head from time to time, only to prove ephemeral. Demand from Ireland grew steadily, punctuated by short and sometimes sharp depressions which were naturally worrying to the west Cumberland owners. The rise in demand can be attributed to two factors. One was the extensive exploitation of Ireland's woodlands in the seventeenth century, largely by the agency of English owners.[5] The Irish were forced to look for alternative fuel supplies. Peat was only used inland, so coal was the obvious substitute in Dublin. The other factor was the phenomenal growth of the Irish capital. From a population of around 60,000 in 1700, it expanded to nearly 200,000 a century later. As a result, it became one of the top ten towns in Europe, and the second town in Britain by a large margin.[6]

Economic progress in Ireland was hampered by the absence of raw materials, particularly coal and iron. Coal trials took place in various parts of the country during the seventeenth century. By the early years of the eighteenth century dissatisfaction in Dublin with the importation of coal from England compelled the government to promote mining. The result was a venture at Ballycastle in north Antrim, which met with some success, and Dublin was reported to be glutted with coal from there in 1722. As resources had also been found at Strangford, which was less than a hundred miles by sea from the capital, it was feared in Cumbria that 'the coal trade of Cumberland seems to be threatened with immediate ruin'. Possibly as a result of this success, glassworks were opened in Dublin and Waterford. But Irish hopes proved to be over-optimistic. Although ships continued to carry Ballycastle coal to Dublin for a few years, further efforts to stimulate the industry met with little success. As late as 1749 trials took place near Belfast, but since most of these efforts ended in failure, or with insufficient success to inspire great confidence, the Cumberland trade was never seriously threatened. In the absence of raw materials, coal-fuel industries could not develop, and the rising demand for coal was almost entirely for domestic purposes.[7]

The threat of competition from Pembrokeshire, Flintshire, Lancashire and Ayrshire never proved to be very serious. Flintshire had provided much of Ireland's supply until the early seventeenth century, while Ayrshire threatened to become a serious competitor when a new pier was built at Saltcoats during the 1680s and 1690s. Although the Scottish coal was not particularly popular in Dublin, by the early 1720s the Ayrshire owners were expanding their trade with Ireland rather more rapidly than the Cumbrians. The threat receded because the Scots had difficulty raising capital, but it was sufficiently real in the early 1720s for Sir James Lowther to contemplate buying the lease of Saltcoats colliery, at least partly as a means of negating the competition. In the end, it was not until the second half of the eighteenth century that exports from Swansea, Liverpool and Scotland began to cut into the Cumberland trade, but the fear was always present that other areas might gain more than a toehold in the Irish market should west Cumberland be unable to meet the demand.[8]

The west Cumberland coalfield is a small one by comparison with the other great mining areas of Britain, with a surface area of only ninety square miles. It runs from Barrowmouth, just south of Whitehaven, to Maryport, fifteen miles to the north, and extends no more than five or six miles inland, except for a prolongation two miles wide and a dozen long, at the north-east end. The area is made structurally complex by faulting, and is constituted, in effect, by a number of coalfields around the towns of Whitehaven, Workington and Maryport.[9] These geographical considerations proved to be crucial, as each town became associated in the eighteenth century with the name of one or more landowning-entrepreneur: Lowther at Whitehaven, Curwen at Workington, and Christian and Senhouse at Maryport.*

Figure 2.1 shows the distribution of collieries in west Cumberland during the seventeenth and eighteenth centuries. The Lowthers' importance was far greater than the number of their collieries would suggest, because their mines accounted for a high proportion of total output. Howgill and Whingill were their main interest at Whitehaven. They acquired Scalegill in 1730, and, by purchasing the manors of Moresby and Distington in 1737, Sir James Lowther gained control of all the collieries served by Parton. The Curwens' interest extended south along the coast from Workington and east

---

* The structure and mechanics of the coal industry and trade will be examined in chapter 3. The reader may find it useful to know at this point, however, that the three elements of the trade – the provision of coal in Whitehaven, its transport to Ireland, and its sale there – were largely separate. The coal owners' profits depended on their selling price to the ships' masters; in turn the masters depended on a good price in Ireland for their profit.

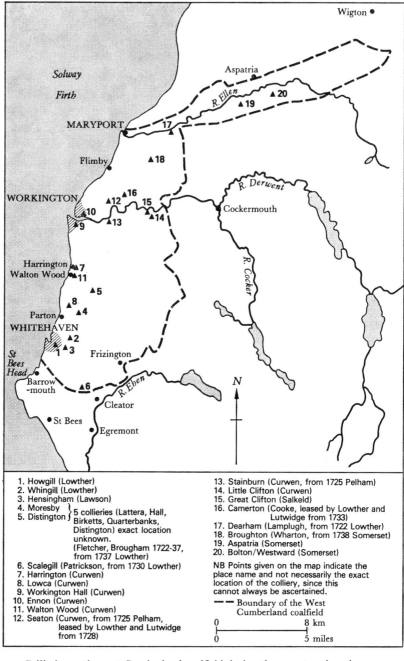

1. Howgill (Lowther)
2. Whingill (Lowther)
3. Hensingham (Lawson)
4. Moresby
5. Distington } 5 collieries (Lattera, Hall, Birketts, Quarterbanks, Distington) exact location unknown. (Fletcher, Brougham 1722-37, from 1737 Lowther)
6. Scalegill (Patrickson, from 1730 Lowther)
7. Harrington (Curwen)
8. Lowca (Curwen)
9. Workington Hall (Curwen)
10. Ennon (Curwen)
11. Walton Wood (Curwen)
12. Seaton (Curwen, from 1725 Pelham, leased by Lowther and Lutwidge from 1728)

13. Stainburn (Curwen, from 1725 Pelham)
14. Little Clifton (Curwen)
15. Great Clifton (Salkeld)
16. Camerton (Cooke, leased by Lowther and Lutwidge from 1733)
17. Dearham (Lamplugh, from 1722 Lowther)
18. Broughton (Wharton, from 1738 Somerset)
19. Aspatria (Somerset)
20. Bolton/Westward (Somerset)

NB Points given on the map indicate the place name and not necessarily the exact location of the colliery, since this cannot always be ascertained.

— — Boundary of the West Cumberland coalfield

0   8 km
0   5 miles

2.1   Collieries on the west Cumberland coalfield during the seventeenth and eighteenth centuries towards Cockermouth. Harrington was developed by Henry Curwen, for exporting coal, in the second half of the eighteenth century. Apart from two collieries at Workington, at the end of the seventeenth century the Curwens also controlled Seaton (two groups of pits on the north bank of the Derwent), Stainburn, Walton Wood and Little Clifton collieries. Near the latter was Great Clifton, owned from the later seventeenth century by Thomas Salkeld, a local Catholic gentleman. Intensive coal mining did not begin near Maryport until the later 1740s. In addition to coal found close by, the port was conveniently situated to serve several inland collieries, particularly Dearham (bought by the Lowthers in 1722), the Duke of Somerset's interests, and the Duke of Wharton's Broughton colliery.

The coal trade passed through a number of stages during the seventeenth and eighteenth centuries. To begin with, the Lowthers established themselves as the dominant coal owners, and Whitehaven as the major outlet. This, essentially, was Sir John Lowther's contribution, but the situation did not change in any substantial way until about 1720. Six years of depression, 1718–24, together with fears concerning the coal supply at Whitehaven, led to a rethinking of the one-port structure. To the accompaniment of calls for the opening up of Workington and Maryport, Sir James Lowther set out to convert the dominance he enjoyed as owner of the major collieries and the major port into a virtual monopoly of the whole west Cumberland coal trade. Reluctance to spend sufficient money, coupled with powerful resistance from other vested interests, ensured that although he retained the position of dominant owner, his control was never absolute. By the last decade or so of his life, he was ready to work with the other coal owners to promote the trade. The net result of his policy was to encourage his rivals to mine their resources. Each of these shifts must be examined in order to make clear the course of the coal trade in the seventeenth and eighteenth centuries.

Two entrepreneurs were active in west Cumberland during the 1630s: Sir Christopher Lowther at Whitehaven, and Sir Patricius Curwen at Workington. Some 2400 tons of coal were sold by Lowther in 1636, and his total profits between 1631 and 1637 amounted to £220. Curwen worked coal at Clifton and iron ore at Harrington.[10] These early efforts soon lapsed. Sir John Lowther's long minority curtailed developments at Whitehaven during the 1640s and 1650s. Curwen died in 1664 and his successors failed to build on his pioneer work. Indeed, in 1676 a commentator wrote that Workington harbour 'was not then frequented with ships and the colliery was decayed'. Henry Curwen, owner of the estate between 1673 and 1725, sank a number of pits, but his interest in the coal trade was desultory. In any case, he was abroad with James II between 1688 and 1696. Harrington, Lowca, Seaton and Little Clifton collieries were leased out in the early 1720s, producing a fixed rent of £315 per annum.[11]

Such lack of interest worked in Sir John Lowther's favour, since the one family from whom he apparently had most to fear remained inactive. As their interest did not revive until the later 1720s, and no other owner was able to raise the capital or enthusiasm to stake a serious claim, the Lowthers came to dominate the trade. It grew under their management without the crippling competition which bedevilled the coal industry in Northumberland and Durham. Not that no one else tried. William Christian, a Newcastle hostman, leased several collieries near Whitehaven in the 1680s, but his interest does not seem to have outlived the century.[12] Thomas Lamplugh and Thomas Patrickson, who sold Lowther their interests in Distington and Scalegill collieries respectively, could not afford the cost of mining.[13] Thomas Salkeld owned and worked Great Clifton colliery, but ran into financial difficulties. His profits totalled £170 in 1711/12, but only £145 in 1713, £63 in 1714 and £20 the following year. Then, in 1716, came the melancholy news of how 'the colliery was lost this year by water and no profit made thereof'. However, this was not the end, and the colliery was leased out for £60 the following year.[14] Gilfrid Lawson of Brayton claimed that his colliery was worth £500 a year in 1722, but five years later he was ready to let it for £100 per annum, and in 1730 the seam was reported to have failed.[15] In 1723, Sir Wilfrid Lawson's Hensingham colliery was said to have been worth £100 a year in the past, but it was not then being worked; indeed, there is no direct evidence of it being worked before the 1760s.[16] Humphrey Senhouse of Netherhall made various attempts during the 1720s to find coal on his estate near Maryport. He even sent men to study the techniques used in Dearham colliery (after Lowther purchased it in 1722), but his hopes came to nothing. He had to purchase coal to keep his salt pans going.[17] Significantly, of the fifteen gentry families who sold their estates between 1680 and

1750, six are known to have had mining interests, while three more had estates near to the west coast.[18] Ironically, one of the few 'success' stories amongst the gloom related to the Duke of Somerset's collieries. All three were leased throughout the first half of the eighteenth century, but they were too far inland for it to be economic to move the coal to the coast.[19]

Sir John Lowther was not slow to fill the vacuum left by the failure of west Cumberland's other coal owners, opening new pits and sinking shafts just as quickly as his limited resources allowed. Output or sales figures do not survive prior to the mid-1690s, but, as figure 2.2 shows, his profits rose steadily from 1665. Assessing the state of the trade simply on the basis of Lowther's profits is unsatisfactory, but in the absence of other evidence such figures do provide a general indication of the trend. The rapid upswing during the 1680s, following the more modest increase since 1665, probably resulted from the introduction of cartways to cut the cost of transporting coal to the harbour. According to one commentator, cartways 'gave Sir John command of the coal trade'.[20] The cutback of

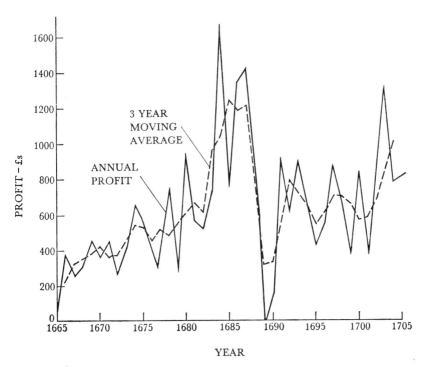

2.2   Sir John Lowther's colliery profits, 1665–1705

the 1690s was the result of two factors: wartime conditions, which hampered trade across the Irish sea, and a reduction in the sale price of Sir John's coal. He actually made a loss in 1689. Subsequent arrangements gave sufficient protection to the shipping for the trade to continue, but evidently on a lower level than previously.[21] Output figures begin in 1695. That year 19,000 tons were raised from Sir John Lowther's three working collieries (Howgill and Greenbank at Whitehaven, and Lattera in Moresby). By 1705, the last full year of Lowther's life, production had increased to 33,000 tons. These figures illustrate the industry's dependence upon the Irish market, 82 per cent and 85 per cent, respectively, of the 1695 and 1705 output, being sold in Ireland.

This upward trend continued after Sir James Lowther succeeded to the Whitehaven estate in 1706. Perhaps not unnaturally, he had certain reservations about his father's approach to mining. In particular, he believed that too many pits had been worked at the same time. Although concerned 'that new works be timely laid open before the old ones are run out',[22] he decided to begin his tenure of the estate by rationalizing his interests. Production stopped at Greenbank and Lattera during 1707. For the next seven years coal was only mined at Howgill colliery. In 1714 Lowther purchased the lease to Gunerdine colliery (Distington). He proceeded to work this colliery, together with Lattera, taking advantage of the newly built pier at Parton.* At the same time he reopened Whingill, an old colliery to the east of Whitehaven, which had been leased out in the later seventeenth century but had lain unused since 1706. John Spedding 'had some old workmen to inform me how the coal has been wrought' in 1712, and two years later production recommenced.[23] Output at Howgill and Whingill collieries totalled nearly 66,000 tons in 1717, of which 94 per cent was sent to Ireland. A further 7000 tons were raised in Lattera and Gunerdine collieries.

If these figures reflected the steady growth of demand from Ireland, they also provided ample justification for the land accumulation and investment policies pursued by Sir John Lowther and extended by his son. Figure 2.3, which gives export sales from the Whitehaven collieries between 1695 and 1750, shows the generally upward trend, occasionally interrupted by depressions. These statistics are the only detailed figures covering the whole period.

---

* See chapter 6. The output figures quoted in this chapter are reproduced in full in appendix 4.

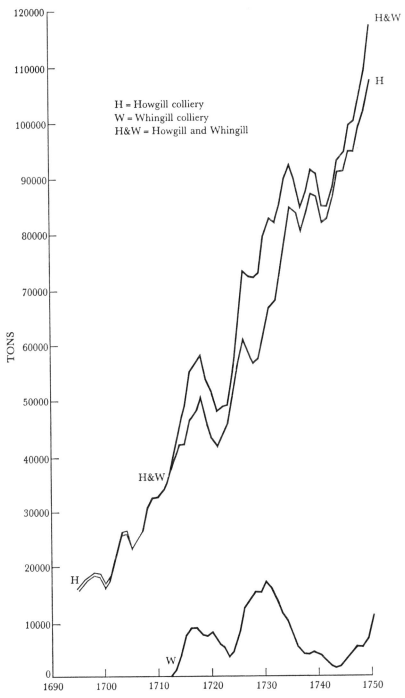

2.3 Export sales from the Whitehaven collieries, 1695–1750 (3 year moving average)

They cannot be used as an absolute guide to the state of trade, since by the 1730s and 1740s significant quantities of coal were being shipped from other outlets. They do, however, provide an indication of the trend, because Howgill colliery was the most productive, and the major export colliery in west Cumberland throughout the eighteenth century. It was also sensitive to changes in the level of demand. The only supplementary evidence is the shipping statistics which can be drawn from the port books.*

The upward trend in sales temporarily ended in 1717, to be succeeded by several years of depression. Coinciding as it did with changed circumstances in the trade, this had far-reaching effects. In simple statistical terms, the shortfall in demand need not necessarily have been a disaster. Sir James Lowther's export sales at Whitehaven topped 61,000 tons in 1717, a figure not exceeded until 1725. Sales between 1720 and 1724 were 12 per cent down on 1715–19 levels. A similar pattern is suggested by the number of vessels involved in the trade. Such a measure is only a rough guide to fluctuations, since vessels varied in size and capacity, but the figures do indicate a similar downward trend; voyages between Whitehaven and Dublin fell from 352 in 1716 to only 308 in 1720. Yet it was a combination of circumstances which forced a fundamental reappraisal of how the trade should be run. Depression – associated with the successful Irish mining at Ballycastle, the growing competition from Ayrshire, and fears about the viability of Howgill colliery – raised doubts about the future. Lowther found himself faced with an unenviable choice; either he could reach an agreement with the other local owners on prices and output, or he could go it alone. In the event he opted for the latter course.

The situation at Howgill appeared to be serious. In 1719, Lowther

* Port books survive for the years 1687/8, 1706–20 and 1738–43. They are annual, covering the period Christmas–Christmas, and include entries for the whole port. For the years to 1720 the place of origin is given for each vessel (Whitehaven, Workington etc.), but this information is not available thereafter, which makes it more difficult to distinguish between the trade of the various outlets. The many problems associated with the use of port books need not be repeated here. (See, for example, D. M. Woodward, 'The Port Books of England and Wales', *Maritime History*, iii (1973), pp. 147–65.) Owing to a statistical illusion, the port of Whitehaven stood second only to London in tonnage clearances for most of the eighteenth century, well ahead of ports whose main concern was the colonial trade. This was because coal exports to Ireland were counted as foreign trade, even though they were only liable to coastal duties. See G. Jackson, *Hull in the Eighteenth Century* (1972), p. 67, and J. E. Williams, 'Whitehaven in the Eighteenth Century', *Economic History Review*, 2nd series, vi (1956), p. 398.

expressed his fear that 'all my coals to the north of Howgill will be almost quite wrought out in four years, after which there will not above half the coals come down as do now'. A pamphlet circulated locally at about the same time made known these sentiments to the inhabitants of west Cumberland.[24] Admittedly this was not the first time that questions had been asked about the colliery. In the 1690s Sir John Lowther had been confronted with the same problem, and had considered buying Humphrey Senhouse's estate at Netherhall, near Maryport. Had the worst come to the worst he could then have moved the centre of his interests to what he thought was a highly promising area for future mining.[25] Sir James Lowther also thought about moving. He repeated his father's enquiries about Maryport in 1719, and in the early 1720s considered buying the lease of Saltcoats colliery in Ayrshire. The latter was a tactical move designed to counter the growing influence of the Scottish coal owners, whilst at the same time enabling him to regulate the trade to Ireland. Serious negotiations were undertaken with the lessee, Philip Peck, in the 1720s. Reports were prepared on the viability of the colliery, and Carlisle Spedding was asked whether he would be prepared to go to Scotland as manager. In the end, however, Lowther baulked at the asking price.[26]

The alternative course of action was to mine further inland, by extending the levels eastwards into Harras and Hensingham. This raised several problems. Sir John Lowther had built up a dominant position in the trade by effectively controlling the coal exports from west Cumberland's different outlets. Forty of the vessels which cleared the port of Whitehaven with coal for Dublin in 1706 were from Workington, and 46, 69 and 68 in 1711, 1716 and 1720 respectively, between 14 and 16 per cent of the total. Obviously, since the Lowthers owned no collieries at Workington, they could never completely eliminate this competition, but they could undercut it by supplying ample quantities of the best coal. Whitehaven coal was generally the most popular in Dublin, selling for around a shilling a ton more than other coal. Great care had been taken to maintain the standard, sometimes by bringing coal from Lattera colliery to mix with the Howgill produce as a means of raising the quality.[27] Even with better coal, the increasing share of the market being taken by Workington was worrying to Lowther. According to the customs collector, writing in 1720, Henry Curwen's decision to lease several of his Workington collieries had 'occasioned a very

C

great resort of shipping there'.[28] Moving inland was likely to erode Lowther's price differential since the cost of carrying coal from the pit head to the harbour rose proportionate to the distance involved. Whereas, in the early days of mining, packhorses had been used to carry the coal, cartways were necessary by the 1680s, and it was now thought that only wagonways would enable Lowther to compete. These were costly, and the outlay had to be recouped through the price charged to the ships' masters at the quayside. Furthermore, it would take time to complete the necessary alterations. To win time, Lowther could step up production at his Moresby collieries; 'I could supply some of our ships at Parton with 15 or 16,000 tons of coal yearly, as might easily be done from Lattera, Birketts and Gunerdine.'[29]

Lowther could not buy time in this way, because Parton pier had been destroyed in a gale during November 1718. Instead of doing all that he could to ensure its speedy reconstruction, he had chosen to indulge in what turned out to be a six year legal battle over responsibility for repairs, during which time no coal could be exported. This, together with fears about the viability of Howgill, seriously undermined his position. Quite apart from those masters now going to Workington, others were fetching coal from Maryport, Flimby (north of Workington) and Walton Wood (near Harrington). All three outlets were accessible to the smaller vessels during the summer months, and Maryport gained particular advantage from the congestion at Whitehaven following the destruction of Parton pier. Suggestions were being made by the summer of 1719 that two more customs officials were required to cope with the extra trade.[30] With Whitehaven apparently in decline, and Parton out of action, it was not long before the case for opening up other parts of the coalfield was being argued. Only if the precaution was taken of improving harbour facilities before the Whitehaven supply failed could west Cumberland hope to nullify the competition from Scotland and Wales.[31]

The queue for coal at Whitehaven had been a source of frustration to the masters before the Parton disaster. At a time when their profits were being squeezed by low prices at Dublin, they could ill-afford to wait any longer, as they inevitably had to do. More, rather than fewer voyages, was their solution to the problem.[32] No attempt was made to extend the facilities at Whitehaven during these years because of financial difficulties, while Lowther's suggestions for riding out the crisis were inadequate. He put forward the idea of building vessels more suited to the trade, but Spedding pointed out that these would cost no less than £1600 each, 'which is too great a sum for anybody to think of getting friends to raise in these melancholy times'.[33] The masters were equally unimpressed by Lowther's plea that they should search for new markets, while the one positive step taken in an effort to protect those masters whose primary interest was the coal trade, was not very effective. This was a two-tier price system for summer and winter, introduced in 1721 in an effort to exclude from the trade those masters mainly concerned in the colonial trade. They only took coal to Ireland during the winter months, and tended to depress the price even further by accepting low profit margins.[34] Lowther agreed to sell coal at a lower price to those masters who continued to carry coal to Ireland during the summer months, to compensate for the less favourable returns that they received in Dublin, and to induce them not to leave the trade.

Given these circumstances, it is hardly surprising that considerable support was mustered for improving Workington and Maryport harbours. It proved more difficult to turn good ideas into practical reality. Talk of legislation to develop Workington came to nothing, although a voluntary agreement was reached to implement several alterations. However, at Maryport, Humphrey Senhouse, the major landowner, would have nothing to do with any changes. His opinion was that he would rather see the harbour 'quite blocked up'.[35]

Yet it would have been folly on Lowther's part not to have recognized the threat to his position, and as a good businessman he was unlikely to bury his head in the sand. Logically, his best course of action was to reach an agreement with the lessees of the Curwen collieries around Workington to regulate output and prices. He could then have begun working further inland without the fear of being undercut for price. Such agreements were normal practice on Tyneside during depressions. The 'Grand Allies' came together in 1726 for just this reason, and effectively ran the trade until about 1750. A parallel agreement was reached on the Wear in 1727. The difference in west Cumberland was that Lowther had a much more dominant position than any single owner in the north-east. Even when the Grand Allies renegotiated their agreement in 1733, the three of them only supplied 57.1 per cent of the vend.[36] Although precise figures are lacking, Lowther's position was clearly much stronger. In addition, he found the Tyneside example unedifying.

As he told Spedding in 1725, 'there are terrible disputes among the coal owners at Newcastle, and so there must be where there are several coal owners joining together with great purses'.[37] Under the circumstances, Lowther decided that he should stake out a claim to the Workington and Maryport trade. By leasing, or, in an extremity, buying the major export collieries serving the two ports, he would be able to control the vend and prices. He would do on his own what the Grand Allies had done between 1715 and 1726 in preparation for their agreement: purchase good coal lands and strategic way-leaves, so as to control the factors of production and erect barriers against new entrepreneurs. The near monopoly which his father had created through the quality of the Whitehaven coal, the indifference of the other coal owners, and heavy capital investment to ensure that he could meet demand, would now be extended to the whole coalfield.

Lowther first adopted this new policy in 1722, although he had been considering expanding his horizons for about three years. His justification was that 'as there is no other coal owner that will take care of the coal trade, it is better both for me and the coal trade that I should have more collieries'. He told Spedding: 'I will bid for anything on the coast from Whitehaven to Elnefoot [Maryport]'.[38] Without doubt Lowther was aided in reaching his decision by the availability of Broughton colliery, which was put up for sale in the spring of 1722. One of the major collieries east of Workington, this was regarded by Spedding as second only to Howgill in west Cumberland. It was geographically well suited to using Maryport as its outlet, a point which Lowther was undoubtedly aware of when he bought his cousin Richard Lamplugh's estate at Ribton and Dearham during the summer of 1722. If he could link Broughton and Dearham collieries, Lowther would establish a considerable interest at Maryport. In actual fact he never acquired Broughton, although this was not for want of trying.

An immediate result of his decision was to give a new significance to the discussions about improving Workington and Maryport harbours. 'The coal trade will be immediately ruined', Lowther informed Spedding, 'if harbours are not improved.' For good measure he added, 'I hope one way or other we shall increase the exportation of all the harbours that I shall have the shipping more in my power and be able in time to make the coal trade increase and lessen at the different harbours as I see cause.' By 1730 he was convinced that 'there is experience enough in our country that nothing is to be made of collieries or harbours where the trade is in several hands'.[39] Such opinions became well known in Cumberland during the years that followed. According to Walter Lutwidge, Lowther viewed the coal trade as 'his royalty in Cumberland'.[40]

Lowther's new strategy contained two elements. First, he had to buy more property around Whitehaven, in order to give himself the room to expand laterally. Hence the purchases of the later 1720s and 1730s, noted in chapter 1. This was his safety valve; having already put considerable capital into the Whitehaven collieries, it was hardly sensible to risk everything on being able to lease, and then mine, elsewhere. Wagonways were constructed to serve the inland mines. Secondly, Lowther had to persuade the other coal owners, particularly Henry Curwen, Thomas Salkeld (Great Clifton colliery) and the Duke of Wharton (Broughton) to lease or, if necessary, sell him their interests. He could then work the mines to raise total output in west Cumberland. Alternatively he could use them as 'blocking' collieries; by leaving them inoperative he would ensure that his investment at Whitehaven was not wasted. Even if these tactics were successful, however, Lowther was still faced with the possibility that the temporary mining successes enjoyed by the Irish would become permanent, and that the Ayrshire enterprises might continue to expand. Fortunately for him, both of these projects ran into difficulties by the later 1720s. His major headache proved to be in west Cumberland, where the other owners initially refused him leases and later set up in competition.

The formula for success was to move quickly. If this also meant paying high prices, then so be it. Unfortunately, events were against speed, while Lowther's predilection was not conducive to paying the prices and rents demanded. Even so, he came close to complete success in 1728, and eventually created a network which was sufficiently comprehensive to maintain his dominant influence throughout the coalfield.

Events in 1722 ensured that Lowther would first move to secure Maryport. He kept the newly purchased Dearham colliery in production, and made clear his intention to bid for the Wharton estates in order to secure Broughton. Immediately he ran into difficulties. Humphrey Senhouse's attitude towards Maryport augured ill for future harbour development, while legal technicalities prevented the Wharton trustees from selling the property until 1727. When it eventually came under the hammer, Lowther was the highest bidder at £12,400. But this success proved to be hollow, because a legal dispute still had to be settled as to the ownership of part of the property. Lowther eventually withdrew from the contract in 1734, and the estate was readvertised three years later.[41]

Just as frustrating were the barriers Lowther encountered in his efforts to block Workington. He enquired in 1723 as to whether the lessees of Seaton colliery might be prepared to part with their lease, but the response was negative.[42] However, his prospects seemed brighter when Henry Curwen died in 1725. A bachelor, Curwen had fallen out with his Sella Park relatives, who were the natural heirs to the property. He could not prevent them from inheriting the settled estates (those south of the river Derwent), but he could dispose of the rest as he chose. His nominated heir, Charles Pelham of Brocklesby in Lincolnshire, came into something like £800 of the total rental (£1400) along with two collieries, Seaton and Stainburn. Since this division reduced the overall investment capacity, and all the existing leases were voided by the change of ownership, Lowther decided that the time was ripe to stake a claim. Negotiations were opened for both Seaton and the south bank collieries. Pelham at first seemed agreeable to Lowther's proposals, but then let Seaton back to the former proprietors. Henry Curwen of Sella Park was prepared to lease, but here Lowther found himself in competition with another local coal owner, a Mr Porter. This was probably Joseph Porter of Weary Hall, whose property included the manor of Crosby three miles from Maryport. He claimed that Curwen had offered him a lease of Workington Hall, Walton Wood and Little Clifton collieries for a fixed rent of £300 a year. Lowther was only ready to offer £200, or at most £220, for all of Curwen's interests. He was disconcerted to find that the asking price was £340, but he raised his offer to £300 for a twenty-one year lease. Curwen decided in the end to let Clifton back to the original lessees and work Walton Wood himself.[43] In 1726, Porter leased Thomas Salkeld's Great Clifton colliery.[44]

By the autumn of 1727 five years of monopoly hunting had achieved very little. The fact that Lowther had increased production at Whingill colliery may indicate that some of the fears about Howgill colliery were being realized. However, the situation changed rapidly towards the end of the year, for in December 1727 Broughton colliery was provisionally sold to him. At the same time, Henry

Curwen died. His brother and heir, Eldred (1692–1745) instituted trials at Workington Hall colliery, and let Little Clifton to Porter for £80 a year. In 1728 Lowther offered to lease all the collieries (except Little Clifton), and Curwen was sufficiently agreeable for a draft lease to be drawn up. When news leaked out that Curwen intended to agree with Lowther for a rent of £300 on a thirty-one year lease, he was severely criticized. Throughout March and April Curwen prevaricated, first asking that the commencement date of the lease might be put back, and then that it should be voided, on the grounds that his agreement had been secured 'in a drunken bout'. Finally, he offered Spedding £100 to be quit of the whole affair. He evidently had no intention of executing the lease, and although Lowther considered taking legal action the matter was eventually dropped. Possibly Lowther hoped that any attempt by Curwen to 'go it alone' would fail, and he would then consider leasing.[45]

This was a setback, but in April 1728 the partners working Seaton agreed to sell the remainder of their lease to Lowther. Accordingly it was transferred to Spedding, Walter Lutwidge and Thomas Benn, a local attorney.[46] (As with all these manoeuvrings Lowther preferred not to have his own name mentioned since this would make his intentions more obvious.) Consequently, in the early months of 1728 he was close to success. Broughton and Seaton collieries were apparently safe, while he was within an ace of securing the Workington collieries. But for the legal complications which thwarted the Broughton transactions, and a slightly increased rental offer to Curwen, Lowther might have achieved his aim.

Certainly the events of these months gave Lowther cause for optimism, and with Walter Lutwidge, who retained a one-third interest, he spent the next few years consolidating the Seaton holding. In 1732 they leased several parcels of land to facilitate drainage, and the following year took a thirty-one year lease of Richard Cooke's Camerton colliery. For the latter they were to pay a dead-rent of £20 a year, which would double if they decided to mine. Further land was leased at Camerton in 1745, which suggests that by then they were working in the area.[47] If so, it was probably in conjunction with Seaton, and another interest, Great Clifton. Porter's lease of Great Clifton expired in 1735, when Salkeld renewed it to Messrs Cookson and Williams, ironmasters. Lowther and Lutwidge contracted to purchase 7000 tons of coal annually from the colliery, in return for which Cookson and Williams were not to compete in the export trade. This was a major breakthrough for Lowther. Spedding believed that it had 'broke the heart of the coal owners at Workington and must put the trade of that place entirely into your hands'. He even hoped Curwen would reconsider his decision not to lease.[48]

Whilst these negotiations had been proceeding, little had happened at Maryport. Only when he had secured the Workington interest by the mid-1730s did Lowther's attention revert to his interests at the northern end of the coalfield. In 1735 he leased from the Dean and Chapter of Carlisle all royalties in their lands at Dearham. The following year he reached an agreement with Humphrey Senhouse on wayleaves. In return for a rent of £5 a year, Lowther was to have liberty to move his Dearham coal to Maryport across Senhouse's land. He was also to have forty square yards of staithing (storage) space in the village. In return, Senhouse agreed to refrain from mining. Lowther purchased the royalties of Fletcher Partis' land at Dearham in 1737, and of John Brisco's land in the manor of Crosby (just north of Maryport) two years later.[49] In 1738 he lent money to William Beeby and William Blennerhasset, both of whom had estates at Flimby, south of Maryport. He may well have been hoping that the day would come when he would be able to foreclose the mortgages, particularly on Blennerhasset who, according to Lowther, had 'turned projector . . . such wild notions as he has are not cured without wasting a little money'.[50] Finally, he again showed interest in the Wharton estates when they were readvertised in 1737.[51] However, a year later they were sold to the Duke of Somerset, possibly after some tacit agreement was reached to lease Broughton colliery to Lowther. In a letter written in November 1738, Lowther noted that according to Thomas Elder, the duke's steward, 'Somerset takes it very kindly of me that I would not bid against him for the Duke of Wharton's estate. He [sic] will do me any service about Broughton colliery and thinks it his grace's interest to let them to me on a long lease.' In the event, no lease was ever forthcoming. Possibly Somerset refrained under pressure from other local coal owners anxious to thwart Lowther, or because his favourable disposition turned sour when he recognized Lowther's growing interest in his own borough stronghold of Cockermouth.[52]

Although the interests that Lowther put together did not represent the monopoly that he had originally had in mind, by the early 1740s he was the major figure in the coal trade at all four ports along the coast. As he told John Spedding some years later, 'Mr Senhouse is to blame not to encourage such as me to carry coals to Elnefoot [Maryport] who have so much power to turn the channels of the coal trade'.[53] His own parsimony was a major reason why the position that he had created was not stronger. As William Brownrigg put it in 1765, 'could he have been prevailed on to lay out some of the profits of this trade in advantageous purchases, he had the fairest opportunity of securing it entirely to himself'.[54] The fact is that a higher rent might well have secured Curwen's collieries in 1728, while Charles Pelham would almost certainly have parted with the Seaton estate to Lowther had the money been forthcoming. Lowther was always keen to 'treat for the whole' of Pelham's property because this would have given him Stainburn colliery. Furthermore, it included a number of detached properties: the manor of Rottington, intermixed with Lowther's property at St Bees, an estate south-east of Whitehaven, and property near Maryport. The possibility of leasing Stainburn colliery had first been proposed in 1728 when a rent of £100 or £120 a year was mentioned. Further hopeful expressions of interest were made in 1740, 1743 and 1752. In the course of these negotiations Lowther made several offers aimed at tempting Pelham to sell out, and concentrate his attentions in Lincolnshire. The stumbling-block was the price; Lowther insisted that his offer of twenty-eight years' purchase was a high one, but Pelham adamantly refused to accept anything less than thirty years. When Sir James Lowther of Lowther finally bought the estate in 1758 he paid £55,000, over £17,000 more than his predecessor had valued it at in 1751.[55]

Perhaps the most significant result of Lowther's activities was the revival of competition amongst the coal owners. Lowther can hardly have approved, but by the mid-1740s he showed some willingness to work with other entrepreneurs, apparently content that he had secured a sufficiently dominant position to dictate terms. Eldred Curwen, having backtracked on the 1728 lease, began to mine around Workington. Initially he worked with Porter,[56] but the latter's influence waned after the Great Clifton lease passed to Cookson and Williams in 1735, and Curwen took Little Clifton colliery in hand the following year. By the mid-1730s Curwen's concerns were flourishing, although he apparently told John

Spedding in 1735 that he had 'made nothing by working them himself'. Precise details of his activities over the years that followed are lacking, only a few snippets of information having survived. Spedding informed Lowther in 1736, for example, that Curwen 'had laid out a great deal of money in opening an old colliery at Clifton chapel where he now gets about twelve tons a day'. In 1751 he was attempting to reopen Lowca colliery, which had not been worked since the 1720s. By the 1740s Curwen seems to have been on amicable terms with Lowther, reaching joint decisions on convoying vessels across the Irish sea after war broke out with France in 1744.[57]

At the end of the 1740s the new town of Maryport was founded by two local landowners, Humphrey Senhouse II, and Ewan Christian of Unerigg. Lowther believed that the property around the town was too divided for effective mining, but this did not stop the two men looking for coal. Senhouse's hands were tied by his father's 1736 agreement with Lowther, which was not due to expire until 1757. Lowther had made it partly to block Senhouse's father in anticipation of a Broughton lease. Since this now seemed less likely to materialize, he agreed to amend the contract so that Senhouse could mine.[58] Ewan Christian died in 1752. John Christian, his brother and heir, instituted local trials, and after some initial disappointments, succeeded in finding and working a number of small pits.[59] Senhouse and Christian, with four other partners, secured a lease of Broughton colliery in 1755. The term was twenty-one years at an annual rent of £200. The partners agreed to provide the necessary wayleaves so that the coal could be transported to Maryport. Christian was to extend the levels of his existing mines to facilitate drainage. In 1763 he took over the lease from the other five partners and he and his son worked the colliery for the rest of the century. More than 30,000 tons were being raised yearly in the 1760s and 1770s, thus confirming John Spedding's optimistic comments back in 1722.[60] The Christians and Curwens were united by marriage in 1782, bringing together in one family two of the major colliery interests in west Cumberland.

All this post-1720 manoeuvring in the industry was inevitably reflected in output and sales. Judging by Lowther's Whitehaven figures (fig. 2.3, p. 47), the 1718–24 depression was succeeded by a decade of rising demand. New peaks were reached in 1725, 1726 and 1727, with the 1724 figure being surpassed by 53 per cent in the latter year. 1728 was a bad year because of a long combination by the masters during the autumn. However, new peaks were attained in 1730, 1731, 1734 and 1735. A customs report of 1736 noted that there were at Whitehaven 'near 100 sail from 20 to 190 tons burthen ... concerned in the coal trade to Ireland'.[61] The cyclical nature of demand is best illustrated by the years 1736–43. Lowther's sales fell by 5·6 per cent 1736–38, more than recovered to reach new peaks in 1739 and 1740, fell back by over 20 per cent in 1741 and 1742, and returned to the 1740 level in 1743. By this time Whitehaven's trading interests were sufficiently diversified for cutbacks in demand not to have the same damaging effects as two decades earlier, whilst in any case these were shorter depressions. Coal voyages from White-haven and Workington tripled between 1707 and 1743.[62]

In the last few years for which figures have survived Lowther's sales rose fairly steadily, the record being broken in 1746 – when sales to the masters topped 100,000 tons for the first time – 1747, 1749 and 1750. Nearly 118,000 tons were sold to the masters in this final year. Demand was continually threatening to outstrip supply. Scalegill colliery was linked to Whitehaven by wagonway in 1739 to provide extra coal. Even this was not enough; in the 1750s produc-tion was increased at Whingill and a wagonway built to service the colliery. By these and other improvements, Lowther and his suc-cessors increased supply to meet the Irish requirement; 218,000 tons were sent to Ireland in 1772 according to Pennant, while the peak year was 1785, when Whitehaven supplied 227,000 tons.[63] Over the whole period 1695–1750 sales to the ships' masters grew at an annual compound rate of 3·6 per cent. In addition, Lowther had the sole interest at Parton from 1737. Although no figures have survived, it is possible that this supplemented his Whitehaven trade.

Perhaps more interesting than this steady growth at Whitehaven was the impact of mining at Workington and Maryport. In 1736 Workington had 'upwards of 35 sails of ships ... besides several strangers that use that place' involved in the coal trade. By 1741 forty ships were regularly engaged in the trade, and a couple of years later more than fifty. Such was its trading position by 1743 that calls were made for it to have separate port status, independent of Whitehaven. The harbour was improved during the 1750s, and Henry Curwen calculated in 1756 that more than eighty vessels were constantly employed in the coal trade, a figure repeated four years later by the traveller John Crofts. Pennant described the trade as being 'considerable' in 1772. Much of the supply must have been from Seaton colliery. According to the customs collector in 1736, 'a very great coal trade [was] carried on . . . especially on the north side of the river where the wagonways are laid'.[64] From under 6000 tons in 1728 Seaton production rose to more than 12,000 tons in 1732, 34,000 tons in 1739 and 39,000 tons in 1753. It is impossible to be sure whether or not these figures included any of the 7000 tons a year Lowther and Lutwidge contracted to buy from Great Clifton colliery, although as early as October 1736 the agreement had run into trouble over the tonnage Lowther and Lutwidge had actually collected.[65] In any case, these figures made this Lowther's most important colliery interest apart from Howgill, even after Lutwidge's one-third share was deducted. Lowther exported 87,000 tons of coal at Whitehaven in 1736 when 100 vessels were said to be involved in the trade. Given that the number of vessels operating out of Working-ton is known, it is possible to suggest that Lowther and Lutwidge could have been supplying c. 80 per cent of the coal shipped there in the 1740s.

Developments at Maryport only started in the last years of Lowther's life, but some of the coal exports undoubtedly came from Dearham colliery. Twelve or fourteen tons were being mined daily in 1723, most of it for local sale. Production cannot have increased very much before Lowther began to expand his Maryport interests in the mid-1730s. By 1740 anything up to 4000 tons a year was being sold at the colliery.[66] It was possible to export through Maryport before the harbour improvements began in 1749, but by the follow-ing summer thirteen or fourteen vessels could use the harbour at any one time. The collector of customs believed that more officials were needed. A further increase of trade was noted in 1751 when fourteen or fifteen ships were frequently in the harbour together, some of them from Ireland and the Isle of Man. By 1777 the town had some seventy or eighty vessels of between 30 and 250 tons operating in the coal trade.[67]

In 1725 Sir James Lowther told John Spedding that 'there is nothing so ridiculous as to insinuate I aim at a monopoly'.[68] This was hardly a denial which would have gained much credence in west Cumber-land; to all intents and purposes Sir John Lowther had established an effective monopoly of the trade, and his son was unlikely to relinquish the grip voluntarily. Few can have doubted that Lowther would attempt to extend his influence once the trade moved to new outlets. However, he could not be prevented from cornering a large share of the market. By 1750 his collieries may have been producing 170,000 tons of coal annually, the great bulk of which was sold in Ireland. This could have represented as much as 90 per cent of the total west Cumberland export, although such a figure is no more than a speculative estimate.* He certainly had complete control of the Whitehaven/Parton trade, although the latter was never very significant even after its pier was rebuilt in the 1720s. According to the customs collector, in 1736 its trade was carried on 'by six or seven colliers to Ireland and Isle Man'.[69] In addition, Lowther was the dominant interest at Workington, and contributed to the much smaller Maryport trade. But the failure to complete the monopoly by excluding all the other owners was to be significant; Lowther's successors found that the competition which he had failed to stamp out was much more vigorous in the second half of the eighteenth century.

---

* These 'guesstimates' can be used to compare the volume of west Cumberland's trade with that of Tyneside and Wearside. If Lowther (and Lutwidge) supplied c. 80 per cent of the export supply at Workington in the 1740s, this would have represented around 94 per cent of the total from Workington and Whitehaven. Assuming some drop in this proportion (since the number of vessels operating out of Workington apparently increased more rapidly than the supply from Seaton), it is possible that Lowther's total export sales in 1750 (118,000 tons from Whitehaven plus c. 39,000 from Workington) represented about 90 per cent of the trade. This implies an overall export of around 175,000 tons. Coal shipments from Newcastle and Sunderland in 1750 amounted to 1,192,500 tons (B. R. Mitchell and P. Deane, *Abstract of British Historical Statistics* (Cambridge, 1962), pp. 108–10). Even allowing for the fact that no account has been taken of any sales from Maryport, it would seem that the west Cumberland trade was around 15 per cent of that enjoyed by the north-east.

3

Coal: the Structure of Trade and Industry

Behind the overall pattern of growth in the coal trade lay a complicated system of organization comprising production, transportation and marketing. These functions remained separate for much of the period. The coal owners, the Lowthers in particular, were generally individualists, investing in their collieries to the limit of their financial abilities, facing up to such problems as drainage and transport to the quayside, and regulating their profits according to capital expenditure. Before the mid-1730s they had little direct interest in shipping, but sold at the quayside to the ships' masters. (Cumberland had no equivalent of the Tyneside 'fitters'.) In turn, the masters disposed of the coal in Dublin, usually to middlemen, for marketing. As a result of this structure, the skippers tended to be squeezed between the two land-based interests. Faced with a tacit agreement on prices amongst the Cumberland owners, and an Irish parliament prone to pass punitive legislation if prices in Dublin rose too rapidly, the masters only occasionally succeeded in raising their profits by combined action against either the owners or the market. The fear of cutting off their own livelihood, reluctance to search out new markets, dependence on coal for all profits, and fierce resistance to becoming merely carriers, contributed to an endemic lack of organization amongst the masters. Together these pressures served to ensure that their profits were generally small.

Whilst the component parts of the trade were separate, all three had considerable interests in common, the owners and masters in particular. With only a limited demand for coal in Cumberland, the owners depended on selling in Ireland. As William Brownrigg pointed out in 1765, 'it is the ships and the seamen, in great measure, that here give a superiority in the trade, and were they to remove might draw much of the trade after them'. According to Brownrigg, to ensure that the masters remained content the coal owners had to follow two important maxims: first, they had to protect the masters wherever possible against the full impact of Irish legislation, and, second, they had to act so as to ensure that they did not provoke the masters into combining to stop the trade.[1] Thus masters and owners shared a common bond within the confines of what were, in theory, highly disparate interests. The way this worked out in practice is an important theme running through this chapter.

Coal production in west Cumberland was the province of wealthy landowners working independently. Apart from some co-operation between Curwen and Porter in the 1730s, and the Lowther/Lutwidge partnership at Seaton, the entrepreneurs were completely independent, bearing the full burden of responsibility for investment. The need for heavy capital expenditure hampered the emergence of smaller men, and called for self-sacrifice on the part of the greater. According to William Brownrigg, 'it has been computed that these two gentlemen [Sir John and Sir James Lowther] in the compass of a century . . . have expended in [Howgill colliery] upward of half a million sterling'.[2] The source of his figure is unknown, but as son-in-law to John Spedding, and close confidant of Carlisle Spedding, he was sufficiently involved in colliery affairs for its accuracy to be respected. We shall return to these figures, but first it is necessary to examine the means by which the rapid increase in production was achieved. Some improvement was possible through greater efficiency, but beyond that new technology had to be introduced. Our evidence here is, perforce, mostly derived from the Lowther collieries; management and working conditions in these were probably not untypical of the region, although they were on a larger scale than elsewhere.

Early workings in west Cumberland were shallow and near the outcrops. 'Bearmouths' were driven into the side of a hill, acting both as channels to drain water and passages for workmen to enter the mines. Shafts were sunk so that coal could be raised to the surface. Sir John Lowther hired men on a contract basis for this work,[3] but Whitehaven employees were sufficiently skilled by the later 1720s to carry out the task. The method of mining, 'bord and pillar' was similar to that used in Durham. Headways were cut along the grain of the coal, and from these, at intervals, the bord or stalls of the hewers were cut out. The need to leave large pillars, thirteen or perhaps fifteen yards square, meant that the bulk of the coal was not removed.[4] Coal was worked at the face by haggers and odmen, the hewers of Tyneside. It was then carried to the shaft bottom, in hazel-rod baskets known as corves, by traylers. Specialized brakesmen and winders raised it to the surface where it was placed on heaps. Banksmen then removed slate and other extraneous matter before the coal was transported to the harbour.

Organizing and overseeing the actual process of mining was the responsibility of a three-level management structure. In overall control of all the Lowther mines including, at least nominally, Seaton, was the Whitehaven colliery steward. His second-in-command, from 1717 when the post was created, was the colliery engineer. Supervisors, known as 'overseers underground', constituted the third level of management.

Not a great deal is known about the colliery workers. No use was made of the binding system common in Northumberland and Durham, or the gang system found elsewhere.[5] Payment was daily, rather than by the piece. The total wage bill for one week in November 1709 was £74 14s 7d, when haggers were receiving daily rates of 10d, traylers, brakesmen and winders 8d, and corve makers 1s. These rates had not changed by 1716, but few later figures have survived. The miners were subject to deductions for offences. In 1723, for example, 3s 6d was stopped 'of Corporal pit workmen for picking coal off the pillars', and in June 1732 16s was withheld for a similar offence. Another fineable offence was to contract to work with the 'steel mill' (see below), for which higher wages were payable, and then to use a candle, which provided better light at greater risk. An explosion in 1743 was attributed to this practice.[6]

Numbers of workmen are more difficult to establish. Table 3.1 depicts a single week in November 1705. Unfortunately no later figures have survived with which these can be compared, although it can be assumed that rising productivity was achieved, at least in part, by expanding the workforce.

Many of the Lowther employees were part-time. Most of the underground supervisors had more than one interest, and Christopher Hare was sacked in 1714 for concentrating on his own affairs to the expense of Lowther's. Anthony Richardson had a small farm, acted as a bailiff, and held a lease to operate the water gins at Howgill colliery. Peter Peele, before he became an overseer at Whingill in 1728, had substituted for John Spedding in several roles. Later he held a position as bailiff.[7] Haggers often combined pit work

Table 3.1. *The colliery workforce in 1705.*

Workmen	Howgill colliery	Lattera colliery	Greenbank colliery
Haggers	82	–	12
Odmen	82	16	4
Traylers	108	–	12
Winders	53	20	12
Bankers	22	1	1
Smith	–	1	1
Carpenter	–	1	–
Pumping	–	–	6
	347	39	48

Source: Carlisle Record Office, D/Lons/W St Bees, box 13, list 1.

with a smallholding, while the leaders needed land in order to keep a horse. Although the Lowthers favoured this form of dual employment, it could lead to labour shortages at sowing and harvest times. Men were hired from Durham in 1714 partly because it was hoped that they would be 'more constant in the summer time'. This did not turn out to be the case; in June, Spedding informed Lowther that 'mowing time will take off some of our workmen and some of the new ones are gone off to mow in their own country and attend one of Sir William Blackett's days at the lead mines'.[8]

The Lowthers seem to have experienced little industrial unrest among the labour force. When Sir James Lowther was asked by the Society for the Promotion of Christian Knowledge in 1738 to advise Mr Hartsome of Brosely in Shropshire how 'to redress the enormities of the colliers which he complains of', his reply was that they should be obliged 'to be better husbands of the produce of their labour'.[9]

One group of workers was more prone to take industrial action than the rest: the coal leaders. These were the men who moved coal from the pit head to the harbour in the days before wagonways were introduced. Each man had a single horse and cart, but they normally operated in gangs, the size of which varied according to the pit involved. The strength of their position was considerable. If they stopped work the Lowthers could not move coal to the harbour for sale. The masters would therefore go elsewhere for coal. If colliery workers were laid off to reduce production, they in turn might seek employment elsewhere. This was the type of situation which confronted John Spedding when he attempted to reduce the leaders' payments from 10d to 8d a ton in 1710. They immediately struck, and for ten days only one cart was at work. He found himself with no option but 'to comply with them for the present'. To break similar combinations Sir James Lowther adopted an eviction policy. Since leaders kept a horse, they had to be provided with a smallholding. When they again outmanoeuvred Lowther in 1729 to achieve an increase in their rates, he responded by insisting that they should have land only on condition that the rent was paid weekly. Under such circumstances 'if they leave my business I may secure my rent and turn them out'. He wanted to keep them 'in the greatest dependency'.[10] With the introduction of wagonways in the 1730s their bargaining power diminished.

Underground workers lived a highly dangerous life and accidents were frequent. Many were the result of explosions, but other hazards also claimed victims. A hagger was killed by a falling rock at Lattera colliery in 1728; the colliery engineer, Christopher Fulthrop, died when he fell from a corve being hauled up Saltom pit (Howgill) in 1739; and a man was drowned at Scalegill colliery in 1749. Sometimes the workmen were blamed. An explosion at Corporal pit (Howgill) in 1730 was attributed to 'a workman's unwarily opening a door and going and carrying the candle into an old head . . . to seek out some picks he had hidden there'. A further disaster at the pit seven years later was blamed on 'the workmen getting too great a quantity of liquor at the fair'. An explosion in 1753 was also attributed to the workmen being 'in liquor'.[11] For those who survived the hazards Lowther provided a pension of one shilling a week. In 1733, he had a number of rooms built to accommodate people who had retired from the collieries. They received a pension of 5s a month, and a coal allowance equivalent to 6s 8d a year. Perhaps it is a measure of the mortality rate that the rooms were used mainly by widows of men killed in accidents. Those who already had a house only received the pension.[12]

Seaton was managed slightly differently from the Whitehaven collieries, probably because of its physical detachment and joint working. Lowther and Lutwidge entrusted its management to James and William Gorton, and William Greer, the former lessees, when they bought them out in 1728, but by 1735 the organization was in such disarray that new regulations were needed. It was agreed that

James Gorton should 'superintend the whole affairs of the colliery both underground and above, and that he apply himself with the utmost diligence and care to have the same managed with the greatest frugality and best husbandry that is possible'. John Metcalf was to supervise the work underground; John Moor was to take charge of all business at the harbour, and Thomas Atkinson was to oversee the coal stocks. A couple of years later Lowther and Lutwidge had a serious disagreement over financing the *Cumberland*, a ship built to promote the Seaton trade. Thereafter ill-feeling between them spilled over into disputes about management. In May 1738 Lowther sent Spedding to Seaton to raise the price of coal; Lutwidge was temporarily absent in Dublin at the time. The following year he referred to his partner as 'an audacious griper'. For his part, Lutwidge was constantly complaining that the colliery was underworked and badly managed. In 1740 he accused James Gorton of gross mismanagement, and asked for 'such drunken, whoring fellows as Moor' to be turned out of their posts. When he failed to persuade Lowther to take any action, he suggested that Atkinson, Metcalf and Gorton were too old and infirm to carry on management. A new employee was taken on in 1748; according to Lutwidge, his 'extraordinary zeal' provoked the other managers into encouraging the underground workers to make an attempt on his life. Lutwidge also maintained that Metcalf, now over seventy, was given to carousing and too much drinking, which rendered him unfit to remain at his post.[13]

The extent to which Lutwidge was justified in his accusations about underworking is debatable. In 1728 Lowther had not anticipated having a partner, although Lutwidge's help had been indispensable in setting up the deal. When Lutwidge made known his intention of not assigning the third share that he had bought, Lowther decided that 'it will be a great advantage to have one of the partners in the country when I am in London to help in case of any disputes'.[14] He even agreed to Lutwidge's scheme for a wagonway. But this was not Lowther's main interest. Possibly he had leased Seaton simply to prevent anyone else working the colliery. Certainly it was not advantageous for him to promote it at the expense of his Whitehaven interests. Some evidence suggests that, perhaps because he did not want Seaton overworked, he tolerated inefficiency. Between 1741 and 1748, John Westray held a contract to keep Seaton wagonway in repair. According to one modern commentator he received an exceptionally high rate for the task. However, Lutwidge claimed that Westray was inefficient, and when his contract was due to expire only seventeen of the twenty-two wagons were still usable. Lutwidge complained that this was one result of Lowther's failure to exercise sufficient control over the activities of his servants. There may have been some justification for such an accusation since Westray was involved with the Spedding brothers in the Whitehaven timber company.[15]

The introduction of new technology was of vital importance for coal mining. The fact that Howgill colliery remained the Lowthers' most productive colliery throughout the eighteenth century is ample testimony to the significance of a series of innovations: Newcomen engines for raising water from 1716; gunpowder for blasting from 1717 (two years before it came into use on Tyneside[16]); ventilation improvements from the 1720s; and wagonways from the early 1730s. As a result, mining took place further inland and at deeper levels without becoming uneconomic. Some of the changes during these years simply represented the use of methods already adopted on Tyneside; others were pioneered at Whitehaven and copied elsewhere. The important point is that without them the vast increase in production could not have come about.

Water was always a major problem. Originally mines were drained through the channels which ran from the pit bottom to the side of a hill. As mining progressed, more sophisticated methods became necessary. Sir John Lowther introduced the cog-and-rung gin at Whitehaven in 1685, and gins were used thereafter for raising both water and coal. Occasionally they were installed underground to operate at different levels. As late as 1750 Carlisle Spedding was exchanging notes with the Tyneside viewer William Brown on improvements to gins, but in any case these were not the final answer to the problem of drainage; the steam engine was far more crucial. Sir James Lowther first heard of Thomas Newcomen's successful experiments in 1712. He was urged by John Spedding to investigate the possibility of obtaining a Newcomen engine for Whitehaven because 'if you do not light on something of that kind that will drain the coals . . . at an easy charge, I am sure the price [of coal] will never bear the expense of it in the ordinary way we have hitherto been used to'.[17]

The first Newcomen engine in west Cumberland, the sixth of its kind in the country, was built at Howgill colliery in 1716. It was followed by three more at Howgill during the 1730s, and a number of others elsewhere in the region during the second half of the eighteenth century. In November 1715 Sir James Lowther agreed with the proprietors of the patent for an engine. Built the following year at Stone pit, in an area south of Whitehaven known as The Ginns, it had a 17-inch cylinder. Peter Walker was appointed by the proprietors of the patent as maintenance engineer, thereby originating the position in the colliery management hierarchy. He is known to have made a number of improvements to the engine's operation; indeed, when he died in 1733 Lowther thought that it would be 'difficult to find one so useful in making and fitting things for the engine'. Carlisle Spedding showed a similar talent, and was nearly tempted away from Whitehaven in 1721 to manage another engine. George Richardson (engineer 1733–38) tried unsuccessfully to patent an adaptation of the engine to raise coal as well as water.[18] Lowther bought the engine outright from the proprietors in 1727 and installed a larger cylinder. A second engine was built at The Ginns in 1736, and both were still used in 1769.[19]

Such improvements as the colliery engineers were able to make could not overcome the restrictions imposed by gravity. The maximum lift for a single pump was forty-five yards, and in practice the single lift was usually substantially less. To drain the lower levels a series of pumps had to be placed at different levels in the shaft, to raise the water to a point at which the engine could operate. In 1724 the Spedding brothers were attempting to construct a pump for this purpose, an exercise they abandoned when Lowther told them that such machines were already available in London. He inspected several and even tried working one himself; 'I turned it myself with one hand and raised the water in a two inch bore 85 feet'. But he finally decided that one of the others was a better investment. Once it was used in Whitehaven a number of deficiencies were uncovered, and from 1726 the pumps were made locally to a design by Carlisle Spedding.[20]

Newcomen engines were particularly crucial for sinking Saltom pit, an undertaking linked with Lowther's attempt to create a monopoly of the coal trade in the 1720s. Once he had decided to extend his interests to other parts of the coalfield, and to continue mining at Howgill and Whingill, he had to reach a decision on how to supply coal to the Whitehaven ships' masters. The choice available was twofold; either he could mine further inland or go deeper.

Lowther chose both, and Saltom was the result of his decision to mine at a lower level. The idea was to sink a shaft in Saltom Bay (a mile or so south of Whitehaven) and mine out under the sea. John Spedding described the project as 'perhaps the boldest thing that was ever undertaken', and Sir Thomas Lowther of Holker told his cousin in 1732 that 'by all accounts your works at Saltom are the finest in England of their kind'.[21] Work began in 1730, and a Newcomen engine with a 17-inch cylinder was erected the following year. This was soon replaced by a cylinder twice the size, which in turn gave way to a 42-inch cylinder in 1737. Since more power was still needed, a second engine, also with a 42-inch cylinder, was built in 1739. Carlisle Spedding fixed the engines to work simultaneously. After renovations in 1751 they were reported in 1756 to be 'pretty constantly at work'. A single, larger engine was introduced in 1782. As a feat of engineering Saltom was an immense success: more than 15,000 tons a year were raised from the pit between 1734 and 1751, a total output in excess of 270,000 tons. Sir John Clerk of Penicuik was greatly impressed by the works when he visited Whitehaven in 1739; 'the sink goes down perpendicularly', he wrote afterwards, 'eighty fathoms below the sea, and many underneath it. Sir James' riches in part swim over his head for ships pass daily above the ground where his colliers work.'[22]

Various engines were installed elsewhere in west Cumberland as a result of Lowther's successful pioneer work. In a history of coal mining written for the Victoria County History, R. W. Moore maintained that it was the use of engines in the 1730s and 1740s which made possible the Curwens' achievements. John Spedding informed Lowther in 1742 that 'Mr Curwen talks of setting up a fire engine [sic] at Workington, and for that purpose lately sent some of his officers to Newcastle and brought back an engineer ... to whom it is said he has paid fifty guineas towards providing materials'. However, the first direct evidence of an engine at Workington dates from 1769. Nine years later engines were in use at Moorbanks and Chapel Bank collieries, while six Boulton and Watt engines are reputed to have been built at Workington during the 1790s. The Broughton lease of 1755 gave liberty to erect New-comen engines, but whether or not this was acted upon is unknown. By 1769 engines were used at Greysouthen and Parton.[23]

No less of a problem than water were the poisonous gases known as 'fire-damp' which killed and maimed men working underground.

Explosions were the single most important cause of death and injury in mines during the eighteenth century; among those who died at Whitehaven were Carlisle Spedding in 1755, and two engineers, George Richardson in 1738 and Joseph Iredale in 1753. The steward ran the greatest risk, since the workmen would only return to the coal face after an explosion if he would demonstrate his confidence that the trouble was over by leading the way. Thus John Spedding told Lowther in 1730 that 'my brother is forced to be constantly among them', and further examples of Carlisle's bravery were recounted in 1736 and 1737. Lowther compensated the maimed and paid funeral expenses for the deceased. Burnt men were usually given between five and ten shillings. He also financed medical treatment; the catalogue of injuries was sufficiently long by the early 1730s for him to pay an annual retainer of £10 to Apothecary Smith 'for curing burned men'. By 1741 Mr Hamilton was receiving £20 for this task. Fortunately, because not many men worked together multiple deaths were rare, although five men died in 1753, and in the worst accident of all, at Corporal pit in 1737, twenty-two people lost their lives. Lowther distributed £100 to the relatives of those who died in this latter catastrophe.[24]

Ventilation problems multiplied in proportion to the depth of pits, but vital improvements were made in the Whitehaven collieries as a result of the practical inventiveness of Carlisle Spedding and the scientific genius of Dr William Brownrigg. Spedding's importance for the Lowther collieries was aptly summarized in an obituary which appeared in the *Newcastle Journal*. Much of the credit for the developments of these years was attributed to his 'uncommon abilities, assiduous application and intrepid conduct'.[25] He is best remembered for having invented the 'steel mill', alternatively known as the 'flint and steel'. This machine consisted of a small steel disc which was made to revolve rapidly against a piece of flint by means of a cogwheel and pinion. The stream of sparks emitted produced a glimmering light which was sufficient for haggers to work by, and which, unlike candles, did not ignite the fire-damp. Dr John Dalton commemorated the mill in verse when, describing the mines at the end of the day, he wrote:

> Nor strikes the flint, nor whirls the steel,
> Of that strange spark emitting wheel,
> Which, formed by Prospero's magic care,
> Plays harmless in the sulpherous air,

Without a flame diffuses light
And makes the grisly cavern bright.[26]

Quite when the mill was invented is uncertain, although it may have been in connexion with the Saltom pit project. Whereas exploratory trials were abandoned at Saltom in April 1729 because of the risk of explosions, it was possible to resume them a year later after experiments carried out by Spedding at another pit. Whether or not the invention was made at this time, it was not outdated until the Davy lamp was introduced in 1815.[27]

Spedding was also responsible for several other improvements, mostly to do with ventilation. The first was a method of 'coursing the air', by 'conveying air from one passage to the other to prevent the damps [sic] and stagnations', as Dr William Stukeley, the antiquarian, described it in 1725. Saltom pit was Spedding's biggest challenge. In effect he sank two shafts. Fresh air was forced down one to blow out the gunpowder smoke which accumulated after every underground blast. In addition, a tube or pipe was introduced through which bad air was drawn off from the pit bottom and discharged into the atmosphere at the pit head. Similar pipes were used by 1743 at Gameriggs and Thwaite pits (Howgill). Pipes were used at all the pits by 1747. Dr Richard Pococke described how these pipes operated in an account compiled following a visit to Whitehaven in 1750:

The foul air is very common in these pits, and in order to carry it off they enclose a shaft and place three or four wooden pipes in it about four inches square, which are carried up to the surface, and all the foul air going into this shaft is conveyed up the pipes, to which there are small funnels at top, about two inches diameter, by which one may perceive the air comes up; on them lay a plate of iron, with holes made through it: if they put a candle to it, or any flame, the air takes fire, and continues burning: 'tis observable that the fire put to it must be at four or five inches distance from the place where it comes out, or it will not take fire, which seems to prove that in this case it requires the air above to mix with it to make it take fire. It is also necessary that the pipes which convey it should not be more than four inches square, because if it was the air below might take fire, and they find by experience it will not when they are of this size, it being probably too much condensed as at first coming out. They have funnels like chimneys in many of the pits to convey away the air.[28]

In some mines a small amount of water was allowed to run down one of the shafts 'which, spreading over the pit, has a surprising effect in carrying the fresh air down the pit along with it, and so keeps a constant course . . . through the works which is so full of foul air which the fresh air drives out'. Underground air doors and boarded partitions also helped to circulate the air.[29]

Spedding's work was practical, but in an attempt to find out where the gas originated, and how explosions might be predicted, two experiments were performed before the Royal Society in the 1730s. After the opening of Saltom, bladders filled with air collected in the pit were sent to Lowther. Sir Hans Sloane, his friend and physician, 'fired' them before the Royal Society in 1733. A paper from Carlisle Spedding was presented at the same time, and later published in the *Philosophical Transactions* under Lowther's name. Three years later Lowther, by now a Fellow himself, conducted a similar experiment using gas collected at Swinburn pit. Although the learned gentlemen showed great interest in these experiments, no suggestions for countering the effects of gas were forthcoming. Another paper from Spedding was read before the Society in 1741 but not published.[30]

More positive progress was made when Dr William Brownrigg returned to Whitehaven from several years of study on the Continent, in the wake of the 1737 Corporal pit disaster. Brownrigg, the son of a local gentleman, was trained as a medical practitioner, but his interests ranged widely. He soon began to work with Carlisle Spedding; by 1741 the two men were 'daily consulting about managing the air', and two years later Brownrigg was described by John Spedding as being of great use to his brother 'in contriving how to deal with the damps'. As a result of his work, Brownrigg presented a series of papers to the Royal Society in 1741 and 1742, and was elected a Fellow. He refused to publish the papers immediately; indeed, recognition of his achievements only came in the 1760s. A paper on gases at last appeared in the 1765 *Philosophical Transactions*, and as a result he was awarded the Society's Copley Medal for the best original publication of the year. To facilitate his research, a small laboratory was built in 1743 close to the collieries. Air from the pits was conveyed to it along pipes constructed by Carlisle Spedding. Lowther met half the cost of the laboratory, and it was here that Brownrigg discovered how a fall in barometric pressure increased the risk of explosions.[31]

The work of Spedding and Brownrigg did not prevent explosions, which continued to happen occasionally at Whitehaven. When M. Jars visited Workington in 1765 he noted that they were still a frequent occurrence. However, the innovations were important, and by the mid-1760s Spedding's ventilation improvements were widely used on Tyneside. They were not superseded until the intro-duction of John Buddle's 'split-air' system in 1810.[32]

The final technological advances were in transportation. Coal was carried to the harbour by packhorses in the early seventeenth cen-tury. This mode continued to be used at Lattera colliery until it was temporarily closed in 1707, but cartways were introduced at How-gill in the 1680s. Carts, pulled by horses, were used as early as 1677, although proper cartways (or 'causeways' as they were known) consisting of wooden rails, bounded by baulks, on which the wheels could run, were only constructed during the following decade. Such a system of transport was unusual, but it was successfully employed at all Lowther's collieries by 1714, and on other parts of the coal-field thereafter.[33] The drawback to this form of transportation was that each cart was pulled by a single horse. The greater the distance covered, therefore, the greater the transport costs.

Consequently, once Lowther decided to mine further inland in the early 1720s, cartways became uneconomic. Wagonways, which utilized declivities to 'run' the wagons to harbour, and were much less dependent upon horse power, had to be built if the movement inland was to be a success. Initially they were used underground at Whitehaven, being installed at Corporal and Swinburn pits (How-gill) in 1722 and 1725 respectively. By 1756 underground wagon-ways were in use at all the Lowther collieries.[34] John Spedding first suggested the introduction of overground wagonways in 1725. At that time Lowther was wary of laying out money whilst he was unsure of an interest at Workington. If the coal owners there started mining, and built wagonways in imitation of Whitehaven, any initial advantage would be lost. Once Lowther had a stake at Workington, in the form of Seaton colliery, the situation changed, and it was here that the pioneer project took place. In 1732 a wagonway was constructed from Seaton to a purpose-built staith on the north bank of the Derwent at Workington, from which ships could be loaded. Built by a Newcastle engineer, it was extended to Great Clifton colliery in 1735 following Lowther and Lutwidge's agreement with Cookson and Williams. In 1740 it ran to 6977 yards. During the following seven years 3073 yards were added, and 2799 removed, reflecting changes in the mining area. Twenty-two wagons were used.[35]

Before the Seaton wagonway was completed Lowther authorized the construction of new sales facilities at Whitehaven. A wagonway modelled on the Workington prototype was built to link Corporal and Swinburn pits (Howgill) to Quay staith, a large new storage building on the quayside at Whitehaven. The staith was 120 yards long and could hold 3000 tons of coal. Its completion in 1734 heralded a change in the structure of coal production. The wagonway served Howgill colliery where four or five pits had normally been worked simultaneously. The number now doubled, with annual average output rising, as a direct result, from 71,000 tons between 1730 and 1734, to 84,000 tons between 1735 and 1739. The coal was either emptied into the staith to increase the stock, or discharged directly into the ships' holds through five spouts, or 'hurries', which protruded from the staith 'at such a distance apart that a ship of 300 tons can be under each and receive a loading at the same time'. After visiting Whitehaven in 1772, Pennant described how the coal was 'discharged out of the wagons into the holds of the ships, rattling down with a noise like thunder'. By contrast, production at Whingill colliery fell in the mid-1730s, and the colliery mainly supplied local demand. Its country sales rose from 10 per cent of total sales between 1722 and 1733, to 25 per cent in 1735 and to over 50 per cent in 1737. It remained at this level during the 1740s.[36] Whether or not the new sales structure improved turnaround times in Whitehaven harbour is debatable, but at least it overcame some of the difficulties Lowther encountered in supplying the masters.

To complete his reorganization, Lowther built a small pier and staith at Saltom Bay to service the new pit. The coal was raised close to the shore line, and he hoped to increase his profit margin by exporting from the site rather than incurring additional transport costs by moving the coal to Whitehaven. In turn, this would offset some of the heavy capital expenditure. The pier was completed in 1732, and in a letter written the following March Lowther referred to 'the quick loading of the *Ann and Mary* at Saltom'. However, the new quay soon proved to be hazardous. The colliery accounts record shipments there only in November 1735 and June 1736. By 1738 the pier had been more or less abandoned, 'scarce a ship a year', took on coal there, 'it being a dangerous place'. As a result, Lowther was faced with what must have been the galling prospect of having to move his coal overland to Whitehaven, along a route parallel to the sea.[37] This was achieved through the construction of a wagonway to Quay staith in 1734. But it rather negated the idea that more money could be spent on sinking when transport costs were negligible. Wagonways, after all, were only designed for inland collieries such as Scalegill, which was linked to Quay staith in this way in 1739.[38]

Lowther considered further wagonways. After acquiring the manors of Moresby and Distington in 1737 he gave some thought to the possibility of building a wagonway between the collieries and Parton harbour. This idea was never acted upon. However, a wagonway was constructed to Whingill colliery in 1754, after Carlisle Spedding had made improvements to the braking system used on the wagons to enable them to descend the steep declivity into Whitehaven harbour. Unsolved technical difficulties dictated that the final section was only completed early in the nineteenth century.[39]

Elsewhere in west Cumberland wagonways were introduced in the 1750s. Eldred Curwen was still managing with packhorses and carts at Workington in 1738, but improvements may have been made to coincide with harbour alterations in the 1740s. A wagonway had certainly been completed by 1760. The Broughton colliery partners constructed a wagonway to Maryport after the lease was executed in 1755.[40]

All the improvements described here were not only necessary, they were also expensive. It was the cost of mining which drove the smaller landowners out of business, as is clear from a few examples. Between 1716 and 1727, £18,470 was spent by Sir James Lowther recovering, and then mining, the prior band (i.e. seam) at Howgill. Saltom pit cost £4255 between 1729 and 1732, which included £1777 before any coal was brought to the surface, and another £950 in 1733 'to drive the air race in the bannock band'. The new coal staith and wagonway built between 1732 and 1734 cost £1400, and the two Newcomen engines at Saltom £1146 and £1202 respectively.[41]

More specifically, it is possible to ask searching questions about the total expenditure, and whether or not the Lowthers really laid out the £½m suggested by Brownrigg. The records vary in quality, but overall figures for the Whitehaven and Moresby/Distington collieries for the period 1695–1750 (to 1737 in the latter case) are given in table 3.2. Since these figures are not strictly comparable,

Table 3.2. *Income, expenditure and profit from the Lowther collieries, 1695–1750.*

	£
Total income	608,332
Total expenditure in the collieries	412,508
Total expenditure on land	37,196
Total profit	£158,628 (26%)

Source: Carlisle Record Office, D/Lons/W Colliery Abstracts.

it is more meaningful to separate the groups of collieries (table 3.3). The contrast between the figures is surprising. It shows that even a wealthy entrepreneur could not always make his collieries pay, and the extent of the Lowthers' dependence upon Howgill. If expenditure figures for the period 1664–95 had survived, the overall outlay might well have been shown to be close to Brownrigg's figure.

Table 3.3. *Income, expenditure and profit by colliery, 1708–50.*

Location	Years	Gross income £	Gross expenditure £	Profit £	% rate
Whitehaven					
Howgill	1708–50	482,953	320,705	162,248	33·6
Whingill	1714–50	57,948	37,071	20,877	36
		540,901	357,776	183,125	34
Land purchase†			20,872	−20,872	
			378,648	162,253	30
Moresby and Distington					
Lattera	1714–37	13,472	10,973	2,499	18·5
Gunerdine	1714–28	2,264	1,974	290	13
Birketts	1718–23	725	1,243	−518	–
Quarterbanks	1725–37	2,125	2,259	−134	–
		18,586	16,449	2,137	11·5
Land purchase†			11,575	−11,575	
			28,024	Loss 9,438	

† Whilst it is impossible to be certain that every purchase included in these figures was an integral part of the mining venture, the policy described in chapter 1 makes it intrinsically likely. Property evidently outside the coalfield has been excluded.
Source: Carlisle Record Office, D/Lons/W Colliery Abstracts.

How do these figures break down? The Lowthers budgeted so as to ensure that investment was more or less proportional to the tonnage mined in each colliery. The abstracted accounts make no distinction between day-to-day expenditure and capital investment, while weekly accounts survive only spasmodically. These show that labour, capital costs, harbour duties, and incidentals (for example, a pen and ink required by the colliery steward), were lumped together for accounting purposes. The modern concept of depreciation and saving for future investment was not employed.* Consequently the best means of indicating the rate of return over time is to calculate the expenditure on each ton of coal mined, against the selling price to the masters. Such figures are most relevant for Howgill as the major export colliery, and the barometer for all other changes. Missing years in table 3.4 are for those in which prices did not stay constant during the course of a quarter. The data clearly has deficiencies; it is obviously unsatisfactory, for example,

Table 3.4. *Profitability at Howgill colliery over time.*

Years	No.	Sale price per ton	Total cost £	Tonnage	Average cost per ton	Profit %
1708–12	5	2s 8d	17,839	186,897	1s 10d	42
1716–19	4	3s	18,642	199,269	1s 9d	42
1720	¾	3s	3,002	32,328	1s 11d	37
1721	½	3s	1,846	20,733	1s 9d	42
1721	¼	3s 4d	941	10,831	1s 9d	48
1722	½	3s 4d	2,153	20,814	2s	40
1723	½	3s	2,633	26,831	1s 11d	37
1724	½	2s 10d	2,355	24,257	1s 11d	33
1724	½	3s 2d	2,246	19,391	2s 4d	27
1725–27	3	3s 2d	19,609	173,266	2s 3d	29
1729–33	5	3s 4d	47,795	328,015	2s 10d	15
1734–38	5	3s 4d	49,418	421,620	2s 4d	30
1739–43	5	3s 4d	51,360	406,038	2s 6d	25
1744–48	5	3s 4d	52,303	466,782	2s 2d	35
1749–50	2	3s 4d	23,229	199,798	2s 3d	33

Source: Carlisle Record Office, D/Lons/W Colliery Abstracts.

* This was not only true of coal. C. K. Hyde has found the same for ironworks accounts: 'There is no notion of capital costs or of depreciation in these accounts [three overlapping manuscript collections relating to South Yorkshire and Derbyshire between 1690 and 1785]. Large expenditures on repairs were always charged against one year's operating expenses, causing costs to fluctuate violently in particular years.' *Technological Change and the British Iron Industry, 1700–1870* (Princeton, 1977), pp. 221–2.

to have very short time periods in the 1720s. Even so, a number of conclusions can usefully be drawn. The figures indicate a long-term rise in costs. This was inevitable in view of the movement inland with the expansion of Howgill colliery, and the undertaking of expensive projects such as Saltom pit. In addition, the figures demonstrate the level of Sir James Lowther's profits, generally around or in excess of 30 per cent. Such rates were probably not untypical; certainly they stand comparison with data for the south-west Lancashire coal field in the seventeenth and eighteenth centuries. However, as costs rose in Lancashire, profit margins fell.[42] Lowther experienced such a trend in the late 1720s and early 1730s as he reorganized his colliery undertakings. If land purchases are taken into account, his average profit between 1729 and 1733 was only 5 per cent. But the extent to which he dominated the industry, even if it did not amount to a true monopoly, is reflected in his ability to keep profit margins over 30 per cent thereafter. It is also clear from the figures for the early 1720s (even allowing for their inaccuracy) that Lowther's domination of the industry ensured that he did not suffer. Although demand fell back in Ireland, and the trade was distressed, Lowther's per ton profit margins were only reduced when he reluctantly agreed to drop his price in 1724. In the light of such figures, his comment in 1725 that 'it is not my business to raise the prices at Dublin to an extravagant height, but to help the masters that follow the trade to constant business' rings just a little hollow.[43] In mitigation of his position, however, price rises do seem to have been associated with cost changes. A rise of 2d a ton in 1728, for example, which provoked the masters into a three month combination, was justifiable on the grounds that his costs had increased by 7d a ton since 1724. He may also have been anticipating the high expenditure of the 1729–33 period.

What did this level of profits mean in monetary terms? Sir John Lowther's profits have been shown in figure 2.2 (p. 45), which, like figure 3.1, does not take account of property purchases. Figure 3.1 reflects the depression between 1718 and 1724, the cutback in trade around 1740 (coupled with heavy expenditure on a Newcomen engine), and the low profit margins when Saltom was being sunk and wagonways built in the period 1729–33. Total annual profits rose to a peak of £8500 in 1749, which certainly gives the lie to Walter Lutwidge's claim two years before that 'Seaton is a better colliery than Sir James' Whitehaven colliery by which he clears

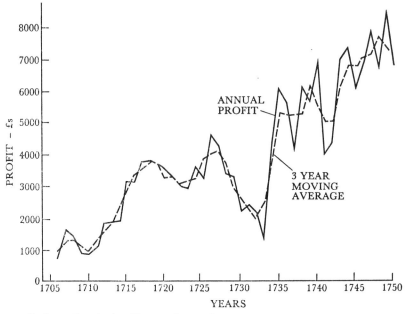

3.1 Sir James Lowther's colliery profits, 1706–50

£13,000 or £14,000 per annum'.[44] Moresby and Distington apart, Lowther's other colliery interests are less well documented. Profits at Dearham ranged from £130 in the first year in which it was worked by Lowther (1722/23), to less than £30 in the decade after 1726/27, but rose again from 1738 when Lowther expanded his interests in the area, to stay above £50 thereafter.* During the first five years that Seaton was worked by Lowther and Lutwidge, losses amounted to £3000. However, this was a period of considerable capital investment, and by 1736 the colliery was showing a profit of £719. Three years later it was about £2000, and although by 1743 Lowther was still claiming that he had not been reimbursed his initial outlay, profit that year amounted to £1256.[45] Finally, Scalegill gave Lowther profits of £260 in 1737 and £146 a year later. The introduction of a wagonway in 1739 pushed up the figure to £568, and profits remained at that level over the next couple of years.[46]

Simultaneous figures for all the Lowther collieries do not survive. Table 3.5 gives the nearest set of complementary data, and an estimate can be attempted for 1750. Howgill and Whingill profits

* Detailed figures for these collieries are given in appendix 4.

Table 3.5. *Lowther's colliery profits c.1737.*

Colliery	Profit £
Whitehaven–Howgill } –Whingill }	4,133
Moresby –Lattera } –Quarterbanks }	− 100
Scalegill	260
Dearham	16
Seaton/Great Clifton*	479
	£4,788

* ⅔ of 1736 profit.
Source: see appendix 4.

averaged £7407 between 1746 and 1750, and Dearham £118 over the same period. Less coal was being brought from Scalegill to Whitehaven, which suggests that profit there may have fallen to around £200 a year. Seaton profits, after deducting Lutwidge's share, will have brought Lowther at least £1200. Even if nothing at all is allowed for the Moresby/Distington collieries, Lowther must have cleared around £9000 overall in 1750. It must be stressed though that these figures do not take account of land purchases, which were separately accounted. By way of comparison, this profit level was nearly twice the amount Lowther was receiving from all his landed property in rents and estate income.

Finally, when placed alongside the Curwen evidence, these figures show that Lowther had by far the largest profit of the west Cumberland entrepreneurs. Henry Curwen's profits from the two collieries he worked between 1725 and 1727 are given in table 3.6. Eldred Curwen soon found that his decision not to lease his collieries to Lowther was a wise one. In 1736 he made a profit of £793 from his mining ventures, more than twice the rent Lowther had offered him. In 1742 and 1743 the figures were £2142 and £2218. His son Henry was receiving an annual average profit of £5500 when he died in 1778.[47]

The second component of the coal trade was the actual process of transporting coal from west Cumberland to the market, which for

Table 3.6. *Henry Curwen's colliery profits 1725–27.*

Colliery	Dates worked	Gross income £	Gross expenditure £	Profit £	% rate
Walton Wood	July 1725– February 1728	2,047	1,373	674	33
Ennon	August 1726– February 1728	592	560	32	5

Source: Carlisle Record Office, D/Cu Family Records, Ledger Walton Wood 1725–8.

the most part was in Ireland. Control was vested in the ships' masters. They hired seamen for their vessels, bought coal at the quayside in Cumberland (sometimes obtaining credit from the owners), and re-sold it at the market. Their profit depended on the selling price, which was probably the most significant factor in the whole trade.

The master was both mariner and businessman, responsible for his crew in all conditions, and yet himself only an employee of the vessel owners. If he owned a share in the vessel it was seldom more than one-eighth. Some of the more enterprising masters went on to become merchants, most notably Walter Lutwidge. Their origins varied, as indeed did those of the seamen, coming from a geographical area which included not only the west Cumberland hinterland, but also southern Scotland and Ireland. Lutwidge, for example, was of Irish extraction. The seamen who sailed their vessels constituted one of the largest occupational groups in eighteenth-century west Cumberland. Even so, at times demand for seamen outran supply. Some ships could not get hands in 1721 despite the recession, which Spedding blamed for the loss of between 150 and 300 seamen from Whitehaven by 1727. Consequently twenty vessels were laid up in the latter year; twelve were unemployed in 1729, and the shortage was commented upon in 1730, 1732, 1735 and 1738.[48]

The colliers themselves were broad-based vessels similar to those used on the Tyneside–London route. According to one source, twenty-five vessels belonged to Whitehaven in 1664, while other evidence suggests figures in the region of 100 by 1716 and 260 by 1755.[49] Workington's fleet expanded less rapidly. Surviving estimates put the number of vessels owned by the port at eleven in

1682, thirty-five in 1728 and over eighty in 1756.[50] The vessels became more efficient over time, increasing in size while employing less labour. None of the Whitehaven colliers exceeded 75 tons burthen in 1679; by 1702 thirty-nine vessels were of more than 100 tons, thirty were of between 50 and 100 tons, and only ten under 50. In 1736 the range was from 20 to 190 tons. The maximum tonnage manned by eight men in 1711 was 70 tons burthen, whereas by 1755–57 a similar size of crew was the average for a vessel of 100 tons.[51]

Greater efficiency in the trade was also obtained by other means, of which perhaps the most important was the regulation of the 'turn'. The rules about queuing at Whitehaven were altered in 1719 so that masters were guaranteed their place according to the order in which they passed the Isle of Man *outward* bound for Dublin. The purpose of this measure was to keep prices as high as possible. If a master had difficulty selling his coal, he might decide to cut his price and dispose of the coal rapidly at little profit. He could then return to Whitehaven so as to be well placed in the queue and obtain the best coal, which, he hoped, would attract good prices. Such a practice tended to depress prices. If, however, his place was secured before he even reached Dublin, then he could bide his time and await a good price. Yet to give the impression that greater efficiency brought with it increasing profitability may be misleading. Only a few figures exist from which to examine the state of the trade in quantitative terms, and these may provide a distorted picture.

Essentially two pieces of evidence can be used. The first is a pamphlet published by the leading coal masters in 1720.[52] On the basis of a detailed statistical analysis the masters claimed that the long queue at Whitehaven following the destruction of Parton was reducing some vessels to only three voyages a year. They calculated that eight was a more realistic figure if a master was going to have any reasonable hope of keeping his vessel in the trade, and concluded that carrying coal was not a very profitable exercise. The other evidence is from Lowther's shipping accounts.[53] The *Liffey* averaged over ten voyages a year between 1728 and 1753, while the *Resolution* managed more than nine annually between 1748 and 1755. These figures suggest that turnaround times were considerably faster by the 1730s and 1740s. Furthermore, some of Lowther's vessels were very profitable. The *Liffey* netted £635 from its sixteen years in the trade; the *Devonshire* £668 between 1737 and 1758, and the *Dublin* £692 between 1742 and 1758. Taken together, these two pieces of evidence suggest poor returns in the early 1720s, which is no surprise given the depression between 1718 and 1724, but a much improved situation in the 1730s and 1740s. The figures for Lowther's vessels certainly appear to give the lie to a recent claim that throughout the eighteenth century the coal trade was 'distinctly an unprofitable business'.[54]

To draw such a conclusion on the basis of this evidence, however, is possibly misleading. The masters' complaints in 1720 were at a time of particularly severe depression in the trade. When the coal trade expanded again in the later 1720s, and the alternative trading routes to America and the Baltic picked up during the 1730s, much of the slack disappeared. Even so, the Lowther figures cannot be taken to represent the state of trade in the 1730s. Lowther held a majority share in most of his vessels so that he could dictate the trading pattern they were to follow. He may also have ensured that they jumped the loading queue. Certainly the *Devonshire* was loaded from the quayside using coops in 1739, which suggests some bending of harbour rules.[55] Such advantages are likely to have inflated Lowther's profits, while the examples cited were not necessarily typical of the vessels he owned. Ten of the vessels in which he had a controlling interest made an overall loss. One of these was the *Cumberland*, built jointly with Lutwidge to promote the Seaton trade. It proved to be uneconomic to operate in the coal trade, and Lowther sustained an overall loss of £1122 on his investment when it was taken by the French in 1745.[56] It is probably safe to conclude that more profit was being made in the coal trade by the 1730s, but that the exodus of vessels into other trades during the summer months strongly suggests that coal was not the most lucrative of the various alternatives.

The fact that the trade was never particularly profitable can be attributed to a number of factors. Profits were affected by the pressures from land-based interests in both Dublin and Whitehaven; the trade was plagued by internal disagreements and affected by the natural problems of bad weather and adverse conditions in wartime (see below). Three factors, however, stand out as being most significant: disclaimed responsibility, dependence on a single market, and the masters' individuality.

The lack of responsibility for the trade was of considerable significance. Multiple ownership of vessels, with many of the share-holders living away from the ports and taking little personal interest in the ships, did not make for good management. The absence of direct participation in the trade by the coal owners, at least prior to the mid-1730s, was detrimental in that it ensured that they felt little sense of obligation towards the masters in terms of profits. The situation was not uncommon; writing of Northumberland and Durham, Hughes found 'incontestable evidence' that in 1729 'the shipping interest was quite distinct from the coal owners'. The same was true of north Lancashire.[57] Finally, the masters' sense of responsibility might have increased if they had owned a greater financial stake in their vessels; Lowther thought that this would at least have ensured that they kept the vessels in a better state of repair.[58]

Secondly, the trade was almost entirely dependent on one market. The masters had effective control of the colliers because of the pattern of dispersed ownership, and they were not easily persuaded to search for markets other than Dublin. Since wind direction determined when the vessels could sail, whole fleets would arrive in the Irish capital at the same time, ensuring low prices for everyone. Such a disadvantage might have been partially offset by securing return cargoes. However, these were scarce, and more often than not to Bristol and Liverpool when they were obtainable. In part, this was the result of legislation in 1667 which banned all English and Welsh ports from importing Irish cattle and wool. Sir Christopher Lowther had appreciated the benefits of importing Irish goods in the 1630s; he had even suggested that iron could be brought back from Ireland in vessels carrying cattle, 'so it may lie under the beasts' feet without hindering anything'.[59] The cattle ban was temporarily lifted between 1679 and 1681, and the wool ban between 1697 and 1699, but unlimited trade was only restored in the 1750s. Some smuggling was inevitable; an investigation of 1704 found that despite the prohibitive legislation, 'the country here is in a great measure supplied with beef and other provisions from Ireland'.[60] Almost certainly these were smuggled, although the level of customs evasion inevitably remained uncertain. Of course a few ships did bring a legitimate return freight. The *Prosperity* of Whitehaven cleared outwards with sixty-five chaldrons of coal on 1 December 1708, and entered a return cargo of 'six ordinary chairs' on the 23rd: hardly a windfall, admittedly, but this was more than most. Since a ship was no more likely to return with a cargo if it took coal to a port other than Dublin, little additional incentive existed for searching out new markets.[61]

A third factor conditioning profit margins was the masters' individuality, and the absence of any regulations governing the trade other than the harbour rules. Masters and shipowners alike valued independence: the right to buy and sell, and to run the trade as they pleased. Although Lowther proposed in 1725 that 'we must talk already of my contracting with a number of ships to carry all the coals',[62] the drawback to such arrangements was made clear by Brownrigg in 1765:

> Our masters and owners of ships, while they looked upon themselves as principals in this trade, have heretofore been encouraged obstinately to pursue it for seven years together, with constant loss, until at length they gained their point, which was securing the trade to themselves. But had they only been employed as carriers, they would have been as ready to carry for one as for another, and all the expense of supporting the trade would have fallen on their employers.[63]

To complicate the matter still further, no regulation existed governing the number of ships involved in the trade. Whilst the total number did not outstrip the tonnage of coal to be moved, the trade remained profitable. A downturn in demand revealed the narrow margins within which it worked. The 1718–24 depression, for example, showed that the trade was 'exceedingly overbuilt in shipping'.[64]

The masters' independence and lack of co-operation worked to the benefit of the coal owners since they could not agree on concerted action either to force up the selling price in Dublin or to alter the price in west Cumberland. Efforts to regulate the Dublin market were generally unsuccessful. Evidence survives of an attempt in 1684, although the outcome is unknown. In 1716 an agreement was reached to stop the trade for a fortnight before sending fourteen ships to test the demand, but twenty-six masters refused to conform. During the 1718–24 depression various discussions took place as to how minimum prices of 18s a ton in winter and 16s a ton in summer could be extracted at Dublin. Nothing positive came of these talks.[65] The masters tried to keep the price steady in 1726 by sending a few ships at a time. Lowther feared that such a move would provide the Irish with an excuse to pass further restrictive legislation; it was tantamount to 'putting a knife into the hands of the Irish to cut their throats'. He instructed Spedding to load out of turn, and to allow those masters ready to continue with the trade on a normal basis a regular supply of the best coal.[66] Other proposals followed; according to Brownrigg, 'when our traders have been at variance with the city of Dublin by attempting to fix the price of coals, or on other accounts, they have talked much of agreements'.[67] Such discussions were seldom productive, and 'each man for himself' was the general rule. The corollary was periodic glutting of the market with consequential low prices.

Ironically the masters' greatest success in working together came with combinations designed to prevent a rise in the owners' selling price. The Lowthers' predominance in the market ensured that no other owner could effectively undercut them by supplying enough coal at a cheaper rate, and some sort of tacit understanding on prices seems to have been observed along the coast. But even the best laid plans for monopolizing the market were likely to come to grief should the supply fail, and this point was not lost on the masters. They recognized that the owners were more likely to submit to pressure than the Irish. The owners depended on the masters; the Irish could revert to legislation as a means of controlling the price. Sir John Lowther was forced to reduce his price from 3s* a ton, to 2s 8d during the 1690s. When he tried to restore it to 3s in 1698 the masters refused to buy and Lowther had to back down.[68]

Sir James Lowther decided to charge 3s a ton from Michaelmas 1714, and the masters struck immediately the price rise came into force. No coal was taken for 'above five weeks', but Lowther would not change his mind, and the masters eventually submitted. A further crisis came in 1721 when Lowther introduced a two-tier price system. This was partly to exclude the tobacco ships from the coal trade, because their masters tended to accept low prices and depress the market, and partly to act as an incentive to those masters who continued to trade with Whitehaven coal during the summer months. Coal was to be sold at 3s 4d a ton between October and March, and 3s during the remaining six months of the year. To institute the policy Spedding raised the price to 3s 4d a ton in January 1721. A more inappropriate time to raise the price could

* The masters' expectation that they should pay 3s a ton in Whitehaven and sell at 18s in Dublin suggests a high rate of return. However, in addition to victualling costs, duty payments and vessel depreciation, the masters had to make an allowance for the larger size of the Dublin ton. The subject of measure is examined in appendix 4, but it is worth noting here that the Whitehaven ton was approximately three-fifths of the Dublin ton.

hardly have been found, coming as it did hard on the heels of a pamphlet produced by the masters in 1720 which purported to show that the economic viability of the coal trade was in serious doubt. Within a few days Spedding reported Whitehaven to be 'all in an uproar', with 'almost a general combination to refuse taking at 3s 4d'. The strike lasted until mid-February, only ending when Spedding began giving sacks well filled with the best coal to anyone prepared to buy. Lowther kept his word and reduced the price to 3s a ton at the beginning of April.[69] The two-tier system remained in operation until a further amendment became necessary in 1723. Because the price at Dublin was low in October that year, Spedding put off raising the Whitehaven price for a month. However, the Dublin price continued to fall, and the masters stopped buying altogether. Spedding, with Walter Lutwidge's support, persuaded Lowther to alter the pricing system to 2s 10d and 3s 2d, for summer and winter respectively. The new arrangement ran until 1725 when, despite fears of a combination, Lowther stabilized the price at 3s 2d all the year round.[70]

When he restored the price to 3s 4d a ton in 1728, Lowther brought on the most protracted dispute at Whitehaven in the whole period. Spedding raised the price by 2d at Michaelmas, and the masters struck. Invitations were sent to the Scots and Irish to send ships to carry coal to Dublin, and Lowther enlisted the help of his cousin Sir Thomas Lowther to try to find masters at other ports who would be willing to help out. Masters refused to break the strike because they feared for the lives of their seamen and the safety of their vessels. Even John Spedding's brother Lancelot, master of the *Speedwell*, was not prepared to offer any help. Distress produced 'a devilish spirit' in Whitehaven, and by December the town was in 'unexpressible calamity'. Three ships broke the strike. Lowther considered letting other masters take at 3s 2d 'for the sake of helping the poor to victuals', but this was simply a rationalization of his desire to get coal to Dublin by any means. Eventually, on 3 January 1729, the masters called off the strike. Spedding, unhappy that they should have ended it in such a rational manner, gave orders to load any 'foreign' ships in the harbour first. He soon rescinded the order for fear of restarting the combination, and because of the danger posed to life and property by starving seamen. The coal leaders then threatened to stop carrying the coal to the harbour unless he raised their allowance. Under the circumstances

Spedding had little alternative but to comply with their demands.[71]

The impact of the combination was far-reaching. When vessels began to arrive in Dublin during January 1729, the masters sold their coal at 30s a ton. The lord mayor used his authority to cut the price, first to 20s, and later to 16s a ton.[72] The Irish Parliament, anxious to prevent a repeat performance, hoped to lessen dependence on west Cumberland by constructing a canal from Lough Neagh to Newry. Legislation authorizing the canal was passed in 1730, the intention being to bring county Tyrone coal to Dublin by water. The canal was completed between 1731 and 1742, but it never played a particularly significant role in the movement of coal.[73] Perhaps most significantly, however, the combination revealed that at a time of buoyancy in the trade – Lowther's 1727 sales were more than 50 per cent up on 1724 – the masters were capable of mounting an effective combination. Possibly it is significant that Lowther did not raise his price again, although in terms of profit margins he had no real need to do so, except perhaps in the period of heavy expenditure around 1730.

If the figures in Lowther's shipping account can be taken to suggest that the coal trade was more profitable in the 1730s than in the depressed years of the early 1720s, the reason was almost certainly bound up with a fundamental restructuring of its organization. The ships' masters may have been reluctant to search for new coal outlets, but they were well aware that Whitehaven's trading links with America and the Baltic might offer more lucrative employment. In part this reflected the seasonal nature of the different trades. Whatever the general state of the Dublin market, the best prices were obtained during the winter months. Low summer prices coincided with the opportunity for masters to set their sights on different trade routes, and quite a number of vessels could be used for more than one purpose. Furthermore, even the larger vessels specifically designed for the trans-Atlantic route could adapt to carry coal in the winter. Thus fewer ships were normally on the Dublin run during the summer than in the winter, which was fair enough given the pattern of demand. However, by the mid-1730s summer numbers had dwindled to the point where the continuation of the trade was threatened. Spedding could find only thirty-seven vessels *not* engaged to visit the American colonies or the Baltic in the summer of 1736. A year later he estimated that only twenty-three ships were left on the coal trade.[74] This trend was not altogether surprising, given the rapid expansion of the tobacco trade from about 1735 (see chapter 4), but increasingly the summer coal trade was coming to depend on the Irish sending their own vessels to White-haven. This was just the type of situation which would give the Scottish and Welsh competition an opportunity to invade the market.

Two possible courses of action were open to the coal owners: the unpopular one of hiring masters to carry their coal, or, more practically, buying vessels of their own. Provided that they pur-chased at least a 50 per cent holding in any vessel, the owners could dictate the course of trade to be followed by the master, thereby circumventing some of the problems noted above. As a bonus, they could use the vessel to help break combinations. Lowther was aware of both advantages. He told Spedding in 1736 that 'I think when any ships that are to be sold that will do for the coal trade, I should buy 9/16ths of some of them to keep them constantly in the coal trade all the year round.' He preferred 'middling' ships, 'the better to deal with the perverse masters that we might have always one or more to load and to break in upon their combinations'. Large vessels might be more economic to run, but they could not be used so effectively for this latter purpose. Overall, his aim was to 'make sure of a large exportation of coals and also drive the masters to follow the example of my own ships to enable them to do better'.[75]

It was Walter Lutwidge who first persuaded Lowther of the benefits to be derived from owning vessels. A former ship's master, and primarily a wine and tobacco merchant, Lutwidge wanted to promote Seaton colliery by acquiring shares in one or two vessels. He persuaded Lowther in 1733 that they should buy a one-eighth interest in the *Hope* of Workington, financed in proportion to their holding in the colliery. Two years later the partners agreed to meet the cost of building a ship to carry Workington coal to Ireland. The *Hibernia*, built at Workington in 1735 for an outlay of £1027, was launched on 20 January 1736. By April it was on its third voyage to Dublin, carrying about 140 tons of coal. It had made thirteen voyages by April 1737 bringing a clear profit of £134. The project was an encouragement to all the owners, although in any case, by the end of 1735, Lowther had decided that he would 'provide ships of our own against next summer and make the voyages on our own account'.[76]

Lowther's intention was to acquire what he termed 'floaty' vessels, ones 'that draw little water in proportion to the coals they carry'. He even suggested to Spedding that 'as for the shares I have of other ships in the common way of building, it is best to dispose of them as opportunity offers'. He held one-eighth shares in three vessels, one of which was sold in 1739, by which time his interest in the other two (the *Lucia* and the *Bonetta*) had been converted into more than a 50 per cent holding. Between 1735 and 1738 he bought two vessels outright, shares of more than 50 per cent in a further six (although one was re-sold in 1737) and jointly financed the building of two new ships with Walter Lutwidge. There followed a four-year break, but he resumed purchasing in 1742, and by 1749 had acquired shares in a further nine vessels, of which six were of more than 50 per cent. By the time the shipping account was closed in 1758, five of the vessels had been lost, three sold, one laid up, and one wrecked, leaving thirteen in service, of which Lowther had more than a half share in ten.[77]

The other coal owners concerned in the Irish trade followed Lowther's lead. Eldred Curwen launched his first vessel, the *Charming Jenny*, in December 1736. He bought a second vessel in 1737 and talked of building others. By 1745 he owned three ships outright, and had shares of one-sixteenth or one-thirtysecond in a further seven. Humphrey Senhouse and John Christian also took a financial stake in the trade once they began mining.[78]

The impact of the owners' intervention was mixed. It certainly did not resolve all their problems. Spedding complained in 1743 that 'we have few ships left at home for the coal trade', and a year later he was again at a loss to know how exports could be maintained. Throughout the decade the trade was partially dependent upon the Irish fetching coal from west Cumberland.[79] Nor did intervention prevent combinations. A dispute at Workington in 1749 demonstrates the continuing power of the masters. Lowther and Lutwidge had collected 2d from the masters for each ton of coal sold to them at Workington, 'to make and repair our own wharf'. The masters became increasingly unhappy about how the money was used, and agreed in January 1749 to buy no more coal until they received a satisfactory explanation. They insisted that the duties should 'be immediately applied to cleansing and repairing the harbour'. Lowther was incensed by such 'illegal combinations to impose upon the coal owners', but the dispute had been resolved to the masters' satisfaction by the following month, although the outcome is unknown.[80]

Lowther certainly ensured that his vessels prosecuted the trade with vigour. Evidence about their activities is limited, but the *Liffey*, the *Resolution* and the *Boyn* made all their voyages in the coal trade (166, 75 and 51 respectively), and all but four of the *Felicity*'s 108 were with coal to Dublin.[81] The *Lucia* provides perhaps the best example of how an owner converted a vessel for the trade when he took it over. Lowther bought a one-eighth share for £101 in 1723, and between then and 1738 it made eleven voyages to Virginia and the West Indies, one each to Norway and Holland, and nineteen with coal to Ireland. He then bought the other seven-eighths of the ship for £405, sold a quarter to the master, and used it exclusively in the coal trade until it foundered at sea in 1742.[82]

Before examining the market, some additional comments are needed on the important relationship between ship's master and coal owner. One of the most crucial areas of co-operation concerned the customs. The Lowthers made efforts to discover the state of the trade by having an informer in the customhouse. Sir John Lowther obtained the important post of customs surveyor in the port of Carlisle (with special responsibility for Whitehaven) for Thomas Tickell in 1666. From that time he received 'a monthly account of the entries in the customhouse, thereby the better to judge the state of trade'. Not surprisingly, he tried to obtain a similar position for William Gilpin. As it transpired he failed, but his son obtained the position of comptroller of customs for Gilpin in 1706. Sir James sought a similar position for John Spedding in the 1720s. Although Spedding was appointed to a post at Berwick in 1727, as a stopgap until a suitable position at Whitehaven became available, he never obtained a place in Cumberland.[83]

In addition to assessing the state of trade, the owners took pains to protect the ships' masters against the full impact of customs duties. When Howgill wagonway was built in the early 1730s Spedding had a four-ton wagon made – the usual size was three tons – as a means of circumventing the watchful eye of the officials. The masters preferred to take coal directly from the hurries, rather than out of the reserve stock in the staith, but by using the four-ton wagon Spedding could induce them to take the latter, since one ton of coal was duty free.[84] Furthermore, the Lowthers owned the customhouse. It was built in 1695, and leased to the customs commissioners, together with a watchtower on the pier, for a fifty-one year term. In 1745, when the lease was near to expiring, Spedding advised Lowther that in the event of a new lease being granted it would be advisable to exclude the watchtower. Since the building of Quay staith the tower had given the customs officials a particularly good vantage point from which to view the quantity of coal being put on board each ship. This had led to bargaining between masters and officials, with the masters paying one shilling a voyage bribe to prevent themselves being fully rated to the duty. Spedding feared that if the collector got wind of this illegal arrangement,

we shall be in danger of having the ships charged to the full. . . . This is really a matter which concerns you both as a convenience for your own buyers, and also to deprive the custom house officers of so easy and certain a way of coming at the knowledge of the coals really shipped, and therefore I beg leave to recommend it to you that upon no account whatsoever you grant them any longer term in the watchtower.[85]

Lowther took the hint; although a new lease was not settled until 1752, the watchtower was omitted.[86]

Another important area which called for co-operation between masters and owners was the state of trade in wartime. Ships could be lost to become naval transport vessels,[87] seamen were press-ganged to man ships of war, and those colliers left in the trade were harassed in the Irish sea by enemy privateers. With wartime conditions existing for long periods (1689–97, 1702–13 and 1739–48), and rumours of war in 1718, 1726, 1727 and 1733, it was important to have someone on the spot in London to request protections and organize convoys. 'Protections' were certificates issued by the Navy Board through the Admiralty Office to seamen in 'reserved occupations', which exempted them from being pressed; the Whitehaven colliers usually received protection similar to that granted to their counterparts in Northumberland and Durham.[88] Seamen refused to sail, and went off into hiding once a press was suspected, so that speed in obtaining protections was vital if supplies for Ireland were to be maintained.

The Lowthers took upon themselves the responsibility of procuring protections. Sir John Lowther benefited from contacts he established as an Admiralty commissioner between 1689 and 1694. A Mr Gordon, whom he had promoted, helped to obtain protections during the 1690s and 1700s. In 1711, however, he was 'like to leave the Admiralty Office . . . for a better preferment', an untimely move because the war was still in progress. According to Sir James Lowther, writing to Gilpin, this made it 'the more necessary to give the doorkeeper a guinea to forward those matters, and if I find it necessary to give one of the under clerks two or three guineas I shall let you know'.[89] Lowther was remarkably persistent in seeking protections, although he expected the masters both to pay for them, and to refund him any out of pocket expenses. He went to the Admiralty every day for over a month in 1711 to make sure that his requests were not forgotten. When rumours of war circulated towards the end of 1726 Spedding sent Lowther a list of ships likely to need protections. Although Lowther refused to solicit for the Workington vessels in case this damaged his Whitehaven interest, a stipulation he not unnaturally dropped after he obtained the Seaton lease in 1728, he was ready to go to the Admiralty 'every post day' to solicit protections for Whitehaven vessels. In the event the press was called off and none were issued. A year later, in 1727, Lowther was 'daily at the Admiralty office' to see if his were ready. Once the press began, the Whitehaven protections were issued so quickly that Spedding reported the masters to be 'vastly surprised you should get them so soon, and even without their particular application to you'.[90] He again requested a list of ships in 1733, and as a result received his protections on 7 March 1734, 'the first day protections were issued . . . before the members for Durham and Northumberland'.[91]

Protections were not wholly satisfactory. Men were occasionally pressed in spite of them, and the Admiralty was reluctant to limit the numbers who could be pressed by covering too wide a range of men. Lowther supported legislation in 1740 to protect all seamen under eighteen and over fifty-five, but he was still not satisfied, and considered an appeal to the King and Privy Council for relief in 1741. New rules were introduced in 1742. These could not prevent men being pressed illegally, but they were some help; Lowther believed that 'the seamen may depend upon it that I shall get them discharged'. His confidence was successfully tested in 1743 when he was instrumental in having two Whitehaven apprentices discharged. Lowther was never completely satisfied. He continued to complain to the Admiralty periodically about the detrimental effect of illegal impressment upon the number of boys apprenticed to go to sea.[92]

The colliers were often subject to harassment from privateers when they crossed the Irish sea in wartime, and convoys were regarded as essential. Sir John Lowther made representations to the

Admiralty during the 1690s, usually in response to requests from his Whitehaven stewards. After his retirement to Whitehaven in 1698 this became more difficult. When no action was forthcoming in 1702 in response to his letters soliciting a convoy, he asked his son to make a personal request at the Admiralty. Convoy vessels could not always be spared, and a Cumberland ship was converted for the purpose; between 1710 and 1712, the *Whitehaven Galley*, of which Walter Lutwidge was the master, was the protecting vessel.[93] War scares in 1718 and 1727 made the masters wary of sailing without a convoy, but the most serious problems occurred during the 1740s. Convoys were requested from the time that war broke out with France in 1744. Lowther told Spedding 'I shall do all that ever I can to get good convoys for our coal trade', but it proved to be a difficult task. Spedding suggested that a Whitehaven vessel be fitted out with sixteen or twenty guns. In 1744 Peter How, a tobacco merchant, allowed the *Howard*, one of his ships outward bound for Virginia, to act as a convoy guard for colliers going to Dublin. Twenty-one vessels were escorted and the success of the venture prompted Lowther to suggest fitting out the *Cumberland* for the task. A similar scheme was under way at Newcastle to equip a local vessel to protect the colliers plying the London route. However, it was an expensive business. Spedding estimated that it would cost £549 to fit out the *Lowther*, a 70 ton brigantine, with guns and small arms for fifty men. Nevertheless, the *Cumberland* was converted for convoying during the summer of 1744, as were the *Devonshire* and the *Augusta*, two other vessels in which Lowther had an interest. Other masters borrowed guns from returning Virginia-men, but when it became apparent that the Navy would be unable to supply regular convoys, more permanent measures were needed. The *Adventure* was chartered to the Navy commissioners in June 1745 to act as a convoy protection vessel, and ships involved in the coal trade provided the crew. Such measures were only partially successful; amongst the ships which fell into enemy hands was the *Cumberland*, in 1745.[94]

The Lowthers also regarded their membership of Parliament as an instrument for protecting local trading interests. They opposed legislation passed by the Irish House of Commons, although Sir James Lowther complained that the ships' masters took all too little interest in measures under debate in Dublin. Not until 1725 did he persuade them to employ a solicitor in Ireland to attend the Parliament and 'take care of the affairs of the coal trade'.[95] In fact, of course, Lowther also stood to lose if unfavourable bills were passed, and he was better placed than the masters to oppose such measures. Poynings Act of 1494, which remained in force until 1782, provided that legislation drafted in Ireland could be altered, without the possibility of re-amendment by the Irish Parliament, or suppressed altogether by the king and council in London.[96] It was up to an English MP who objected to Irish legislation to make representations to the Privy Council. Lowther 'attended early . . . the committee of the lords of the council' in 1710, and 'apprized several more of them of the unreasonableness of the [yarding] bill' (see below). He claimed to have gained alterations to another act in 1719 as a result of using similar tactics.[97]

In the English Parliament the Lowthers were particularly interested in national measures likely to have an effect on the coal trade. A good example relates to seamen. The periodic shortages at Whitehaven were a matter of concern to Sir James Lowther. He therefore opposed a bill introduced into the lower house in 1739 for the compulsory registration of seamen, on the grounds that the government might use such information to second men in wartime. Such a situation would have reduced the numbers available for the coal trade. When the matter was again debated in 1741, Lowther argued that 'nothing would do in the present emergency but a greater bounty, for that more force and violence than the present way of pressing, and especially giving power to search for them and break open private houses would destroy the breeding of seamen'. By contrast he sponsored a bill introduced in December 1739 designed to ensure that one-quarter of the crew *must* be British, but three-quarters *might* be foreign. He saw this as a means of increasing the number of seamen.[98]

Measures likely to impose additional taxation on the trade in some way were also opposed by the Lowthers. It was agreed in 1706 that for the safety of Whitehaven ships a lighthouse was needed at St Bees. Sir James Lowther undertook to find out from Trinity House the procedure to be followed, making clear at the same time he would expect to be paid a rent and to have sole right to supply coal, if the house was built on his land. The lighthouse was not completed until 1718, at which point the masters believed their safety to be assured. Consequently they objected the following year when a Mr Trench sought legislation to establish a lighthouse on the Isle of Man, to which he would expect them to pay duty. Preparations were made to oppose his bill, with finance for the resistance being collected at the rate of 2d for every chaldron of coal exported. Eventually Trench dropped the project, which left the masters to squabble over what to do with the money.[99] This was not the end of the affair since Trench owned a lighthouse at Skerries, near Holyhead. After his death in 1725 this was sold, and in 1729 a Mr Morgan applied to Parliament for legislation to enforce the payment of duties. Again a fighting-fund was established, and Lowther was commissioned to oppose the proposition. After a certain amount of manoeuvring, he agreed with Morgan on a compromise measure whereby the Whitehaven masters would pay the duty on only one voyage a year. Legislation to this effect was passed in 1730.[100]

Once coal reached Ireland it still had to be sold, and the marketing mechanism was crucial, in view of the importance to the masters of the price. The lack of formal organization in the trade has already been shown, but a marketing structure was vital because a number of vessels normally arrived in Dublin at the same time. If the masters sold their coal at the mast, none of them would attract a reasonable price. A form of stockpiling for later sale had already come into use by the early eighteenth century, with coal being off-loaded into storage containers known as gabards. Legislation passed by the Irish in 1705 was intended to prevent this practice, on the grounds that it was designed to influence prices. As a result, the masters began to 'yard' their coal: that is, sell it to the keepers of yards to retail. Once again this offended the Irish, and further legislation was passed in 1710 despite a petition from the Cumberland masters alleging that any attempt to curb yarding amounted to an attack on the whole trade. The new regulation stipulated that not more than 1000 tons of coal was to be held in one yard. Although the limit was raised to 1500 tons in 1719, such a restriction was hardly designed to aid rational organization of the trade. In any case the 1719 legislation made matters worse by ordering the masters to sell their coal within eight or ten days of arriving at the quayside.[101]

Restrictions of this nature were distinctly unhelpful given the depressed state of the coal trade in the early 1720s. The situation altered when conditions in the trade changed towards the end of the decade. The legislation seems seldom to have been enforced after

1728, which would imply that the market was no longer glutted. A scheme of 1737, however, suggests that the masters were by no means happy with the marketing procedures available to them. That year Thomas Bacon was appointed, on a salary of £150, to oversee the Dublin sales procedure. Twelve Dublin pursers were contracted, at £40 a year, to handle all the west Cumberland coal and were made responsible to Bacon. This was the first rational marketing structure to be organized from west Cumberland, and it involved masters from both Workington and Whitehaven. Unfortunately it collapsed within a year because the pursers proved to be dishonest, and because of local disagreements among the west Cumberland masters.[102]

The Irish seized any opportunity that they could to regulate the price, hence the dangers of combinations in west Cumberland. Dublin's lord mayor intervened to restrict the price following the 1728 combination, and it was feared that his action would be followed by legislation. This did not happen, although it was again anticipated in 1738 when the lord mayor of London was granted the right to set the price at which coal might be sold in the capital, and to fine anyone exceeding the limit. However, no effort was made to obtain similar powers for Dublin, and the legislation was not renewed after a year.[103]

Although Dublin undoubtedly took the great majority of west Cumberland's supply, the owners were well aware of the need to diversify the trade. Perhaps not unnaturally, talk of new routes tended to be most noticeable in periods when the trade was depressed. The idea was conveniently forgotten once recovery began. To make matters worse, the masters were generally unwilling to go elsewhere. John Spedding found them reluctant to leave 'their old beaten road to Dublin', and it was in fact a sensible business policy to stay at home and wait for a rise in the Dublin price. As a result, some of the other Irish ports had to send their own vessels to fetch west Cumberland coal, even before the shipping difficulties of the 1730s and 1740s. In 1715/16, for example, vessels came from Belfast, Cork, Wexford, Wicklow, Londonderry, Newry, Kinsale, Killyleagh, Dundalk, Downpatrick, Bangor, Bray and Carlingford. More than seventy vessels cleared the port of Whitehaven in 1743, with coal for places in Ireland other than Dublin, some 8 per cent of the total.[104]

It was in the owners' interests to persuade the masters of the benefits they could derive from finding new outlets. With peace in prospect, as the Spanish Succession war drew to a close in 1712, Lowther foresaw the possibility of a coal trade to the south-west of England and the southern Irish ports. He even acquired letters inviting the Whitehaven masters to trade to Plymouth and Falmouth. A few masters took up the offer: the *Love and Anne* cleared for Plymouth in March 1716, and for Penzance three months later. Also in June 1716, the *Henry* carried coal to Falmouth.[105] However, most of the masters preferred to concentrate on the Irish route, at least until the 1718–24 depression produced a spate of new ideas.

With the onset of depression in 1718 the Whitehaven 'turn' was adjusted to aid those masters willing to look for new outlets for the coal trade. Masters were allowed to jump the queue if they entered into a bond, commensurate with the size of their vessel, but usually about £20. The bond, which obliged the master to trade with places other than Dublin, was sufficient to make the voyage unprofitable if he failed to comply with its terms. It was forfeit if he went to the Irish capital after all. The system could easily be abused, and tended to be suspended when prices rose in Dublin; indeed, it was suggested that there should be 'a rule that when coals sell above such prices [i.e. those that would guarantee the masters a reasonable profit] no ships shall load out upon bond'. The scheme was suspended in 1725 when too many masters wanted to load on bond, following the return of the Baltic vessels in the autumn. How much it was used thereafter is unclear, although Lowther remarked in 1752 about 'putting a stop to the ships having liberty to load out immediately for foreign parts upon bond'.[106] Also during the 1720s depression, Lowther made enquiries about the possibility of a trade to France, where coal was needed because of a scarcity of wood.[107] The drawback was that the duty of 4d a ton was twice the Dublin rate.

Further pious words were spoken when the trade temporarily declined at the end of the 1730s, but it was only in the 1740s that the coal owners really began to appreciate the unhealthiness of depending on the Dublin market. Despite the continued growth in sales during the 1740s and 1750s, Lowther remained interested in diversifying the trade. Coal was used as ballast by ships carrying tobacco to France in 1744. With the coming of peace in 1748 Lowther hoped to persuade the masters to sail to southern Ireland, where they could sell to French skippers. His idea here was that the latter would find it advantageous to buy Whitehaven coal on such terms, since they would halve the duty payable by purchasing direct from Newcastle. Negotiations continued into 1749, at which point Lowther decided to promote the trade himself by sending the *Shannon*, in which he had a five-eighths interest. The possibility also arose of sending coal to Spain and Portugal in 1752 and 1754, while in 1753 consideration was given to loading Baltic-bound vessels with a cargo of coal for Denmark.[108]

Although none of these schemes appears to have met with any great success, the Lowthers were always hopeful of promoting the coasting trade, and a few cargoes of coal were sent coastwise each year, mainly to southern Scotland. Sir James Lowther's most positive promotional effort came in 1738, partly because of a reduction in Irish trade. Lowther declared himself ready 'to labour to get off the coast duty . . . I have more and more hopes of succeeding'. By December that year a report was circulating in Wigan that he intended to farm the waterborne duties in the port of Lancaster. It was believed that his intention was to 'stock all the country with his own coals free of duty in regard the trifling rent he would pay as farmer of this branch of the revenue'. Although nothing was immediately forthcoming, in 1741 Lowther hoped that a petition from Cornwall to the House of Commons might prove to be 'a foundation for a union of the members of all the maritime countries that have mines of copper, tin, lead, coal etc to graft somewhat upon for relief about the coast duty on coals'. Legislation followed allowing a rebate of duties on coal sent for use at the tin and copper mines. This does not appear to have made much difference to the pattern of west Cumberland's coasting trade, despite the benefit gained by Tyneside.[109]

Writing in 1765, William Brownrigg described how

the late Sir James Lowther perfected what his father had planned out and carried the trade to such an height that neither the Welsh, who before him were in possession thereof, nor the Scotch at Ayr, Irwin or Saltcoats, who long strove to gain it, nor the Irish from Newry or Ballycastle . . . could stand in competition with him therein.[110]

His conclusion was perceptive; despite the hazards which confronted the trade during the later years of the seventeenth century and the first half of the eighteenth century, Whitehaven in particular, and west Cumberland in general, still dominated the Dublin market.

Lowther, as the major entrepreneur responsible for providing a large proportion of the coal supply, and as the owner who took the most active interest in the smooth running of the trade, deserved such praise. In true entrepreneurial style he had run the risks and filled any gaps which threatened to disrupt the trade, as with his purchase of shipping shares in the 1730s, for example. He had encouraged the masters to look for new markets, opposed Irish legislation (something the other coal owners were not in a position to do), and generally expended considerable energy in order to keep the trade going, whatever the circumstances. In the process he had acquired for himself a considerable income. Ironically, one of his most significant contributions was to show the other coal owners the possibilities open to them. Where he had led the others followed, hence the competition of the later eighteenth century. But whilst the coal trade was the staple from which all else developed in west Cumberland during this period, it was not the only economic activity. New trade routes and new industries, either directly stimulated by coal or merely coincidental, developed; it is on these that attention must now be focussed.

4

The Expansion of Trade

Ports in west Cumberland developed in a remarkably similar way to those on Tyneside and Wearside. The coal trade was the staple, supplemented by a trading link with northern Europe. But they also differed: west Cumberland's trade to the Baltic did not match that of the north-east and neither did it develop coal-based industries on a significant scale. On the other hand Whitehaven* took its place alongside Bristol, Liverpool and Glasgow in the trans-Atlantic trade. For a while in the 1730s and 1740s this offset some of the imbalance which resulted from relying so heavily on a single economic function. However, just as Tyneside failed to sustain the momentum of its industrial development, so Whitehaven's new trade proved to be a short-lived phenomenon. Although west Cumberland continued to trade with areas well beyond Europe for the rest of the century, these new connexions never threatened to displace the economic underpinning provided by the coal trade. To quote the customs collector in 1820, 'the business of this port continues in the same state it has for some years past, the principal trade being that of exporting coal to Ireland, the Isle of Man and foreign parts'.[1] Nonetheless, the expansion of other trades should not be understated. New employment opportunities were provided and local manufacturing was stimulated, to cite but two of the effects. In addition, a merchant community emerged which took

* Distinguishing the port from the town is not easy, particularly after 1720 when the port books no longer differentiate between the coastal towns. Whitehaven (town) was the dominant outlet in the developments described here. Statistically this is evident from the pre-1720 port books, while Spedding's letters to Lowther in the 1740s suggest that, while Workington vessels plied similar trade routes to those of Whitehaven, they did so on a much less significant scale. (See especially his letters of 1 April 1742 and 26 October 1743, Carlisle Record Office, D/Lons/W.) Unfortunately there is no means of checking the accuracy of his claim. This chapter relates to the whole port, but references to 'Whitehaven' normally mean the town, and the term 'west Cumberland' is used for general references to the port.

considerable interest in the further development of the region. This proved to be particularly important, simply because the Lowthers, or to be more accurate, Sir James Lowther, chose to concentrate on the coal trade. Although Sir James appreciated the need for diversification, all his financial involvement was in the coal trade.

Ostensibly the development of new trade routes was not surprising since, as Sir John Lowther pointed out in the 1690s, 'where ships are the whole world is the market'.[2] Once the coal trade to Ireland had been established in the early years of the seventeenth century, the more enterprising ships' masters began to look for new trading outlets in which they could employ their vessels, a search encouraged by the relatively poor returns from the coal trade. A small-scale coasting trade operated for most of the seventeenth century. Grain and coal were the chief commodities exchanged in a geographical nexus incorporating Carlisle and southern Scotland, Liverpool and Bristol.[3] By the 1680s more distant links were being established. Thomas Denton, during his tour of Cumberland in 1688, noted that 'they import French wines and brandy from Bordeaux and Nantes'. Wine imports remained significant until about 1720, fourteen ships entering at Whitehaven in that year. Perhaps because of smuggling, the trade – or at least the legitimate side of it – fell away.[4] But it was the trans-Atlantic and northern European routes which were the most significant. West Cumberland was conveniently situated to trade with America and the West Indies, while the demand for timber and other shipbuilding materials, stimulated by the increased trading activities of the port, produced a regular trade to the Baltic.

The significance of this trading diversity was considerable in terms of local prosperity and the repercussive effects on employment in both shipping and related industries. However, Whitehaven could not compete for long with Glasgow in the tobacco trade, it never remotely matched Liverpool's interest in the sugar and slave trades, and it could not generate sufficient demand to trade with the Baltic on the same scale as Tyneside. Consequently the prosperity, particularly during the 1730s and 1740s, proved to be short-lived.

The expansion of the Cumberland coal trade in the seventeenth century coincided with changes in England's trading pattern which encouraged trans-Atlantic connexions. The Navigation Laws of

1660 and 1671, along with the evolution of a protectionist tariff, ensured that goods passing to and from the colonies would have to be carried in English vessels, a situation which opened up a variety of new opportunities for English shipping.[5] Tobacco from America and sugar from the West Indies were the chief commodities brought across the Atlantic, their prices tumbling once the colonialists stepped up production in the seventeenth century. The great majority of the import was re-sold in Europe, where semi-luxuries soon became near necessities. Bristol and Liverpool built up considerable interests in all the trans-Atlantic routes. At Liverpool, for example, vigorous trading gave the merchants a strong interest in the sugar and slave trades, quite apart from a considerable tobacco trade.[6] Whitehaven's Atlantic trade was heavily weighted in favour of tobacco, with never more than three vessels bringing sugar (from Barbados, Antigua and Jamaica) in any twelve month period. The slave trade was almost completely ignored, at least before the 1750s.[7]

Liverpool and Whitehaven were particularly well placed in the later seventeenth century to take advantage of the colonial connexion. They built up their trans-Atlantic links in the war-torn years after 1689 when eastern, southern and south-western ports were particularly vulnerable to privateering attacks. Ships' masters preferred to use the safer route north of Ireland, a fact which was advantageous to the north-west.* Whitehaven had two further advantages: its link with Ireland, which provided a ready source from which to acquire goods (especially linen) for sale in America,[8] and its proximity to Scotland. The Glaswegian merchants had established direct links with the colonies in 1665, but tobacco imports were forbidden by the 1671 Navigation Act, unless they first passed through an English port. Rather than give up the trade, Scottish merchants began to freight Whitehaven ships to America as a means of circumventing the law. This practice became increasingly

---

* Liverpool and Whitehaven developed along remarkably similar lines in these years. Both needed to extend their harbours early in the eighteenth century, and both were granted their first act of Parliament to facilitate this in 1709. Both had to return to Parliament within a few years to arrange for additional borrowing. Furthermore, both had to extend their harbours again in the 1730s, and acts were passed for Liverpool in 1738 and Whitehaven in 1740. At both places new industries developed in the early years of the century, and they had similar trading interests. Perhaps the major difference was Liverpool's greater overall interest in the colonial trade. See F. E. Hyde, *Liverpool and the Mersey 1700–1970* (Newton Abbot, 1971), and P. G. E. Clemens, 'The Rise of Liverpool, 1665–1750', *Economic History Review*, 2nd series, xxix (1976), pp. 211, 217.

popular when frigates were sent to the Clyde in 1689 to stop and search vessels suspected of illegally trading directly to America.[9]

Whitehaven's tobacco trade passed through four distinct phases: rapid growth from the 1680s until 1707; a reduction in overall activity in the three decades which followed; rapid growth in the 1730s and 1740s; and a long decline thereafter. The earliest evidence of a west Cumberland vessel taking a direct interest in the tobacco trade dates from 1683, when the *Resolution* crossed the Atlantic. By 1686 the Bristol merchants were complaining of 'the shifting of the plantation trades of late years to the northern ports, Chester, Liverpool, Workington and Whitehaven'. Four ships entered at Whitehaven with tobacco in the first six months of 1688, and that same year the customs officials asked for a new customhouse owing to 'the increase of our plantation trade'. Financial returns were high. The *Resolution* had made at least seven voyages to America by 1693 when Sir John Lowther, who had owned a one-eighth share in the vessel since 1680, had made a profit on his investment of £146.[10] An indication of the scale of the trade during the 1690s is given by table 4.1.

Table 4.1. *Vessels expected at Whitehaven from Virginia.*

Year	Number
1693	10
1694	10
1695	14
1696	11
1697	20

Source: Carlisle Record Office, D/Lons/W William Gilpin to Sir John Lowther, 5 March 1694, 28 September 1695, 4 November 1696, 1 November 1697, John Gale to Sir John Lowther, 2 July 1693, Whitehaven Papers, bundle 14.

The union with Scotland in 1707 dealt a severe blow to the English tobacco trade from which it took many years to recover. The direct intervention of the Scottish merchants in the re-export business was especially harmful to Whitehaven, as table 4.2 makes clear. It was quickly recognized that 'the said trade is much lessened since the Union'. The reason was thought to be connected with the high duties on imports.[11] After the initial impact of the Union had

Table 4.2. *Vessels entering at Whitehaven with tobacco, 1706–20.*

Year	Number
1707	22
1708	12
1711	11
1716	13
1720	20

Source: Port Books (see bibliography).

passed the trade showed signs of recovery. Re-exports to Dublin continued, and smaller amounts of tobacco were sent to the Isle of Man and Norway. However, the cutback was real enough. Imports of tobacco at Whitehaven averaged 1·5m pounds (of which 80 per cent was re-exported) between 1698 and 1702, but only 1·2m pounds between 1722 and 1726.[12] Ironically the Scottish merchants afforded the Whitehaven trade some relief in the 1720s. They did not have enough vessels of their own, and so began to employ the Cumberland masters again. According to the customs collector, by 1721 the Scottish trade was 'mostly carried on by ships and sailors hired from time to time from hence by the Glasgow merchants, having twenty-four sail from us this year of ships of good burthen'. According to Spedding, at least forty-two vessels had gone to America 'of which about fourteen are to discharge here . . . the rest for Glasgow'.[13] The practice was curtailed in 1723 when Glaswegian and Whitehaven merchants clashed over alleged customs frauds. With only one vessel hired in 1724, and the coal trade still depressed, some masters looked to Ireland for a freight to America, a practice normally resisted because of bad returns.[14]

During the 1730s and 1740s Whitehaven's tobacco trade expanded at a phenomenal rate, as the merchants began at last to exploit the major European markets in Holland and France. For a while in the 1740s Whitehaven outpaced Liverpool, Bristol and Glasgow, to stand second only to London in the size of its tobacco import; a third of the total import of the four western ports passed through Whitehaven. The Dutch had been purchasing in England since the Navigation Laws were passed. In the later seventeenth century they bought anything up to half the tobacco re-export, and they never took less than a third during the eighteenth. From the mid-

1730s the Whitehaven merchants started to exploit this outlet, and by 1740 Holland was recognized as 'their chief market'.[15] Two years after this an even more lucrative market opened up in France. From the time its tobacco import became a state monopoly in 1674, France gradually increased its share of the British market, and in the 1730s it surpassed Holland. Until the 1740s the French bought little in the north-west, but they were attracted to White-haven and Glasgow with the outbreak of war in 1739. The two ports were able to provide cheaper tobacco, and had firms which were large enough to make substantial sales, but were not sufficiently strong to demand extortionate prices.[16] The result of moving into these new markets is clear from table 4.3.

Table 4.3. *Recorded imports and re-exports of tobacco at Whitehaven, 1726–50.*

| Years | Imports (lbs) | Exports (lbs) | | | | | |
		Holland	Ireland	Norway	France	Other	Total
1726–30*	1,836,200						
1738	3,168,000						
1739	3,942,000	3,441,372	1,102,245	25,641	–	15,779	4,585,037
1740	4,457,000	4,020,693	1,198,309	–	–	–	5,219,002
1741	5,413,000	4,783,838	929,521	35,388	–	260,000	6,008,747
1742	6,970,000	3,170,728	793,707	–	3,024,332	30,391	7,019,158
1743	9,443,000	3,403,096	1,132,612	–	5,434,719	650	9,971,077
1744	9,359,000						
1745	7,073,000						
1746	9,145,000						
1747	9,266,000						
1748	10,622,000						
1749	10,556,000						
1750	9,013,000						

* Average.
Source: J. M. Price, *France and the Chesapeake* (Ann Arbor, 1973), pp. 590, 596, 599.

Apart from demonstrating the extent of customs frauds by the under-recording of imports, these figures reveal the remarkable speed with which the trade expanded. In 1739 twenty-six vessels entered with tobacco at Whitehaven, thirty-six entered the following year, and fifty-seven in 1743. Whitehaven was 'reckoned the second port in England for importation of tobacco', a statement of Lowther's amply borne out by the figures for the 1740s. Spedding described the trade in 1745 as 'the very life and soul of Whitehaven'.[17]

But the boom was not sustained. Despite the high level of imports throughout the 1740s, by the end of the decade Whitehaven was being outpaced by Glasgow. In 1749 and 1750 the Scottish merchants imported over 60 per cent more than their west Cumberland counterparts. For a while the trade continued to be profitable; in 1759 a visitor to Whitehaven noted '140 ships in the Virginia trade. A very large import of tobacco, greatest part of which is sent to France by Mr Hall [sic] a contractor here.' Already, however, the cracks were appearing, and Peter How, the man responsible for forging the French connexion, failed in 1763. His bankruptcy coincided with a crisis at Amsterdam, to which the merchants had attempted to re-transfer their loyalty after 1758. In the early 1770s Thomas Pennant noted how 'formerly about 20,000 hogsheads were annually imported from Virginia; now scarce a fourth of that number; Glasgow having stolen that branch'. He exaggerated slightly – imports were about a third of their 1743–49 level – but Whitehaven now handled only about 6 per cent of the total export of the four western ports; three decades earlier the figure was nearer 33 per cent.[18]

The Baltic trade was an additional and often profitable interest for the Cumberland merchants and masters, although it experienced nothing comparable to the spectacular expansion of the tobacco trade. As the coal trade expanded a greater number of ships were required, and even though by no means all of the west Cumberland vessels were built locally, a significant demand existed for ship-building materials. The complementary development of coal mining raised the demand for ropes. These were manufactured in White-haven using hemp brought from the Baltic. Although the Baltic connexion tended to be a secondary interest for merchants, it was a regular business with as many as twenty vessels visiting ports in northern Europe in some years.

The trade originally developed in the 1680s because of the in-convenience of bringing shipbuilding materials and hemp overland from Newcastle. Thomas Denton noted in 1688 that 'they import . . . fir, sails, pitch, tar and cordage, from Denmark and Norway'. Tanning bark and iron were brought from thence four years later. The expansion of English trade to the Baltic in the 1680s was facilitated by the decline of the great trading companies. The failing powers of the Eastland and Russia companies threw open the Baltic to competition, and the north-east and west Cumberland were among the areas which built up their links before wartime disruption overtook the trade in the 1690s.[19] The Whitehaven rope company, for example, had a scheme in 1694 for a regular trade to the Baltic, which almost certainly fell victim to the war. The company intended to employ two vessels. First, the ships were to take a freight to Virginia and return with tobacco, of which the worst could be sold in Newcastle and the best in Holland. Second, they were to go on to the Baltic to collect goods, mainly hemp, for Whitehaven.[20]

The brief interlude of peace between 1697 and 1702 saw a minor resurgence of the Baltic trade, but although ships continued to visit the Baltic during the Spanish Succession War, complete recovery came only after 1731 (table 4.4). In the absence of port books little

Table 4.4. *Ships entering at Whitehaven from the Baltic.*

Year	Number
1707	2
1716	4
1720	23 (18 Whitehaven 5 Workington)
1739	11
1741	16
1743	10

Source: Port Books (see bibliography).

is known about the trade between 1720 and 1739. Despite the figures, it was claimed in 1740 that 'above twenty' vessels sailed for Norway annually. 'A good many' had gone there in 1744, according to John Spedding, and the development of shipbuilding, ropemaking, and the iron industry in the 1740s and 1750s, was largely dependent on imports from the Baltic.[21]

Some of the west Cumberland ships' masters, having carried coal to Dublin, obtained a freight from Ireland for the Baltic. This was a stand-by interest, the main disadvantage of which was that rates tended to be low. In 1724, for example, with both the coal and tobacco trades in recession, twenty ships turned to Ireland for freights, thereby ensuring low rates. By contrast, rates could become sufficiently competitive to endanger the smooth running of the coal trade, a situation which is known to have occurred in 1732 and 1749.[22]

Although the new trade routes developed independently of the staple coal trade, some interconnexions were inevitable, of which shipping was the most obvious. Merchants and coal owners were shareholders in vessels, which gave them at least a passing interest in each other's concerns. More significantly, many of the vessels were versatile, and masters could move from one trade to another depending upon where they expected to make the greater profit. Hence the paradoxical situation whereby many vessels were underemployed when the coal trade was depressed early in the 1720s, but too few vessels were available to keep the coal trade going during the summer months when the tobacco trade was expanding in the 1730s and 1740s.

Generally speaking, however, the merchants and coal owners were remarkably detached in their interests. Few merchants took any part in the coal trade, although Peter How, the wealthiest and most powerful of them in the 1740s, sounded out the possibility of exporting coal to Spain in the 1750s.[23] The Lowthers took little direct interest in the tobacco trade. Sir James Lowther, though ready to venture £1000 with his father in the Virginia trade in 1703, refrained from any investment of this kind after inheriting the Whitehaven estates, on the grounds that he did not live in Cumberland.[24] Thus his only financial involvement was an indirect one. Vessels in which he owned less than a 50 per cent share undertook non-coal voyages: the *Friendship*, the *Hope*, the *Concord* and the *Experiment*, for example, all made a number of visits to the Baltic. Only two of those in which he held a majority interest were involved in other trades, the *Union* and the *Cumberland*. Both were sent to Virginia during the 1740s, on the grounds that they were too cumbersome to operate in the coal trade during wartime.

If the Lowthers' financial interest in the new trades was negligible, they certainly appreciated the advantages of diversification and took steps to help the local merchants. In the 1690s, Sir John Lowther was encouraging the Baltic trade by acquiring letters of introduction for ships' masters. His son was active on behalf both of

Whitehaven's trading interests, and also individual merchants. He spoke in the House of Commons when the tobacco trade was under discussion, and presented a number of petitions from Cumberland about the state of the trade.[25] He attended at the customhouse in London on behalf of the merchants; indeed, he only ever went there 'upon the business of our merchants'. When war broke out with France in 1744, Lowther obtained passes to allow the tobacco trade to continue.[26] He investigated the problems of individual merchants. In 1725, for example, he was asked to find out the fate of one of Walter Lutwidge's vessels, 'seized at Bordeaux'. When the ship was released in July that year, Lowther claimed that it was 'upon the application I made, while other ships of the like circumstances were still detained'. He helped Lutwidge again in 1733, persuading the Russia Company, by his own account, to drop an intended prosecution on payment of 20 guineas towards their costs.[27]

Lowther made a significant contribution by lending small sums of money to merchants with cash-flow problems. Credit was not easily obtained in eighteenth-century Cumbria, and merchants had few people to whom they could turn apart from Lowther. Peter How and William Stephenson borrowed £270 in August 1739; with Richard Kelsick, How borrowed £1000 in 1741 and 1742; and on his own, How borrowed a further £1000 in 1742 and 1743.[28] Walter Lutwidge called on Lowther for rather more help than most. He borrowed £300 in 1720, £200 in 1726 'upon the coming home of his ships', and £300 in 1731. None of these sums had been repaid when his affairs reached a crisis in 1737. James Arbuckle, his son-in-law and Belfast agent, was on the verge of financial ruin, and in an effort to save him Lutwidge borrowed a further £1000. His total debts to Lowther, together with unpaid interest, were brought into a mortgage of his estates, which he did not finally clear until 1745.[29]

In helping the merchants the Lowthers were indirectly aiding the overall economic development of the region. Where they fell short in terms of encouraging new trades and industries to supplement coal, the merchants filled in. Wealth accumulated in trade was divided between conspicuous consumption to acquire the trappings of local social status, and new enterprise in industry and commerce. In this their role might have been more significant had the expansion of the tobacco trade in the 1730s and 1740s not been short-lived. Relatively few personal and business papers have survived from which to make an assessment of the local merchant community, but some account of their contribution is necessary to make sense of the overall developments of these years.

The merchant community was not a large one, as table 4.5 demonstrates. In a year when Whitehaven stood second only to London in the quantity of its tobacco imports, just twenty-one men are known to have been directly involved in the trade. The largest firm, How and Kelsick, supplied 34 per cent of the 5.4m pounds re-exported to France. William Hicks provided a further

Table 4.5. *Tobacco entries for Whitehaven merchant companies, 1743.*

	Place of call*				
Company	Virginia only	Maryland only	Virginia + Maryland	Other	Total
Peter How and Richard Kelsick	6	1	1	1	9
Joseph Adderton	1	2	2	–	5
John Lewthwaite	3	2	–	–	5
Edward Tubman	3	1	–	1	5
William Gale	3	1	–	–	4
Robert Gilpin	1	2	1	–	4
William Hicks	3	–	1	–	4
Thomas Hartley and Timothy Nicholson	1	–	1	1	3
Thomas Lutwidge	1	2	–	–	3
William and Thomas Gilpin	–	1	1	–	2
Walter Lutwidge	1	–	–	1	2
James Milham	1	1	–	–	2
Timothy Nicholson and Daniel Stephenson	–	–	2	–	2
Mathias and William Gale	1	–	–	–	1
Henry Littledale	1	–	–	–	1
Timothy Nicholson	–	1	–	–	1
Thomas Patrickson	–	–	1	–	1
James Spedding	–	1	–	–	1
James Spedding and John Ponsonby	1	–	–	–	1
Edward Tubman and Thomas Hartley	1	–	–	–	1
	28	15	10	4	57

* The distinction between Virginia and Maryland was significant in that the French refused tobacco from the latter as 'not being under the same rules in the country and often very bad'. (Carlisle Record Office, D/Lons/W John Spedding to Sir James Lowther, 14 May 1742.) Most of the Maryland import must have gone to Holland.
Source: Port Books (see bibliography).

15 per cent. Many of these merchants had capitalized on the trade from small beginnings. Informal co-operation, with several men combining to freight a vessel, was an early hallmark of the trade. Some of the partners on these occasions were ships' masters: Walter Lutwidge, Edward Tubman and Richard Kelsick, all began their careers in this way before moving on to higher things. Kelsick's father had skippered the first Whitehaven-financed vessel known to have crossed the Atlantic ocean, in 1683. William and Thomas Gilpin were respectively grandson and son of William Gilpin, Sir John Lowther's steward. William Gale was the younger son of Lowther's former colliery steward, while James Spedding was the son of Sir James' long-serving steward.[30] Some grew very wealthy, particularly Peter How. In 1742, at the beginning of the French trade, he called upon his London drawer George Fitzgerald for £30,000 in just eight months. John Spedding thought that the trade would raise him a 'monstrous fortune', and at his death in 1772 the *London Daily Advertizer* described him as 'for forty years one of the most principal merchants in the north of England'.[31] William Hicks was described after his death in 1758 as having 'acquired a very considerable fortune and purchased several freehold estates of about £10,000 value as well as large stock and trade and personal effects in Virginia'.[32] His whole fortune was estimated at about £20,000. John Gale, eldest son of Sir John Lowther's colliery steward, left at his death in 1726 a plantation at Kingston in Maryland, shares in six ships, and a freehold estate at Egremont.[33] Walter Lutwidge claimed in 1754 to be 'worth £20,000 or more'.[34]

Such success stories need to be carefully balanced against the reverse side of the trading coin. Thomas Lutwidge, one of Whitehaven's most respected early merchants, overstretched his resources and seems to have ended his days in a Dublin debtors' gaol, sometime in 1744.*[35] Robert Gilpin, a leading tobacco merchant in the 1740s, failed in 1751. Later that same year Lowther wrote of 'so many bankruptcies at Whitehaven', and, two years later 'these many bankruptcies at Whitehaven', after Daniel Stephenson failed.[36] The case of Benjamin Lowes may not have been untypical. He probably started trading in the mid-1740s, but quickly ran into

---

* The Thomas Lutwidge referred to as a major tobacco importer in 1743 was almost certainly the eldest son of Walter Lutwidge. Thomas junior established himself as one of Whitehaven's most important merchants during the 1740s, but it is not known whether he had any connexion with the business interests of his elder namesake.

financial difficulties. By 1754 he had a mortgage to Lowther for £300, and when he died four years later left debts totalling £3584, mainly to other merchants. Since his assets of £1919 were insufficient to pay the debts, an exchequer bill was entered against his widow by Peter How and Thomas Lutwidge. Most spectacular of all was How's own failure in 1763 for between £40,000 and £50,000.[37]

Merchants were well aware of the uncertainty of their occupation, and at all the major ports they were to be found investing in local property to give their fortunes a secure base. At Hull, for example, 'no merchant of any consequence was without his seat or estate, large or small, in the East Riding or Lincolnshire', while land was the largest single investment of Glasgow merchants after commerce.[38] Whitehaven was no exception. When Peter How failed in 1763, he owned a variety of properties including freehold land in Egremont and St Bees with a rental value of £166 a year.[39] In 1737 Walter Lutwidge had an estate in Ireland, houses in Whitehaven, and a customaryhold property at Rockcliffe, near Carlisle. Despite financial troubles he was reputed to have bought property at Ravenglass in 1739, and the following year he claimed to be 'about purchasing an estate that will cost me £3000'. Also in 1740, he bought an estate at Beckermet, a few miles south of Whitehaven, for £811. He purchased another property at Woodhouse in 1741 for £421.[40] James Spedding, son of Lowther's estate steward, was just 22 when he began trading in tobacco in 1741. His timing was fortuitous, and by 1750 he had been able to spend more than £2000 on property. As a result, his eldest son was a country gentleman with no attachment to Whitehaven.[41]

Industry was another area into which the merchants pumped money, especially with the development of their prosperity in the later 1740s. Walter Lutwidge had interests in Seaton colliery, rope, glass and brickmaking in Whitehaven, and a ropewalk in Workington. William Hicks was his partner in the glasshouse project begun in Whitehaven during the 1730s, and a member of the consortium which established an iron forge near the town in 1750. The senior member of this partnership was Peter How, who also developed an important tobacco manufacture locally. Whitehaven merchants were prominent in setting up Maryport furnace in 1752, and two of them partnered John Christian and Humphrey Senhouse in the Broughton colliery lease of 1755. The link between

THE EXPANSION OF TRADE

trade and industry was often close; indeed, some of the merchants were simply Whitehaven manufacturers importing raw materials for their businesses. During the 1740s Thomas Hartley, one of Whitehaven's leading ropemakers, regularly freighted a ship to St Petersburg for hemp. Similarly, at least four of the eleven ships which entered at Whitehaven from Norway in 1739 brought timber for Thomas Patrickson, a local shipbuilder.[42] Interestingly, neither man could escape the lure of tobacco. A vessel entered at White-haven with tobacco for Patrickson in 1743, and Hartley had shares in two vessels which came from Virginia that year.*

A potential problem for the merchants was that of discounting bills of exchange payable on London. English trade was able to develop because there existed negotiable instruments of credit devised for use in overseas dealings. However, they were usually payable in the capital. Clearly, it was inconvenient for merchants to discount them for cash, and then have to transport coin and notes long distances. Consequently, in the absence of banks before the later eighteenth century, the Whitehaven merchants needed to meet someone in west Cumberland with money to remit to London. They could then sell them the bill in exchange for cash. In turn, the person involved could discount the bill for cash in London.

Remittances arrangements in Cumbria presented the merchants with no real problems before the later 1730s. The customs and ex-cise receivers, and the receivers-general of taxes, had more than enough money to return to London. Indeed, they experienced some trouble in obtaining bills. In 1702, the collector of customs could not acquire bills nearer than Newcastle, and complaints were frequent in the 1720s and 1730s. It was reported in 1734 that 'the collector sent to Manchester, Lancaster, Leeds and other trading towns in Yorkshire near 100 miles off to see what remittances could possibly be had there'. The following year, and again in 1737, bills could only be obtained in Manchester.[43] Central government was sufficiently aware of the remittance problems in the north-west to allow the receiver-general of taxes an extra 3d poundage, as compensation for the problems that he faced in obtaining bills.

An influential factor creating the bill famine was the amount of money Sir James Lowther remitted to London from his estate. Like the receivers he had great difficulty with returns. For many

* The merchants' industrial activities are dealt with in greater detail in the next chapter.

years he relied on one important client, Nehemiah Champion of Bristol, who supplied south Wales with iron produced at Backbarrow. William Rawlinson, who dealt with Champion on behalf of the company, preferred to fetch his money from Whitehaven, rather than bring it overland from Bristol or London. His first transaction through Lowther was in January 1716, when £872 changed hands. Thereafter the business became a regular one: £1060 in December 1717, £900 in January 1719, £1000 in December 1719, £525 in January 1726, and £1400 in January 1727. The importance of this connexion is evident from the events of January 1729. Money was scarce at Whitehaven following a long combination in the coal trade during the previous autumn. Knowing this, Lowther told Spedding, 'you must try all ways that Mr Champion may not be disappointed'. A few days later he reasserted the instruction in a different way: 'I would not have Mr Rawlinson disappointed'. Spedding made a number of local enquiries, and was eventually helped with £300 from John Fletcher, the land tax receiver. The Backbarrow link remained important even when Champion withdrew. John Becket, like Champion a Quaker ironmaster, took over the business, and in January 1734 remitted two bills through Lowther for £1237.[44]

Lowther was well aware of the competition; he sought to offer better terms than the customs officials, and to neutralize the receivers by having friendly parties appointed to the post. Thus his distant cousins Charles Highmore and John Fletcher acted as receivers more or less continuously from 1716 until 1743. Lowther expected them to use the cattle drovers' bills, and not interfere in the Whitehaven market. When Fletcher considered resigning in 1740, Lowther thought it would be best to replace him with a Carlisle man 'who would fall in with the drovers and not get our merchants' bills'. The drovers' bills were unreliable, and both Highmore and Fletcher went bankrupt. In trying to keep Highmore solvent, Lowther became involved in a mortgage which troubled him for many years. This improvement, together with the various places in government service that he obtained for the Fletchers, may indicate a twinge of conscience on his part.[45] As long as he could keep them away from the merchants he was happy.

The opening up of the French tobacco trade was particularly significant for the bill problem. In the early 1730s Lowther's demand for money in London continued to outrun the supply available in

Cumbria, and he was by no means pleased when Peter How was appointed to the excise receivership in 1739.[46] The leading tobacco merchant now became a rival for bills in Cumbria, a situation which Lowther could only have viewed with apprehension. How's intention was to meet the remittances with balances accumulated in London for tobacco bills discountable there, using money he collected in Cumberland to give himself a ready cash flow. By importing tobacco (through his company, How and Kelsick) and buying from the other merchants for cash, he was ideally placed to meet the French demand. Consequently, when the new trade opened up in 1742, the bill supply situation changed dramatically. Spedding was able to assure Lowther in 1745 that 'the French tobacco trade gives an opportunity of remitting ten times more money than you have occasion for. Mr How is often straitened for money.' Such was the transformation that, whereas in 1740 Lowther had wanted John Fletcher replaced as receiver-general for taxes by a Carlisle man, when he was finally forced to retire in 1743 the post went to How, with Lowther's active support. Despite having both the excise and the taxes to remit, How was one of Lowther's best customers. He needed cash to pay his fellow merchants for the tobacco he purchased from them on behalf of the French. In 1745, for example, he sent a bill to Lowther on his London correspondent for £735. Spedding paid the cash to his own son James, and to William Hicks, both of whom had sold tobacco to How. Three months later How remitted a further £2265 through Spedding, of which he received only £1050. Similar transactions continued throughout the 1740s; for example, in January 1749 he remitted bills of £1550, £1050 and £800 respectively.[47]

An accurate impression of how important the expansion of trade was for west Cumberland cannot be derived simply from trade statistics. In 1743, at the commencement of the tobacco boom, a total of 1200 outward clearances from the port of Whitehaven was matched by only 300 inward. Obviously these figures reflect the greater number of voyages that colliers could make in the same time that a tobacco vessel was traversing the Atlantic. They reveal nothing about the relative values of the trades. To assess the real impact of trade diversification, the historian has to look behind the figures, at the benefits derived from the generation of wealth among the merchants, the increased employment offered in shipping, and the related industries which developed in the wake of new trade routes. Some of these will be examined in the next chapter, where the men who developed these new routes will also reappear. The demands of the new trades forced the merchants to promote new industries and better communications in the region in much the same way as their contemporaries in other ports. In so doing they became significant figures in the local community, although almost inevitably their interests clashed with those of Lowther. This tension was reflected in a series of disputes relating to town government in Whitehaven, harbour improvement, and priorities for future development in the region. At least they tried to fill in the gaps left by Lowther's abrogation of responsibility for anything other than coal, and in doing so they ensured that the region's economic foundations were not as insecurely based as Sir James Lowther was prepared to leave them.

5

The Development of Industry

According to Parson and White's directory of Cumberland and Westmorland, published in 1829, 'amongst [Whitehaven's] manufactures are linen, sailcloth, checks, damasks and drapier, cabinet goods, earthenware, colours, copperas, snuff and tobacco, soap, candles, anchors, cables, nails etc etc'.[1] Such a list reflected the port's maritime interests, and the demands of overseas trade. Yet there are some notable omissions for a region abounding in coal and iron ore, and conveniently situated for smelting copper, lead and other metals. The absence of heavy industries from the list was at least partly the result of failure to build upon the advantages provided by coal in the first half of the eighteenth century. The importance of diversifying was certainly recognized locally, most notably by the Lowthers. Sir James Lowther claimed in 1721 to be 'providing to have proper manufactures put forward at Whitehaven and [to be] ready to join in promoting the same at other places'. Like his father, he was aware of the 'absolute necessity of setting up manufactures to keep the people employed at Whitehaven after the near coals are wrought out'.[2] Recognition of the problem was one thing; positive action was another. Various coal-consuming industries were promoted in eighteenth-century Cumberland, but many of these were short-lived and local industry remained generally small-scale. The region continued to depend on the coal trade for its prosperity. In relying on a single economic function west Cumberland was not altogether untypical; other regions similarly placed also had great difficulty widening their horizons, notably Tyneside and Shropshire.[3] West Cumberland's shortcomings were related to the structure of the local economy, the size of population, the inadequacy of enterprise, and a shortage of capital.

Geography and location were natural disadvantages which hindered industrial progress in west Cumberland. The region was, after all, isolated from the rest of England: hence Whitehaven's development as an entrepôt, re-exporting the great majority of its trans-Atlantic imports. However, the significance of geography needs to be kept firmly in perspective. In an age greatly dependent upon coastal transport, especially for moving heavy goods, it was not a vital economic factor. The psychological barrier of distance from the heart of England was most crucial. Only when inland communications were improved in the second half of the eighteenth century did west Cumberland's isolation become a serious economic drawback.

More to the point was the relative underpopulation of the region. Whitehaven's trade may have matched Liverpool's and Bristol's, but its population did not keep pace. It grew from a town of probably no more than 300 inhabitants in 1660, to 3000 in 1702, and to over 9000 in 1762. Workington developed less rapidly, but a population of 945 in 1688 had expanded to over 6000 by 1801. Maryport, from insignificance in 1749, had a population of 1200 in 1765 and 3800 in 1831.[4] By contrast, Liverpool was a town of 10,000 people in 1720, and twice that in 1750; Bristol had 20,000 inhabitants at the beginning of the eighteenth century.[5] How can this relatively slow growth in population be explained?

One important reason was the relatively sparse population of the hinterland around the west coast ports. Cumbria offered little by way of a surplus upon which the coastal towns could draw, although the 'pull' of Whitehaven is clear from the declining population of some west Cumberland parishes. Whicham, Whitbeck and Lamplugh, shed 30, 11 and 13 per cent of their inhabitants respectively between 1700 and 1750.[6] Daniel Dickinson, a prosperous yeoman from Lamplugh, discovered that the growing town of Whitehaven offered him a number of benefits. He had nine children. John, the the eldest, married into the local yeomanry, although not until after he had been on sea trips to Dublin and Virginia. Joseph (b. 1680) and David (b. 1682) probably died at sea, while both Isaac (1686–1756) and Abigail, Dickinson's second daughter, died in Dublin. Dickinson's eldest daughter, Faith, married John Hamilton, who was described in the 1694 marriage settlement as a 'navigator'. Yet another son, Joseph, was apprenticed to Hamilton in 1697 'to learn the art and mystery of mariner and navigation'. Several of John Dickinson's eleven children also benefited from the proximity of Whitehaven, while the family's increased prosperity during this period in spite of numerous progeny may well have been facilitated by finding employment for younger children in the growing port.[7]

Whilst Whitehaven undoubtedly exercised a pull on the immediate hinterland, the geographical range from which migrants were attracted was limited. Eighteenth-century migrants seem to have travelled relatively short distances,[8] and at times the demand for labour in west Cumberland outran supply. Sir James Lowther occasionally sent his stewards to recruit coal-face workers from Tyneside. When an iron furnace and forge enterprise was set up at Frizington in the later 1720s, labour had to be attracted from forty miles away. Lowther claimed that many of his men were tempted away to Frizington, forcing him to raise wage rates and, as a result, prices. According to one local resident 'that [is] wrong, there being labourers enough to attend both their affairs'.[9] Even so, problems of labour supply occurred relatively frequently, inhibiting the establishment of new industries. The absence of alternative employments led to people leaving the region when the staple coal trade was depressed. According to John Spedding, writing in 1726, 'a good many of all sorts of people must be gone to other places in the troublesome times we have had of late years. This causes a good many houses to stand empty, and the rents consequently to fall.'[10] No quantitative evidence survives to prove the point, but the new industries do not appear to have added a great deal to the stock of available employment.

Natural drawbacks cannot be held entirely responsible for the slow industrial expansion of Cumbria; human failings were also important. Heavy industry and improved communications required considerable capital investment. Sir James Lowther could have provided this, but he chose not to. No one else had similar resources, at least until late in the period, and his decision to opt out of certain crucial areas left the region short of enterprise.

Although the overall picture was a gloomy one, this did not mean that the region was completely devoid of industrial development. Expansion and diversification took place in several sectors of the economy, but with only limited success. Clearly coal-fuel industries were a priority, and they were commonly found in mining regions. Glasgow and Newcastle, for example, both had copperas and salt works, and the latter was a centre for glassmaking.[11] In west Cumberland, John Gale despaired in 1697 'of seeing any manufacture flourish here unless built upon the basis of coal-fuel'. Many years later Sir James Lowther wrote that 'it will be difficult to get a much greater consumption of coals without having lead, copper or iron works to supply about Whitehaven or in Ireland'. He hoped to see the region 'get into most of the manufactures that they have at Newcastle for the consuming of great quantities of coal'.[12] In point of fact the region did copy Newcastle, but not on a similar scale.

A second area of development was the manufacture of goods marketable in America and the Baltic, together with the processing of imports for local consumption. Considerable quantities and varieties of manufactured goods were exported to the colonies. For example, the *Peace*, which cleared for Virginia in 1707 with a cargo of thrown silk, mohair, haberdashery, quilts, pewter, leatherware, iron, leather gloves, wool stuffs, rugs, blankets, woollen stockings, cottons, felt hats, fustians and spirits.[13] In terms of transport costs, it was advantageous for merchants to purchase locally produced goods. The demand was a potential stimulant to local manufacturing industry. In the 1690s Sir John Lowther hoped that by setting up tanneries and 'increasing our manufactures of shoes, saddles, harness etc', Whitehaven and its surrounds would be able to supply 'all or the greatest part of our export of those commodities to Virginia'. Similarly, he suggested to William Gilpin in 1694 that 'if some hemp and flax were bought and put out to spinning and a weaver set up I do not see but something might be produced of use for the West India trade'. As Gilpin pointed out in reply, this would have a dual purpose since 'a spinning manufacture might do well here to employ the coal workers' wives etc'.[14] Sir James Lowther did not encourage manufactures specifically as a means of supplying cargoes, although he was 'very glad' in 1725 when Spedding informed him that a man was hoping 'to set up one here for nails, haws and other things proper for the plantations'.[15]

Quality and quantity, however, were the all-important factors, and it was in the interests of local entrepreneurs to ensure that their production matched the required standards. Some specifically geared their manufacture to colonial needs. Lord Lonsdale opened a small workshop at Lowther in Westmorland in the 1740s. In 1742, encouraged by a government bounty on exports, he switched from producing woollen cloth to linen. Walter Lutwidge was asked to advise on the most suitable product for the colonies, and the Whitehaven merchants claimed that Lonsdale's was the best linen that they could acquire; Peter How, William Hicks, and William and

Thomas Gilpin, all bought linen there over the years which followed. From 1748 Lonsdale turned to selling in Liverpool, although his reasons for this move are not altogether clear.[16]

Service industries and traditional local occupations were also ripe for development as the west Cumberland ports grew in the eighteenth century. Several of the former served more than one purpose. Ropes, for example, were required on board ships, and for use in the mines. Nails, apart from having a similar double function, also constituted a valuable export commodity. Shipbuilding and repairing provided local employment, and ensured that masters could know all about their vessels. Finally, a growing population stimulated the traditional local occupations of fishing, brewing and building. Taken together with a variety of miscellaneous employments, these interests gave the region a highly varied occupational structure. Each sector can be analysed in turn, although the investigation is hampered by an almost total absence of statistical data.

Given the predominance of the coal trade, west Cumberland would have stood to gain considerably from developing coal-fuel industries, not least because of the local availability of iron ore, copper and salt water. For the Lowthers the advantages would have been considerable, as they could anticipate a solid local market for their coal. This would help to even out the boom–slump pattern which characterized the coal trade and affected profits. The relative lack of success of the industries can be attributed to shortage of demand, undercapitalization and entrepreneurial failings.

Coal-fuel industries needed a market outside the immediate region if they were to be developed on an economic scale. In theory, conditions were propitious. No shortage of demand existed for English bar iron, particularly for manufacturing processes such as nailmaking. West Cumberland was even better situated than Furness for establishing an iron industry, because in addition to deposits of iron ore it already had adequate coastal transport facilities. Haematite ore, of the type found in Furness, was located around Cleator, Frizington and Egremont, near Whitehaven. The major disadvantage of west Cumberland was a shortage of suitable charcoal timber. The region was also conveniently situated for smelting non-ferrous metals including copper and lead. With the introduction in the seventeenth century of the reverbatory furnace, it became possible to smelt the ores with coal. As much greater quantities of coal were required than ore, it was also advantageous to move the ore to the fuel, rather than *vice versa*. Demand from Ireland stimulated salt-making in the early seventeenth century, although a hundred years later west Cumberland could not compete with the expanding Liverpool trade. When Sir James Lowther entered the business in the 1700s, however, he hoped 'to have the sales of all that part of the country (as far as Bowness) as also to Penrith and Appleby, and part of Yorkshire', which suggests that local demand was not negligible.[17] Glass made at Whitehaven during the 1730s was sold in London, Dublin and the Baltic, while copperas, manufactured on a small scale from 1718, went to markets as far distant as north America. But selling at a distance was not easy; one reason for the failure of the Whitehaven glassworks in 1738 was that the company involved did not establish warehouses in London and Dublin.

Undercapitalization and entrepreneurial shortcomings were related phenomena which owed much to Sir James Lowther's attitude towards new industries. Sir John Lowther was a pioneer with a finger in most industrial pies. In 1693 he was appointed first governor of an incorporated company 'for making iron with pit coal' in west Cumberland. He was also heavily involved in salt panning, although he claimed in 1705 to have taken away 'many of the salt pans of his own that were very beneficial to him because they annoyed [the townspeople]'.[18] By contrast, Sir James Lowther's recognition of the need to establish new industries was more often backed by pious words than hard cash. He had interests in salt and glassmaking, but generally refrained from projects in which he lacked monopoly control, or which seemed likely to prove costly. This was the case with iron. In 1737 he was prepared to 'lend a little money without interest for some few years upon undoubted and ample security to promote the iron manufactures at Whitehaven'. However, 'a little money' turned out to be £400 or £500, but only 'if other folks would raise a stock of £3000 or £4000'. For his own part, he told Spedding, 'I will do all I can in the world without entering into partnerships with them to encourage all persons that will engage to promote iron manufactures at Whitehaven.'[19] He was true to his word. The journey between Whitehaven and London afforded him an opportunity to visit ironworks in the Midlands. In 1736 he visited Wolverhampton and Birmingham, and two years later he inspected a slitting mill at Holmes Chapel. Having met the ironmasters on their own territory he was able to negotiate further with them in London, where he could also converse with people from areas he is not known to have visited, such as Sheffield. The story was always the same: 'there is no danger of any people that are bred up to manage naileries coming to settle at Whitehaven', he told Spedding with heavy irony in 1739, 'I find the like from others that they have such a mean opinion of the country by reason of its remoteness from London.'[20] Midland entrepreneurs would almost certainly have expected some financial incentive if they were to move north. Since this was not forthcoming, their reluctance is hardly surprising.

Lowther did not opt out completely, but his general failure to invest threw responsibility on to west Cumberland's lesser gentry, and its *nouveau riche* element, the overseas merchants. A few of the local gentlemen took an interest in such ventures as salt panning, but it was the merchants who made the most significant contribution. In so doing they played a role not dissimilar to that played by their contemporaries elsewhere: tobacco capital was crucial to the early stages of industrialization around Glasgow; Liverpool merchants improved the local communications network in order to control salt deposits in Cheshire; and the merchants of Hull were willing to invest wherever the opportunity arose.[21] Several of the more substantial Whitehaven merchants were involved in industrial concerns from the 1730s, despite a complaint by Lowther in 1737 that they would do little or nothing to promote manufactures. The opening up of the lucrative Dutch and French markets gave the merchants sufficient finance to move into industrial enterprises, including ironworks at Whitehaven and Maryport.[22]

In the seventeenth and eighteenth centuries the Cumbrian iron industry consisted of three elements: an export trade in iron ore; bar iron production at several sites; and the manufacture of iron wares for local and export purposes. Leaving aside the Furness industry, west Cumberland had a number of interests which were significant even if they were not on the same scale. Iron ore was exported through both Whitehaven and Workington in the seventeenth century. Most of the ore passing through Whitehaven came from Egremont, and was sent to Ireland, to the Duddon furnace near Millom in southern Cumberland, to Frodsham in Cheshire (for transportation to the Vale Royal), and to Wick in Scotland. More than 1000 tons were sent coastwise annually between 1672 and 1687. The mines were worked until the early 1720s when they could no longer compete with the Duke of Montagu's interests in north Lancashire.[23] Ore was again being raised at Frizington in the 1740s, some for smelting in west Cumberland, and the rest for transportation to Shropshire.[24]

Iron production in Cumberland was hampered by the frustrations of trying to smelt in the furnace with coal. Hardly surprisingly, with iron ore and coal readily available, and charcoal timber in short supply, new concerns invariably began with confident words from the proprietors about using coal. This 'philosopher's stone' of the industry eluded almost all of them. The industry had expanded in Cumberland during the course of the seventeenth century, although it was still a minor concern in 1700. Output in 1660 was about 250 tons a year, roughly one-hundredth of total national production. Bloomeries were used for smelting until 1694, when the region's first blast furnace was established at Cleator, an enterprise which may have lasted until 1699. Efforts to smelt with coal failed, and the operation had to revert to charcoal. As a result, the proprietors found themselves forced 'to buy up all as far as Dalegarth (fifteen miles south east of Whitehaven), and are also purchasing in Scotland'. Another attempt is known to have been made to smelt with coal at Whitehaven in 1698.[25]

The major eighteenth-century works were short-lived; indeed, when Isaac Fletcher came to write an account of the iron industry in the later nineteenth century, he could find 'little to be said on the subject'.[26] The more enterprising ironmasters who began their careers in the north-west generally established their reputations only after moving south. Isaac Wilkinson, father of John Wilkinson, started his career at Clifton furnace (Workington). He was described as 'a very notable man' after he moved to Backbarrow in 1728. Later he established himself in Denbigh and Shropshire.[27] Anthony Bacon, best known for his interests in south Wales, also started out in west Cumberland, as did Charles Wood. With his brother, Wood patented the 'potting and stamping' process in 1761.[28]

Clifton ironworks, established in 1723, served a market both locally and on Tyneside. A blast furnace was erected on the banks of the river Marron at Clifton, a few miles east of Workington. Messrs Cookson and Williams, the proprietors, intended to produce pig iron from local ore. Initially the ore came from Branthwaite, south of Clifton. Later it was brought from Frizington. Like other hopeful entrepreneurs, Cookson and Williams intended to use 'pit coal in smelting the iron stone', and they actually found a means of using coal in the process. The fact that they leased Great Clifton colliery in 1735 is suggestive, especially as, in their agreement with Lowther and Lutwidge, it was calculated that they could consume 10 tons of coal daily 'at the furnace'. Apparently they had discovered a technique for producing cast iron with 'pit coal and some wood charcoal', a method still being used in 1752.*[29] Apart from selling pig iron, the company produced a variety of castings, despite the competition from Backbarrow. Production at the furnace was described in a letter written by John Spedding to Sir James Lowther in 1738:

the largest of their castings at Clifton are pans containing about 150 gallons which weigh about seven or eight hundredweight. From that weight downwards they cast pans of all sizes. Their other wares are backs for chimneys, bushels for wheels, furnace bars, plates for ships, fireplaces called gambouses, wagon wheels and many other such things. They have also attempted to cast large boilers for salt pans. . . . Mr Cookson says they make in the whole about 120 tons of pigs and castings and that their pigs when mixed with the pigs that come from the plantations is a great improvement on the latter. He sent about fifty ton of pigs and castings to Newcastle last summer and will send about seventy ton this summer amongst which there is to be a great many wagon wheels, which he says are likely to take very well there.[30]

Lowther bought most of his wagon wheels at Clifton. No bar iron was produced at Clifton, although it is possible that some of the pig was taken to a forge at Eskdale. Virtually nothing is known about this beyond the fact that it was operating in the 1720s under the management of a Mr Russell, and used charcoal.[31] Clifton became uneconomic by the 1760s, and was replaced by a furnace and forge works at Seaton.

Furnace and forge works were established at Frizington in the

* In a recent study of the British iron industry, Charles K. Hyde has suggested that 'costs alone explain the timing of the adoption of coke-smelting. It was cheaper to use charcoal rather than coke in the smelting process until around mid-century, so ironmasters were acting rational in shunning coke-smelting and continuing to use the older techniques.' Hyde rejects the standard interpretation of T. S. Ashton that 'the technical limitations of coke-smelting, particularly the poor quality of the product, prevented its adoption for nearly a half-century': 'The Adoption of Coke-Smelting by the British Iron Industry, 1709–90', *Exploration in Economic History*, x (1973), pp. 397–8. He takes the argument further in his recent book, *Technological Change and the British Iron Industry 1700–1870* (Princeton, 1977), see especially chapter 2. However, given that charcoal was scarce in Cumbria, and coal sufficiently plentiful for the local ironmasters to exploit a series of interim stages between charcoal and coke-smelting, there seems to be at least some grounds for Ashton's conclusion from west Cumberland.

1720s as part of the spectacularly fraudulent scheme dreamed up by William Wood to revolutionize the British iron industry through the creation of the first £1m industrial corporation.[32] Wood leased an iron mine at Frizington in 1723 for £20 a year, as the innocuous base from which to launch his project for smelting iron with coal. The ready availability of ore and coal was an obvious attraction, while he may also have hoped that the co-operation of Sir James Lowther would lend legitimacy to the project. Early in 1727 Wood obtained a patent to make pig iron from ore using coal, but at this stage his main problem was capital. The really significant breakthrough came in 1728 when he signed a contract with the Mines Royal and Mineral and Battery Works, guaranteeing financial backing for him to produce 10,000 tons of the best malleable iron annually. Since most of this was to be smelted at Frizington, the local inhabitants were 'in hopes of being in a little time the richest part of the kingdom'.[33] Wood also obtained a new patent which effectively enabled him to produce bar iron. This overcame the inadequacy of the original patent which had referred simply to pig iron.

With the guarantee of finance and the security of a patent, Wood and his sons began to develop Frizington. Work began in 1728 and the first iron was produced early the following year. By the summer of 1729 eleven furnaces, three or four forges and a variety of other buildings had all been erected on the site. Wood claimed to have spent £10,000. Already, however, considerable doubts were being expressed about the quality of his product. Such fears were apparently confirmed when some bar iron, smuggled from the works for testing by a Whitehaven smith, proved to be useless: hence the local belief that if the Woods were making good iron, it must have been fraudulently smelted with charcoal. In October 1729, 1426 bars of iron were shipped to London, a mere 10 tons of the contracted minimum of 1000. It was overdue by two months, it was the only recorded shipment, and it was poor iron. When, at the end of 1729, the Woods applied for a charter of Incorporation under the name of the Governor and Company of Ironmasters of Great Britain, at least in Cumberland few people were prepared to entertain their claims.

No more iron was made at Frizington, and the failure of the scheme was a blow to hopes of establishing profitable production in west Cumberland. Lowther had good reason to wish to see the works succeed. In July 1726 he had agreed to sell coal to the Woods at his country sale price of 2s 2d a ton. The following winter he discussed with William Wood the possibility of some sort of partnership. He was prepared to be involved himself, and 'believed he could engage others to come in with great sums when the profit was made appear', but only if Wood started by making trials with a single furnace. Lowther withdrew his support when Wood refused to back down from his original proposal of building a hundred furnaces. Lowther also turned down a proposed contract to supply 20,000 tons of coal annually from Whingill colliery because the Woods offered no security. Typically, he made sure that he could meet the demand should it materialize; production at Whingill was stepped up from just over 4000 tons in 1724, to nearly 18,000 in 1727.[34]

An additional drawback of the project's failure was the impact on employment. According to John Spedding, the Woods employed 'several hundred men', many of whom came from a distance. This high level of employment had a temporary inflationary effect on local wages and the cost of living, but in October 1728 Wood 'turned off 70 or 80 of his labourers . . . it is said he'll discharge a great many more labourers tomorrow [2 November]'.[35] Having appeared to offer considerable employment opportunities, the Woods served only to flood the labour market at a time when it was already overstocked because of the long coal trade combination in the autumn of 1728.

Lowther's forthright opposition to the project, once he discovered its worthlessness, reflected the damage caused by the Woods to the west Cumberland economy. As early as December 1727 he was 'persuaded Mr Wood is not able to do anything considerable in his project . . . and that he designs only to make use of his patent to draw in people to advance money for carrying on his other schemes'.[36] Late the following year he became a deputy-governor of the Mines Royal and Mineral and Battery Works. Such a position enabled him to advise the company, and to ensure that the directors were not totally dependent upon the Woods for their knowledge of events at Frizington. He resigned in 1729 when his governorship was twisted by the Woods into being an endorsement of themselves. Lowther renewed his opposition when they petitioned for a charter of Incorporation. 'I have within this week set all the chief nobility and greatest commoners in the kingdom against [Wood]', he told

Spedding only a month after the application was submitted. He paid £2 10s to James Crowley, younger half-brother of Sir Ambrose and clerk of the works at Frizington, for helping to expose the fraud. Then in 1731 he was a member of the prestigious committee set up to inspect the Woods' iron. He attended the final trial on 11 May which exposed the project.[37]

Given these circumstances, it is hardly surprising that some years passed before further ironworks were established in west Cumberland. However, in the 1750s two works were set up on the basis of merchant capital. The first was at Low Mill, near Whitehaven, where a forge was erected in 1750. Peter How, William Hicks and Gabriel Griffiths, all of them Whitehaven merchants, were partnered by Charles Wood.* Each man advanced £2000 initial capital with which to build the forge. Early business involved producing bar iron from imported American, Russian and Swedish pig iron, but the company ran into considerable difficulties, both technical and financial. Lack of charcoal was the first drawback. In 1751 Lowther was promoting a scheme to grow suitable wood on the estates of local landowners, in a bid to keep the forge in fuel. About the same time, however, the company hit on a new method of forging 'with pit coal, iron ore and scrap iron mixed'. This technique was apparently used with some success over the next couple of years, and may have prompted them to mine ore at the Duke of Somerset's Egremont mines. How had leased these in 1749, possibly with the intention of building a furnace as well as a forge. Although the mines were not worked consistently, more than 10,000 tons of ore were raised between 1753 and 1759.[38]

From its early years the company ran into financial difficulties. The partners borrowed £5500 from Lowther in 1753 and 1754 – a rare loan to an industrial project, and a reflection of the good relations he enjoyed with Peter How. By 1758 the partners had borrowed a total of £11,400 from various sources. Possibly fuel

* Charles Wood was the son of William Wood. After being heavily involved in the fraud, he had been bankrupted in 1733. He stayed in Whitehaven after the works failed (Carlisle Record Office, D/Lons/W Spedding to Lowther, 12 February 1735) but apparently spent some time over the following years in the West Indies. He married William Brownrigg's sister, and was involved with his brother-in-law and Anthony Bacon in the Cyfarthfa ironworks during the 1760s. With his brother, Wood patented a new process for producing wrought iron with coal called 'potting and stamping'. A recent commentator has argued that it was this 'rather than puddling [which] enabled the refining sector to expand output and increase its share of the domestic bar iron market over the period 1750–1790', C. K. Hyde, *Technological Change and the British Iron Industry, 1700–1870* (Princeton, 1977), p. 77.

remained a problem. In March 1754 Lowther sent news that iron was being made with coal at Coalbrookdale. He told Spedding that 'Mr Salter was at Coalbrookdale and saw their ironworks, which he says are prodigious and that they make very good iron there with pit coal only, which I shall get him to enquire more exactly into.' In September two of the partners, Griffiths and Wood, toured the west Midland forges noting production methods. They found coal being used at eight of the eleven forges that they visited. Before the end of the year Lowther heard that 'Mr How and Company seem to be in earnest to put forward the making of iron from the ore with pit coal'. However, the company remained unprofitable, being indebted for a total of £32,068 when Peter How failed in 1763. How himself was owed £12,410.[39]

The second iron project based on merchant capital was at Maryport. A seven-man consortium leased from Humphrey Senhouse a site adjacent to the river Ellen, in order to erect furnaces and forges. At least three of the partners – Edward Tubman, John Gale and Thomas Hartley – were Whitehaven merchants, and they had Lowther's blessing, if not his financial support. A furnace began to blow in 1754. No forge was ever erected, so that cast iron products must have been the main output. Much of the ironstone was procured locally. Despite financial difficulties, the works functioned until the mid-1780s.[40]

The production of ironware for overseas and domestic consumption was also characterized by good intentions rather than practical innovations. According to Lowther, writing in 1738, 'in time iron manufactures will be the chief business of our side of the country [sic] from Whitehaven to Broughton and Dearham, and all the adjacent villages'. That year he was engaged in a series of consultations in London; 'there is hardly a day', he told Spedding in March, 'but I meet with somewhat which shows more and more that iron manufactures will do at Whitehaven'.[41] Yet nothing much happened, as the abortive effort to establish naileries at Whitehaven illustrates.

The nail industry was the most important of the secondary iron trades in the early eighteenth century, and the largest single consumer of English bar iron. A considerable demand existed at Whitehaven from the collieries, the shipbuilders and the merchants. The latter included nails among their export cargoes. Since little initial capital was required to start a nailery this was an obvious business to promote at Whitehaven. Although the town always supported a number of nailers, six or eight in the 1730s for example, Lowther believed that a much greater supply of the product would be justified by sales. However, very little transpired from the various attempts to increase the number of nailers. In part, this must have been because suitable bar iron was not available in west Cumberland, but it was also partly a labour supply problem. Various schemes were contemplated. In 1725, for example, a man described as having 'a considerable iron manufactory on the Borders of Scotland' talked of setting up a nailery. In 1736 William Rawlinson of the Backbarrow Company had similar ideas, and Lowther met a Mr Sparrow at Wolverhampton who promised to find someone willing to start nailmaking at Whitehaven. But none of these projects came to fruition. Lowther was pleased when two new naileries were opened in 1739, although he still believed that the town could support more production.[42] Nails were made in Whitehaven throughout the eighteenth century, but the failure to attract skilled and entrepreneurially-minded labour inhibited production.

The smelting of non-ferrous metals (copper, lead and tin) raised different problems. Unlike iron they were not often found close to coal. With the introduction of the reverbatory furnace, however, it became common practice to smelt on a coalfield, and the coastal proximity of Cumberland coal was advantageous. Since the region also possessed copper and lead deposits it had a firm foundation upon which to build the industry. Copper resources had been worked in the sixteenth century by the Mines Royal, and mining was still in progress at Coniston in Furness.[43] In Cumberland neither copper nor lead was exploited on an appreciable level in the eighteenth century, and again Lowther was partly to blame. He acquired a copper mine with the estate Richard Lamplugh sold to him in 1722, but this was never worked; indeed, Lowther eventually sold it in 1750.[44] For the most part local efforts were concentrated on attracting ore from a distance for smelting in Whitehaven.

Attempts to stimulate the industry took place in the 1690s, the early 1720s, and the later 1730s and 1740s. None was particularly successful. During the course of a general expansion of the English copper industry towards the end of the seventeenth century, a company was formed in Cumberland in 1694. However, it was a further three years before any smelting took place, with the building of a reverbatory furnace at Moresby. The idea was to smelt ore brought from Millom, in the south of the county. Sir John Lowther visited the works in 1699. He inspected the furnace and noted how 'the fuel is on one side and the funnel on the other, the ore in the middle so that the flame in passing over the ore runs it in a few hours'. He hoped that the Duke of Somerset might guarantee the success of the furnace by reopening the Keswick copper mines which had been worked with great success in the sixteenth century. He probably failed to respond since nothing further is known of the furnace after 1699.[45] In the early 1720s Sir James Lowther not only had the opportunity to mine his own copper, but he also planned a scheme to attract copper ore to Whitehaven from America, north Africa, Norway and Cornwall. Since this was to be in conjunction with Thomas Lamplugh, with whom he was never on good terms, and since Lamplugh sold his interests to John Brougham in 1722, it is hardly surprising that nothing further was heard of this ambitious scheme.[46]

Attempts were made in the later 1730s and 1740s to attract both lead and copper to Whitehaven for smelting. William Brownrigg was persuaded to request a relation of his with copper mines at Wicklow in Ireland to consider sending his ore to Whitehaven for smelting, rather than to Bristol or Warrington.[47] In 1740 and 1742 Lowther had talks about bringing Welsh ore to Whitehaven. He also opened negotiations, in 1742, to bring ore from the Earl of Breadalbane's mines near Loch Lomond to Whitehaven. These particular consultations went on until 1745. In 1746 Lowther was hopeful of reaching an agreement with John Vaughan, a London merchant who leased a lead mine at Nantycreiau in Cardiganshire at about this time, to bring the ore to Whitehaven for smelting. Subsequently Vaughan did very little with the mine, and like all the other projects this was abortive.[48] As far as the evidence allows, it is safe to conclude that despite the variety of these schemes, they were singularly unproductive.

Salt was produced by evaporating seawater in large pans, and consequently it was a convenient and profitable way of using poorer quality coal. It was panned at several places from Maryport to Saltom Bay, while one of the foremost textbooks on the subject of making salt from seawater was written by Dr William Brownrigg.[49] Little evidence has survived about output and profit, while the absence of port book entries suggests that production was mostly for local requirements.

Salt panning began under Lowther influence in the early seventeenth century, with much of the produce going to Ireland. The executors of Sir Christopher Lowther made a profit of £156 on the sale of salt in 1646. During the course of the seventeenth century, however, west Cumberland lost its competitive edge to Liverpool. In the 1660s Sir John Lowther was working his own pans at Whitehaven, and also those of the Duke of Somerset, which he had leased. By the last decade of the century he no longer found it profitable to manufacture salt, and sub-let the interest. Another projected scheme in the 1690s, at Parton, also failed. The proprietors aimed to work 'the rock salt there which they bring from Cheshire'. Rock salt, discovered in Cheshire in 1670, could be moved from the saltfield for refining elsewhere, and it became attractive to do so following the reimposition of the excise duty on salt in 1694. This was particularly lenient on the rock trade, and may well have encouraged the Parton proprietors. However, the tax inequalities were ironed out in 1696, and possibly as a result the Parton scheme achieved little.[50] This decline ensured that the industry was never as significant for west Cumberland as it was to prove at Liverpool and Newcastle.

Between the 1690s and the 1720s the industry lost its way. Various entrepreneurs set up in business, but few achieved very much. A good example concerns the Duke of Somerset's pans at Bransty. Sir James Lowther did not renew his father's lease of the pans, and they were let in 1710 to a consortium headed by John Radcliffe. Initially Radcliffe met with success. An additional excise officer was appointed in 1714 to attend 'a new saltworks at Bransty'. By 1725, however, the pans were reported to be 'quite worn out', and work had stopped. Radcliffe bought out the other partners in 1729, and renewed the lease, but it seems unlikely that he continued panning for very much longer.[51]

Revival in the industry came about as the result of enterprise on the part of the local gentry, Sir James Lowther in particular. West Cumberland did not recapture the Irish trade, but it did find a considerable local market to serve. In 1733 Robert Lamplugh of Dovenby was working two salt pans at Crosscanonby, Humphrey Senhouse was working two at Netherhall, Adam Craik was working two more at Flimby, and Eldred Curwen and John Brougham worked one each at Walton Wood and Parton respectively. Spedding expected Brougham to make £40 a year when he started panning in the 1720s,[52] and table 5.1 shows that both the Curwens and Senhouse made a profit.

Table 5.1. *Curwen and Senhouse salt pans.*

Pan owner	Years	Income £	Expenditure £	Profit £	Sales (bushels)
Henry Curwen (d. 1727)	1725–7	—	—	34	—
Eldred Curwen	1727–8	—	—	9	—
Humphrey Senhouse	1732–3	290	317	loss 27	1,275
Humphrey Senhouse	1733–4	503	438	65	2,217

Source: Carlisle Record Office, D/Sen Salt Pans account books; D/Cu Estate ledger 1725–46, f. 55.

The fact that several gentlemen were involved in the manufacture of salt suggests that they were able to attract good prices. This was probably the factor which persuaded Lowther to enter the industry. Inevitably his concern was to dominate, and although he did not create a monopoly he certainly forced several of his rivals out of business. Rather than resume panning at Whitehaven, where his father's energies had been concentrated, Lowther set up salt pans at Saltom Bay. Work began in November 1734, and by May the following year two pans were at work. A storehouse was built, and water was pumped to the pans by the Newcomen engines used in the coal mine. By utilizing the waste coal on the site for salt panning Lowther avoided the expense of transporting it to Whitehaven. Spedding hoped that eighteen or nineteen bushels would be made daily at each pan. By the end of 1736 he was confident that Lowther was winning over the trade: 'the salt trade seems to be centreing here very fast, and all the other pans may soon be laid idle'.[53]

This was not merely speculation. Humphrey Senhouse and Robert Lamplugh were forced out of business when Curwen and Brougham lowered the price in 1736, presumably as a result of Lowther's intervention. Senhouse sold one of his pans to Lowther, and leased him the others. Brougham sold all his interests to Lowther the following year, and Radcliffe failed to complete his lease of Bransty pans. The site was used for a snuff mill from 1733. Only Lamplugh was not permanently deterred; he was working his pans again in 1738. Given this success, Lowther may also have brought the

Whitehaven pans back into use; Sir John Clerk saw several pans in the town in 1739, although he did not record any information about their working.[54]

Lowther evidently took over a considerable share of the west Cumberland supply. He was successful possibly because he could undercut several of the other gentlemen in terms of fuel costs – Humphrey Senhouse, for example, had to continue buying coal to work his pans because he had no success locating it on his estate – and because working alone, Lowther was prepared to invest more energy and finance than when he was involved in a partnership. He used a sloop, the *Bee*, to carry salt to north Cumberland and Lancashire, and he built a storehouse on the quayside at Whitehaven. By 1748 he was paying duty of £9 a week on salt manufactured at Saltom. But although this was a successful business for Lowther it was not a monopoly; a traveller of 1746 commented on Henry Curwen's new pans at Harrington, although the old ones at Lowca, which had been operating in 1725, were 'tumbling into ruins every spring tide'.[55]

Copperas, a green vitriol (ferrous sulphate) used in dyeing and in the making of ink, was made from iron pyrites, or 'marcasites' as they were known, which were found with coal. As a result copperas works were often found on coalfields. The pyrites were placed in heaps and dissolved by exposure to rain and oxygen; this produced a liquid solution which was boiled with rusty iron until it crystallized. The benefits of such an industry were not lost on the Lowthers: they could expect to provide both the fuel and the pyrites. When William Gilpin heard of the export potential of copperas, and knew that pyrites were available on the Whitehaven coal banks, he suggested to Sir John Lowther that copperas manufacture would be suitable for Whitehaven. Lowther made a number of enquiries in London as to exactly what was required, but nothing appears to have come from Gilpin's suggestions, and copperas manufacture only started in 1718.[56]

Thomas Robinson, a Chester merchant, reached an agreement with Sir James Lowther in 1718 to establish copperas works in Whitehaven. Robinson was to use only marcasites found in Lowther's coal, and to pay 3s 4d for every ton of copperas manufactured, in addition to a rent charge of £2 15s for the land let to him by Lowther in Gin Lane. When it became apparent that Lowther could not supply enough marcasites the agreement was amended, enabling

Robinson to bring additional marcasites from elsewhere. In 1723 he contracted for 800 tons in Poole and Portsmouth.[57] Lowther's supplies to the works are given in table 5.2. Although no records

Table 5.2. *Marcasites and coal sold to the copperas works by Sir James Lowther.*

Year	Marcasites* (tons)	Cost	Year	Coal (tons)†	Cost £
1719	112	£ 9 6s 8d	1736	310	41
1726	230	19 3s 9d	1737	336	44
1730	8	13s 4d	1738	381	50
1731	12¼	1 1s 3d	1739	453	59
1732	12	1 0s 3d	1740	375	49
1733	18	1 11s 3d	1741	333	43
1734	87	7 6s 2d	1742	360	47
1736–55	1,134	94 9s 2½d	1743	465	60
			1744	705	92
			1745	534	69
			1746	591	77
			1747	567	74
			1748	531	69
			1749	669	87
			1750	359	47

* At 1s 8d a ton, as per the amended agreement of 1719.
† At 2s 8d, Lowther's price for local coal sales.
Source: Carlisle Record Office, D/Lons/W Colliery Abstracts.

have survived, the port books show that much of the produce was exported coastwise and to Dublin. Some went to New England in 1742, while in 1750, according to Dr Richard Pococke, much of the produce was 'put in hogsheads and sent abroad'.[58] Copperas remained a small-scale manufacture at Whitehaven, but it was one of the town's more successful coal-consuming interests.

Glass manufacture also came to be located on coalfields once the coal-fired furnace was introduced in the seventeenth century. Sir John Lowther hoped to see glass made in Whitehaven during his lifetime, and within a few months of inheriting the estate his son made it known that he saw 'nothing so likely to take for a consumption of coals as a glasshouse' (the technical name of the place of manufacture).[59] However, glassworks are first known to have been established at Parton in 1719. The project floundered before the end of 1721, partly because of the outstanding arrears on coal purchases from Lowther.[60] When John Brougham bought the manor of Moresby in 1722 he intended to revitalize glass manufacture. Apparently he was successful since two ships left Parton with bottles in August 1725. Another vessel, carrying bottles to London, was lost off the Isle of Wight two months later. Losses such as this may have been too great for the business to absorb, and it had been wound up before the end of the decade.[61]

The best-documented scheme was the Whitehaven glasshouse, established in 1732 on a site adjacent to the copperas works. Lowther, a partner, let a plot of land to the company (table 5.3) on which to

Table 5.3. *The Whitehaven Glasshouse Company, 1732.*

Partners	Share	Initial stock 1732	Second advance 1734	Third advance 1735
Thomas Lutwidge (merchant)	$\frac{1}{4}$	250	250	100
Walter Lutwidge (merchant)	$\frac{1}{4}$	250	250	100
Sir James Lowther	$\frac{1}{8}$	125	125	50
John Spedding	$\frac{1}{8}$	125	125	50
Abraham Chambers (merchant)	$\frac{1}{8}$	125	125	50
William Gilpin (merchant)	$\frac{1}{8}$	125	125	50

Source: Carlisle Record Office, D/Lons/W Estate ledger 1737–58, fos. 85, 216.

build the premises. He charged a rent of five guineas a year plus five shillings for the right to take sand from the seashore. A Mr Verney was appointed manager. The company's intention was to produce bottles to be sold in both England and Ireland, but the failure to establish marketing facilities in London and Dublin proved to be a drawback. Indeed, the company soon ran into production difficulties. Some bottles sold in London in 1735 were found to be 'weak in the neck and abundance break on corking'. The capital stock twice had to be replenished, and the partners were continually disagreeing. William Hicks, who bought Gilpin's share, complained in 1735 that Walter Lutwidge was 'making advantages of it he ought not', only to find when the accounts were examined that far from misapplying funds Lutwidge had been using his own money for the company's benefit. Lowther, who had entered the partnership in the hope of promoting coal consumption in Whitehaven (table 5.4), was annoyed by the company's failure to

Table 5.4. *Coal purchases by the Glasshouse Company from Sir James Lowther.*

Year	Tonnage
1735*	1,587
1736	2,406
1737	2,343
1738	621
1739	9
1740	834
1741	1,377

* Half-year only.
Source: Carlisle Record Office, D/Lons/W Colliery Abstracts.

pay for the coal that it used, and periodically asked for the debt to be reduced. Hicks and Chambers refused to advance further capital in 1736, while Thomas Lutwidge's financial worries were such as to force him into borrowing from Lowther.[62]

After heeding Spedding's advice that to close the glasshouse would mean incurring a fairly substantial loss, Lowther decided to put up a further £600, two-thirds of the insurance value. He hoped that this would give him sufficient additional influence to put the business into what he regarded as acceptable management. His gamble failed, however, and by the summer of 1738 the partners' disagreements had become so severe that the company was wound up. The capital stock of £2400 was effectively lost. A year later the glasshouse was sold by auction, and conveyed to Lowther for £420. Walter Lutwidge closed the accounts by repaying Lowther's £600.[63]

In similar fashion to the iron industry, Lowther now attempted to attract outsiders into Cumberland to run the glasshouse as a going concern. Again he found them reluctant, and he actually let it to the Spedding brothers in 1740 and 1741. According to Lutwidge, writing some years later, they made £1200 or £1400 profit. Although this cannot be substantiated, the port books show that glass bottles were exported to Belfast, Dublin and Norway in 1741, and sent to Dumfries, Wigton, Lancaster, Carlisle and Kirkcudbright the following year. Since the last shipment was not until mid-1742, and the Speddings had given up the glasshouse before the end of 1741, some of this glass may have been manufactured elsewhere. Despite various efforts by Lowther to attract lessees, the works do not seem to have been used again. In 1754 the buildings were being used to store hay.[64]

The general failure of coal-fuel industries is best illustrated by figure 5.1. Less than 10 per cent of the Lowthers' coal sales between

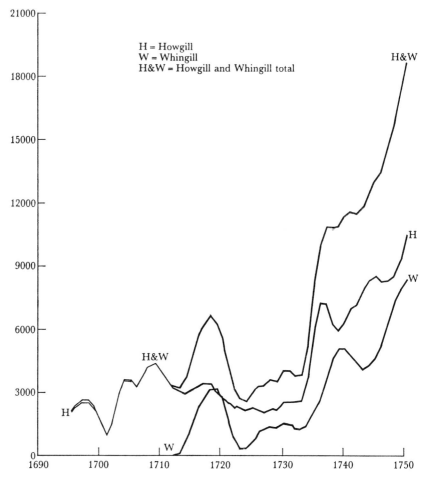

5.1   Local sales at Howgill and Whingill collieries (3 year moving average)

1695 and 1750 were local. Consumption rose from an average of 2000 tons between 1695 and 1700, to nearly 16,000 tons between 1746 and 1750, but this represented an increase of only 2·4 per cent (from 10·6 per cent to 13 per cent) in the proportion of local to total sales between the same years. The booms and slumps may have coincided with population changes rather than industrial expansion.

Local sales constituted 4·6 per cent of the total between 1726 and 1730, for example, perhaps reflecting the migration out of the region as a result of the coal trade depression. Table 5.5 adds further weight to the suggestion. Glassmaking in the 1730s pushed up local sales. After the Whitehaven company folded in 1738, the tonnage of coal specifically delineated in Lowther's accounts as being sold to industrial concerns fell away. Even so, local sales rose steadily throughout the 1740s.

Table 5.5. *Lowther's local coal sales from Whitehaven collieries, 1735–50.*

Year	Total (tons)	Industry (tons)	% of industry to total	Year	Total (tons)	Industry (tons)	% of industry to total
1735*	6,502	1,794	27·6	1743	11,121	564	5·1
1736	10,544	2,673	25·4	1744	13,475	750	5·6
1737	11,137	2,679	24·1	1745	13,304	588	4·5
1738	11,238	1,002	8·9	1746	12,954	642	5·0
1739	10,399	462	4·4	1747	14,629	630	4·3
1740	11,461	1,209	10·5	1748	16,175	666	4·1
1741	12,590	1,788	14·2	1749	16,457	834	5·1
1742	11,145	537	4·8	1750	18,652	594	3·1

* Half-year only.
Source: Carlisle Record Office, D/Lons/W Colliery Abstracts.

The major drawback to generalizing from these figures concerns the supply of coal to local salt and iron works. Salt pans used the waste coal, and this may never have passed through Lowther's accounts at Saltom. However, Humphrey Senhouse had to buy coal from Dearham colliery for his pans.[65] Of the major ironworks, Clifton furnace was supplied by Clifton colliery, Low Mill by a small colliery at Bransty near Whitehaven (leased by Peter How from the Duke of Somerset), and the Maryport furnace by Broughton coal from 1755. Only William Wood bought coal from Lowther.[66] Evidence about quantity is scarce, but at Clifton in 1735 the proprietors expected to use 3000 tons annually 'at the furnace'.[67] This was an estimate; whether or not they actually used that amount of coal cannot be confirmed. The evidence is not adequate to draw any firm conclusions as to whether the Howgill and Whingill figures were in any sense representative of local sales. However, such sales from Lowther's Moresby and Distington collieries represented just 9 per cent of the total sales between 1714 and 1737, while at Seaton the figure was 5 per cent in the years 1728–32. Lowther expected Scalegill colliery to 'supply all the south part of the country [sic] from Whitehaven', but this proved to be uneconomic. A nailery to consume the surplus coal was suggested in 1737, and when this scheme came to nothing a wagonway was built to link the colliery with Quay staith in Whitehaven.[68] All that can safely be concluded, therefore, is that given their small size and ephemeral nature, coal-fuel industries in this period did not consume a great deal of coal, nor did they provide very much employment. Overall, they failed to supplement the coal trade in such a way as to protect the region from the vagaries of trade fluctuations.

West Cumberland's second industrial sector was the production of goods for sale in America or the Baltic. Eighteenth-century ports often developed as service centres for their hinterlands: Bristol was 'the metropolis of the west in the eighteenth century'; Hull developed on the basis of service rendered to the Yorkshire woollen industry and Sheffield iron; Liverpool was the servant of industrial Lancashire.[69] Such service was not, however, crucial. Glasgow, for example, developed originally as an entrepôt rather than as the seagoing outlet for the west of Scotland. As with west Cumberland, the improvement of land communications came relatively late, a fact which reflects the absence of hinterland dependence in both ports. Only 11 per cent of Scottish linen output was being exported through Scottish ports in the 1740s.[70] The merchants had to assemble much of their export cargoes from considerable distances. According to William Gilpin, writing of the Whitehaven merchants in 1696, most of their cargo was 'provided beforehand, and of several persons in Holland, Cumberland, Newcastle, Kendal, and (of late especially) in Ireland'. Later the more substantial merchants retained agents in several towns to help assemble their goods. Walter Lutwidge, for example, had factors in Newcastle, Kendal, Darlington, Belfast, Dublin, Liverpool, Bristol and Manchester.[71]

Although Sir John Lowther was among those who recognized the advantages for west Cumberland of producing for the overseas market, it seems unlikely that the proportion of locally produced goods was ever very great. Detailed evidence is almost non-existent. Penrith, Cockermouth and Carlisle, all of them textile towns, were expanding in the eighteenth century, which may indicate a response to overseas demand. Certainly the surviving journal for one Cockermouth merchant reveals that in 1749 he was sending goods to Jamaica, Barbados and the Baltic,[72] while Lord Lonsdale specifically geared his workshop at Lowther to the needs of the overseas market. On the other hand much of the cloth produced in Kendal, the most important woollen town in Cumbria, seems to have been exported through Liverpool, despite Sir John Lowther's efforts to attract it to Whitehaven in the 1690s. A Barbados merchant in Liverpool had been sending 'Kendal cloths' for twenty years before 1692. In 1770 over 4000 pieces were exported through Liverpool, of which a little over two-thirds went to Virginia and Maryland. Thomas Pennant noted in 1769 that Kendal produced worsted stockings and 'a coarse sort of cloth, called cottons, for the Guinea trade'.[73]

Obviously the sparse population of the hinterland limited the region's capacity to supply a large proportion of the export demand, but the situation was compounded by the unsuitability of locally produced goods. With a relatively high value commodity such as cloth the cost of transport was correspondingly low, which enabled the merchants to be discriminating in their purchases. It was, therefore, particularly unfortunate that the Cumbrian textile manufacture was generally unsuited to the colonial market. Domestic textile production took place on a small scale throughout the seventeenth and eighteenth centuries; linen, sacking, coarse woollens, stockings and hats, were all being manufactured by the 1680s. Sir John Lowther was in the forefront of efforts to encourage these and other manufactures, on the assumption that this would increase the employment opportunities open to the poor, whilst at the same time providing goods for overseas export. The real need, however, was to make full use of Cumbria's own wool rather than, as was then the case, sending it out of the county, untreated. According to one estimate, in 1752, 'four-fifths at least of all the wool annually produced within the county are sent out of it unmanufactured'. The reason was quite simple: on its own the Cumbrian wool was not suitable for manufacturing quality goods. It needed mixing with 'wool of a finer growth'.[74] Mixed with Irish wool the Cumbrian produce could be made into good quality cloth, but from 1667 Irish imports were banned. Apart from a temporary lifting of the restriction between 1697 and 1699 the supply was effectively cut off.[75]

The export potential of woollen goods using a mixture of Cumbrian and Irish wool is clear from Sir John Lowther's efforts to establish manufacturing during the temporary import de-restriction of 1697–99, various discussion in the years that followed as to the possibility of asking Parliament to reconsider its decision, and the claims of a pamphlet circulated in 1752. Sir John Lowther seized the opportunity to promote the making of fine woollen cloth using Irish produce mixed with local wool when the ban was lifted in 1697. He told Richard Stainton, the man he commissioned to manage the project that he had in mind, that he would provide

money to buy wool, English or Irish, the latter rather, that this wool be delivered out to some who can card or comb it, then delivered over to others who can spin it and lastly to a third person who can weave or knit the yarn so spun, each of which persons having other employments may by doing this at their leisure hours, afford their work cheaper than if they had nothing else to depend upon, and this put in a way and found practical I would then erect tenters and a fulling-mill.[76]

Lowther proposed a cautious start – a 'small entrance' – in the hope that 'it will be encouragement enough to proceed, and as hands increase to bring some master workmen among them and to erect some common workhouses for instructing of others'. Production commenced in March 1698, with spinners and knitters being brought from Kendal to instruct the local employees in carding and combing, spinning and weaving. Thirty-two spinners were employed initially, and a weaver began work in June. Enquiries were made about attracting skilled French refugees to Whitehaven, while the local merchants assured Stainton that they would 'buy all the goods can be made whether bad or good, and if our cottons exceed those made in Kendal they will advance the price accordingly'.[77] The Irish wool, however, was vital, and when the ban on imports was reimposed in 1699, Lowther could see no alternative but to end the scheme. Stainton was paid off in 1700. Even without government intervention the project might not have lasted. Lowther's stated aim was simply 'to break the ice and to help others, not dip deep in anything myself'. Although he advanced at least £100 on the project, he could evoke little enthusiasm for the formation of a company.[78]

In the years that followed, the great bulk of Cumberland wool was sent from the county unmanufactured, although the drawback of being unable to mix it with Irish imports was fully appreciated;

indeed, Spedding told Lowther in 1724 that 'most of the town would be glad to have this a port for bringing in Irish wool, but none will advance anything towards the charge of getting an act'. The suggestion was mooted by Peter How in 1737 that coarse wool and linen might be manufactured in a large house in Whitehaven, the produce to be sold in America. Lowther favoured the proposition, 'and would help to encourage it', but he correctly predicted that it would not come to pass.[79] His own attitude to textile manufacture was little different from the opinions he expressed about the coal-fuel industries. In effect, it was left to the merchants to promote any new schemes, if they so wished.

Consequently it is hardly surprising that merchant pressure can be discerned behind the eventually successful efforts to have the wool embargo lifted. A paper, published anonymously in 1752 but known to have been the joint work of William Brownrigg and Andrew Hudleston, a local gentleman, suggested that the 'huge demand for wool' in the West Riding of Yorkshire was good reason for opening up Whitehaven to Irish wool imports. The recent expansion of trade with America had increased the demand for the type of woollen goods which could be made from a mixture of Cumbrian and Irish wool, while in the absence of locally produced woollen goods, the merchants had to look well beyond the region for supplies.[80]

The paper opened up a debate. Lowther himself responded with a splendidly abstract appeal to the local gentlemen, altogether typical of his 'encourage rather than invest' attitude. His paper, 'for exciting the lords and gentlemen to encourage manufactures', stressed 'the great benefit of improving the woollen manufacture', but offered no positive commitment to investment. Only in a private letter to Spedding did he admit to being willing 'to join in a subscription to encourage the woollen manufacture by a mixture of Irish wools with ours'.[81] Another anonymous pamphleteer worked out the financial gains of manufacturing woollen cloth in Cumbria.[82] Success came in the form of a general act of 1753, which allowed Irish wool to be imported at any English port. Lowther, perhaps recalling his father's efforts, at last declared his willingness to join in a subscription, but no evidence survives to show what, if anything, transpired.[83]

Less difficulty was encountered in establishing import processing manufactures. Raw sugar was boiled in the town before being re-exported, or being sent coastwise to southern Scotland and Carlisle. Sir James Lowther persuaded a Mr Barwise to set up a sugarhouse in Whitehaven in 1712, to refine small amounts for local consumption. Lowther's motives were far from disinterested for he sold coal to Barwise. The boiler continued in operation until 1726 when Barwise moved to Workington. It was then taken over by William and John Gilpin, the former a son and the latter either a son or a brother of Lowther's former steward. Sugar boiling continued thereafter, although the evidence is sparse and Lowther's accounts do not specifically record sales of coal to the works. The sugarhouse is depicted on several views of Whitehaven drawn during the 1730s (see frontispiece). Its management still seems to have been in the hands of the Gilpins early in the 1740s. Two ships entered at Whitehaven in 1739 with sugar for William Gilpin and Company, and another vessel in 1741.[84]

Tobacco processing was the other import-based industry developed in these years, which facilitated local consumption and encouraged coastal sales. In 1718 the family of a Whitehaven man were reported to have 'set up to spin tobacco'. Although they were probably not alone, the most important undertaking in the town was Peter How's snuffery at Bransty. In 1733 he had 'lately set up to manufacture tobacco, by making it into cut, roll and snuff'. Two years later Lowther granted him liberty to erect a water mill for grinding snuff 'for benefit of trade he carries on in manufacturing tobacco'. By the time How failed in 1763 this was a substantial business, although few details relating to it have survived.[85]

Various service trades developed in Whitehaven in response to commerce and the demands of the collieries. Ropemaking, shipbuilding and repairing, anchor, sail and blockmaking, all came to be part of the town's manufacturing activities. In addition, ropes were made at Workington and Maryport in the later eighteenth century, while ships were built at all the main outlets along the coast. Sir John Lowther was involved in a rope company in the later seventeenth century, but his son exercised the normal balance between encouragement and investment. However, through the Spedding brothers, who were concerned in both ropemaking and shipbuilding, he was able not only to keep abreast of activity in the town, but also to exercise some influence on the course of events.

Ropemaking was established in Whitehaven early in the seventeenth century. A print of the town in 1642 shows two ropewalks, and three ropers were active by the end of the century. Since ropewalks demanded considerable space they were gradually moved further north to release land for additional housing. Demand for ropes was considerable: they were needed on board ships and in the mines, and for reasons of safety had to be regularly replaced. The miners, for example, started to ascend and descend the pit shaft in the corves, and this practice led them to 'insist upon having the ropes fresh and good, their lives depending upon it'.[86]

Three rope companies were operating in Whitehaven in the 1690s, two at Braconthwaite and one at Bransty, on the north side of the town. Sir John Lowther was a partner in the 'Whitehaven Rope Company'. Hemp was brought overland from Newcastle, and the desire to obtain it more directly helps to explain the efforts to restore the Baltic trade once the war ended in 1697.[87] This level of ropemaking continued into the eighteenth century. As with most local activities the early 1720s proved to be a difficult time. Several ropers failed, with the result that only two companies were operating by the end of the decade (table 5.6). Lowther acquired his ropes from John Spedding's company (table 5.7). This partnership ran into difficulties during the 1740s; Lutwidge claimed that he was

Table 5.6. *Whitehaven rope companies, 1727–56.*

Braconthwaite ropewalk no. 1			Braconthwaite ropewalk no. 2		
Company	Term	Lease rent	Company	Term	Lease rent
John Spedding ⎤ Walter Lutwidge ⎪ John Hamilton ⎬ Joseph Littledale ⎦	Christmas 1727– Christmas 1746	£12 10s 0d	Thomas Hartley	Candlemas 1728– Candlemas 1749	£9
John Spedding	Christmas 1746– Christmas 1755 (Renewed for 21 year term)	£12 10s 0d	Thomas Hartley	1750– 'at will'	£9

Source: Carlisle Record Office, D/Lons/W Estate ledger 1737–58, fos. 37–8.

147

Table 5.7. *Lowther's known rope purchases from the Braconthwaite no. 1 company.*

1728 Dec	To paid the New Ropery Company for ropes	£83 19s 11½d
1729 Dec	A bill for ropes since Xmas 1728	128 3s 9½d
1730 Dec	Ropery bill for all collieries this year	123 18s 2½d
1731 June	Ropery bill since Xmas last	49 19s 10½d
1731 Dec	Bill since Mids. last	75 15s 9d
1740 Dec	To Ropery Company for ropes per account for last year	262 3s 2d

Source: Carlisle Record Office, D/Lons/W Colliery ledger 3, 1727–32 (various entries), MSS History of Whitehaven Collieries, fos. 106ff.

owed £700 or £800 expenses for procuring hemp and flax, Spedding and the other partners (both described as 'mariners') disagreed, arguing that he had acquired the goods during the normal course of his business. No settlement could be reached, so in December 1746 the three partners dissolved the company, splitting the capital between them. According to Lutwidge they pretended that 'I have the company's money in my hands to pay myself, though . . . I am not doubtful but to make it appear they are upwards of £1500 in my debt besides my quarter of the capital'. Lutwidge entered a bill in Chancery against Spedding, who countered with a special writ claiming £400 plus interest on an outstanding promissory note. When Spedding's case was heard in November 1747, Lutwidge failed to make a defence and judgment was given against him of £400 plus £117 interest. From 1746 Spedding ran the company alone, Lutwidge concentrating his efforts at Workington. Spedding's executors sold the company in 1765 for £1800.[88] Little is known of Hartley's ropewalk beyond the fact that in the later 1730s he was importing hemp from St Petersburg.

Shipbuilding and repairing were commonly found in English ports. Although the naval requirement was fulfilled in Chatham and Portsmouth, ships used in trade (less than 150–200 tons) were often built in the places from which they would later operate. In west Cumberland, shipbuilding dates from the later seventeenth century, although the region was never self-sufficient. Vessels were built at Whitehaven from 1677, at Workington by 1721, at Parton by 1724, and at Ravenglass, some miles south of Whitehaven on the Cumberland coast, in the mid-1730s. Later in the century ships were also built at Maryport.[89] By no means all the tonnage owned in the port of Whitehaven – it rose from 7200 tons in 1702 to 52,300 tons by 1788[90] – was built in west Cumberland, but this was an important local interest.

Throughout the eighteenth century vessels were built along the water-edge at the north end of Whitehaven, although shipbuilding was a fluctuating business until the expansion of the tobacco trade. William Gilpin reported the launching of the *Cumberland Merchant* in 1696, but even though several vessels were being built for Whitehaven the following year, none of them was constructed in west Cumberland. Six ships were on the stocks in 1712, and the following summer plans were in hand to build a further six or seven. Depression in the coal trade hit the industry early in the 1720s. Only one ship was built in 1720, and one ordered for the following year.[91] This situation changed abruptly when demand for vessels increased in the 1730s to meet the new trade requirements. A number of vessels were acquired in America.

The shipbuilding company which gained the most considerable benefits from the demands of the 1730s was one run in partnership by Thomas Patrickson and the Spedding brothers, known as the 'Timber and Brewery' company. Again Lowther could exercise influence through his stewards, and he lent the company £630 in 1737, a sum which was still outstanding in 1755. Timber supplies were the company's major problem. Five ships entered at Whitehaven with timber in 1739 and two in 1741. In 1740 Patrickson was buying timber in Scotland,[92] while the following year he was the highest bidder for a consignment of wood made available by the trustees of the Greenwich Hospital's Keswick estates. Patrickson's offer of £4100 was turned down by the Hospital, who valued the timber at £5000 and suspected a confederacy in west Cumberland not to bid against Patrickson. The transaction went through later in the decade, and the company was supplying timber for Maryport harbour in the 1750s. To expand their business the company leased part of a timber yard from Lowther in 1745.[93]

Throughout the 1740s the industry was buoyant. Lowther commented in 1744 that 'the trade of building and repairing ships . . . seems to have increased much of late years'. When Patrickson died in 1746 he feared that 'the building of ships will hardly go on so well as it did'. However, Patrickson's son, another Thomas, replaced him, and the company continued to expand its dealings. It was reformed in 1748 when Patrickson sold his share to William Fletcher and William Palmer, John Spedding made over his share to his son James, and Carlisle Spedding split his holding with his son James. Lowther granted the company a lease of the rest of the timber yard to facilitate their activities, and made available ground for additional buildings. Other shipwrights were also active in Whitehaven. Between 1749 and 1752 Lowther gave leave, for a consideration of 10s 6d a time, for the building of eleven ships on 'ground behind Tangier street walled in from the houses', and in 1751 he reached agreements with Henry Benn and John Wood, shipwrights, which enabled them to enclose parcels of ground for use in shipbuilding.[94]

All this activity was clearly beneficial to the industry, and by implication to the town, although some of the momentum seems to have been lost in the last years of Lowther's life. 'We were in a good way of business for building and repairing ships', he wrote only weeks before he died, 'but the masters of the coal ships have ruined that business.' His reasoning here is obscure, but any decline in activity was not permanent. At the end of the century six ship-builders were at work in Whitehaven, with often ten or twelve new vessels on the stocks at a time. In 1790 3690 tons of shipping were built in the port of Whitehaven, making it the eighth largest ship-building port in England, by tonnage.[95]

The subsidiary shipbuilding trades are not well documented, largely because Lowther had little or no stake in them. Few people were apparently engaged in sailmaking during the first half of the eighteenth century. Perhaps not surprisingly, therefore, little evidence survives of sailcloth manufacture. Twine was spun at a walk situated behind a staith at Braconthwaite. Lowther leased this out in 1738 for a rent of 8s a year. The rent was raised to 10s in 1744. Anchors were made in Whitehaven. Of the four anchorsmithies on the quay in 1700 – two let for £3 each and the other two for £2 10s, all by Sir John Lowther – three were pulled down in 1732 to make way for Quay staith. The existing iron ore staiths, unused for some years, were then converted into smithies, the net result of the operation being five smithies, all of which were situated below the new coal staith and let for £3. These shops were too small to make large anchors, and Lowther spent £100 building a larger one in 1739. He leased this to Robert Bowman. Also on the quayside was a blockmaker's shop, let by Lowther.[96]

As the population in and around the west Cumberland towns

grew, the traditional occupations were stimulated. Physical growth provided many opportunities for people with building skills. Houses, warehouses, harbour extensions and road improvements, all required labour. Fishing, which had been west Cumberland's major trading concern according to a sixteenth-century survey, had almost died out by the later seventeenth century, but was revitalized in the eighteenth. Additionally, the growing population increased demand for consumer goods, and stimulated tertiary interests in food and drink processing.

Most building work was undertaken on an individual contractual basis. The masons and carpenters awaited commissions. Failing that, they built to sell on their own account (chapter 7).[97] Evidence relating to building, as indeed to most of the traditional occupations, is sparse, but the trend can be measured from brickmaking in the town. Despite the physical expansion of Whitehaven, the trade was not always profitable, particularly when trade depression led to migration from the town in the 1720s. Three brickmakers, Richard Robinson, Thomas Anderson and Thomas Moor, were all bankrupt at their deaths in 1724, 1726 and 1728 respectively. But by the mid-1730s business had improved: Thomas Hassel sold all the bricks that he could make in 1734, and was hoping for 'a great consumption' the following year. In 1737 he leased additional land to extend his enterprise. However, he must have glutted the market or overstretched his resources, since the lease was soon terminated. Lowther's coal sales to the manufacturers in the 1740s provide a yardstick which indicates rising production (table 5.8). Walter

Table 5.8. *Lowther's sales of coal to the brickmakers, 1742–50.*

Year	Tonnage
1742	39
1743	36
1744	30
1745	54
1746	51
1747	63
1748	135
1749	165
1750	135

Source: Carlisle Record Office, D/Lons/W Colliery Abstracts.

Lutwidge was involved in brickmaking in 1751, fraudulently as it transpired. By 1754 bricks were being manufactured on Lowther property at Moresby, and at two locations in Whitehaven.[98]

'Fishing', according to William Gilpin in 1698, 'is but a poor trade and followed by none but poor people, and only then when they cannot get other employment.' The variety of alternative opportunities available in west Cumberland had enticed away many of the better fishermen, and thwarted Sir John Lowther's hopes of encouraging the industry.[99] However, eighteenth-century evidence shows that it was not completely lost. Sir James Lowther expressed his willingness in 1734 to allow 'a convenient place . . . on the back of the pier for the fishermen to lay up their boats in',[100] and he was responsible for encouraging a new scheme in the 1750s which involved Whitehaven vessels in the herring fishing industry. During the first half of the eighteenth century herring fishing had been almost completely taken over by the Dutch. In an effort to revive the English industry, an incorporated joint-stock company was formed in 1750, with a capital of £500,000. Seventy-ton fishing busses (herring boats), built in British ports and manned by British crews, were to fish off the Shetlands between June and October each year. A government bounty was provided to encourage the company. Since part of the capital could be subscribed by a 'chamber' formed in an individual port, Lowther saw this as an opportunity to diversify Whitehaven's interests. The busses could be built locally, and net and line making would provide additional employment.[101]

The Whitehaven chamber was formed in 1751. By the end of the year one vessel had been built, and a second was on stocks. The latter, launched the following spring, was named the *Lowther*. The busses sailed for the Shetlands in 1752, in time to join the main fleet. On their return they called at the Isle of Man to 'manufacture' the herrings for sale in Cumberland, and their claim to customs immunity produced a dispute between the chamber and the island authorities. They were accused of fishing within the unwritten territorial waters of the Manx fishermen, and threatening their livelihood. Four Whitehaven busses joined the Shetlands fleet, in both 1753 and 1754. This renewed interest in fishing during the 1750s encouraged some of the merchants to diversify their interests; just two days before he died Lowther wrote that 'Mr [Anthony] Bacon is mightily for our merchants engaging in the whale fishery and I am glad Mr How and others are going into the Newfoundland fishery'.[102]

Sir John Lowther recognized a demand for cheap consumer goods. He thought that pottery would be a suitable product, and told William Gilpin in 1697 that he was 'extreme impatient for some manufacture' to be started. He suggested that two brickhouses in the town, not then let, could be used for the production of pottery. Gilpin's reaction was to lease them himself, in order to make clay tobacco pipes. He sent Lowther encouraging reports of his progress, but these seem to have been largely fictitious since he gave up pipe-making within a few months 'being a loser'. Another group, which included John Spedding's father, was planning to make pottery in 1698, but this project also seems to have come to nothing. Sir John Lowther attempted to make pipemaking more systematic by building proper facilities in 1699. A 'pipehouse' was built, to which he made improvements a couple of years later, and which was let throughout the first two decades of the eighteenth century. Nothing further is known about pottery making until Thomas Atkinson set up as a potter in 1740. He purchased 200 tons of coal from Lowther in 1742 and 1743, but by 1746 he had not made any pottery for two years and the lease was terminated. The pothouse was not let again until 1755.[103]

Some of the problems associated with Whitehaven's food supply will be analysed in a later chapter, but the town's alcohol needs also had to be satisfied as the population grew. The coal miners, in particular, were not noted for their sobriety. At a celebration in 1714 of George I's arrival in London, they 'drank a great many loyal healths over [Lowther's] barrel of ale, which put a good many of them past coming to work next day'. But the town had no brewery until Thomas Lutwidge established one in 1730. He ran this, together with a distillery, until financial problems overtook him in 1736. Some time between then and 1741 the distillery was leased and the brewery ceased production. A Mr Salter proposed in 1743 to start a small brewery in the town, but despite Lowther's encouragement nothing came of the project, and when a new brewery was set up, it was under the auspices of the Patrickson/Spedding timber company. One advantage of this arrangement was that the company could benefit from cheap grain, since Lowther imported supplies at this time to relieve local shortages. A second brewery was opened in 1754.[104]

Other products may have been manufactured about which, for want of evidence, little or nothing is known. What can be stated with confidence is that the major local interests provided a certain amount of stimulation for industrial and manufacturing concerns in and around Whitehaven. Trade stimulated service industries such as ropemaking and shipbuilding, while the mere growth of population had a significant effect on traditional occupations. However, with the coal-fuel industries, and the production of goods suitable for sale in America, it proved none too easy to turn possibility into reality. The iron industry was hampered by the absence of an effective means of smelting with coal; efforts to smelt copper and lead, whilst theoretically possible, were not in practice very successful; glasshouses were expensive failures; domestic textile production was restricted by legislation barring Irish imports, while nailmaking never developed on a significant scale. Except for a few years during the 1740s when the tobacco trade was at its height, west Cumberland never really cut free from its economic dependence upon the coal trade. Hence the omissions in the list of local manufactures provided by Parson and White in 1829.

Although the reasons for the relative inability to develop new interests are complicated, the problems of enterprise and population were crucial in determining the success, or (as was usually the case) failure of efforts to diversify west Cumberland's industrial concerns. The decision of Sir James Lowther to offer words of encouragement rather than investment (with the notable exception of salt manufacture, and briefly, glassmaking) was vital in the long run. Responsibility was thrown on to other local people, or outsiders. The gentry played some part in establishing salt panning, while the merchants had an important role to play in iron manufacturing. However, merchant capital was not readily available until the later 1740s because of the uncertain nature of the tobacco trade. Lowther might complain that the merchants took insufficient interest in local manufacturing industry, but they were not in a position to do so. Once their situation altered they took the lead. In the absence of gentry capital, and in the delay while merchant capital was accumulated, west Cumberland was forced to rely on outsiders. Such dependence raised additional problems. Quite apart from the willingness of offcomers to settle in what they regarded as a remote area – a notable example being the failure to attract nailmakers in sufficient numbers – those who came were not necessarily trust-worthy. Frizington ironworks, organized by William Wood, was probably the most ambitious scheme financed from outside Cumbria, but it had a negative effect on the region's economy. Only the small but profitable copperas works was organized with any success by an offcomer. But the entrepreneurs were not wholly to blame, since the small size of population was always likely to hamper rapid growth. West Cumberland, like Tyneside, was hampered in its development by a small local market and a slowly increasing population; hence it was unable to establish consumer goods industries which could compete in the overseas, or even the national market.

6

Communications

The developments in industry and trade analysed in the foregoing chapters have illustrated the vital importance of good communications. Service centres such as Liverpool and Hull could only have grown in the way that they did because communications were improved. Economic development was inevitably hampered in regions poorly served by transport. North Wales, for example, made considerable progress until about 1760, but thereafter improvement was impeded as harbours silted up, and the lie of the land made canals and railways difficult to build. Similarly, Shropshire's iron industry suffered because the area was not linked to the main canal system before the mid-1830s.[1]

The need to ensure that Cumbria had the best possible communications network was recognized in the region. Sir James Lowther was 'mightily glad' when he heard in 1744 of proposed plans to turnpike several of the local roads, because of the benefits that this would bring to trade.[2] However, the nature of development in west Cumberland brought with it particular problems. Nationally, inland routes were normally improved at roughly the same time as harbour extensions took place; indeed, the pace of such developments quickened noticeably in the later seventeenth century, and was greater between 1695 and 1725 than at any comparable earlier period.[3] In Cumbria the situation was atypical. Harbour extensions followed the national pattern, with Whitehaven, Workington and Parton all being extended, but it was not until the 1740s and 1750s that roads were improved. The position of Whitehaven was almost unique among major British outports. It was neither a natural haven, nor was it located on a river, a fact which bears witness to the way in which economic development was based on coal rather than on service to the hinterland.

Underlying this pattern were the different aims and motives of west Cumberland's two major interest groups, the coal owners and the overseas merchants. Since coal was mined close to the coast, and the owners provided their own packhorses, cartways and wagonways, their major concern was with the harbour facilities. The ill-fated quay built at Saltom in 1732 illustrates the importance for coal owners of providing shipping facilities close to the coal. Their main consideration in terms of transport was that all the vessels involved in the trade should be able to find harbour accommodation, so that masters would not be tempted to go elsewhere for business. Even the coal-fuel industries which developed during the eighteenth century were situated near to the coast, or (for obvious reasons in the case of iron) on a river. The overseas merchants were using facilities made available for the coal trade, but if harbour developments were therefore less of a worry for them, it was in their interest to see local roads improved. If they were to exploit the – admittedly limited – resources of the hinterland, good communications were vital. According to a pamphlet printed in 1752, one of the two principal obstacles to improving Cumbria's woollen industry was 'the want of a ready and easy communication with the principal seaport by reason of the badness of the roads'.[4] Insofar as merchants lacked the capital for industrial investment until the 1740s, they also had insufficient resources to devote very much to road improvement schemes. As with the promotion of new industries, Lowther, who had the resources, did not require the facilities. Significantly, the local merchants were heavily involved when schemes to encourage road improvements were finally put forward.

Partly because the aims of the two groups differed, tension and conflict arose both within and between them. Amongst the coal owners, the monopolistic intentions of the Lowthers affected the pattern of development. The conflict began with Sir John Lowther's efforts to close off the area around Whitehaven by preventing the building of a harbour at Parton, and extended from the 1720s into disputes between the coal owners over changes at Workington and Maryport. Between coal owners and overseas merchants the struggle was fought out in Whitehaven. Once the tobacco trade became an integral part of the town's economy in the 1740s, the merchants were no longer prepared to bow unquestioningly to Lowther dictates about harbour developments. Everybody agreed that the harbour needed to be extended; where they differed was that

Lowther favoured lengthening the quays to accommodate more (coal) vessels, whereas the tobacco merchants wanted to spend whatever money was available deepening the outer harbour to allow their larger volume ships to enter at low tide. The result was a struggle between the two interests which highlighted the personal antipathy between Lowther and Walter Lutwidge, and spilled over into Whitehaven's local government affairs.

Harbour developments in west Cumberland reflected the shifts and changes of the coal trade. First, Whitehaven's facilities were improved in line with its position as the major export outlet. Later, when Sir James Lowther turned his attention towards controlling all the west coast collieries, Workington and finally Maryport harbours were extended. Parton, a relief outlet for Whitehaven vessels, generated a good deal of heated argument regarding its position in the coal trade, but was never particularly important in terms of the quantity of coal handled. In consolidating their interests the Lowthers faced considerable opposition. Their efforts to ensure that Whitehaven remained the only outlet at the southern end of the coalfield produced conflict with those supporting the development of Parton, at least until Sir John Lowther decided that it had become in his interest to have a harbour there. Despite dominating the export trade at Workington in the 1730s, Sir James Lowther found himself unable to control the course of harbour extensions in the way that he might have hoped to have done, while he was more or less excluded from participating in the improvements at Maryport. Finally, at Whitehaven, the Lowthers' original bastion, the merchants secured a voice in deciding on changes as early as 1709, although they did not positively intervene in affairs until the 1740s.

Both Parton and Workington had operational harbours at the beginning of the seventeenth century, whereas the Whitehaven landing stage was only a heap of rubble and stone. Troops embarked for Ireland from Workington during the first decade of the century, while coal was exported through Parton until the pier collapsed in the early 1630s.[5] Between 1632 and 1634 a proper pier was built at Whitehaven by Sir Christopher Lowther, with government financial support. It was eighty-five yards long, and was constructed of irregular stones which were held together with timber. Evidence gathered for an exchequer bill in 1679 suggested that the pier had cost £700 to build. One man remembered seeing '60 or 70 men daily at hard labour'.[6]

As coal exports from Whitehaven grew in the seventeenth century it became clear that Sir John Lowther's efforts to create a monopoly of the trade from Whitehaven were resented, at least in part because he failed to improve the harbour facilities. The first signs of conflict came in the 1670s. William Fletcher, lord of the manor of Moresby, began to rebuild the old pier at Parton, which lay a mile north of Whitehaven. This was outside Sir John Lowther's jurisdiction, and the project was designed to enable the smaller coal owners to use Parton rather than continue dependent on the facilities provided further south. For Lowther this represented a threat to his monopoly. To prevent Fletcher from succeeding, he obtained a Crown grant of the foreshore in the manor of Moresby, and secured White-haven's appointment as a member port under the head port of Carlisle. These moves effectively prevented the building of any wharfs or quays within the jurisdiction of the port of Whitehaven, which included Parton. As a result, Lowther was able to obtain an injunction in the exchequer court to bring Fletcher's building programme to an abrupt halt.[7] At least this exercise produced one positive result, improvements at Whitehaven. Between 1679 and 1681, with the help of money levied on coal exports, and after con-sultations with the masters, Lowther added a fifty-yard extension to the pier.[8] Thus he survived the first threat to his position, and actually strengthened his hand. But attempting to control the trade by such means was certain to create further conflict as long as he was not the only local owner.

Lowther's monopoly was again challenged in the 1690s, this time because of expansion in the tobacco trade and increased mining activity at Parton. Discussions about building a new pier at White-haven were inconclusive,[9] but efforts were made to improve con-ditions at other harbours along the coast. In 1696 Henry Curwen was reputed to be intending 'to bestow a great sum in recovering a harbour' at Workington. Two years later he was considering en-larging the harbour and encouraging some Whitehaven merchants to settle there. Clearly he was attempting to promote the tobacco trade through Workington, but it seems unlikely that the project met with any success.[10] At Parton, another attempt was made to break the Lowther grip by William Fletcher's son Thomas, and by Thomas Lamplugh, to whom he leased Distington colliery (Gunerdine) in 1693. As Sir James Lowther was later to discover, it was not economic to move coal from Gunerdine to Whitehaven. When Fletcher and Lamplugh began rebuilding the pier at Parton in 1695, however, Sir John Lowther obtained an injunction to stop them. But by this time he had acquired, and begun working, Lattera colliery in Moresby. Consequently he could see the advantage to be gained from having an outlet for his coal at Parton. As a result, and much against the advice of his stewards, Lowther allowed Lamplugh to build upon the old foundations at Parton. A pier was constructed capable of accommodating seven or eight vessels – ten by one account – and Lowther was soon its major user.[11] When it suited him, Lowther was ready to allow another outlet to be developed, but such a policy created a dangerous precedent if he again tried to invoke his right to control local harbour developments.

Just how dangerous became abundantly clear in 1704 when Fletcher and Lamplugh decided to seek legislation enabling them to raise money for improving and extending Parton harbour. Apart from being a direct affront to Lowther, this raised important questions about the problems of having two large harbours in close proximity. Lowther used this as his strongest argument, claiming that to expand Parton would threaten the livelihoods of many Whitehaven people. He cited other instances where Parliament had refused to allow two adjacent places to develop harbours simultaneously, and stressed the additional problems to be expected in 'preventing the running of prohibited and uncustom'd goods; the natural effect of having two ports so near one another'.[12] Clearly, however, the Parton promoters were in a stronger position. Apart from stressing that harbour facilities were inadequate at Whitehaven, they did not hesitate to argue that Lowther's real motive was his desire to retain the right to regulate the coal trade by controlling the local harbours. This smacked of private interest being employed to forestall public good. Their position was enhanced because neither Lowther nor his son was in Parliament at the time. By contrast Lamplugh, then sitting for Cockermouth, was ideally situated to steer the bill through the lower house. James Lowther was at least in London, but what limited opposition he could put up disappeared when Sir John Lowther died early in 1706, and he went north to claim the inheritance. The bill passed: twenty-nine trustees were appointed, with power to raise loans to the value of £1500. With this they were to finance the construction of a harbour capable of accommodating fifty vessels; the capital was to be repaid from the duties of 4d a ton on coal exported over the following eleven years.[13]

It looked in 1706 as if the Lowther monopoly had been broken. Work was quickly put in hand to extend the facilities at Parton, and by May sixty men were employed there ten hours a day. It was widely believed that Whitehaven harbour lacked sufficient accommodation for vessels, despite Lowther's claims that he was ready to 'lay out considerable sums of money every year for the improvement of it'.[14] In fact, turning theory into practice proved to be no easy task. Lowther was faced with the problem that his father had never resolved: how to control all the outlets when the need to mine further from Whitehaven made new harbours necessary? The difference was that, whereas Sir John only had to cope with the problems of Parton, his son would also be faced with trying to control Workington and Maryport.

Given these circumstances, it is hardly surprising that Lowther's initial move was to cut his losses by concentrating on his Whitehaven collieries. The success of the Parton project almost certainly depended on Lowther exporting coal. His decision in 1707 to step up production at Whitehaven, and to stop mining at Lattera was a setback. For the next few years he made little or no use of Parton, but took positive steps to improve the harbour facilities at Whitehaven. Breaking with his father's policy, Lowther allowed control to pass into the hands of a board of trustees. 'I would know . . . how the town likes my willingness to give them any accommodation about the harbour', he told Spedding, 'which they could hardly have obtained of my father.' He steered a bill through the House of Commons in 1709 by which twenty-one trustees were appointed to raise money for harbour improvements.[15] Its terms soon proved to be inadequate, and supplementary legislation was passed in 1712.[16]

Lowther was hardly acting in a disinterested fashion. Fourteen of the trustees were to be elected triennially from amongst the masters of vessels, the owners of not less than a one-sixteenth share in a vessel belonging to the port, or inhabitants dealing in goods subject to the payment of duties. Lowther nominated the other seven. He also had the power to veto decisions, and he took considerable pains to ensure that anyone unfavourable to his views was not elected to the board. He manoeuvred John, Mathias and Ebenezer

Gale off the board in 1722, and Walter Lutwidge in 1752, on both occasions when his views were opposed.[17] John Spedding was appointed harbour treasurer, which was another advantage to Lowther. Rather than await the lengthy deliberations of the trustees on harbour repairs, Lowther could instruct Spedding to put them in hand; in this way he effectively underwrote improvements. In a formal sense Lowther lent only £720 out of the £3970 borrowed on the strength of the 1709 and 1712 acts, just 18 per cent. Through Spedding, however, he advanced money from time to time for paying wages, buying materials and generally ensuring that work could continue. By 1735 the amount owed to him was £1156. Although this had been reduced to £773 a year later, the problem was to repay this when the temporary duties levied according to the terms of the acts expired in 1737. The trustees agreed that the masters should continue to pay the duties on a 'voluntary' basis, but this was hardly satisfactory and a third act was passed in 1740.

Once new legislation had been obtained, the trustees' first task was to settle Lowther's account. Lowther 'lent' them £1000 with which to pay outstanding debts (including those to him) and begin the improvement fund. In return he received the first ten £100 harbour bonds. Since the planned improvements were mainly for the benefit of the overseas interests, Lowther now formalized his relationship with the trustees. He agreed to lend £100 for each £200 put up by other trustees, reflecting his nomination of one-third of the board members. As a result, between 1740 and 1753 he purchased a further thirteen bonds valued at £1340. Altogether sixteen were redeemed during his lifetime, leaving £740 outstanding when he died.[18] Lowther ensured that, though powerful factions in Whitehaven might oppose him, and, through fortuitous circumstances in 1750 actually hold up the implementation of his ideas, they could never prevent his policies from being carried through. As Walter Lutwidge expressed it in a letter written to Lowther in London, following the passing of the 1740 act, 'I don't see how it is possible . . . to do anything before you come down.'[19]

The trustees' first task in 1709 was to have the harbour deepened, and a countermole constructed as a sea defence on the northern side of the harbour (figure 6.1). After some discussion it was decided that the latter should run from the foot of Duke Street. Work started during the summer of 1710. It soon became apparent that on its own the countermole would be inadequate, and consequently new

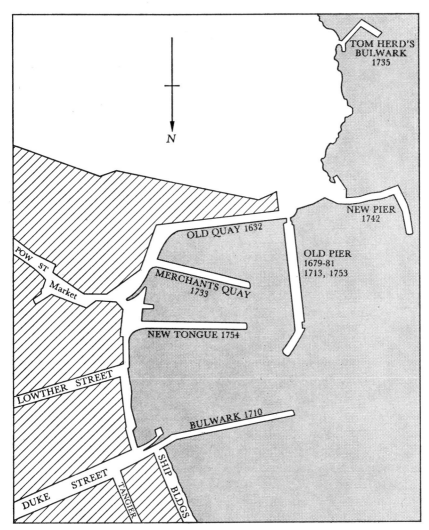

TOM HERD'S
BULWARK
1735

N

NEW PIER
1742

OLD QUAY 1632

OLD PIER
1679-81
1713, 1753

POW ST

Market

MERCHANTS QUAY
1793

NEW TONGUE 1754

LOWTHER STREET

BULWARK 1710

SHIP BLDGS

DUKE STREET

TANGIER

6.1 Whitehaven harbour looking south (showing additions)

borrowing plans were drawn up in the summer of 1711. Cleaning
the harbour and building the countermole had cost £1694 by then.
The trustees decided to apply for an extension of the temporary
duties granted in 1709, to pay for the capital expenditure. To this
end Lowther steered another bill through Parliament in the winter
of 1711/12. As a result, work on finishing the countermole went
ahead, and the old pier was extended. Both projects had been
completed by 1713.[20]

The extensions at Whitehaven undermined Parton, where lack of finance and bad weather caused considerable disruption. Late in 1707 John Spedding informed Lowther of 'the damage done at Parton in the late stormy weather . . . all the work which [Lamplugh] did this year is entirely ruined and nothing of it appears but like a heap of rubbish'.[21] Even so, the pier was completed over the following years, and Lowther's acquisition of Lamplugh's lease of Gunerdine colliery in 1714 entirely altered the situation. Lowther now had a vested interest in seeing the works completed, but the pier was found to be badly constructed. It was thought to be on the verge of collapse in 1715, and major repairs were needed when the extraordinary duties granted in 1706 expired in 1716. Although further legislation was considered, the duties were eventually re-imposed on a voluntary basis for a twenty-one year term so that £500 could be spent on the harbour. The project was in considerable financial difficulties, however, and it was brought to a dramatic conclusion when the pier collapsed in November 1718.[22]

The situation as the coal trade went into recession in 1718 was certainly not propitious. Parton pier was in ruins, and neither Lowther nor Lamplugh was prepared to take responsibility for its repair. The agreement between the two men in 1714 had proved unsatisfactory, but its amendment in 1715 included a very significant alteration. Lamplugh sold all his remaining mining rights to Lowther. With no coal to raise, Lamplugh now had little incentive to carry out his side of the 1714 agreement to transport Lowther's coal to the harbour and to maintain the pier. Lowther refused to accept that Lamplugh could be let off since this would make the price that he had paid in 1714 appear extortionate. The result was that an impossible situation arose in 1718. Lamplugh claimed that he could not rebuild the pier without the duties from Lowther's coal exports, and Lowther pointed out that he could not export because the facilities did not exist. Lamplugh gambled that in view of Parton's importance to Lowther he would not want a long dispute. Since Lowther refused to back down, a six-year legal tangle ensued.[23] To complicate the situation still further, the implementation of a decision by the Whitehaven trustees in 1718 to add thirty yards to the old pier had to be postponed owing to lack of finance and a labour shortage. Coupled with Lowther's supply problems at Whitehaven, there seemed to be a real possibility that the level of exports would not be maintained, whatever the state of demand.

Lowther's decision to search for a monopoly, both to increase overall output in west Cumberland, and to enable him to work further inland at Whitehaven, had two effects for local harbours. First, he became a supporter of developing other ports, since he would now expect to make use of them. Congestion at Whitehaven had led many masters to use Workington, Maryport and the smaller creeks. Although Humphrey Senhouse vetoed any alterations at Maryport, a voluntary agreement to finance improvements was reached by the Workington masters in 1719. When Henry Curwen let Seaton colliery in 1721, it was on condition that the lessors paid 4d for each chaldron of coal shipped at Workington, the money to go towards harbour upkeep. A further agreement was reached between the Workington masters and coal owners two years later, and Lowther heard that they had 'two foot more water at Workington, are building a ship and two new houses'. By this time he was interested in leasing collieries in the area. Consequently he was a firm supporter of such changes 'in order to keep the prices of coals more reasonable for the shipping than they were like to be if there was only one harbour'.[24] Secondly, if he was to mine inland around Whitehaven, Lowther had a vested interest in seeing the harbour improved, and in encouraging the rebuilding of Parton pier. The Whitehaven depression was at least partly responsible for the absence of any further changes there before the 1730s, but his desire to promote the Moresby collieries ensured that rebuilding would take place at Parton once the legal dispute was settled.

Lowther's dispute with Lamplugh over Parton was a matter of considerable local significance. When Thomas Fletcher decided to sell the manors of Moresby and Distington in 1722, Lowther refused to bid for them on the grounds that to purchase them would compromise his position over Parton. However, he approached a number of his relatives in the hope that they would buy the manors with money provided by him on a fictitious mortgage. All refused, particularly his younger (indebted) cousin, Lord Lonsdale, who wrote,

your dispute with Mr Lamplugh, as it is about a matter of public nature must be well known to all those who have any interest or concern in the coal trade, which includes a great number of people, and besides at this juncture, as he has a considerable stake in the county election, and holds his interest from you on account of this difference, your quarrel with him is talked of almost quite round the county. . . . Can you imagine that if it is bought in the manner you propose, that it wont be discovered to be for your use and advantage, and then you will have the odium of commanding two harbours with this addition, that this manner of purchasing was an invention found out for evading the obligation you are under to Mr Lamplugh of paying two pence a ton for all the coals you ship at Parton.[25]

In fact, not only did Lowther's ingenious schemes fail when the manors were sold to John Brougham, but, as Lonsdale had predicted, the matter became an issue in the 1722 county election, and Lowther was unseated.[26] The case was not finally settled until Lowther and Lamplugh reached an out of court agreement in January 1725, although by then plans for rebuilding Parton pier were well in hand.[27]

Brougham intended to mine at Moresby, so that he appreciated the importance of restoring Parton. He reached an agreement with Lowther over restoration work, and a new act was obtained early in 1725, this time with Lowther steering the legislation through Parliament against the wishes of the two Cumberland MPs (he was sitting for Appleby at the time). The temporary duties which had lapsed in 1716 were revived for a further twenty-one years, allowing money to be borrowed for the pier to be rebuilt. Lowther wanted to avoid what he saw as Thomas Lamplugh's mistake of trying to to build a more extensive harbour than the slender resources would permit. The 1706 legislation had stipulated that the harbour should be capable of accommodating fifty vessels, but to keep costs to a minimum Lowther suggested that the new pier should be built to hold thirty ships, with room for expansion if necessary. After some dispute over planning and costs, rebuilding began in 1726, and £1900 was spent during the course of that year.[28]

With the southern end of the coalfield secured, Lowther could turn his attention to Workington, particularly as Henry Curwen's death in 1725 augured well for changes. Little was done immediately, although Eldred Curwen was anxious to develop the harbour when he inherited the estate in 1727. He consulted Lowther about the possibility of obtaining legislation, but by the time he came seriously to contemplate an act of Parliament in 1731, he and Lowther were no longer on good terms. The abortive 1728 lease, from which Curwen had extracted himself with difficulty, and Lowther's activities on the north bank of the Derwent after acquiring the Seaton lease, had produced distinctly cool relations between the two men. In any case Lowther and Lutwidge were building a wagonway and staith by 1732, which made harbour improvements less necessary to them. Curwen made his initial moves to obtain legislation without consulting Lowther; indeed, by the summer of 1733 the two men had become overtly hostile towards each other. Lowther considered that it would 'be proper one way or other . . . entirely to confound all prospects that Mr Curwen may have of getting an Act of Parliament next session by proposing scheme after scheme'. In the end Curwen abandoned the quest for legislation, and a voluntary agreement was reached in 1734 whereby duties were to be collected for upkeep of the harbour.[29] If anything, it was Curwen who had most to lose, since Lowther was successfully looking after his own interests on the north side of the river.

Meantime the Parton project ran into further problems when Brougham's enthusiasm waned. His Moresby mining interests proved more difficult to work at a profit than he had anticipated, with the result that he began to regret his financial commitment to Parton. Twice he asked Lowther to take over the whole project; each time he was met with a firm refusal. The two men finally agreed on further legislation, because the rebuilt harbour proved to be too dangerous for constant use. An act was passed in 1732 empowering the trustees to borrow another £2500 so that the pier might be lengthened by forty yards.[30] Lowther finally bowed to the inevitable and bought out Brougham in 1737, thereby acquiring the holding for which his father had begun the search back in the 1690s. He now had full control of both Whitehaven and Parton. With Maryport unimproved, and Workington using only a voluntary agreement, he had been at least partially successful in controlling port developments.

This situation lasted until the later 1740s, at which point Lowther's loosening grip on the coal trade was paralleled by a growing challenge to his supremacy in harbour developments. First, the tobacco boom at Whitehaven produced calls for a restructuring of harbour facilities to cater for the tobacco vessels in preference to coal ships. Secondly, Lowther found himself largely excluded from developments at Workington and Maryport as the two harbours were improved to cater for the increasing volume of traffic that they were handling. Although he emerged in control of Whitehaven, his overall loss of influence was clearly borne out by the growth of Workington and Maryport in the later eighteenth century, largely free of Lowther control.

Once the coal trade picked up in the later 1720s Whitehaven harbour again became congested, even with the relief afforded by Parton. The situation was compounded in the mid-1730s by the expansion of the tobacco trade, which revealed the inadequacy of the harbour for dealing with the increased traffic. In 1732 the trustees decided that a new mole was required, and the 'Merchants' Quay' (figure 6.1, p. 163) was built during the summer of 1733. It was extended the following summer. Additional work on deepening the harbour and building a new bulwark was undertaken in 1735 and 1736. All of this cost money. Temporary duties authorized by the 1709 and 1712 acts came to an end in 1737, at which point £15,522 had been spent on the harbour; £777 was outstanding in unpaid debts. From 1737 routine maintenance was supposed to be met from the perpetual duties granted in 1709, but these were at a lower rate, and yielded insufficient money to meet day-to-day costs, let alone pay off the deficit. Hence the trustees' decision to seek a new act in 1740, which extended the temporary duties for a further twenty-one years.[31]

The trustees intended to pay off outstanding debts and to construct a new outer harbour for the benefit of vessels trading to America and the Baltic. The argument for an outer harbour rested on the depth of water: although the existing harbour had been deepened several times, it still had only seventeen feet of water at spring tide, and ten feet at neap tide. As a result, some of the larger vessels could often be immobilized in the inner harbour for all but six or seven days either side of a spring tide. One effect was to prevent colliers from reaching the coal hurries. By erecting a new pier and mole out beyond the old pier, the trustees would make provision for twenty vessels to shelter at a point where the water was sufficiently deep for them to float on both spring and neap tides. Work on building the new pier began in 1740, the trustees lending the required finance in equal proportions. Engineering difficulties forced the trustees to employ an outside consultant, but the work was completed in 1743.[32]

Although this arrangement satisfied both Lowther and the merchants in 1740, by separating the two interests the trustees were storing up contention for the future as to which area of the harbour needed repairs and improvements. The storm broke towards the end of the 1740s when both inner and outer harbours required attention. In 1747 it was evident that the new pier and countermole needed strengthening, but plans to lengthen the latter were thwarted by a shortage of both capital and workmen. Expansion in the coal trade necessitated further improvements to the inner harbour. Carlisle Spedding put the number of colliers 'belonging to the town more than the harbour will contain in safety' at sixty. Lowther inevitably favoured extensions to the inner harbour. He proposed a thirty-yard extension to the old pier, and the building of a new mole in the inner harbour should this not prove to be sufficient. The net effect would be to allow another sixty-six colliers to moor in the harbour. This plan required the support of seventeen trustees including Lowther. Only sixteen signatures could be mustered; two places on the board were vacant, and three trustees (including Walter Lutwidge) preferred a rival plan. They proposed that the outer harbour should be completed before any extensions to the old pier were considered. According to Carlisle Spedding this 'would cost several thousand pounds more than our duties upon the present act would raise'.[33]

Such an impasse infuriated Lowther, and if Carlisle Spedding is to be believed, led to considerable feeling among the ships' masters against the recalcitrant trustees. Two further schemes were considered and rejected, so that the 1752 trustees' election turned into a battle of local loyalties. The fact that only three of the elected trustees had stood out against the Lowther plan, and that it had been supported by a number of the most influential merchants, is an indication of the considerable support for enhancing the interests of the coal trade. As a result, in August 1752 Lutwidge and his supporters were ousted from the board. Within a few days an agreement was reached to add an additional thirty yards to the old pier, work which was completed during the summer of 1753. Since a new tongue was still needed, this was built the following summer.[34]

Lowther's control at Whitehaven was paralleled at Parton. From 1724 he and John Brougham advanced money in proportion on £100 bonds. By the time Lowther bought Moresby and Distington in 1737 both men had invested £1900. Lowther acquired Brougham's share as part of the transaction, giving himself custody of the whole outstanding debt. Annual interest of £171 was payable from the harbour duties; it was paid in 1738 and 1739, but the 1740 interest was only paid in 1753, and that for 1741 in 1756.[35] Such figures may give an indication of how little the harbour was used after 1737. Lowther considered selling his Whingill coal there in

1750 when Lutwidge was holding up harbour improvements at Whitehaven. When Curwen began working Lowca colliery in 1754, the least expensive course would have been for him to export through Parton. Instead, he developed Harrington. Parton underwent a brief revival in the 1760s, and Thomas Pennant described it in 1722 as 'intended for shipping; a new creation of Sir James Lowther [of Lowther]'. Five years later the county historians, Nicolson and Burn, commented that it was a convenient harbour for exporting Moresby coal, and it probably remained in use until 1795, when it was destroyed in a gale and not rebuilt.[36]

By contrast, Lowther was able to exercise relatively little control at Workington and Maryport. In part, this was hardly surprising in view of his known intentions from the 1720s. Sir John Lowther's moves to deny William Fletcher the right to build at Parton during the 1670s, followed by his compromise in using the restored pier in the 1690s, and then his about-turn in opposing the 1706 bill for personal reasons, had not gone unnoticed. Neither had Sir James Lowther's energetic opposition to the 1706 bill, followed by a similar *volte face* to become an active promoter of Parton. Such a record inevitably made the sponsors of improvement at Workington and Maryport wary of his intentions. Moreover, Lowther did not help the situation by his failure to reach an agreement with Eldred Curwen in the early 1730s, or by his general scepticism about proposed schemes. When asked to contribute towards improvements to the town and harbour of Maryport in 1749 he wanted first to know the overall cost. A petition was presented to Parliament in February that year, and the bill which followed became law within six weeks. The main purpose of the legislation was to give legal backing for duties collected in order to finance harbour developments. Lowther sat on the committee, but told Spedding that 'they might have got it a good deal cheaper, but shall not find fault, they may go on their own way'. Despite his later claim to have been 'hearty' in aiding its smooth passage, Lowther's scepticism is also apparent from other references to the new town. The overriding belief which had lain behind the policy of 'laying things together' at Whitehaven proved to be his undoing elsewhere. He was sure that the property around Workington and Maryport was too divided for the owners to consult together for improvement schemes. Certainly no one owner stood in the same relationship as he did to Whitehaven, but this was not necessarily prohibitive of

change. However, Lowther was adamant, and even when he had
evidently been proved wrong by 1754, he still maintained that 'it
is not likely that any great matter will be done either at Workington
or Elnefoot [Maryport] the property is so divided, though the
country will be for everything but parting with their money upon
which all depends'.[37]

His scepticism proved to be incorrect. Work was quickly put in
hand at Maryport once the bill passed, and simultaneous improvements took place at Workington. In January 1749 Henry Curwen
sounded out Lowther as to the possibility of obtaining legislation
to improve Workington. Although Lowther claimed that he was
willing 'to promote any good bill', his attitude towards Maryport
may have discouraged Curwen, and a further voluntary agreement
was reached to replace the one which had operated since the 1730s.
Fifty-six masters signed an agreement to collect two pence for each
ton of coal exported (the same rate as Maryport). The money was
to be apportioned for harbour upkeep by a number of trustees.
Regulations about harbour use were also introduced. The agreement turned out to be highly successful, and the Merchants' Quay
planned in 1748 was completed in 1754. Lowther wrote in 1751
that the money spent at Workington had put the harbour 'into so
good a condition that they have no scheme at present for applying
for an Act of Parliament'. Indeed, no legislation was passed for
Workington until the nineteenth century.[38]

Harbour developments clearly followed the pattern of the coal
trade, with only the dispute at Whitehaven in 1750 showing any
real attempt by the overseas merchants to bring about change.
The growing importance of the Curwens, Christians and Senhouses
in the coal trade by the later 1740s, was reflected in their control of
events at Maryport and Workington – a control which eventually
enabled the two ports, together with Harrington from the 1760s, to
compete with Whitehaven. Whereas in 1772 Whitehaven owned
197 ships, and the other three 185, fifty years later the respective
totals were 181 and 293. By 1792 Whitehaven's proportion of the
total coal export from the four west Cumberland harbours (assuming
little was being sent from Parton) had slipped to 41·5 per cent.
Seventy, or even eighty per cent of total English sales to Ireland had
been exported from there in the 1750s.[39]

Lack of incentive was the major obstacle to improved inland

communications. The coal owners had little reason to encourage improvements, while the overseas merchants were not in a position to spare the capital for what was always likely to be a small return. The one attempt to promote river navigation was greeted without much enthusiasm. This was the 1722 act to make the river Eden navigable from the Solway Firth to Carlisle. Sir James Lowther favoured the measure because he believed that it would enable coal to be transported to within three miles of the town. Apart from increasing his own sales during the trade depression, he hoped that it would stimulate manufacturing industries. He even wrote to the Corporation 'to propose the raising a stock of £1000 for beginning a manufacture, without interest for seven years. I have offered to lend £200 upon such terms.' Not everyone shared his optimism. Vessels could already navigate the river at high tide, and Lord Lonsdale was sceptical as to whether the bill would make much difference. Lowther complained of Lonsdale's lack of support in seeing the bill through the House of Lords, and nothing more was heard of the scheme after 1722.[40]

For many years the same problem of working up enthusiasm restricted any improvement of the region's roads. As late as 1735 Lowther complained that he could muster little support for promoting a turnpike bill, and this lack of interest was compounded by the nature of the existing roads, both in terms of their direction and their physical state. Generally they ran north–south through Cumbria, rather than east–west (which would have suited the merchants rather better). John Ogilby recognized only four in 1675: one connected Kendal with Carlisle via Shap; a second joined Egremont and Carlisle through Whitehaven, Workington and Cockermouth; a third stretched from Carlisle to Kendal through Keswick and Ambleside; and a fourth ran east from Carlisle to Newcastle. Since most goods were carried by packhorse, it is unlikely that any of these roads were usable by wheeled traffic.[41]

The state of the roads was a subject of considerable comment. Celia Fiennes described travel in 1699 as 'tedious' because of the 'illness of way'. Robert Molesworth, writing from Edlington near Doncaster to his wife in Ireland in 1704, told her 'you must by no means think of sending anything by Whitehaven. It is almost 100 miles from us, filthy way, ten times worse than that from hence to Chester.'[42] Even local inhabitants were scathing. In Westmorland, Benjamin Brown, high constable of Kendal ward, could not find a word of praise for any of the roads in his district when he inspected them in 1730 and 1731. Lowther described the highways around Whitehaven in 1734 as 'prodigiously out of repair'. He feared that the town might be fined by Quarter Sessions for neglect. Sir John Clerk complained in 1739 that 'the last three miles to Whitehaven are monstrously bad, rough and narrow'. The House of Commons committee considering a turnpike petition in 1740 was told that the roads were so narrow, and the banks so high, that in many places a single horseman could not pass by a cart or a laden horse.[43]

Taken together, these circumstances ensured that only increased use of the existing roads, both by passenger and goods traffic, would bring about any improvement. This was certainly the reason given in 1740 by the Whitehaven harbour trustees, merchants and coal owners. In a petition to the House of Commons they suggested that

the high roads leading to the said town of Whitehaven are very narrow having seldom been made use of by carts and wheel carriages till of late years; but that, since the improvement of the harbour aforesaid, the resort of persons from other parts of the country has been so great, and likewise such increase of carts and wheel carriages as well as loaden horses passing with goods to and from Whitehaven, that the said roads are become ruinous and almost impassable in winter.[44]

Attempts had been made in 1733 and 1735 to stimulate interest in turnpiking the roads around Whitehaven,[45] but legislation was only obtained as part of the 1740 Harbour Act. The four main roads leading into the town, from St Bees and Egremont to the south and south-east, Harrington to the north, and Bridgefoot, near Cockermouth, to the north-east, were to be turnpiked. Of these schemes, the most important was the road to Bridgefoot, since this provided a link with Cockermouth and the existing, if in-adequate, cross-country route through Keswick to Penrith, where carts could join the London road. The merchants' interest was reflected in the naming as commissioners of Peter How, Thomas and Walter Lutwidge, William Hicks, Robert Gilpin, Thomas Hartley, Richard Kelsick and Thomas Patrickson. Work was quickly put in hand, and by August 1744 the roads to Egremont and Bridgefoot were almost completed. A traveller in 1746 described how 'the roads leading to [Whitehaven] are equal to the best turnpikes about London and are every day improving'. Lowther lent a total of £655 to the £2000 borrowed by the trust. Of this, £355 was still outstanding in 1755. No documentation survives regarding other contributors.[46]

If full advantage was to be taken of this scheme other roads needed attention. First, and most crucially, east–west communications across Cumbria needed to be improved if the west coast ports were to take advantage of local domestic production and consumption. Secondly, it was necessary to improve the road to Carlisle and from there across country to Newcastle. This would make the overland route to the north-east more viable. Thirdly, the roads north–south through Cumbria needed improving to speed up the flow of traffic. In fact, little happened of a positive nature for some years after 1740, the most successful scheme between then and 1753 being the turnpiking of the Egremont to Millom road by the terms of an act passed in 1750.[47]

The cross-country turnpike from Bridgefoot to Penrith was the first to be canvassed following initial hostility to the Whitehaven turnpike, which only died away when its success became apparent.[48] At the Cumberland Quarter Sessions in September 1744, agreement was reached on a petition to Parliament for legislation to turnpike the road from Bridgefoot through Penrith to Brough in Westmorland. Lowther presented the petition, but the scheme went no further. In a dispute surprisingly reminiscent of the 1970s, contemporaries argued the case for the road to go either via Caldbeck, or Keswick. Subsidiary to this, though little less important, was the question of whether there should be one or two sets of trustees for the whole length of the road. Consequently, further petitions to Parliament in 1747 and 1750 were equally unsuccessful in bringing any positive action. An act was eventually passed in 1753 to turnpike the Penrith–Caldbeck section of the road, but the Penrith–Cockermouth route was only approved in 1762. Such prevarication may indicate the absence of pressing need for improvement. Be that as it may, it certaibly meant that the two parts of the county were not linked until the tobacco trade had passed its peak.[49]

Attempts to improve the links between Bridgefoot and Carlisle began in the wake of the 1745 Jacobite uprising. General Wade's inability to relieve Carlisle, because of the state of the roads from Newcastle, highlighted the inadequacy of communications across the north of England. Furthermore, substitute cannon had been moved to Carlisle from Whitehaven. This operation had served to demonstrate just how poor the road links were between west Cumberland and the county town. When the government assumed responsibility for building a military road between Carlisle and Newcastle to prevent any repetition of the events during 1745, local gentlemen in Cumberland canvassed the idea of having the road extended to Bridgefoot. Apart from providing the necessary overland link with Newcastle, this had the subtle advantage that the road would have been built with government money. Grand though it was, and attractive though the scheme must have been to many people, the idea was stillborn.[50] The link from the west coast to Carlisle was only prepared with the passing of a turnpike act in 1753 to improve the road between Workington and the county town.

The north–south links through Cumbria were the oldest, but that did not mean the roads were in very good condition. Traffic south from Cumbria either passed over the Pennines and down through Yorkshire, or went through Lancashire. Normally it passed along the Carlisle–Penrith–Kendal, or Carlisle–Penrith–Brough axes, which highlighted the need to improve the Carlisle–Penrith road. Legislation was only passed in 1753. Attempts to turnpike the road from Penrith over the Pennines began in 1742, but only produced legislation eleven years later, the same year in which the Penrith–Lancashire road was covered by legislation (table 6.1).

Table 6.1. *Turnpike Acts relating to Cumbrian roads (see also fig. 6.2).*

Year	Roads	Act reference
1740	Whitehaven–St Bees, Whitehaven–Egremont, Whitehaven–Bridgefoot, Whitehaven–Harrington	13 Geo. II c.14
1750	Egremont–Millom	23 Geo. II c.40
1751	Carlisle–Newcastle	24 Geo. II c.25
1753	Penrith-Caldbeck	26 Geo. II c.1
1753	Carlisle–Penrith–Eamont Bridge	26 Geo. II c.4
1753	Carlisle–Workington	26 Geo. II c.13
1753	Hyning Syke–Kendal–Eamont Bridge	26 Geo. II c.16
1753	Brough–Eamont Bridge	26 Geo. II c.31
1753	Keighley–Kendal	26 Geo. II c.50
1762	Penrith–Cockermouth–Keswick–Kendal	2 Geo. III c.61

The plethora of legislation in 1753 raised obvious problems of financing the new roads. Lowther suggested that local members of Parliament and peers with considerable estates in Cumbria should put up the money, but in fact little seems to have been accomplished in his lifetime.[51] His own energy in steering the bills through Parliament was remarkable. On 19 January 1753 he reported the committee proceedings on the Penrith–Caldbeck petition to the House of Commons, and also presented a petition for the Carlisle–Penrith turnpike. He saw the latter through committee in February before presenting a petition for the Penrith–Brough turnpike. On 3 March he and John Stanwix, the Member for Carlisle, moved for the Carlisle–Workington bill. And so it continued; not surprisingly, by the time all six bills had passed on to the statute book, Lowther was able to claim that 'hardly any other members attend so much as I

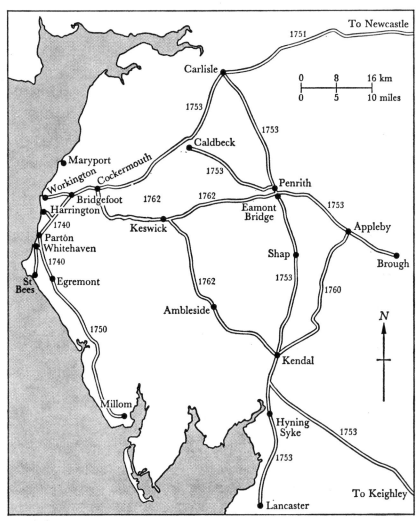

6.2   The establishment of Turnpike Trusts in Cumbria

do because of these six turnpike bills'.[52] Such a record was impressive for a man nearing his eightieth birthday. For their part the merchants acted as commissioners for the Whitehaven turnpike, and almost certainly lent money to the project, although evidence about the working of the trust has not survived. Lowther consulted Peter How about the proposal to turnpike the Penrith–Keswick road in 1744, an indication that this was a scheme in which the merchants had a positive interest.[53]

The dominance of coal in the west Cumberland economy was highlighted by the pattern of change and development in the communications network. Particularly apparent was Sir John Lowther's monopolistic desire regarding harbours, and his son's single-minded pursuit of the coal trade. The board of trustees for Whitehaven harbour exercised little real power; Sir James Lowther continued to exercise almost total control, and even the most substantial merchants accepted his right to do so. His own belief, that the coal trade was the backbone of west Cumberland's economy and the overseas ventures were transitory, ensured that the direction of harbour improvements favoured the colliers. Even the duties payable towards the upkeep of the harbour were weighted against the overseas traders. By comparison with Liverpool, all too little was done to produce the deep-water facilities which were crucial for the continuation of the colonial trade. Proposals for building a proper dock were vetoed by lack of support among the trustees in 1751, and in consequence the port failed to develop the facilities required for its non-coal interests.[51] By contrast, the natural harbours at Workington and Maryport were not centres of development until the overseas trade had peaked.

This same dominance of coal is apparent in regard to inland communications. Road improvements were left to the discretion of merchants since coal owners provided their own overland transport: hence the later developments. Admittedly Lowther played an active role in Parliamentary proceedings, but this reflected his beliefs about the role of a county member rather than any obvious desire on his part to improve the roads. As with the extensions to the outer harbour at Whitehaven, he was scrupulously correct in offering to lend a proportion of the money needed. Honourable though this attitude may have been, simply supporting schemes in this way was no guarantee of action; after all, three acts of

Parliament were passed for promoting Parton harbour within the space of twenty-six years, but the business transacted there was never particularly important. Workington, by contrast, was much more significant although no legislation was passed during the eighteenth century. In the final analysis financial backing was the crucial determinant of improvements: hence the atypical pattern in west Cumberland, where four harbours were operational by 1755, but no adequate road link existed with the east of the county.

7

Creating New Towns: Urban Growth

Urban growth was one of the most striking features of English social change in the later seventeenth and eighteenth centuries. Some of the more important 'new' towns were those associated with industry and trade: they usually developed a single economic interest, rather than diversifying their activities; they were often found close to a supply of raw materials; they were usually unplanned; and they experienced severe teething troubles in the form of ineffective social control, which in turn reflected the absence of municipal authority. In this latter aspect they provided a striking contrast to the older established towns.[1] West Cumberland hardly had a settlement which could justifiably be termed 'urban' in the mid-seventeenth century. Whitehaven had something under 400 in-habitants, and Workington probably few more. Both were little more than villages, even by contemporary standards. They lacked the specialized economic function which is often taken to be the simplest criterion of a town. By 1801, however, they could boast populations of more than 10,000 and 6000 respectively, while Mary-port was a rapidly emerging third town. The other outlets used for exporting coal at different times – Parton, Walton Wood and Flimby – had remained small centres. A comprehensive picture of urban growth in the period can only be drawn for Whitehaven, because of the limitations of the evidence. However, this reveals many of the stresses inherent in town development in what was in many ways one of the more significant new towns of the period.

Whitehaven's growth was typical of its *genre* as a new industrial town. It had a specialist economic function, coal mining, and – a feature more reminiscent of the sixteenth century than the eighteenth – a low level of capitalization, with wealth being concentrated in the hands of a minority. The Lowthers, together with the growing merchant community in the eighteenth century, constituted the minority. Whitehaven was bedevilled by the absence of effective local government, the machinery of the manor court proving quite ineffective for the purpose. As a result, the question of government was constantly being brought to the fore on issues varying from the allocation of housing plots to the nature of harbour extensions, from growing poverty and crime to the chronic failure of the town to feed itself. The most atypical feature of Whitehaven (and this was also true of Maryport in the mid-eighteenth century) was in being planned, rather than growing in the haphazard manner of many new towns.

Whitehaven was a planned town because one family had a prevailing control of the site. The dominance of the Lowthers was by no means a bad thing, since they put considerable energy into developing the town. Whitehaven was often in Sir James' mind. After a great storm struck southern England in November 1703 he wrote from London expressing his concern about possible damage in Whitehaven. Following another gale in southern England in 1735, he told Spedding 'it was well it was a neap tide when I thought of Whitehaven'. He pronounced the town a 'very good wife' to him, and was always concerned about symptoms of decline.[2] Contemporaries and historians recognized the Lowthers' role. William Brownrigg described Sir John Lowther as 'the founder of that town'. Sir Thomas Lowther of Holker told his cousin Sir James, after a visit to the town in 1735, that he hoped to come again 'for the great improvements you have made about Whitehaven ought not to be seen in too much haste, especially as taking the whole together the like cannot be seen anywhere else in England'. Sir James Lowther's successor, Sir William Lowther, had it recorded on his benefactor's tomb that he had 'achieved by his superior counsel that this town . . . has grown into a splendid city'. William Hutchinson, the later eighteenth-century historian of Cumberland, described Whitehaven as the brainchild of Sir John Lowther, whose 'great plan was brought to perfection' by Sir James.[3]

Such comments partly reflect the inflexible control that the Lowthers chose to exercise, which had both good and bad implications for Whitehaven. On the plus side, Sir John Lowther contrived to have the town develop as a planned town, something he was able to do because he possessed the two vital pre-requisites for town planning: absolute ownership of the site and a large amount of capital which he was willing to put at risk.[4] The Lowthers' dominance enabled them to arbitrate in disputes. In 1736, for example, the table of customs fees which had been used since 1698 was found never to have been legally confirmed. It was decided that the merchants and customs officers should produce a new table, and in the case of disagreement 'the final end and determination' was to be by 'Sir James Lowther, John Christian esq and Thomas Benn, gentleman, or any two of them, Sir James being one'. The table was drawn up while Lowther was in Whitehaven, and he took it with him to London that autumn.[5] Against these benefits, however, must be set the disadvantages. In particular, as Sir James grew older he lost control of town developments, allowing some of the original plans to be ignored or abused. He simply could not control the burgeoning town from his London home, and one result was a series of social problems in the 1740s.

Whitehaven in the 1640s was no more than a hamlet. A print of 1642 (see frontispiece) shows a scattering of houses nestling round the harbour in what today is the south-west corner of the town, a small harbour, several ropewalks (running through the fields where Sir John was later to create the new town) and a chapel. In the forefront of the print are packhorses, doubtless depicted to indicate that they were carrying coal to the harbour. Expansion beyond this small area came only in the 1680s. At Sir John Lowther's instigation a scheme was drawn up which made Whitehaven one of the first planned towns in England since the Middle Ages. As a Member of Parliament since 1664, and a regular attender at the House of Commons, it is more than likely that he had sat through the inconclusive debates about rebuilding London in the wake of the great fire of 1666. Furthermore, as a Fellow of the Royal Society, he would have come into contact with such notable figures as Sir Christopher Wren. These influences may well have been important in persuading Lowther that his new town should be planned.[6] Certainly he knew the theory; he wrote in 1698 that

uniformity is best when a town spreads from the centre to the circumference, but if it happens that the outskirts of a town are first built, the centre will follow quickly, only care must be taken that the first buildings do not interfere with what may succeed. But the best way of all is to mark out several streets and to set different rates and let them choose where they will.[7]

In the 1680s, Lowther commissioned Andrew Pellin to draw up a plan. Pellin had originally come to Whitehaven as a serge weaver, but later turned his energies to teaching mathematics. He produced a gridiron scheme which is still visible in the town today. Lowther Street, the central axis, ran west–east from the harbour to Flatt Hall; indeed, it was a symbol of the paternalism with which the new town was built that the Hall was visible along its whole length. This was the widest street, some sixteen yards across, and was reserved for buildings 'above the ordinary'. Running parallel, to the north and south respectively, were Duke Street and Roper Street; four streets ran between them, crossing Lowther Street at right-angles. These streets were all ten yards wide. The land between the streets was divided into numbered building plots, all fifteen feet wide.[8]

The town grew outwards from the harbour, with Lowther Street the most popular for building purposes. Sir James Lowther commented in 1751 that 'the town is got as near my house as I ever thought to let them come in my time'. He resisted the final move, which would have extended Lowther Street past Flatt Hall, but Sir William Lowther agreed in December 1755 that it should be completed through his gardens to join the old road from Corkickle.[9] It thereby became the main entrance to the town from the east. Sir James Lowther took personal responsibility for laying out the new streets. In 1734 he told Spedding 'not to build more [in Tangier Street] yet a while till I come into the country'. Occasional changes were made in the plan, and in the 1740s it had to be extended so that houses could be built at Braconthwaite, the area on the north side of the existing town. Increased trading activity stimulated an exceptional demand for housing during the decade.[10]

As a result of this planning, Whitehaven developed in an orderly fashion. Even Sir James Lowther, not a man noted for emotional outbursts, was moved to describe it as 'one of the prettiest towns in England'. After passing through in 1772, Thomas Pennant reflected that it was 'one of the handsomest [towns] in the north of England'. The very orderliness of Whitehaven was calculated to please the aesthetic tastes of rational eighteenth-century men. As a poet of 1752 expressed it, 'That all is beauty, all is order found'.[11]

Something of the reason for such admiration can be derived from the surviving copies of Matthias Read's 'Bird's-Eye View' paintings of the town, which were drawn between 1732 and 1738 (see frontispiece). Read drew the town from Braconthwaite hill on the north side, roughly the same position as the illustrator of 1642. His prints show only minor variations, and all give a distinct impression of the regular manner in which the streets were laid out. St Nicholas' church stands prominently in the centre of the town, with Holy Trinity less obtrusively located away on the perimeter. Presbyterian and Quaker chapels are shown, along with Flatt Hall, the dominant mansion. The town's trading and industrial activities are not neglected: the crowded harbour, the ropewalks (resited since 1642), the sugarhouse, the copperas works, the glasshouse, and one of the Newcomen engines, are all shown. The wagonways can be seen winding their way into Sir James Lowther's Quay staith. In sharp contrast on Read's paintings is the haphazard building of the original village way in the distance.

Read's picture provides an accurate, if possibly idealized view of the town as he saw it in the 1730s. It continued to grow thereafter, having spread its boundaries considerably wider by the time of the next map in 1794. One of the results of Sir James Lowther's loss of control towards the end of his life was that the idyllic picture of houses, all with their own gardens, neatly laid out and built to specific regulations, was rudely spoilt. Overcrowding brought cellars into use as separate residences, despite the fact that this was contrary to the regulations by which the houses were legally held. Gardens were built over to provide more housing. But if the vision was tarnished, the fundamental street plan remains as a tribute to Sir John Lowther's vision and enterprise in the 1680s.

Designating the streets and numbering the plots did not produce a town. Anyone wishing to build a house, warehouse or shop, had to buy or lease a plot from the Lowthers, and conform to regulations regarding height and construction. Surviving evidence shows that Sir John Lowther made a total of 88 grants, and his son a further 477, although it is possible that these figures are incomplete. Sir John Lowther was anxious to provide accommodation for offcomers attracted to the town. He had 'a great mind to be a builder at Whitehaven, not for any profit, being even content to sustain some loss, but rather to draw people thither'. He wanted to ensure 'that newcomers may never want a place to receive them', and intended in 1698 'as fast as I sell one house always to build a new one'. In addition, he was ready to lend 'any inhabitant of Whitehaven who has a house built or building to engage for security such sums as they shall have occasion for at 5 per cent'. Yet his contribution to town building cannot have been great. Gilpin pointed out in 1698 that Lowther's intervention was not really necessary since plenty of private enterprise was available in the building trade. 'The masons and carpenters', he informed Lowther, 'when out of other work build to sell.' Sir James Lowther took more notice of this caution than his father. Apart from erecting almshouses in 1732 to accommodate retired colliery workers, he refrained from building. He even sold the twelve stone cottages which his father had erected especially for miners.[12]

The grants of land made by the Lowthers were a source of contention in Whitehaven. Sir John Lowther made a number of grants in customaryhold tenure, a practice which was widely resented. A legal case brought by several inhabitants in the later 1670s to test his right to make such grants ended with judgment given in his favour. Ill-feeling could not so easily be removed,[13] and in 1695 Lowther reluctantly agreed to let the people affected buy out the freehold of their properties. However, the asking price of sixty times the rent deterred all but a few from responding. Gilpin told him that the tenants had formed 'a sort of confederacy to beat down the terms of their freeholds'. Nothing much was achieved until the 1720s. Sir James Lowther was always willing to sell customary tenures into freehold – at a price – but he made no great effort to encourage such sales until after his defeat in the 1722 election. The realization that selling into freehold would give many people the vote at future county elections spurred Lowther to adopt a more positive policy, since he assumed that the newly enfranchised would cast their votes in his favour. He believed it would be 'a great credit to the town to have a strong body of freeholders'. Enfranchisement (sales into freehold) 'at an easy rate' was offered to 250 or so tenants in 1725, and all plots were granted in freehold thereafter.[14] The response was less enthusiastic than Lowther had anticipated. Twenty-two people bought out their freeholds in 1726, including John Spedding and several of the town's merchants. Lowther blamed the slow response on the inefficiency of Richard Gilpin, his attorney. He complained in 1730 that had Gilpin only acted a reasonable part 'the whole town would have bought free before this'. By then the immediate need for enfranchisement was over, Lowther having been returned unopposed for Cumberland in 1727. Having begun, he decided that the policy should be maintained, and a number of tenants bought the freehold of their property in every year between 1726 and his death. By 1741 there were 496 freeholds in Whitehaven, and 260 customary tenures. Altogether, the estate ledgers record 290 enfranchisements, which netted Lowther the tidy sum of £4399.[15]

Apart from houses, the new town required what Sir John Lowther referred to on one occasion as 'domestic conveniences'.[16] Whitehaven had been granted the right to hold a market during the Interregnum, and had possessed a chapel and school in the 1630s and 1640s. The Lowthers' contribution in the century after 1660 was to ensure that such facilities expanded in line with the growth of the town. Market, cultural and recreational facilities were necessary adjuncts if the new town was to be in any real sense a community.

Whitehaven's status as a market town was confirmed after the Restoration. Sir James Lowther promoted facilities to supplement the original market, and three are depicted on a map of the town for 1794.[17] Marketplaces provided an arena for the exchange of grain and meat, but, as the town grew, a variety of shops were opened as well. In 1720, a 'haberdasher of hardware' had a store in Whitehaven, and by 1732 a gunsmith had set up in business. Lowther told Spedding in 1738 of a baker willing 'to set up a great bakehouse . . . for bread and biscuit', and of a whitesmith who was also anxious to establish a business in Whitehaven. A watchmaker had a shop by 1745.[18] Finally, the town held an annual fair in the first week of August each year. This right was confirmed in the marketplace patent of 1660, which also authorized the payment of fair tolls to the Lowthers.[19]

Educational facilities were established in Whitehaven early in the seventeenth century. Sir Christopher Lowther bequeathed the interest of £100 'for reading prayers and teaching scholars at Whitehaven'. Sir John Lowther established a new school in the town during the 1690s, a Nonconformist academy was opened in 1708, and a multilateral school in 1748. Plenty of employment also existed for private schoolmasters, particularly those prepared to teach apprenticed seamen studying between voyages. Efforts in 1716 to establish a charity school were unsuccessful.[20]

The Lowthers differed in their attitude to education, with Sir John having a more positive attitude than his son. Sir John helped to restore the sixteenth-century grammar school at St Bees during the 1680s, and in 1693 converted the old chapel in Whitehaven into a school. The building was pulled down a year later, when Sir John donated £100 towards a new school. A plaque was placed above the main door commemorating his munificence. It began as a grammar school, but the curriculum was extended after a couple of years to include navigation and mathematics, thereby providing the practical education which was needed in the town. About forty pupils attended the school, and according to Lowther, writing in 1701, it was 'in very good repute as schools go in this country, most of the neighbouring gentry having their sons fitted either for the university or merchandize in this town'. Generally, Sir James showed less enthusiasm for education. He was concerned in efforts to establish a charity school, but the project failed for lack of finance. Moreover, he was apparently prepared to let his father's school close down in 1724, when Peter Farish retired after twenty-seven years as master. However, when an adequate replacement could not be found Farish resumed his responsibilities in order to secure the school's future. He remained in the post until he died twelve years later, at which time no difficulty was encountered in finding a replacement.[21]

Church worship, both Anglican and Nonconformist, was not neglected in Whitehaven. Three Anglican churches were built within a few hundred yards of each other in the course of only sixty years, and various Nonconformist institutions were established. Whitehaven was in the parish of St Bees, but since the church was inconveniently situated, a small chapel (measuring only 45 feet by 15) was built in the 1630s or early 1640s. By 1678 considerable support existed for building a larger one, but it was another nine years before agreement was reached on financing a replacement, for which Sir John Lowther donated a plot of land on the north side of Lowther Street. Trustees and a works' supervisor were appointed in 1687, but the church, which was dedicated to St Nicholas and could seat 1100 worshippers, was only completed in 1693.[22] Within a few years additional facilities were required, and at a meeting in 1714 £1092 was subscribed towards a second church; including £100 from Sir James Lowther who also supplied a plot of land in Scotch Street. The church, completed within eighteen months at a cost of £1900, was dedicated to the Holy Trinity. In 1738 Lowther gave a burial ground on condition that he was allocated space inside the church for a family vault.[23] Despite an extension to St Nicholas' in 1746, by the early 1750s considerable support was being expressed for a third church. The result was St James' built on the north side of the town at a cost of £3408 in 1752 and 1753. Carlisle Spedding was the architect.[24]

The Lowthers' role in church building is interesting. They were staunch Anglicans; indeed, Sir James wrote in 1751 that 'there is nobody more pleased than I am with the excellency of the church service'. On occasion he offered to finance parochial libraries for Cumberland clergy, and he was instrumental in obtaining Queen Anne's Bounty for St Bees church in 1739.[25] Apart from donating the three plots of land, he and his father made financial contributions towards building the Anglican churches; in return they had considerable interest in the appointment of ministers. At St Nicholas' the pew holders elected two candidates, of whom the Lowthers chose one. Sir James Lowther and the pew holders of Holy Trinity alternated in their right to appoint the minister, while Lowther had the sole right to nominate the minister of St James'. Such responsibility enabled the Lowthers to dispense patronage. When a vacancy occurred at Holy Trinity in 1728 Sir James Lowther was determined to 'have a good deal of regard to the services done me in elections', as a result of which William Brisco was appointed.[26] Carlisle Spedding's son Thomas, whom Lowther helped to finance through college, was appointed first minister of St James'.

Although Anglican by persuasion, the Lowthers were tolerant in their religious outlook. By 1693 Whitehaven had a licensed Presbyterian meeting, and numbers were sufficiently great to have outgrown existing facilities. The idea of using the old Anglican chapel as an additional or replacement meeting-house was strongly canvassed before Sir John Lowther had it demolished to make way for his new school. William Gilpin, himself a Presbyterian, claimed that fifty dissenting families resided in the town in 1694, and that same year sixty people signed a petition requesting Lowther to set aside ground for the building of a new meeting house. Land was allocated in James Street.[27] Sir James Lowther preferred not to be too closely associated with the non-conformists, but he did pass on information to Dr Latham, one of Whitehaven's dissenting ministers, about financial aid available in London. 'Great numbers' of Quakers were in the town when an Annual Meeting of the sect was held there in 1737, but perhaps the most significant influence on religious attitudes was provided by John Wesley. The founder of Methodism first visited Whitehaven in 1749, and he was to return a further twenty-five times before he died. On this first occasion he recorded in his *Journal* that he had been well received, although he believed the interest shown in his preaching to have been of a superficial nature. But the visit revealed the extent of interest in religious matters in Whitehaven, and helped to stimulate demand for a third church. Wesley formed a 'regular society' of Methodists whilst he was in the town, and in 1751 the members asked Lowther for permission to build a chapel. Before the end of the eighteenth century the number of sects had proliferated. In 1772 Pennant noted Presbyterians, Seceders, Anabaptists and Quakers, whilst Hutchinson in 1794 recorded the presence of two Presbyterian meeting houses, a Quaker meeting, a Roman Catholic chapel, a Methodist meeting and an Anabaptist chapel.[28]

Social and cultural life in Whitehaven was enhanced by a number of other facilities. Sir John Lowther was asked in 1703 to set up a cockpit. No reply has survived, but the fact that there was one in Irish Street by 1706 suggests that he agreed. Thereafter cock fighting became a regular amusement, to the disgust of Sir James. By 1706 Whitehaven could boast a bowling green, which was 'much frequented by all the town'.[29] Lowther was pleased to hear in 1736 that John Hayton had taken a plot of land in Howgill Street to build 'an Assembly room for the diversion of the ladies'. Little is known about the playhouse, although Spedding noted in 1737 that 'the players . . . still continue in the town'. The earliest surviving playbill dates from 1756. A new theatre was opened in Roper Street in 1769.[30]

For a few years Whitehaven could boast a weekly newspaper. A Mr Cotton moved to the town in 1736 from Kendal, where he had published the *Kendal Courant*. He intended to keep a stationery shop and publish a newspaper. Spedding lent him £10 to clear off debts, and Lowther promised to send relevant news from London to be included in the paper. The first edition of the *Whitehaven Weekly Courant* appeared on 16 December 1736 as a double sheet, fourteen inches by nine, with a total of twelve columns. A circulation of about 100 copies a week was soon established. Cotton also printed for other people in the town, particularly the shopkeepers, who started to produce catalogues of the goods that they sold. His presence helped to bring about the introduction of printed bills and receipts in the town. He was still printing in 1742, the year before his death, but it is not clear how long the newspaper survived. The fact that from its inception in April 1739 the *Newcastle Journal* had a distribution agent in Whitehaven suggests that the *Courant* may have folded by then.[31]

With the exception of the debate over tenures, the picture of White-haven's development painted so far has suggested orderly but rapid growth. To all intents and purposes this reflected Sir John Lowther's planning, and the willingness of his son to follow the scheme mapped out in the 1680s. In one crucial area, however, Whitehaven failed to develop: the machinery of government remained Lowther-orientated and inadequate for the needs of the growing town. Whitehaven was not incorporated until 1894, and as owners of the manor and demesne of St Bees the Lowthers dictated the terms of government. Their chosen instrument was the court leet, to which all the inhabitants could be summoned. Sir James Lowther ensured that this remained the case by selling off freeholds to 'suit of court'. Against this advantage, the court leet only had the power to remedy nuisances, and not to carry out desirable improvements. Consequently the townspeople found themselves in the subservient position of having to petition the Lowthers for changes, and they had few effective sanctions if no action was forthcoming. Such a situation was not uncommon in new towns (even Manchester was governed by a court leet in the eighteenth century) but it could produce considerable friction.[32]

This inadequate structure of government was directly responsible for a series of acrimonious disputes, which were partly an attack on the Lowther position, and partly the result of differences between Whitehaven's trading interests. Sir John Lowther refused to consider any form of power sharing. His son apparently retreated from this hard line with the passing of the Harbour Act of 1709, but in fact this created additional problems because the extent to which he had really devolved power remained uncertain.

Sir John Lowther certainly came under considerable pressure to allow a measure of representation in town affairs. One reason for the attempt to rebuild Parton harbour in the 1670s was that White-haven people believed Lowther had neglected their own harbour, and that he could only be forced to act if his grip on local affairs was loosened.[33] Perhaps galled by the completeness of his victory, and relieved that he had at last instituted developments at Whitehaven, the local inhabitants made no further moves until an opportunity of obtaining a more acceptable form of government came with the building of St Nicholas' church in the 1690s. A regular means of collecting money was needed to ensure that the new church could be properly maintained. The argument was advanced that separate parish status for Whitehaven would provide both the means of collecting such sums, and also a form of town government. A pamphlet circulated in 1695, and written in the form of a petition to the House of Commons, requested that

> there being no regular provision made for the repairs and support of the said church or for the preservation of the said harbour . . . the said inhabitants, therefore, are now humble petitioners, with the said Sir John Lowther, Baronet, that the said town may be made a distinct parish of itself, and they thereby enabled to finish and support their church and preserve their harbour.[34]

The appearance of Lowther's name is interesting. Both he and his son were in a position to present any petition to Parliament, but the *Commons Journal* has no entry to suggest that one was ever received.

These same issues of harbour and church upkeep remained under debate. When Sir John Lowther returned to Whitehaven in 1698 a nine-man committee was elected to negotiate with him. The strained relations between Lowther and the townspeople are evident from the fact that most of the negotiations, which were in any case inconclusive, took place by correspondence. Lowther was again requested in 1705 to put town government into a more acceptable form. An act of Parliament was suggested 'for their better government and security', to establish an acceptable form of authority to finance church and harbour upkeep.[35]

Sir John Lowther's death in 1706 brought renewed hopes of a change in town government. Rev. Richard Jackson of St Bees claimed in 1708 to have heard that Whitehaven was to be made a separate parish and to have corporation status. In the event it was not until 1835 that parishes were carved out for the Whitehaven churches, and until that time they remained chapels of the parish church of St Bees.[36] But the situation did not remain unaltered for that length of time, because the 1709 Harbour Act changed the terms of reference. One of the chief grievances surrounding upkeep of shipping facilities was now countered, although Sir James Lowther's power of veto was sufficient to eliminate any sense of democracy. In addition to the harbour stipulations, the act had empowered the trustees to appoint a scavenger to remove all dirt, ashes and other annoyances from the town. The court leet did not have the authority to levy rates to pay for town improvements, so that such a clause neatly complemented their authority. In 1711 the trustees levied a scavenger tax of 6d in the pound on all the houses deemed liable to contribute. Nonetheless questions of jurisdiction remained, particularly in regard to the amount of power that the trustees really had in town affairs.

The issue of responsibility remained open until it was tested for the first time in 1717. Since the 1690s one family of Virginia merchants, the Gales, had championed the cause of greater participation in town affairs. Ebenezer Gale was a member of the 1717 jury which decided that it was 'not obliged to intermeddle in the matter of nuisances relating to the streets, being now more properly the business of a scavenger to be appointed, directed and ordered by Mr Lowther and the trustees as the said act [of 1709] requires'. Two years later Ebenezer Gale stood for election to the board of trustees, on which two other members of the family already sat. Lowther unsuccessfully backed Thomas Lutwidge, another merchant, against Gale. Within a fortnight of the election the trustees accepted the responsibility offered to them by the jury in 1717. They passed a motion that 'the marketplace and streets of the town being under the inspection of the trustees and appropriated for public use ought not to be divided, obstructed or impaired upon any pretence whatsoever'.[37]

The breakthrough has to be seen for what it was: a merchant-led challenge to Lowther's autocratic position in town government. By shifting the forum of debate to the partly elected board of trustees the reform group hoped to introduce a measure of democracy into town government. The 1719 successes, however, only provided the arena in which the battle could be fought, as indeed it was during the next three years. Lowther regarded the Gales' move as a cynical attack on his own position. He immediately issued instructions that the next court leet jury should be 'packed', in the hope that it would rescind the 1717 order. This failed. Next, he used his veto to prevent the trustees from acting on town affairs. In 1720, he obtained an order from the King's Bench dismissing two substitute trustees who had been illegally elected, and instructing the board to adhere more closely to the terms of the 1709 legislation. Relationships deteriorated further in the winter 1720–1. After a storm damaged the pier in mid-December, Lowther instructed Spedding to have the necessary repairs carried out without awaiting the deliberations of the trustees.[38]

Faced with this barrage the merchants understandably counter-attacked. They discussed the possibility of obtaining legislation to divest Lowther of the power of veto,[39] and deliberately ignored him in other matters. In 1721, for example, Lowther told Spedding that 'the merchants of the town will apply to everybody to help them but me that am willing to take pains about their business'. He seems to have genuinely feared that they would ruin the already ailing coal trade for the satisfaction of seeing him brought down. He regarded it as sinister that in London, 'Mr Hunt, who is the town's agent about the tobacco trade never owns me'. He also told Spedding to refuse coal to 'such ships as my enemies are chiefly concerned in' (i.e. hold majority shares in), and he pondered how much easier it would have been to dictate affairs if he had retained complete control of the harbour.[40]

To complicate the issue still further, the Gales were Lowther's chief opponents in a separate legal tussle which developed simultaneously with these events. When preparations were taking place in 1687 to build St Nicholas' church, the subscribers and representatives of the town agreed that they would present two candidates from whom Sir John Lowther or his successors were to choose a minister. Contention surrounded the first appointment in the 1690s, and an election was necessary to decide which two names should go forward. Eventually the Rev. Francis Yates was appointed. He died in 1720, and a story circulated in Whitehaven that Lowther would close the collieries if Anthony Wilton was not elected as one of the two candidates. Whether or not the rumour had any foundation, the election in December was a resounding vote against Lowther. Wilton received only fifteen votes, Christopher Bowerbank and Robert Loxham being the successful men. Lowther refused to nominate either, and the church trustees, led by the Gales, instituted Chancery proceedings in an effort to compel him. The case was only resolved in 1725 when a definition of the right to vote in elections was handed down by Chancery.[41]

Lowther's unpopularity goes almost without saying, considering that this was also the time of severe trade depression and the Parton harbour dispute. In the spring of 1722 matters came to a head when he was defeated at the Cumberland election. He recovered his authority remarkably quickly, although since he remained in Whitehaven for most of the summer few letters have survived, and thus it is not possible to analyse events in any detail. However, at the election in August for harbour trustees, all the Gales were unseated, and three days later the board revoked the 1719 decision regarding town government, handing responsibility back to the court leet. By Christmas Spedding was assuring Lowther that the merchants regretted his non-return for Parliament: 'they find they want you in the house'. Finally, the antipathy towards him died away when both the Parton harbour and church disputes were brought to a conclusion in 1725.[42]

The battle may have been won, but the war was far from over; indeed, no peace treaty was likely while town government was so unsatisfactory, as became clear in the 1740s. Whitehaven's streets had become untidy and ill-paved. The 1740 Harbour Act reiterated the power of the trustees to appoint a scavenger, and in the absence of effective court action it was suggested that this be implemented. At a meeting in March 1744 the trustees agreed to make an appointment, and also approved a series of rules about maintaining the streets. A repetition of the earlier dispute seemed inevitable. It was forestalled by John Spedding who persuaded the jury (of which, significantly, he was a member) to pass a series of orders relating to upkeep of the streets.[43] Confrontation between Lowther and the trustees was avoided, but once more the conclusion amounted to little more than a temporary cease-fire.

When matters came to a head at the end of the decade, the coal–tobacco split was again the moving force. Many people, including Peter How, whom Lowther had described as 'a wise and discreet man in everything', had come round to the view that the trustees should be given more effective powers of government. Even Lowther was beginning to concur. He started canvassing ideas in 1748 of supplying the town with fresh water, having the pavements properly laid, and lighting the streets. The last of these proposals involved utilizing a scheme of Carlisle Spedding's to convey the fire-damp from the coal mines into the town. Lowther accepted that if these plans came to fruition it would be advantageous to vest greater powers in the hands of the trustees. He was even ready to promote legislation for the purpose.[44]

The scheme was blocked by the impasse which developed over harbour extensions, a dispute which reminded Lowther of the risks involved in passing power to the trustees. By the time Lutwidge and his co-conspirators were voted off the board in 1752 the situation was very different. The plan to pipe water into the town had proved more difficult to implement than anticipated, and Carlisle Spedding's lighting scheme had also had to be abandoned. Street lights were not introduced until 1781. More to the point, Lowther's attitude had changed. No more was heard of the power-sharing scheme, with unfortunate long-term results. Although later harbour acts empowered the trustees to take action on specific town improvements – in 1761, for example, they were given responsibility for organizing a water supply to serve the town and harbour – the division of authority remained a contentious issue. By the early years of the nineteenth century it was a clear-cut party matter, between the Town (the trustees) and the Castle* (supporters of the Lowthers). Only in 1859 was a comprehensive reorganization of local government undertaken in which the powers of the lord of the manor were curtailed. Not until the charter of Incorporation in 1894 were town and harbour legally separated for administrative purposes.[45]

The significance of these unresolved disputes was considerable. In essence town government remained the personal prerogative of the Lowthers, and, operating as they did from a distance, their control was limited. Sir John Lowther was an autocrat, determined to ensure that all decisions were taken by himself. As his own son freely admitted, he would have been unlikely to have granted even the very limited amount of responsibility conveyed to the trustees in 1709. At the same time Sir John was an active, not to say benevolent ruler, who promoted new churches and schools, and encouraged building. By contrast, Sir James was less effective, and his grip slackened as the town expanded. Partly as a result, Whitehaven was affected by a number of social problems, including poverty, disorder and food supply difficulties.

Although none of these problems was actually new, they certainly became worse in Lowther's later years. William Gilpin was the first to comment upon what he saw as an increase in the number of the poor, when he wrote to Sir John Lowther in 1696 advocating the building of a workhouse. By the time any action was taken things were very much worse. An ominous portent for the future

* Flatt Hall was renamed Whitehaven Castle following extensive renovations by Sir William Chambers in the 1760s.

occurred during the 1720s when the trade depression cut into living standards and forced greater sharing of houses. Sir James Lowther provided almshouses during the 1730s to try to ensure that retired colliery workers would not become a burden on the poor rate, and in the worst years of dearth he gave out money. In 1740, for example, he ordered Spedding to distribute a total of £20 among the workmen. Much of this went to the sailors, judged by Spedding to be the 'hardest pinched'.[46] The problem of the poor was already too great for such *ad hoc* arrangements to be sufficient, and a workhouse was established the following year to cater for Whitehaven and the surrounding villages. Sixty-four Whitehaven people were admitted within a few months of its being opened in 1741, but only another eight came in from the surrounding villages. Of the Whitehaven group, '22 went out to shift for themselves', eleven died, and thirty-one remained in the house, together with two children born to inmates during the year. The building was sold in 1748, and replaced by a new one on the Braconthwaite side of the town. Lowther conveyed a plot of land to ten trustees, and the new building was financed by selling tickets of £25 each. It was still operational in the early nineteenth century.[47]

Disease spread rapidly in the town, partly because adequate medical facilities were lacking until the Whitehaven Dispensary was opened in 1783. Lowther proposed a scheme in 1740, and again in 1752, whereby the local gentlemen would finance the payment of a doctor to attend market days in Cockermouth and Whitehaven, and advise the poor on medical matters. He was prepared to subscribe £20, but the scheme never got off the ground. Eight or ten children were dying weekly during a smallpox epidemic in the summer of 1693. Another outbreak in 1743 caused 'grievous havoc in some poor families where the people are crowded into small rooms and have not proper conveniences'. William Brownrigg, Whitehaven's resident doctor, attended all those in need during the epidemic, and witnessed at first hand the appalling conditions in which some people were living. At one house he found 'one man . . . lying dead, another dying, and a third very ill, all in the same little ground room'. Such were his efforts that he 'fatigued himself unreasonably', and was seriously ill for several days.[48]

Crime and disorder became increasingly serious problems in the town. Spedding commented in 1733 on the rising number of rogues in Whitehaven, and a corresponding increase in crime. In 1740

Lowther's estate office was broken into and £25 stolen. As a result iron bars were put across the window, and Lowther suggested that an armed nightwatchman might be employed, together with a guard dog.[49]

The nature of Whitehaven's population enhanced the likelihood of disorder. Colliers were one of the most important groups of eighteenth-century food rioters. They were prominent during disturbances in Whitehaven in the spring of 1728 when a mob gathered to prevent oatmeal from being sent to Ireland. It was only dispersed on the intervention of troops garrisoned at Carlisle.[50] Seamen were also prone to disorderliness. When men on a tobacco vessel were pressed against their protections in 1742, several shots were fired 'which raised the apprentices of the town who for some hours vapd[?] about with cutlasses etc'. An even more serious fray occurred in 1751 when the masters and seamen quarrelled over pay. The Riot Act was read and Peter How, the acting magistrate, requested assistance from a company of soldiers quartered in the town. Despite their intervention, the mob rescued a number of sailors whom How had earlier committed. Unsure what to do next, How wrote to the secretary-at-war for reinforcements, but the matter subsided before further action became necessary.[51]

The loss of authority in the town was clear by the early 1750s. New houses failed to conform to the regulations and were neglected when completed. Cellars were pressed into service as accommodation for the poor and vagrants. Such facilities proved to be convenient for the sale of cheap liquor. This attracted the ships' apprentices, who were accused of pilfering provisions and stores from their vessels to sell as a means of financing such purchases. The extent of the social difficulties is evident from decisions taken by the court leet. A series of regulations were approved in 1755 for keeping the marketplace clean, but even more positive measures were required three years later. To prevent the nuisance caused by tippling and gaming on pay nights, public houses were ordered to close at 10 pm. To prevent children 'easing themselves in the street . . . all parents, housekeepers, schoolmasters and mistresses who have the care of any children', were to provide 'fitting places and oblige such children to ease themselves within doors'.[52] In an atmosphere such as this, poverty, disease and crime flourished together.

Another problem, and one which was common to seventeenth-century new towns, was the provision of sufficient food. To meet the demands of a steadily growing population, grain had often to be purchased elsewhere and shipped to Whitehaven. This practice began in the 1690s, and it soon became a regular trading feature. The *George and Ann* entered at Whitehaven in February 1707 with 97 quarters of bigg and barley. The *Content* brought potatoes and barley in February and March that year. At least two ships fetched grain from Milford Haven in 1715, and more than 100 bushels of Welsh barley were imported the following year.[53] But what began as an occasional trade became a necessity following a series of poor harvests in the 1720s, which culminated in the food riots of April 1728, Within a few months Lowther was buying grain at Plymouth and making enquiries about the price at Haverfordwest. It was clear to Spedding that this was no short-term crisis. He fitted out a new barn in Whitehaven as a temporary store in 1728, and had proper granaries erected in the early 1730s.[54] Except for very good years, such as 1738 and 1743, grain imports became a regular feature of Whitehaven's coasting trade.

Lowther was prominent in promoting the trade, and for personal reasons he remained a leading figure. But he was not alone. Several Whitehaven merchants joined him in the 1740s, and Welsh masters began to bring cargoes of grain on their own account by the end of the decade. Initially, Lowther employed the *Neptune* on regular runs to the south of England and Wales, but from the mid-1730s he started to employ his own sloops, the *Benjamin* (1735–37) and the *Bee* (1736 onwards) in the trade. The latter was 'kept on foot for carrying salt and bringing corn etc coastways', and normally fetched grain from north Cumberland and Lancashire. Masters of vessels in which Lowther had a controlling interest also purchased grain. In 1737, for example, the *Liffey* returned from Dublin, and the *Cumberland* from Cork, both carrying hay which the masters sold to Spedding.[55]

Several local merchants developed an interest in the trade during the 1740s. In 1741 the *Jane* arrived with barley and malt for William Hicks, and Peter How purchased 1500 bushels of corn in Holland. How and James Spedding began importing grain from Wales in 1744,[56] and table 7.1 shows the origin of vessels arriving in 1745. Eventually the Welsh, increasingly aware of the Whitehaven market, began to send their own vessels with grain. Lowther hoped to encourage them; he told Spedding in 1752, 'I hope our taking of the oats (which the little Welsh ships bring) at such prices as we

Table 7.1. *Grain imports at Whitehaven, 1745.*

Vessel	From	Cargo	For
Lowther	Haverfordwest	Wheat/barley	Thomas Patrickson
Pretty Jenny	Carmarthen	Oats	James Spedding
?	?	Oats (800 quarters)	Peter How
Bessborough	Haverfordwest	Oats (900 bushels) Barley (200 bushels) Wheat (200 bushels)	James Spedding
Elizabeth	Carmarthen	Oats (1661 bushels)	Peter How
Bee	Dumfries	Corn	Sir James Lowther

Source: Carlisle Record Office, D/Lons/W John Spedding to Sir James Lowther, 15 February, 24 March, 3 May 1745; Household Accounts, 1742–6.

can afford to give, will encourage them to bring more.'[57] Surviving figures are insufficiently detailed to give an accurate picture of total annual imports, but a rough calculation based upon the number of vessels, occasional import figures and valuations, suggests that at least 3000 bushels of oats were being imported annually during the 1740s and 1750s. Wheat, barley, hay and beans, all figure from time to time among the imports.

The precise clientele served by the different people importing grain is not entirely clear. Lowther's motives were certainly not wholly disinterested. All the grain that he purchased was stored until the local price rose above a certain level. It was then sold, usually at 4s 6d a bushel, but not to all and sundry. Favoured customers included the Speddings' brewery company, but in general Lowther's main aim was to supply the men who kept horses to use in his employment, either to work gins at the pits, or to pull carts to the harbour. Without such a supply, prices would rise and the men would demand higher wages. In turn this would affect Lowther's profit margins, and he might not easily reduce their payments when conditions improved. During the summer of 1741 Spedding was supplying oats 'to the workmen who keep gin horses and to the leaders'. Three years later he told Lowther 'the badness of the harvest has raised oats from 3s 6d to 6s 6d a bushel, and the country people would raise it much more if I did not supply your workmen at 4s 6d a bushel from your granary'. How far Lowther accommodated other townspeople is more difficult to ascertain. The accounts suggest only that his own employees bene-fited, and yet imports went on rising after the introduction of wagonways in 1732, when fewer horses were required. The merchants may have supplied a different public from Lowther, but in any case, the fact that he was undercutting the market price for a section of Whitehaven's inhabitants ensured that the general level of prices in the town remained reasonable. He made little or no direct profit from the venture, but the value of maintaining a cheap supply was doubtless a sufficient reward since it made an indirect contribution to profits. Certainly his successors thought this, and the same method of supplying the town was still being used in 1772, although by then the selling price had risen to 5s a bushel.[58]

A final problem associated with the town's expansion was the need to defend it from attack, both from the sea, and, in the case of the 1715 and 1745 Jacobite uprisings, from the land. The earliest mention of seaward fortification dates from 1639 when Sir Christopher Lowther bought 'two pieces of ordnance'.[59] A platform was erected during the 1690s, and guns were almost certainly acquired in 1702 when James Lowther used his position at the Ordnance office to promote a petition from Whitehaven requesting cannon. It seems likely that the fortifications were allowed to fall into disrepair and that the platform itself was removed during the 1730s, possibly to make way for Lowther's new coal staith. The guns were fired in 1734 as a salute to Lowther, but they were scrapped soon after, since the town had no fortifications when the Spanish war broke out in 1739. Petitions requesting cannon were presented to the clerks of the council by Lowther, and the harbour trustees agreed in 1741 to build a new platform. Guns were dispatched from London in March that year. The trustees decided that the fortifications were still insufficient, and on their behalf Lowther bought seven additional four-pounders, with ammunition, in London. Since 1739 he had been arguing the need for soldiers to be quartered in the town, but his words were only heeded when France declared war on England in March 1744. Many French vessels had collected tobacco from Whitehaven over the two previous years and fears were expressed that their masters would have noted the undefended state of the town. 'The town in general', wrote Spedding, 'are extremely alarmed at the danger they are in of having their shipping and houses destroyed by the French privateers.' Troops arrived in Whitehaven the following month and issued instructions about defence in the event of an attack.[60]

When a threat of force was posed the following year, it came not from the sea but the land, and at a time when no soldiers were quartered in the town. Whitehaven was not seriously affected by the 1715 Jacobite uprising, but the situation was different in 1745. When news of Sir John Cope's defeat at Prestonpans reached the town late in September 1745 emergency measures were taken. According to the collector of customs, 'the inhabitants met and formed themselves into ten companies of fifty men each for the preservation of the town by quelling any disturbance therein and preventing any small part of the rebels approaching it'. The battery was dismantled and the cannon 'shipped off', to prevent them being captured by the rebels, but at the request of the Duke of Cumberland the ten eighteen-pounders were recalled in December and transported to Carlisle. The ships' masters sent powder to fire the guns. After the county town was relieved it retained the guns and Whitehaven was supplied with new ones.[61] Various additions to the fortifications were made in the later years of the century, partly in conjunction with the John Paul Jones episode of the 1770s. By the early nineteenth century the town had four batteries with ninety-eight cannon.[62]

Whitehaven's orderly growth was a considerable tribute to Sir John Lowther's foresight and planning. Town development kept pace with the expansion of its industrial and trading interests in impressive harmony; indeed, for a town to expand so rapidly along the planned lines, and to allow for social and cultural facilities, was remarkable. The major blot on the picture was the inadequacy of town government, and the social problems for which this was partly responsible. Good reason could be found for devolving responsibility; after all, several of the wealthy merchants were active justices. Lowther refused them an effective role in government, and although some objected, Peter How, perhaps the most crucial man, was apparently happy to toe the line. As a result Lowther retained his dominant position. Nonetheless, it would be less than just to detract from the overall achievement of Sir John and Sir James Lowther in Whitehaven. The transition from village to sizeable town was accomplished with minimum dislocation, allowing plenty of scope for private enterprise. Few people can have queried Hutchinson's description of Sir John Lowther as the brains behind the town, nor the rider which attributed to Sir James the commendation for bringing his father's plans to fruition.

Conclusion

Sir James Lowther died suddenly on 2 January 1755 at the age of 81. The wealthiest commoner of his generation, a giant of the stock market, and the longest-serving Member of Parliament, he was undoubtedly one of the most successful of eighteenth-century entrepreneurs. The west Cumberland he left behind was very different from that of a century, or even a half-century earlier. Whitehaven and Workington, fishing villages in 1660, had grown into important commercial towns, while Maryport, planned along similar lines to Whitehaven, was rapidly emerging as a third centre. Local population had increased substantially; harbours had been improved and extended; even the road network had seen the first evidence of change and alteration. All this was in response to the staple coal trade, which had been growing since the early seventeenth century in line with expanding demand from Ireland. In the wake of this success, although independently developed, the tobacco trade had become an important second interest at Whitehaven. Links had also been established with the West Indies and the Baltic. Partly on the strength of merchant capital new industries at last began to emerge in the 1730s and 1740s. By any standards the developments of the later seventeenth and early eighteenth centuries were impressive; as a port Whitehaven took its place alongside Hull, Bristol and Liverpool among the outports; as an industrial centre it bore comparison – if on a smaller scale – with Newcastle.

All of this augured well for the future, yet today west Cumberland is an industrial backwater. Its harbours have silted up, unemployment is at a high level, and in the absence of alternative opportunities even the industrial outcasts of nuclear research and development have been gladly welcomed. The reasons for this decline lay beyond 1750, and as such outside the scope of this book. Yet arguably west Cumberland was not dissimilarly placed to Tyneside and the west of Scotland when Lowther died. Is it possible, therefore, to isolate factors from the early eighteenth century which retarded, and finally undermined the growth? Why did west Cumberland become, like Derbyshire and Shropshire to name but two, an early starter on the road to industrialization which failed to stay the distance?

In the immediate aftermath of Lowther's death all seemed well for the coal trade. Demand from Ireland continued to grow, with beneficial results not only for Whitehaven, but also for Workington, Maryport, and – from the 1760s – Harrington. Indeed, although Whitehaven's exports grew in absolute terms, the other three ports increased their share of the market; in the 1790s Whitehaven's proportion of the trade was only about 42 per cent. This shift reflected the growing importance of the Curwen and Christian interests at the other three ports, an importance which was firmly cemented by the marital union of the two families in 1782. Despite the growing competition from Scotland, south Wales and Lancashire, west Cumberland's coal trade flourished. Output continued to grow in the nineteenth century, reaching a peak in the third quarter.

Coal mining alone, however, provided only the fuel requirement for an industrial revolution; an extractive industry did not constitute a revolution in itself. The crucial factor restricting the west Cumberland economy was the failure to build upon the base provided by the coal trade. Various reasons for this have been suggested during the course of this book, and the threads can usefully be drawn together by way of conclusion. Three points were particularly crucial: a shortfall in population, the failure of the region to establish for itself a specific role over and above coal mining (a failure partly due to the relative decline of the tobacco trade), and the somewhat contradictory role of Sir James Lowther.

Population simply did not grow fast enough to produce the sizeable consumer goods industries with which the national market could be invaded. West Cumberland did not have a natural drawing area, and in an age when the Lakeland hills were regarded with distaste rather than appreciated as a holiday-making beauty spot, it offered little attraction for skilled workers trained in the Midlands and elsewhere. The frequent labour shortages reflected the vicious circle of population growth: entrepreneurs were unwilling to set up a new business because they could not be certain of a workforce;

migrants were not attracted to the area unless they could be sure of finding employment. While the population grew only slowly it was inevitably a retarding factor in the local economy, and the extent to which the lure of employment was the crucial determinant of migration is evident from the pattern of population growth in Whitehaven. In the 1720s people left the town because no alternative employment was available when the coal trade was in recession. Two decades later the expansion of the tobacco trade, and the development of new industrial concerns as a result of merchant capital being channelled into supplementary interests, produced considerable migration into west Cumberland. So much is clear from the demand for housing in Whitehaven – which led to the laying out of streets on the Braconthwaite side of the town – and the setting up of Maryport. Had Lowther offered to invest with Midland ironmasters in the 1730s, the effect on migration could have been considerable when coupled with the prosperity of the 1740s.

A second reason for the slowing down of expansion in west Cumberland was the absence of a specific role for the port of Whitehaven. Eighteenth-century outports usually developed as service centres, or to perform a specific function. Hull, Liverpool and Bristol, all depended for their prosperity on serving their respective hinterlands. By contrast, the Tyne and Wear ports were developed in order to export locally mined coal. Whitehaven fitted both categories without sitting comfortably in either. The nature of its role as an entrepôt was dictated by the absence of any hinterland which it could usefully serve in the same way as a port such as Hull. At the same time west Cumberland's coal trade was of a different order of magnitude to that of Newcastle; exports amounted to something like 15 per cent of the total passing through the Tyne and Wear ports in 1750. Inevitably the secondary and tertiary effects of the west Cumberland–Dublin relationship would have been correspondingly less than those resulting from the Tyneside–London link.

The similarities with Tyneside, however, were considerable. Newcastle experienced a similar loss of momentum in the second half of the eighteenth century, which reflected a failure to broaden its coal-consuming interests. With Tyneside this did not prove to be crucially debilitating; its saving grace was the railway, and the massive iron and steel works, shipbuilding and engineering industries which grew in the nineteenth century. West Cumberland did not recover. Although iron ore was raised in considerable quantities from the later eighteenth century, most of it was exported to the Clyde for smelting. Lack of good coking coal was given as a major reason for exporting, but it is possible that shortage of enterprise was the really crucial factor. After all, when the iron industry became important in the second half of the nineteenth century coke was brought from south Durham. As a result, pig iron production rose from 48,000 tons in 1855 to 871,000 in 1871 on the northwest coast (Lancashire–Cumberland), making it the fourth largest producing area.[1]

Of the other regions subsequently concerned with the iron industry, west Cumberland perhaps had most in common during the eighteenth century with west Scotland. A suggestion has recently been made that tobacco capital was vital in the early stages of industrialization in that region. Local merchants played a crucial role in promoting ironworks, sugarboiling and glassmaking, although by the time structural change in the economy took place in the later eighteenth century the industrial sector was able to generate its own capital. Consequently tobacco capital was directed towards landownership and trading interests rather than industry.[2] Arguably west Cumberland's merchants played a similar role in Whitehaven's early stages of development. They were to be found investing in ironworks, sugarboiling, glass manufacture, ropemaking, shipbuilding and a host of other activities, particularly as their wealth accumulated from the tobacco trade. They even channelled finance into transport improvements. However, the tobacco trade declined before the new industries reached the stage of being financially self-sufficient. Ironically, Whitehaven lost out to the very Glaswegian merchants who were about to help put the west of Scotland on an economic upswing which would make the region a leading area in the industrial revolution.

The crucial point here was the French decision to transfer their business to Glasgow, depriving Whitehaven of a major outlet. Clearly the Scots were offering better terms, but why was this the case? Two advantages helped to give them the edge over Whitehaven. First, Scottish business laws allowed the Glasgow merchants to form larger partnerships, which gave them greater access to capital resources and an enlarged credit capacity.[3] The Whitehaven merchants matched the Scots in organizing a store system, but they were never able to trade at the same level. Secondly, the

Whitehaven merchants may well have lost out in the complicated business of defrauding the customs. All tobacco ports had fraudulent practices, usually the underweighing of hogsheads. Anything between 15 and 20 per cent of Liverpool's imports did not pay duty.[4] Whitehaven, as has been shown (chapter 4), was no exception; a long investigation during the 1740s revealed considerable irregularities, and four searchers and tidewaiters were dismissed as a result. Such drastic action is a clear indication that the fraud had been sufficiently serious for the government not to be able to turn a blind eye any longer.[5] Even so, legislation in 1747 appears to have worked against Whitehaven. Tobacco was to be lodged in warehouses whilst awaiting re-export, to prevent tampering with the hogsheads. Lowther believed that this would damage the White-haven trade because the merchants would 'no longer be favoured in the weight of what will be landed for exportation again as the hogshead inwards and outwards will be the same'.[6] The Scots, according to their Whitehaven rivals, continued to find means of defrauding the customs. When a bill was introduced into the House of Commons in 1751 'for the more effectual securing the duties upon tobacco', the Whitehaven merchants petitioned Parliament requesting either a reduction in the duties, or 'an inspection by the present inland officers' of the Glasgow trade.[7] If the Scots really were doing better from the customs frauds than the Whitehaven merchants, then this may well have given them a significant price advantage.

The final reason for the retardation in west Cumberland was the position of the Lowthers, Sir James in particular. As entrepreneurs their credentials can hardly be faulted. Both Sir John Lowther and his son sought, and more or less established, a dominance in the coal trade which was tantamount to a monopoly. If Sir James' parsimony prevented him from turning what amounted to effective control of the supply into a monopoly, no one would have attempted to deny his prominence in the coal trade. Both father and son fulfilled all the necessary entrepreneurial functions as instigators and organizers, financiers, risk bearers and market exploiters. They played a vital role in town development, and had a stake at one level or another in most of west Cumberland's business interests. But they were not entirely similar. Sir John Lowther was a polymath interested in any industrial or commercial enterprise which seemed likely to bring a profit. By contrast, as has become clear in this book, apart from the coal trade, and from the 1730s salt panning, his son was only ready to offer encouragement to others. To be fair, however, he brought to bear all the parliamentary influence that he could muster on behalf of merchant interests and transport improvements, and he took full advantage of his residence in London to promote new enterprise. Perhaps the ultimate justification for the policy he pursued was in his annual income. From land, collieries and investments this amounted by 1754 to somewhere in the region of £25,000, while his assets probably exceeded £½m (appendix 2). Although partially excluded from the improvements at Workington and Maryport in the 1740s and 1750s, there can be little doubt that, as Walter Lutwidge expressed it, Lowther was the region's 'centre of motion'.

Yet his position was, to say the least, not entirely consistent. If it was vital that he should have a monopoly of the coal trade because no one else could be relied upon, how then could he expect those same people to run other industries? The profits he made were Irish money, but having attracted capital into west Cumberland he preferred simply to encourage others rather than invest in new concerns. In one sense he can hardly be blamed; why, after all, should he be expected to undertake all of west Cumberland's enterprise? He was entitled to use his money as he wished, and having put a considerable proportion of it into the coal industry and the development of Whitehaven, why should he be obliged to do more? Furthermore, psychologically his concern for the future was limited. He was a bachelor, with no obvious heir to whom he could bequeath his estates.* Thus he had no reason to glorify the

---

* The succession changed periodically. In 1726, Lowther implied that he intended to leave the estates to his distant cousins, Lord Lonsdale and his brother Anthony. (C[arlisle] R[ecord] O[ffice] D/Lons/W Lowther to Spedding, 15 Jan 1726.) By the 1740s it is evident that Sir Thomas Lowther of Holker expected to succeed. (See J. V. Beckett, 'The Lowthers at Holker: Marriage, Inheritance and Debt in the Fortunes of an Eighteenth-Century Landowning Family', *Trans Historic Society of Lancashire and Cheshire*, cxxvii (1978), pp. 60–2.) After his death in 1745 the inheritance was transferred to John Stevenson. (CRO D/Sen Corresp. box 2, Sir William Fleming to Humphrey Senhouse, 16 Jan 1755.) A copy of the not wholly flattering pen portrait of Lowther written by Stevenson in 1742 (see chapter 1) was sent to Lowther in 1750 (CRO D/Lons/L Misc. Letters 1550–1872, Alice Stevenson to Sir James Lowther, 17 Apr 1750), apparently with the intention of souring his opinion of Stevenson. If this was the case it may well have succeeded, since Stevenson was cut out of the will. Eventually Sir William Lowther of Holker was the beneficiary, although outlying properties (including the Westmorland and Middlesex estates) and the reversion were left to Sir James Lowther of Lowther. The death of Sir William Lowther in 1756 brought the estates to Sir James, who was raised to an earldom in 1783.

family, which may explain the lack of conspicuous consumption, such as the building of a larger house and formal garden. Rather than promote risky new ventures in west Cumberland he preferred to rest on his laurels, and enjoy using his wealth in non-productive ways. Part was employed in an abortive effort to establish an electoral interest in the borough of Cockermouth, an attempt he more or less abandoned in the later 1740s for want of a suitable candidate to champion.* The rest was used to promote dealings on the London money market, at which he was particularly adept (appendix 2). His attitude of self-satisfaction was expressed in a comment of 1742; he declined any active involvement in promoting the iron industry because he would 'not take a new load upon me at my years'.[8] Admittedly he was nearly 70 at the time, but he was still active and in good health. Had he had a son to whom the estate would pass, his attitude might have been very different.

It would be foolish to start criticizing Lowther. Other land-owning-entrepreneurs, both in Cumberland and elsewhere, limited their interests in a similar fashion, and in any case his far wealthier successor, Sir James Lowther of Lowther, would be even more culpable. Lowther, and his father before him, deserved considerable credit simply for their successful exploitation of the coal industry, quite apart from their activities in town building and planning. Yet, as one who recognized the necessity of setting the regional economy on a secure basis, Lowther's policy of removing a considerable proportion of his income from west Cumberland to invest in London may have been positively detrimental to the stability of the local economy. He himself recognized that the local gentry were relatively poor, and credit was far from easy to obtain. In 1736, for example, he noted that 'ours is a sad country [sic] for mortgages'. It is arguable that the impoverishment of many of the minor gentry in this period can be attributed to their inability to obtain short-term loans to tide themselves over periods of economic difficulty. It was good tactics to lend locally, and Spedding advised him that money lent out at 4 per cent interest prior to an election was usefully employed. By the later 1730s, with only Lowther and Edward Stephenson – a former East India Company nabob who had bought himself an estate near Keswick – lending money,

* Although of interest in itself, Lowther's pursuit of an interest at Cockermouth is not strictly relevant to this book. See J. V. Beckett, 'The Making of a Pocket Borough: Cockermouth 1727–1756', *Journal of British Studies*, forthcoming.

Lowther was inundated with requests. This he resented, having explained to Spedding in 1724 that everyone expected him to have a considerable amount of money waiting for them to borrow at low interest rates.[9] Quite clearly, until the merchants prospered in the 1730s and 1740s, the capacity for investment in new enterprise was limited. Under the circumstances new industries depended on people in his position putting up money as an inducement for outsiders. Whilst he recognized the importance of attracting capital and entrepreneurs from elsewhere, Lowther's refusal to back naileries in the 1730s deterred would-be manufacturers who might have considered his claims for the region more seriously otherwise.

On reflection, the 1740s were the heyday for Whitehaven. Lured by the expansion of the tobacco trade, and new opportunities in industry, migrants flocked to the west coast and a bright future. Lowther's coal sales went ever upward. It was even considered worthwhile setting up the new town of Maryport. In the end, however, the efforts proved to be wasted. Merchant capital ceased to be available; Lowther decided that age ruled him out of new enterprise; and the loss of the French trade undermined the tobacco interest. For a few years Whitehaven hung on, but the failure of Peter How in 1763 sounded the death knell of an era. By 1792 a local man, Jonathan Boucher, could describe the Whitehaven area in the following pessimistic terms:

I am persuaded, a county cannot be named, more abounding in natural advantages, than Cumberland; nor more deficient in all these advantages, which are the result of human ingenuity and human industry. I cannot at present recollect a single public work of any kind among us, set on foot by voluntary contributions. . . . No, not even a great Trading company, in any large and liberal scale, to promote either Fisheries or Manufactures. From the yet unparallelled cheapness of living among us, our County should seem to be peculiarly well adapted to manufactures; but where are they? We have never yet explored to a sufficient extent or accuracy, the bowels of the earth, which are known to abound with one production of more real value, perhaps, than all the mines of Potosi; and which also, there is good reason to believe, contain various ores well worth the searching for. We seem entirely to have lost the making of salt; which once made something like a show of enterprise and business along our coasts; nor have we any longer any considerable glass houses, or iron works; though from the plenty of fuel, our county might be thought particularly favourable to all those works which require large fires.[10]

In the final resort the region was too small, the new trades too ephemeral. By the time west Cumberland recovered in the second half of the nineteenth century, it was too late to catch up the lost ground; once the iron and coal became uneconomic to mine, the region became the depressed area of today.

The Lowther Family

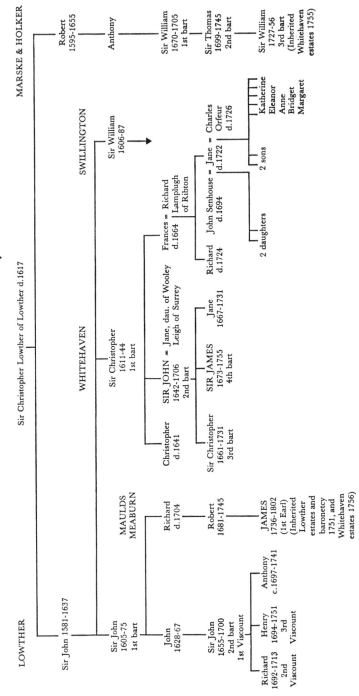

Sir James Lowther's Investments

Sir James Lowther was one of the most important financiers of his day. According to the figures given by P. G. M. Dickson,[1] Lowther's holdings of stock in the 1740s were the largest of all among the 7 per cent of proprietors who lived outside London and the home counties (although, strictly speaking, he should perhaps not qualify for this category since he was born in the capital and spent much of his life there). What is probably an apocryphal story has it that the Earl of Sunderland, First Lord of the Treasury 1718–21, intended to offer Lowther a Treasury post because of his reputation in financial affairs. He apparently changed his mind on finding Lowther to be 'a mean fellow'.[2]

Not a great deal is known of Lowther's activities as a financier beyond his role in the South Sea Company during the 1730s. He was amongst those who believed that the Company should not actually engage in trade, and a proponent of a scheme debated in the early 1730s to have part of the stock turned into annuities. The extent to which Lowther was the instigator, or simply followed where others led, is hard to determine with accuracy. He is known, however, to have been involved with the scheme both in Parliament and at meetings of the Company's general court.

The conversion scheme originated at a meeting 'at the Ship Tavern by Temple Bar' on 22 March 1732. Lowther was amongst those who 'agreed to oppose the directors' scheme for paying a million of Bonds and annihilating $6\frac{1}{4}$ per cent of the stock'. The directors got wind of the plot, and tried to turn it to their own advantage. However, the point was carried at a meeting of the general court, after which Lowther 'proposed . . . my scheme for turning four-fifths of the stock into annuities and putting all the trade and debts on the other fifth part, which is the greatest security against future frauds . . . the scheme is generally liked and I hope will be taken'. He spoke in favour of the scheme during a debate in the House of Commons on 6 April. At a general court two weeks later a motion was carried to petition Parliament for legislation to implement the scheme. With only one material amendment from the original proposal – the proportions of stock to be converted into annuities and left as trading stock were changed from four-fifths/one-fifth to three-quarters/one-quarter – the scheme was presented in a petition to Parliament. It made little progress during the session and was dropped until the following year.[3]

Lowther was unsuccessfully nominated for a sub-governorship of the Company in the election of January 1733, but the following month he was elected to a directorship. He took this to be a great endorsement of his scheme. He soon found that 'both Sir Robert [Walpole] and most of the new directors are at the bottom against my scheme for annuities but I hope we shall force it through by means of my being in the direction'. Over the weeks that followed Lowther regularly attended directors' meetings, and it was he who presented to the House of Commons a petition for a bill on 26 April, and the bill itself on 8 May. On the 11th he reported to the court of directors that the bill had received a second reading, and when it passed the House on the 28th he carried it to the House of Lords. It was approved in the upper house on 9 June, after which Lowther claimed to 'have got great commendation and thanks in all places, the whole town ascribing the success to my great pains and conduct of it through many difficulties'. Two days later he stood down as a director.[4] He led – by his own estimation – a move during 1734 and 1735 to have the final quarter of the Company's stock turned into annuities, a scheme approved by the general court but never carried into effect.[5]

Lowther's investments can be estimated with some accuracy. According to an executors' account, at his death in 1755 Lowther had £150,000 in Bank stock and annuities, East India stock and bonds, £140,000 in South Sea stock and annuities, and £130,000 lent on mortgages and bonds.[6] These figures have clearly been rounded, but they provide a starting point for an assessment of his wealth.

1. Bank stock and annuities, East India stock and bonds

Lowther owned Bank stock from 1708, and at his death the nominal amount held was £19,400. He also opened a Bank of England private drawing account in 1736. When he died, he had £8344 17s in this account. From 1726 Lowther invested in a variety of government annuities. Most of these were converted* in the early 1750s, and his holdings must be viewed against this background (table A2.1).

Table A2.1. *Lowther's annuity holdings, 1755.*

3%s 1726 (unsubscribed in 1752)		2,500
Reduced Threes – 1st subscription (Feb 1750) 1746 4%s		2,000
(Purchased further £3,100 in 1753)		3,100
– 2nd subscription (May 1750) 1748 4%s		4,000
1746 4%s		6,000
Consols – subscribed, November 1752	1731 3%s	3,650
	1742 3%s	5,000
	1743 3%s	7,000
	1744 3%s	12,200
	1745 3%s	3,000
Total Holding		£48,450

Sources: Carlisle Record Office, D/Lons/W Cash Transactions Book 1703–54, fos. 14, 105, 107, 108, 115–17, 126. Bank of England Record Office, Bank Stock Ledger no. 41 (1753–61) f. 935, Private Drawing Office Ledger 119 (1735–7) f. 3575, Ledger 196 (1754–6) f. 3221, 3% Annuities 1726 Ledger B (1733–44) f. 607, Reduced Threes Ledger E 1st subscription (1752–9) f. 3416, Reduced Threes 2nd subscription (1752–8) Ledger B f. 854, 4% Annuities 1748 2nd subscription Ledger f. 294, Consols Ledger no. 1, f. 2809.

Lowther's holdings in the East India Company were not as substantial. He purchased £1000 capital stock in 1719, which he retained throughout his life. In addition, he had £500 of Company bonds by 1750. As part of its agreement with the government to accept the reduction of interest brought about by Pelham's conversion scheme, the Company was allowed to raise funds to pay off some of its debts. This was done by exchanging its existing bonds

---

* Henry Pelham's conversion scheme was implemented by an act of Parliament passed at the end of 1749. His aim was to reduce the interest paid on government debts to the Bank of England, East India and South Sea Companies from 4% to 3%. Under the scheme, the government consolidated all 4% stocks of 1746 and after as 'Reduced Threes' (3½% stock converting to 3% in 5 or 7 years), while consolidating the 3% annuities issued earlier in the 1740s, in 1752, as 'consolidated 3% annuities' (known as 'Consols'). Only the 3% annuity of 1726 was excluded. The scheme, and how it operated, is described in P. G. M. Dickson, *The Financial Revolution in England 1688–1756* (1967), chapter 10.

for annuities and new bonds. Half of the value of the bonds surrendered was to go into 4 per cent annuities from Michaelmas 1750, reducing to 3½ per cent in December 1755, a quarter into 3 per cents from Michaelmas 1750, and the final quarter into new 3 per cent bonds. Thus Lowther would have been credited with £250 3½ per cents (to which he added a further £18,000 by three purchases in July 1751), £125 3 per cent annuities, and £125 3 per cent bonds. His Hoare's bank account reveals that interest was paid on £18,250 3½ per cents and £125 new bonds, but no mention is made of the 3 per cent annuities, although these were retained until 1755 according to the India Office records. The probability, therefore, is that at his death Lowther had the holdings shown in table A2.2.

Table A2.2. *Lowther's East India Company holdings, 1755.*

Capital Stock	1,000
3½% East India Annuities	18,250
3% East India Annuities	125
3% East India Bonds	125
Total	£19,500

Sources: Hoare's Bank, Ledger S f. 30, Ledger X f. 314. India Office, L/AG/14/5/4–12, 253, 257, 329. Carlisle Record Office, D/Lons/W Cash Transactions Books 1703–54, fos. 52, 122.

Taken together, Lowther's holding totalled £95,694 17s which, though a substantial sum, was something less than the executors' figure. The missing value cannot be made up from Lowther's other holdings in 1755. Two of these dated from the 1690s: a survivorship on the life of Sir John Lowther's servant Lancelot Lowther, which was taken out in 1693, and a 14 per cent annuity on Sir James' life taken out by his father. There was also a £2000 Salt Order dating from 1744, paying 3½ per cent interest, and a £45 annuity from 1745, which Lowther had taken out on the life of Sir James Lowther of Lowther.[7] Part of the problem may be that the executors' figure represented what they considered to be the market value of Lowther's securities, rather than the nominal amount, but there is no way of telling this. The discrepancy must, unfortunately, remain unexplained.

One interesting point about Lowther's investment was his involvement with the Charitable Corporation. This was established in 1707 with the intention that it should lend small sums of money to the poor at 10 per cent interest. By the early 1730s the Corporation had a capital of £300,000. Such a scheme was almost guaranteed to appeal to a man with Lowther's ideas about charity and helping the poor, and he first became involved in November 1730. He purchased £2000 of notes that month, and a further £1000 in December. Possibly he favoured the decision attributed to Denis Bond, one of the Corporation's directors and previously one of Lowther's debtors, to use its money in the city. Be that as it may, the scheme collapsed in 1732, when the Corporation was exposed as having operated for the financial benefit of its projectors. William Wood's supporters took 'a great deal of pains to put about the town that I was a director of the Charitable Corporation and also a vast loser in the stock and bonds'. Lowther did not record how much he lost. The possibility of a new subscription was debated in the House of Commons in 1732. Lowther spoke in the debate, and his interest in the Corporation continued thereafter.[8]

2. South Sea stock and annuities

Lowther was an original subscriber to the South Sea Company, investing £3562 in 1711, and, in spite of the Bubble, he continued to invest in the company for the rest of his life. It was his opinion as early as February 1720 that the conversion scheme, which led directly to the Bubble several months later, was ill-conceived: 'great estates will be made, and numbers of families undone when it falls again'.*[9] Consequently he generally held back from the scramble for stock during the ensuing months. He sold £2000 of his own stock for £5359, leaving £3170 in addition to taking a profit of £3359. Like so many investors, Lowther unwisely accepted the Company's terms for converting government debts into South Sea stock, and he probably lost on the transaction. Although his accounts are not clear on this point he was not tempted to sell. Once the Company had stabilized its affairs in 1723, Lowther again became

---

* The Bubble came about because of an ambitious scheme to convert £31·5m from long and short term annuities (expiring 1792–1807 and 1742 respectively, and known as 'irredeemables') together with ordinary government stock ('redeemables') into South Sea stock. However, the scheme was riddled with hypocrisy and double dealing. Dickson has described those who accepted the terms of conversion offered by the company in May and August 1720 as having shown 'blind enthusiasm reminiscent of the Gadarene swine'. *The Financial Revolution*, pp. 133–4. The scheme, how it was conceived, and why it failed, is discussed by Dickson in chapters 4–8.

a regular investor, and his holdings are set out in table A2.3. The total holding was probably rounded up by the executors to £140,000. These bare statistics hardly do justice to his activity in buying and selling stock. The entries in his own record of transactions run to eighteen closely written pages (12 × 8 inches).

Table. A2.3. *Lowther's South Sea Company holdings, 1755.*

Capital Stock
Midsummer 1723 Holding = £29,400. Half of this was then converted to
Redeemable Annuity stock (see below) leaving £14,700.
Midsummer 1733 Holding = £34,201. Stock division ¾ (£25,651) = New
Annuities; ¼ (£8,550) = Capital stock
1755 Holding   5,199

South Sea Old Annuities (Redeemable Annuity stock)
Midsummer 1723 Holding = £14,700 (see above)
1752 Subscribed at the 2nd subscription a total holding of £35,760
1754 Further purchases since 1752 = £9,200
1755 Holding   44,960

New Annuities
Midsummer 1733 Holding = £25,651 (see above)
1752 Subscribed at the 2nd subscription a total holding of £41,889
1754 Further purchases since 1752 = £9,300
1755 Holding   51,189

Further Subscriptions
1750-3 Old South Sea Annuities subscribed at the 1st subscription   17,300
1751-3 New South Sea Annuities subscribed at the 1st subscription   19,100

Total   £137,748

Sources: British Library, Harleian MSS 7497 f. 4. Carlisle Record Office, D/Lons/W Cash Transactions Book 1703-54, fos. 6, 11-13, 29, 30, 61, 65, 91, 117, 123, 125. Bank of England Record Office, Ledger 58 South Sea Old Annuities 1st subscription (1753-8) f. 139, Ledger 135 New South Sea Annuities 1st subscription (1752-8) f. 142, Ledger 58 South Sea Old Annuities 2nd subscription (1750-8) f. 348, Ledger 139 New South Sea Annuities 2nd subscription (1750-8) f. 374.

3. London Mortgage Market

Lowther occasionally stressed his willingness to lend money to impoverished Cumbrian gentry. In 1711, for example, he told William Gilpin that 'I had rather lend to gentlemen of the country', and in the early 1730s he was 'resolved to lend a good deal of money in the country'. In fact, though he was often approached for loans, Lowther did not actually lend a great deal. As he put it in 1725, the drawback was that 'there is such hazard and trouble in meddling with mortgages in our country [sic], one does not know who to trust, if one be not also on the spot'.[10] By contrast, the London money market offered him the secure, long-term mortgages that he preferred. As he told John Spedding in 1726, 'I can have my choice of the whole town to deal with and meet no disappointments'.[11]

Lowther first offered to lend on a mortgage in 1704, to his father. He was prepared to make £3000 available with which Sir John could pay off debts and buy additional property. Although he stood to inherit any land which Sir John might have bought, James Lowther still expected to be paid the common rate of 6 per cent interest on the loan. Perhaps not surprisingly, his offer was ignored. It was in 1720, when he lent Sir William Codrington £4800 on the security of an estate in Gloucestershire that Lowther entered the mortgage market. Thereafter his involvement grew to be substantial. He lent £11,000 to the Earl of Sussex in 1728 on the security of property in Yorkshire, and £4000 to Lord Vane, taking an assignment of a mortgage on an estate in Buckinghamshire. The following year Lady Carew borrowed £10,000 on the security of estates in Leicestershire and Surrey. And so the list goes on: £16,000 to Sir Thomas Reynell in 1736 (which eventually brought him the Laleham estate); £13,000 in 1742 and 1743 to the Duke of Kingston, all of which was later incorporated into a mortgage of £31,000; £24,000 to the Duke of Bedford in 1745; £10,000 to the Duke of Somerset in 1749; £3000 to John Earl Granville in 1752; and, most remarkably of all, £60,000 between 1748 and 1751 to the Earl of Carlisle. Such sums gave Lowther considerable influence; when the Earl of Carlisle hoped to extend his electoral interest to the second seat for the borough of Carlisle in 1752 (he already had an accepted right to nominate to one seat), Lowther quieted his pretensions by threatening to call in the mortgage.[12]

Apart from mortgages, Lowther also lent occasionally on the security of stock. David Solomons and Galfindus Mann borrowed £8000 and £6000 respectively on the security of South Sea annuities in 1748. Samson Gideon, one of the most famous stockjobbers of the first half of the eighteenth century, borrowed £12,000 on the security of £10,000 East India stock in five months in 1747, and a similar account on the security of £8000 for a year in 1748. Altogether there is evidence, in Lowther's own book of transactions, of loans to thirty-four individuals. The total still outstanding at his death was £125,000, which, with the £12,077 lent out in Cumberland, amounted to slightly more than the £130,000 (plus an additional bond of £4000) mentioned in the executors' account.[13]

With these figures, an attempt can be made to calculate Lowther's overall wealth, in terms of both his annual income and the realizable capital value of his property.

A rough calculation can be made for Lowther's income from land, coal and personal estate in 1754. His gross income from land amounted to about £4580, from which approximately 12 per cent should be deducted to produce a net figure of £4030. This does not take into account repairs to property. Lowther's colliery income was approximately £9000 in 1750. His income from personal estates is set out in table A2.4. Taken together, these figures suggest an annual income in the region of £25,000 by 1754.

Table A2.4. *Lowther's annual income from personal estate, 1754.*

	£	s	d
Bank Stock 19,400 @ 4%	1,309	10	0
Annuities			
1726 3%s	75	0	0
Reduced Threes	528	10	0
Consols	925	10	0
2000 Salt	70	0	0
Survivorship	52	0	0
14% Excise	70	0	0
East India stock	40	0	0
$3\frac{1}{2}$% annuities	638	15	0
3% annuities	1	17	6
3% bonds	1	17	6
South Sea capital stock	207	19	8
Annuity stock	786	19	0
New annuities	1,466	2	10
Old South Sea annuities	302	15	0
New South Sea annuities	482	0	0
Mortgages/bonds			
London	4,705	0	0
Cumberland	449	4	0
Harbours/turnpikes	210	4	6
Ships' dividends paid in 1754	171	6	4
Total	£12,494	11	4

Capital value is not easy to calculate. Lowther's personal estate is given in table A2.5, although, as has already been pointed out, the Bank annuity, and East India Company holdings may have been worth more than their nominal value. To this figure must be added the value of his property. Lowther's gross rental amounted to approximately £4580. Freehold land in the Midlands and south of England was selling for approximately twenty-seven years purchase in the 1750s,[14] and it was probably little less than that

Table A2.5. *Lowther's personal estate in 1755.*

	£
Bank Stock	19,400
Bank of England drawing account	8,345
Annuities	48,450
East India Company holdings	19,500
South Sea Company holdings	137,748
London money market	125,000
Mortgages in Cumberland	12,077
Turnpikes and harbours	4,895
Glasshouse (investment not expected to be recovered)	581
Total	375,996

in Cumbria because of the tax advantages. This would suggest a total value for Lowther's landed estate of approximately £124,000. According to a valuation of the Seaton estate owned by Charles Pelham in 1751, collieries in Cumberland were valued separately from land. The rate for the two collieries, Seaton and Stainburn, was put at seventeen years' purchase.[15] If this were to be repeated for Lowther's collieries, assuming a profit figure in the region of £9000 is correct, the collieries would have been worth around £150,000. Taken together, these figures suggest a capital value in the region of £650,000.

The Lowthers' Land Transactions

1. *Acquisitions by Sir John Lowther in Cumberland*

Year	Property	Vendor	Consideration		
			£	s	d
1661	Corkickle – Craister's tenement	Thomas Craister	700	0	0
1667	Corkickle – Crosthwaite's closes	William Crosthwaite	20	0	0
1670	St Bees – estate	Thomas Wybergh	850	0	0
1672	Whitehaven – tenement	William Hodgson	110	0	0
1675	Whitehaven – the Flatt	Sir George Fletcher	1,000	0	0
1675	Mirehouse tenement	John Gale	320	0	0
1675	Stubscales colliery	John Banks	30	0	0
1675	Distington – royalties	Anthony Walker	13	6	8
1675	Stubscales – royalties	Henry Fletcher	53	0	0
1676	Ulgill colliery	William Gyllyat	35	0	0
1676	Whitehaven – several houses	Thomas Jackson	100	0	0
1676	Corkickle – royalties	Richard Patrickson	20	0	0
1679	Standingstones – house	John Banks	20	0	0
1679	Lattera – royalties	Richard Sanderson	300	0	0
1681	St Bees – Harras Park	William Fletcher	550	0	0
1684	Hensingham – half the royalties	Anthony Benn	217	13	9
1685	Moresby – coals at Lowholme	William Fletcher	260	0	0
1685	Distington – advowson	William Fletcher	200	0	0
1685	Whitehaven – several houses	Thomas Jackson	312	2	9
1685	Whitehaven – house	John Benson	650	0	0
1685	Moresby – half of Lowcommonyeat tenement	William Fletcher	100	0	0
1686	Moresby – royalties of ditto	William Piper	80	0	0
1686	Whitehaven – Sandhills tenement	Christopher Grayson	60	0	0
1688	Hensingham – Cross tenement	James Grayson	200	0	0
1688	St Bees – parcel of land	Edward Cooke	132	0	0
1688	St Bees – Stonehouse tenement	Richard Rawlinson	240	0	0
1688	Moresby – Gillhead tenement	Thomas Grayson	190	0	0
1688	St Bees – Moor Raw tenement	John Gale	20	0	0
1689	St Bees – parcel of land in Whitehaven banks	William Woodhall	10	0	0
1689	St Bees – lands	Robert Milburn	40	0	0
1690	St Bees – tenement	Nicholas Myrehouse	80	0	0
1691	Sandwith – tenement	George Richardson	80	0	0
1691	Moresby – Goosegreen coals	William Lawrence	300	0	0

Year	Property	Vendor	Consideration		
			£	s	d
1691	Braistons – freehold tenement	Nicholas Bragg	80	0	0
1691	Hensingham – Galemire	Anthony Benn	120	0	0
1691	St Bees – tenement	John Hutchinson	80	0	0
1691	Stubscales – tenement	George Dickinson	80	0	0
1691	Moresby – coals at Howgate, a quarter share	Thomas Addison	500	0	0
1692	St Bees – five closes	William Bowthorn	30	0	0
1692	Whaw meadow	?	14	0	0
1692	Moresby – Piper's tenement	William Christian	150	0	0
1693	Hensingham – manor	John Senhouse	215	0	0
1693	St Bees – land	Joseph Lucas	80	0	0
1693	Woodhall's tenement – part	William Woodhall	75	0	0
1694	St Bees – parcel of meadow	Thomas Braithwaite	31	0	0
1695	Moresby – lands	Henry Birkhead	775	0	0
1695	Woodhouse – estate near Whitehaven	Henry Singleton	264	0	0
1697	Corkickle – tenement	Eleanor Langhorn	50	0	0
1699	Braconthwaite – house	? Senhouse	100	0	0
1699	Moresby – high and low Hesleheads	Richard Sanderson	25	0	0
1699	Distington – various royalties	Edward Woodhall	60	0	0
1701	Moresby – Middlegill tenement	Henry Birkett	170	8	0
1701	Arrowthwaite – parcel of ground	Richard Skelton	20	0	0
1701	Moresby – a close	George Dickinson	6	0	0
1703	Sandwith – house	Robert Edgar	12	12	6
1704	Distington – three tenements	Thomas Fletcher	100	0	0
1704	Blearbank – mines	William Asbridge	300	0	0
1705	Whitehaven – tenement	Anthony Richardson	220	0	0
1705	Parton – parcel of ground	William Tyson	30	0	0
1705	Moresby – Crofthead tenement	Francis Whiteside	205	5	0
1705	Corkickle – Gibson's tenement	Peter Gibson	340	0	0
		Total	£11,426	8	8

N.B. The list is not exhaustive. There is evidence in the correspondence for other purchases which cannot be verified (for example, Carlisle Record Office, D/Lons/W Sir John Lowther to Thomas Tickell, 26 July 1684, 11 April 1685, 8 June 1686).

2. *Acquisitions by Sir John Lowther in Westmorland*

Year	Property	Vendor	Consideration		
			£	s	d
1661	Tirril – Great Laithbut and Moorhead Close	William Lancaster snr	167	10	0
1662	Tirril – Harrison's Croft	George Lancaster	23	0	0
1662	Sockbridge – Blawath Close	John Robinson	30	0	0
1663	Tirril – High Close	Edward Idle	48	0	0
1665	Waitby – messuage and tenement	John Orton	48	0	0
1665	Sockbridge – Coatgarth	William Lancaster jnr	24	0	0
1666	Sockbridge – Miller Hill	William Lancaster snr	33	15	0
1670	Waitby – several messuages and tenements	Humphrey Bell	70	16	0
1681	Tirril – house and garth	Elin Brockbank	14	0	0
1686	Penrith – tenement	Anthony Nelson	20	0	0
1698	Sockbridge – land	Thomas Saunder	45	0	0
1698	Sockbridge – tenement	William Robinson	55	0	0
1700	Sockbridge – messuage and land	William Robinson*	55	0	0
1704	Thorpe – land	Henry Clark	33	0	0
1704	Sockbridge – tenement	Thomas Richardson	48	0	0
			£715	1	0

* The two Robinson transactions could be the same property but the evidence suggests that there are two.

3. *Acquisitions by Sir James Lowther in Cumberland* (burgages excepted)

Year	Property	Vendor	Consideration		
			£	s	d
1709	Distington – royalties	John Fearon	37	0	0
1709	Distington – royalties	Henry Fearon	1	1	6
1710	Priestgill and Moresby – royalties	Thomas Fletcher	780	0	0
1710	Distington – Stubscales royalties	Joseph Steel	60	0	0
1711	Distington – Gilhots royalties	Anthony Dixon	162	10	0
1713	Distington – mines and royalties	Thomas Lamplugh	2,400	0	0
1722	Ribton and Dearham – manors	Richard Lamplugh	6,000	0	0
1725	Moresby and Parton – land	Richard Sanderson	360	0	0
1726	Stockhow	Thomas Patrickson	2,252	4	0
1726	Weddicar	John Ponsonby	2,100	0	0
1727	Parton – parcel of ground	Thomas Drape	11	10	0
1727	Parton – parcel of ground	Jonathan Cowman	11	10	0
1729	Moresby – Howgate royalties	Henry Grayson	50	0	0
1729	Moresby – Towlow royalties	William Lister	10	10	0
1729	Moresby – Priestgill royalties	John Benn (exchange for tithes)			
1730	Scalegill and Linethwaite collieries	Thomas Patrickson	500	0	0
1730	Weddicar – Loscow (+ 100 sheep)	John Hudson	500	0	0
1730	Arrowthwaite – Kells Close	Thomas Thompson	50	0	0
1731	Castlerigg – royalties	William Allason	15	0	0
1731	Arlecdon – Pearcefield closes	Thomas Wilson	23	0	0
1731	Seaton – $\frac{1}{3}$ lease	Thomas Benn	700	0	0
1731	Seaton – $\frac{1}{3}$ lease	John Spedding	300	0	0
1732	Seaton – tenement	Richard Richmond	100	0	0
1732	Wreah	James Steel	2,700	0	0
1733	Greysouthen – Sandriggs	Thomas Fisher	85	0	0
1733	Moresby – Blearbank	Isobel Ashridge	340	0	0
1733	Moresby – Priestgill	James Nicholson	392	0	0
1734	Moresby – Goosegreen	John Thomas	360	0	0
1734	Thwaites – parcel of land	Thomas Walker (exchange)	1		8
1734	Corkickle – land	William Wilkinson	1,500	0	0
1734	Thwaites – parcels of land	Thomas Parker	260	0	0
1734	Thwaites – dales of land	George Davy	96	0	0
1735	St Bees – parcels of land	Christopher Skelton	120	0	0
1735	Abbey Holm – three closes	John Barnes	70	0	0
1737	Dearham – royalties	Fletcher Partis	52	10	0
1737	Arrowthwaite – tenement	Anne and John Ribton	280	0	0
1737	Moresby and Distington – manors	John Brougham	6,600	0	0
1738	Coalgrovebank – tenements	Hugh Ashton	775	0	0
1738	St Bees – tenement	John and Prudence Pow	710	10	0
	(Consideration also included an annuity of £28, and a gift of £700 to their children.)				
1738	Barrowmouth – tenements	John Jepson	230	0	0
1739	Arrowthwaite – six tenements	Thomas Parker	840	0	0
1739	Arlecdon – Moorside Park	Frances Lamplugh	1,265	0	0
1739	Bigrigg – two acres of land	Josiah Hird	80	0	0
1739	Corkickle – royalties	Elizabeth Kelsick	92	10	0
1739	Corkickle – royalties	Mary Addison	107	10	0
1739	Moresby – Farmlands tenement	Henry Piper	321	1	0

Year	Property	Vendor	Consideration		
			£	s	d
1739	Crosby – royalties in the manor	John Brisco	150	0	0
1739	St Bees – tenement	Mabel Pattinson	100	0	0
1740	St Bees – customary tenement	William Nicholson	110	0	0
1740	Parton – parcel of ground	Jeremiah Cowman	25	0	0
1740	Bigrigg – land and royalties	John Williamson	250	0	0
1740	Bigrigg – land and royalties	Joseph Williamson	160	0	0
1740	Parton – parcel of ground	Martha Richardson	2	2	0
1741	Arrowthwaite – tenement	William Bird	21	0	0
1743	Arrowthwaite – lands	George Davy	720	0	0
1743	Distington – Barngill	Richard Piper	500	0	0
1743	Arlecdon – Redgate lands near Moorside	Frances Lamplugh	219	0	0
1743	Distington – royalties	Jeremy Cowman	250	0	0
1743	Ribton – three customary tenements	John Pearson	210	0	0
1744	Baccusfield – land	William Littledale	143	0	5
1745	Moresby – advowson	Francis Yates	100	0	0
1745	Bigrigg – New Close tenement and royalties	John Nicholson	370	0	0
1745	Arrowthwaite – three parcels of land	Lowther Spedding	700	0	0
1746	Woodhouse – two tenements	Henry Bowman	617	4	0
1746	Woodhouse – two tenements	James Steel	186	12	9
1746	Distington – West Croft tenement	John Marshall	250	0	0
1746	Foxhouses – house and garth	James Moor	15	0	0
1747	Moresby – Croftend tenement	Robert Grindale	450	0	0
1747	St Bees – one third of Salter closes	Jonathan Bowman	130	0	0
1747	Ribton – customary tenement	Rebecca Stamper	40	0	0
1747	Ribton – lands	John and Eleanor Stamper	460	0	0
1749	Ribton – tenement	William Sewell	210	0	0
1749	St Bees – two thirds of Salter closes	Henry Ponsonby	244	5	0
1750	Ribton – tenement	Henry Harrison	250	0	0
1750	Frizington – demesne	John Williamson	1,400	0	0
1751	St Bees – exchange with Walter Lutwidge		500	0	0
1751	Workington – Cloffocks	Henry Curwen	4,275	0	0
1751	Ribton – customary property	Thomas Dodgson	120	0	0
1754	Weddicar – Croftend tenement	John Steel	575	0	0
		Total	£47,454	12	4

4. Cockermouth burgages purchased by Sir James Lowther

Year	Vendor	Consideration		
		£	s	d
1733	Robert Stainton	66	10	0
1734	Andrew Green	10	10	0
1744	? Winder	130	0	0
1744	Joseph Stanger	36	15	0
1744	John Thompson	84	0	0
1745	? Wilkinson	230	0	0
1745	? Whitelock	80	0	0
1745	?	120	0	0
1745	? Capes	122	0	0
1745	? Witteds	120	0	0
1745	? Hallaway	150	0	0
1745	Joseph Dixon	52	10	0
1745	William Harrison	52	10	0
1745	John Watson	50	1	0
1745	John Capes	48	0	0
1746	? Clark	94	10	0
1746	? Cowman	210	0	0
1747	? Cuthbertson	157	0	0
1752	? Smith	210	0	0
1752	John Wilson	101	1	0
1752	W. Watson	105	0	0
1752	Wilson Watson	305	0	0
1752	? Langton	120	0	0
1753	Robert Stainton	104	0	0
1753	James Battey	105	0	0
	Total £2,864	7	0	

5. Other acquisitions by Sir James Lowther

Year	Property	Vendor	Consideration		
1727	London – house in Queen's Square	Mrs Mary Butler	1,607	0	0
1745	Laleham – manor and estate	Sir Thomas Reynell	23,865	9	0
1745	Laleham – manor and estate	William Gardner	605	9	4
1748	Laleham – Plaisted's tenement	T. Plaisted (£40 p.a.)	2,700	0	0
1749	Laleham – copyhold property	W. Dingley	550	0	0
1750	Laleham – Randall's property	Estate trustees	1,000	0	0
1751	Laleham – customary messuage	Edward Turner	105	0	0
1751	Laleham – common rights	Richard Poole	30	0	0
		Total £30,462	18	4	

225

6. *Sales of property (enfranchisements and building grants excepted) by Sir John and Sir James Lowther*

Year	Property	Vendee	Consideration		
			£	s	d
1688	Fee farm rent in the manor of Roundhay, Yorkshire	John Savile	400	0	0
1694	Whitehaven – old custom house	John Golding	110	0	0
1697	Corkickle – part of Ribton's tenement	Thomas Bank	25	0	0
1700	Hensingham – house adjoining tithe barn	Robert Ponsonby	10	0	0
1714	Waitby (Westmorland) – manor	Mr Monkhouse	320	0	0
1716	Gilbrow	William Graham	260	0	0
1716	Gilhead	Edward Kilner	120	2	6
1716	Moresby – Harris' land	John Collins	160	0	0
1716	Galemire and Whaw meadow	John Matthews	130	0	0
1717	Sands closes	Anthony Benn	113	18	6
1750	Gatesgarth – customary estate	James Spedding	750	0	0
1751	Part of Ribton's tenement	Walter Lutwidge	550	0	0
		Total	£2,949	1	0

Total expenditure on property by Sir John Lowther	12,141	9	8
Total expenditure on property by Sir James Lowther	80,781	17	8
Total	£92,923	7	4

Sources: These tables are constructed from a number of sources in the Carlisle Record Office D/Lons/W collection:

1. Deeds (roughly sorted under manors)
2. Two deeds registers (1611–1705, 1709–59), together with a nineteenth-century index against which purchases can be checked
3. Estate ledgers and cash books
4. Rental for 1754
5. Laleham estate records

Evidence was also found in Sir John Lowther's Commonplace Book, the colliery papers, and correspondence between the Lowthers and their agents.

APPENDIX 4

Colliery Figures

The statistics given below for coal production, sales to the ships' masters, local sales and colliery profits, relate to figures given in the text.

Measurement in the eighteenth-century coal industry was notoriously variable, mainly because the tonnage was calculated from the volume of coal in a container rather than weighed on scales. Thus slate and refuse had to be taken into account, and an allowance had to be made for the coal 'settling', either in the corf (a circular basket used for carrying coal from the coal-face to the pithead) or the wagon. The various different measures used at Whitehaven have produced an anomaly which requires explanation.

Close analysis of the figures given below reveals that from 1719 the tonnage sold from Howgill and Whingill was consistently in excess of the tonnage mined, and by 1750 the discrepancy amounted to more than 200,000 tons. The obvious explanation would be that different measures were being employed for production and sales, and indeed this is known to have been the case. Writing in 1695, William Gilpin noted that 'every 8 tons at the pit makes out 3 more, viz 11, at the ships'.[1] But if the figures are all converted to the same scale by use of the formula:

$$\text{Production} = \text{total shipped} \times \tfrac{8}{11} + \text{total local sale}$$

the discrepancy in the figures is biassed in favour of production to the extent of 500,000 tons. Of course it may have been that Spedding was recording in the accounts coal which was not mined at the two collieries. Coal is known to have been brought from Scalegill – a total of 33,289 tons between 1739 and 1750 – but there is no other evidence of such intercalculations, and this sum alone cannot explain the anomaly. What seems to have been happening, therefore, was that yet another measure was used for moving the coal from the pithead to the staiths in Whitehaven. Evidence in support of this contention is to be found in the Howgill figures from 1735. Coal 'led with wagons to the staith' from the pitheads constantly totalled more than production. But against this argument is the problem of why the discrepancy only begins to appear in 1719. It might also be contended that the absence of any similar pattern in the Parton accounts makes such a suggestion unlikely.

However, the use of such a complicated system of measurements would help to explain what looks at first sight to be an even more bizarre accounting technique. For both Howgill and Whingill John Spedding included in the accounts a column headed 'Banks', which ostensibly appears to be the reserve stock, either heaped on banks at the pit head or stored in staiths. In fact the figures are fictional. They were calculated by the simple formula:

'Banks over' (week A) + total sales (week B) − production (week B) = 'Banks over' (week B)

The only alteration over time was that from 1735 total sales for Howgill were replaced by the sum of 'led with wagons to the staith' plus country sales. Obviously the figure was false; the true formula for calculating the bank should have been (as indeed it was at Parton):

'Banks over' (week A) + production (week B) − total sales (week B) = 'Banks over' (week B)

Spedding was obviously aware that more coal was apparently being sold than produced, but, since this was not allowed for, he was clearly not attempting to produce a true comparison. Finally, inherent in such a means of calculation (remembering that sales constantly outran production) was an inbuilt tendency for the 'Banks over' figure to rise. Consequently Spedding periodically reduced the figure. In 1744 he wiped 23,000 tons from the Howgill account and 2500 from Whingill at the beginning of the Midsummer Quarter. Three years later 30,000 and 2000 respectively were lopped off the two accounts. Such a technique put the 'Banks over' figure into the negative (given in the accounts as 'Banks rests') for a while.

Spedding's motive for these statistical gymnastics is not clear, but it seems likely that the explanation may lie in the problems of different measurement. This was a convenient means of giving him a rough check on the relationship between productivity and sales.

It was not necessary to recalculate all the figures on to the same scale, and while the 'Banks rests' figure decreased, or the 'Banks over' figure increased, he knew the balance between production and sales was about right. If the figures went into reverse then production was outrunning sales. This explanation is not terribly convincing for explaining the discrepancy in the figures for production and sales, but in the absence of any specific reasons it is the best that can be contrived.

For the ships' masters the problems did not end when they bought the coal from Spedding. At Dublin a master could sell about 12 tons for the 20 he had taken on board at Whitehaven, as the result of difference in measurement between the two ports. And if that was not enough, should the wind blow him off course *en route* home, and he decided to call at another port for coal, he had to disentangle a further set of figures:

Almost all places that export coals differ very greatly in their measures, for at Saltcoats and other places in Scotland they reckon 40 gallons to a barrel, and eight of those barrels to what is there called a ton; in Wales their measures are different, and at Workington, where the greatest part of the coals are led in wagons which contain as much within the wood as those at Whitehaven, yet are nevertheless heaped as much as they can lay upon them, and the sacks in use there as well as Parton and Elnefoot [Maryport] contain several gallons more than those few that are still made use of at Whitehaven from some small collieries to which wagonways are not yet laid.[2]

Perhaps not surprisingly, according to Gilpin, in 1697 Whitehaven had two mathematics masters and 'both do well'![3]

1. *Coal Production* (Year from Lady Day to Lady Day) in tons

Year	Howgill	Greenbank	Lattera
1695	15,396	2,321	1,388
1696	13,705	1,783	1,200
1697	18,769	1,864	1,313
1698	17,496	1,803	856
1699	16,022	1,002	2,160
1700	18,656	0	1,584
1701	12,133	2,038	1,996
1702	20,592	2,344	3,127
1703	32,354	2,228	4,533

Year	Howgill	Greenbank	Lattera
1704	28,363	2,878	2,037
1705	27,541	3,055	2,831
1706	23,942	2,472	4,116
1707	33,714	791	4,600

	Whitehaven Collieries			Parton Collieries
				(Moresby, Distington,
	Howgill	Whingill	Total	Birketts, Quarterbanks)
1708	34,209	0	34,209	3,150
1709	37,535	0	37,535	0
1710	40,233	0	40,233	0
1711	35,968	0	35,968	0
1712	38,952	0	38,952	0
1713	42,114	1,257	43,371	0
1714	48,149	4,792	52,941	2,349
1715	42,682	9,869	52,551	6,748
1716	45,778	13,836	59,614	6,752
1717	54,741	10,973	65,714	7,019
1718	48,527	10,366	58,893	6,174
1719	50,223	12,453	62,676	3,915
1720	41,887	9,694	51,581	5,328
1721	41,884	9,193	51,077	5,256
1722	40,693	4,044	44,737	4,933
1723	48,110	3,175	51,285	3,949
1724	43,648	4,200	47,848	4,983
1725	56,383	8,378	64,761	6,652
1726	66,034	15,051	81,085	8,156
1727	50,849	17,850	68,699	6,859
1728	54,931	17,218	72,149	5,532
1729	55,216	15,485	70,701	5,597
1730	61,386	20,501	81,887	5,094
1731	69,777	17,674	87,451	5,104
1732	70,338	13,908	84,246	3,321
1733	71,298	14,015	85,313	4,449
1734	81,408	14,766	96,174	3,220
1735	86,036	7,313	93,349	2,695
1736	95,607	6,360	101,967	2,859
1737	84,031	6,589	90,620	2,461

Whitehaven Colleries

Year	Howgill	Whingill	Total
1738	74,538	8,536	83,074
1739	77,144	8,885	86,029
1740	88,800	8,419	97,219
1741	82,525	7,329	89,854
1742	76,723	5,967	82,690
1743	80,846	4,453	85,299
1744	82,093	5,123	87,216
1745	95,776	6,616	102,392
1746	105,289	9,462	114,751
1747	91,079	11,734	102,813
1748	92,545	12,658	105,203
1749	91,587	11,645	103,232
1750	108,211	17,918	126,129

2. *Sales to the ships' masters*

Year	Howgill	Greenbank	Lattera
1695	15,671	1,209	761
1696	16,271	555	770
1697	18,756	1,811	726
1698	18,205	1,639	511
1699	17,278	2,062	1,787
1700	17,461	0	1,078
1701	11,421	1,135	1,743
1702	21,014	1,107	2,580
1703	29,471	894	3,949
1704	24,172	1,125	1,808
1705	24,780	1,114	2,652
1706	20,417	1,140	3,373
1707	29,624	549	4,100

	Whitehaven Collieries			
	Howgill	Whingill	Total	Parton Collieries
1708	29,211	0	29,211	3,307
1709	32,743	0	32,743	0
1710	35,130	0	35,130	0
1711	30,245	0	30,245	0

Year	Howgill	Whingill	Total	Parton
1712	36,156	0	36,156	0
1713	41,458	129	41,587	0
1714	40,166	3,550	43,716	1,084
1715	44,253	7,189	51,442	6,684
1716	41,690	11,348	53,038	6,202
1717	53,529	7,571	61,100	6,529
1718	49,013	7,071	56,084	4,936
1719	48,511	8,304	56,815	1,497
1720	40,155	6,406	46,561	3,799
1721	40,790	9,089	49,879	5,078
1722	43,518	3,640	47,158	5,881
1723	46,118	2,843	48,961	3,191
1724	47,259	4,155	51,414	5,447
1725	58,590	7,820	66,410	5,728
1726	63,788	11,460	75,248	5,328
1727	60,317	18,274	78,591	5,900
1728	51,221	12,410	63,631	6,516
1729	58,239	15,493	73,732	5,806
1730	62,968	18,260	81,228	5,376
1731	67,250	17,859	85,109	4,705
1732	69,699	11,614	81,313	3,233
1733	66,634	12,278	78,912	4,331
1734	84,143	10,591	94,734	3,156
1735	88,222	7,114	95,336	2,579
1736	81,893	5,053	86,946	2,761
1737	80,898	3,417	84,315	2,214
1738	78,255	4,072	82,327	
1739	90,775	4,631	95,406	
1740	92,032	4,512	96,544	
1741	76,590	2,765	79,355	
1742	76,899	1,841	78,740	
1743	94,906	1,453	96,359	
1744	87,233	1,690	88,923	
1745	91,250	2,699	93,949	
1746	95,240	5,074	100,314	
1747	97,970	5,828	103,798	
1748	91,416	5,498	96,914	
1749	107,943	4,840	112,783	
1750	106,812	10,806	117,618	

3. *Local Sales*

Year	Howgill	Greenbank	Lattera
1695	1,753	459	263
1696	2,526	538	236
1697	2,248	246	78
1698	2,452	422	360
1699	1,951	100	827
1700	1,232	0	89
1701	812	460	66
1702	647	1,407	106
1703	3,450	1,250	197
1704	2,457	1,388	109
1705	3,261	1,300	94
1706	3,328	959	630
1707	3,605	400	251

	Whitehaven Collieries			
	Howgill	Whingill	Total	Parton
1708	4,828	0	4,828	142
1709	4,630	0	4,630	0
1710	4,170	0	4,170	0
1711	3,662	0	3,662	0
1712	3,306	0	3,306	0
1713	3,097	48	3,145	0
1714	3,075	392	3,467	373
1715	2,870	1,716	4,586	673
1716	3,705	2,291	5,996	531
1717	3,657	2,625	6,282	404
1718	3,345	3,219	6,564	692
1719	3,610	3,710	7,320	1,018
1720	2,386	2,649	5,035	579
1721	2,599	1,711	4,310	155
1722	2,781	460	3,241	316
1723	1,741	162	1,903	220
1724	2,563	284	2,847	275
1725	2,217	682	2,899	266
1726	2,188	1,148	3,336	336
1727	2,080	1,607	3,687	360
1728	1,999	1,263	3,262	273

Year	Howgill	Whingill	Total	Parton
1729	2,527	1,502	4,029	188
1730	2,078	1,508	3,586	321
1731	3,033	1,755	4,788	192
1732	2,613	1,381	3,994	129
1733	2,076	690	2,766	129
1734	3,300	1,699	4,999	99
1735	6,094	2,240	8,334	126
1736	8,148	2,396	10,544	185
1737	7,655	3,482	11,137	197
1738	5,977	5,261	11,238	
1739	5,099	5,300	10,399	
1740	6,694	4,767	11,461	
1741	7,358	5,232	12,590	
1742	6,974	4,171	11,145	
1743	7,352	3,769	11,121	
1744	9,249	4,226	13,475	
1745	8,388	4,916	13,304	
1746	8,203	4,751	12,954	
1747	8,358	6,271	14,629	
1748	8,577	7,598	16,175	
1749	8,936	7,521	16,457	
1750	10,375	8,277	18,652	

4. *Colliery Profits* – £ (1665–94, *estimates* only)

Year	Total
1665	58
1666	372
1667	263
1668	322
1669	458
1670	366
1671	448
1672	257
1673	415
1674	663
1675	545
1676	388
1677	423

Year	Total
1678	737
1679	292
1680	909
1681	573
1682	523
1683	731
1684	1,630
1685	788
1686	1,342
1687	1,438
1688	878
1689	57 Loss
1690	145
1691	907
1692	606
1693	895
1694	649

1695–1707, combined figures for Howgill, Greenbank and Lattera collieries:

Year	Total
1695	427
1696	561
1697	875
1698	688
1699	576
1700	832
1701	379
1702	881
1703	1,324
1704	777
1705	812
1706	845
1707	1,622

Year	Whitehaven Colleries (Howgill & Whingill)	Parton Collieries
1708	1,330	68
1709	883	0
1710	847	0
1711	1,044	0

Year	Whitehaven Collieries (Howgill & Whingill)	Parton Collieries
1712	1,822	0
1713	1,857	0
1714	1,894	197 Loss
1715	3,125	181
1716	3,142	211
1717	3,732	102
1718	3,812	193
1719	3,713	72 Loss
1720	3,571	99 Loss
1721	3,277	52
1722	2,984	182

Year	Whitehaven Collieries	Scalegill Colliery	Seaton Colliery	Parton Collieries	Dearham* Colliery
1723	2,913			150	130
1724	3,578			409	67
1725	3,257			104	122
1726	4,589			90	88
1727	4,228			266	11 Loss
1728	3,412		192 Loss	358	6
1729	3,269		205 Loss	118	25
1730	2,202		608 Loss	22 Loss	13
1731	2,411		483 Loss	1 Loss	34
1732	2,133		1,474 Loss	11 Loss	18
1733	1,244			40	38
1734	4,177			42	20
1735	6,089			42 Loss	49
1736	5,578			24 Loss	15
1737	4,133	260	479	100 Loss	16
1738	6,096	146			50
1739	5,599	568	1,333		95
1740	6,922	339			87
1741	3,951	564			86
1742	4,347				41
1743	6,919		837		80

Year	Whitehaven Collieries	Parton Collieries	Dearham* Colliery
1744	7,368		26
1745	6,125		129
1746	6,882		110
1747	7,932		126
1748	6,723		137
1749	8,513		77
1750	6,983		143
1751			19
1752			2
1753			37 Loss
1754			31 Loss
1755 (6 months)			61

*Dearham figures are Michaelmas–Michaelmas.

Sources: Carlisle Record Office, D/Lons/W Colliery Abstracts. Colliery Accounts, Seaton 1727–32. Colliery Accounts, Dearham. Miscellaneous Colliery papers, profit of Scalegill.

Notes

To avoid excessive footnoting certain conventions have been adopted for material in the Lonsdale manuscripts, which are housed in Carlisle Record Office. Documents in the Lowther of Lowther section of this archive are denoted by the call-mark D/Lons/L. All other material is in the Lowther of Whitehaven section D/Lons/W. Four series of letters in this latter collection have been given further abbreviations, viz.

JLLB Sir John Lowther's letter books
LG   Sir James Lowther to William Gilpin
LS   Sir James Lowther to John Spedding
SL   John Spedding to Sir James Lowther

In addition the following abbreviations are used:

Brown LB	North of England Institute of Mining and Mechanical Engineers, William Brown's letter book no. 1
CJ	*Commons Journals*
'Clerk'	W. A. J. Prevost, ' "A Trip to Whitehaven to visit the coal works there in 1739" by Sir John Clerk', *CW2*, lxv (1965)
CRO	Carlisle Record Office
CW1, CW2	*Transactions of the Cumberland and Westmorland Antiquarian and Archaeological Society*, series 1 and 2
EcHR	*Economic History Review*
HMC	Historical Manuscripts Commission
LRO	Lancashire Record Office
Lutwidge LB	CRO DX/ 524 Lutwidge letter books
Pennant, Scotland	T. Pennant, *A Tour in Scotland in 1772* (4th edn, Dublin 1775)
PRO	Public Record Office
SPCK	Society for the Promotion of Christian Knowledge
VCH	Victoria County History
WTB	Carlisle Library, Jackson Collection, Whitehaven Town Book, 1706–82

(Place of publication for books is London unless stated otherwise.)

INTRODUCTION

[1] C. Morris (ed), *Journeys of Celia Fiennes* (1949), p. 146. D. Defoe, *A Tour Through the Whole Island of Great Britain* (Everyman edn, 1962), ii, 269–70. *Camden's Britannia* (1695), p. 836.

[2] Roger North, *Lives of the Norths* (3 vols., 1890 edn), i, 179.

[3] Levens Hall MSS, Box D, Sir Edward Seymour to James Grahme, 14 ? 1700.

[4] G. P. Jones, 'Some Population Problems relating to Cumberland and Westmorland in the Eighteenth Century', *CW2*, lviii (1958), pp. 124–6.

[5] C. M. L. Bouch and G. P. Jones, *A Short Economic and Social History of the Lake Counties, 1500–1830* (Manchester, 1961), pp. 26–7. J. D. Marshall, *Furness and the Industrial Revolution* (Barrow in Furness, 1958), pp. 19–29.

[6] HMC, *Portland MSS*, iv, 578, R. Price to R. Harley, 29 Aug 1710. LS 26 Feb 1754.

[7] J. V. Beckett, 'English Landownership in the later Seventeenth and Eighteenth Centuries: the Debate and the Problems', *EcHR*, 2nd series, xxx (1977), pp. 569–72. These conclusions are elaborated in J. V. Beckett, 'Landownership in Cumbria, 1680–1750' (unpublished University of Lancaster PhD thesis, 1975).

[8] Beckett, 'English Landownership', pp. 571–2.

[9] W. Wordsworth, *A Guide Through the District of the Lakes* (5th edn, Kendal, 1835), p. 58. T. B. Macaulay, *The History of England from the Accession of James II* (1881 edn), i, 135. G. M. Trevelyan, *English Social History* (1944), pp. 302–3.

[10] Durham University, Howard of Naworth MSS, C/173/13–17, 19, 21, 22, 24–6, 28–9, 31, 32, C/171/63, 67, 79, C/181a/6.

[11] J. D. Marshall, 'Kendal in the later Seventeenth and Eighteenth Centuries', *CW2*, lxxv (1975), p. 204.

[12] C. M. L. Bouch, *Prelates and People of the Lake Counties* (Kendal, 1948), pp. 241, 344.

[13] A. H. John, 'The Course of Agricultural Change 1660–1760', in L. S. Pressnell (ed), *Studies in the Industrial Revolution* (1960), pp. 125–55. J. D. Chambers and G. E. Mingay, *The Agricultural Revolution* (1966), p. 42.

[14] These paragraphs are based on a forthcoming chapter on agriculture in Cumberland and Westmorland, which will appear in J. Thirsk (ed), *The Agrarian History of England and Wales*, vol. v, *1640–1750*.

[15] J. Thirsk, 'Industries in the Countryside', in F. J. Fisher (ed), *Essays in the Economic and Social History of Tudor and Stuart England* (Cambridge, 1961), p. 86.

[16] JLLB Sir John Lowther to Thomas Addison, 25 Sept 1686.

[17] G. P. Jones, 'The Decline of the Yeomanry in the Lake Counties', *CW2*, lxii (1962), p. 214. J. D. Marshall, 'The Domestic Economy of the Lakeland Yeoman, 1660–1749', *CW2*, lxxiii (1973), pp. 196, 208–10. J. Bailey and G. Culley, *General View of the Agriculture of the County of Cumberland* (Newcastle, 1794), p. 182.

[18] Marshall, *Furness*. A. Fell, *The Early Iron Industry in Furness and District* (Ulverston, 1908).

[19] E. A. Wrigley, 'A Simple Model of London's Importance in Changing English Society and Economy 1650–1750', *Past and Present*, 37 (1967), pp. 59–60.

[20] Bouch and Jones, pp. 217, 267–8.

[21] LS 22 Nov 1753.

[22] J. G. Williamson, 'Regional Inequality and the Process of National Development: a Description of the Patterns', *Economic Development and Cultural Change*, xiii, 4 part II (1965). David Hey, *The Rural Metalworkers of the Sheffield Region* (Leicester, Department of English Local History, Occasional Papers, 2nd series, no. 5, 1972), p. 49. Marie B. Rowlands, *Masters and Men in the West Midlands Metalware Trades before the Industrial Revolution* (Manchester, 1975), chapter 6.

[23] LS 29 Mar 1746.

[24] Lutwidge LB, Walter Lutwidge to Sir James Lowther, 27 Apr 1740, to Charles Pelham, 25 Sept 1739, to Colonel John Mordaunt, 8 Sept, 8 Oct 1740, to Richard Baynes, 1 June 1748. Brown LB, William Brown to Carlisle Spedding, 2 Nov 1751.

CHAPTER I THE LOWTHERS: LANDOWNING-ENTREPRENEURS

1 J. Langton, 'Landowners and the development of coal mining in south-west Lancashire, 1590–1799', in H. S. A. Fox and R. A. Butlin (eds), *Change in the Countryside* (1979), pp. 123–44.

2 D/Lons/W Estate Memoranda Papers, bundle 21; St Bees miscellaneous.

3 D. R. Hainsworth, *Commercial Papers of Sir Christopher Lowther 1611–44* (Surtees Society, 1977): 'Christopher Lowther's Canary Adventure: A Merchant Venturer in Dublin, 1632–3', *Irish Economic and Social History*, ii (1975), pp. 22–35. C. B. Phillips, 'The Gentry in Cumberland and Westmorland, 1600–65' (unpublished University of Lancaster PhD thesis, 1973), pp. 96, 196–205.

4 An account of the disinheritance is forthcoming in *CW2*.

5 HMC *Downshire MSS*, i, 332. HMC *Portland MSS*, x, 2. *Cal[endars of] Treas[ury] B[oo]ks*, ix (1689–92), p. 800. *Cal State Papers Dom[estic]* (1696), p. 153, (1700–2), p. 209. Levens Hall MSS, Gilfrid Lawson to James Grahme, 14, 30 Sept 1708. Various references to payments to James Lowther are in *Cal Treas Bks*, xiii–xxiv.

6 LS 16 Dec 1746.

7 M. W. McCahill, 'Peers, Patronage and the Industrial Revolution, 1760–1800', *Journal of British Studies*, xvi (1976).

8 JLLB Sir John Lowther to Lord Lonsdale, 6 Mar 1699.

9 D/Lons/W James Lowther to Thomas Tickell, 24, 31 Oct 1691 (with the Lowther/Tickell correspondence). JLLB Sir John Lowther to Lady Lonsdale, 29 Aug 1700.

10 LS 13 Jan 1737, 10 Jan 1727.

11 D/Lons/L Miscellaneous Letters, 1550–1872. John Stevenson to Richard Stevenson, 16 Mar 1742 (hereafter Stevenson to Stevenson).

12 D/Lons/W James Lowther to Sir John Lowther, 18 Oct 1705.

13 Lutwidge, LB, Walter Lutwidge to Jeremiah Smith, 4 Dec 1739, to John Cookson, 18 Jan 1747, to Richard Baynes, 10 May 1748.

14 LS 21 June 1737. D/Lons/W James Lowther to Sir John Lowther, 12 May 1705. LS 14 Apr 1743.

15 LS 10 Mar 1726.

16 LS 21 May 1752.

17 J. Thirsk, *Economic Policies and Projects* (Oxford, 1978), pp. 21–2. Charles Webster, *The Great Instauration* (1975), pp. 360–9.

18 JLLB Sir John Lowther to Dr Lancaster, 17 Nov 1688. LS 16 Mar 1734.

19 'Clerk', p. 312.

20 CRO D/Mus/Letters 1710, Sir Christopher Musgrave to Gilfrid Lawson, 10 Oct 1710. Stevenson to Stevenson. Lutwidge LB, Walter Lutwidge to Richard Baynes, 1 Mar 1748. W. King, *Political and Literary Anecdotes of His Own Time* (1818), pp. 102–3.

21 D/Lons/W Memoranda Books, 'My Advice to those that come to my Estate at Whitehaven'. D/Lons/L Check List 16/47.

22 LS 10 Jan, 5, 9 Feb 1740, 10 Jan 1727, 3 June 1742.

23 D/Lons/W Miscellaneous Correspondence bundle 20, R. Mayo to James Lowther, 12 June 1718; bundle 39, Henry Newman to Sir James Lowther, 21 June 1739. St Bartholomew's Hospital Archives, Ha/1/11, p. 126, Ha/1/12, p. 281. Greater London Record Office, A/FH Rough Minutes, General Court, Subscription Book 1739–72, f. 4, H1/ST/E13/2. *Gentleman's Magazine*, xiii (1747), p. 564. Hoare's Bank, ledger S, f. 435, ledger U, f. 308. LS 2 Apr 1747, 25 Mar, 15 May 1740.

[24] N. Curnock (ed), *The Journals of the Rev. John Wesley A.M.* (8 vols., 1909ff), iv, 101–3, copy of letter from Wesley to Sir James Lowther, 28 Oct 1754.

[25] Stevenson to Stevenson.

[26] J. V. Beckett, 'Illness and Amputation in the Eighteenth Century: The Case of Sir James Lowther (1673–1755)', *Medical History*, xxiv (1980), pp. 88–92.

[27] SPCK, CR1/17/12655, Sir James Lowther to Henry Newman, 9 May 1734 (abstract). LS 21 July 1752, SL 2 July 1752.

[28] LS 14 Jan 1752.

[29] LS 12 Mar 1751. D/Lons/L Check List 16/45, E. Wilson to W. Tatham, 16 Mar 1751.

[30] W. A. J. Prevost, 'A Journie to Carlyle and Penrith, 1731', *CW2*, lxi (1961), p. 223. *Gentlemen's Magazine*, xxv (1755), p. 42.

[31] D/Lons/W Surveys 1701.

[32] D/Lons/W Sir John Lowther to William Gilpin, 21 May 1698.

[33] Sir James Lowther's words, see LS 26 Feb, 31 Oct 1751.

[34] D/Lons/W Misc. Corresp. bundle 40, Sir John Lowther's instructions to Mr Tickell, 19 June 1666; Sir John Lowther to Thomas Tickell, 10 Sept 1666, 21 Apr 1688, 24 July, 15 Sept, 30 Oct 1688, 16 Dec 1690, 28 Mar, 9 June 1691, Tickell to Lowther, 21 Dec 1690. JLLB, Sir John Lowther to John Gale, 28 July 1688.

[35] D/Lons/W William Gilpin (?) to Sir John Lowther, 3 Dec 1704 (found amongst the letters from James Lowther to Sir John Lowther).

[36] D/Lons/W Estate Memoranda Papers, bundles 9, 24, 29, Colliery Papers, bundle 23. LS 13, 15 Feb 1724.

[37] D/Lons/W Sir John Lowther to Thomas Tickell, 9 Dec 1690.

[38] SL 28 Dec 1712, 16 Dec 1739, 14 Nov 1742. LS 15 Aug, 10, 12 Sept 1723, 16 Jan 1725, 15 Nov 1729, 12 Feb 1732, 20 Nov 1744, 22 Nov 1753.

[39] D/Lons/W Sir John Lowther to Thomas Tickell, 15 Sept 1688, 26 Apr, 24 May 1690.

[40] D/Lons/W Deeds, Frizington 25/1/9, 10; Cash Book 1720–2; Estate Ledger 1737–58, fos. 210, 219.

[41] LS 31 Aug, 10 Sept, 24 Dec 1723, 2 Feb 1725.

[42] SL 24 Oct 1742. LS 11 June 1743, 7 May 1747.

[43] SL 7 Dec 1740.

[44] LS 24 Nov 1733. SL 23 Oct, 4 Nov 1741, 29 Oct 1742. North of England Institute of Mining and Mechanical Engineers, Watson Collection 3093.

[45] LG 18 Jan 1707.

[46] D/Lons/L Box 'Various deeds relating to the Sockbridge estate'. D/Lons/W Cash Book (Mr Bird); Sir John Lowther to Thomas Tickell, 14 May 1688. LG 18, 27 Feb 1707. LS 24 Nov, 31 Dec 1726.

[47] JLLB Sir John Lowther to Lady Lonsdale, 4 Aug 1701.

[48] LS 9 Jan 1728.

[49] SL 6 May 1744.

[50] D/Lons/W Sir John Lowther to Thomas Tickell, 23 Mar 1680, 14 Jan 1688, 8 Aug 1691.

[51] LS 6 Nov 1731. LG 22 Apr 1707.

[52] D/Lons/W Sir John Lowther to Thomas Tickell, 14 May 1681. LS 17 Dec 1737.

[53] P. Roebuck, 'Absentee Landownership in the late Seventeenth and Early Eighteenth Centuries: A Neglected Factor in English Agrarian History', *Agricultural History Review*, xxi (1973), pp. 1–17. S. Pollard, *The Genesis of Modern Management* (1965), pp. 209–10.

54 D/Lons/W Misc. Corresp. bundle 25, W. Smith to Sir John Lowther, 18 Apr
1700. SL 17, 24 May 1706, 30 Mar 1707. LS 20 June 1706, 25 Mar, 24 Apr
1707 (in Spedding letter books). LG 17 Aug, 8 Oct, 14 Nov 1706, 27 Feb 1707.
Whitehaven Public Library, MS 30, Token Book vol. 1.
55 W. Jackson (ed), *Memoirs of Dr Richard Gilpin of Scaleby Castle in Cumberland by
Rev. William Gilpin* (1879), p. 40. D/Lons/W Estate Ledger 1706-22. SL 18 June
1725, 9 Nov 1726, 25 Oct, 17 Dec 1727, 17 Mar, 14 Apr 1728. LS 5 Nov 1726,
7 Dec 1727, 31 Mar 1730, 13 Apr 1751.
56 LRO, Inventory of Edward Spedding, 1706.
57 SL 28 Dec 1744. John Stevenson to John Spedding, 23 June 1750 (in LS
bundle).
58 LS 20 Mar, 28 Apr 1739. D/Lons/W Misc. Corresp. bundle 39, Sir Thomas
Lowther to Sir James Lowther, 16 July, 10 Aug 1739. SL 19 Sept 1744, 24 Apr,
5 May 1745. Brown LB, Carlisle Spedding to William Brown, 7 July 1752.
59 D/Lons/W Sir John Lowther to Thomas Tickell, 21 Jan 1682. LS 17, 19, 21,
Sept 1723, 21 Mar 1724, 14 Oct 1726, 31 Jan 1746. Lutwidge LB, Walter
Lutwidge to Sir James Lowther, 16 Feb, 3 May 1747, 21 Mar 1749, to Richard
Baynes, 12 June 1748. LS 21 May 1751. SL 8 Jan 1724. D/Lons/W Misc.
Corresp. bundle 44, Sir Edward Fawkenor to six Whitehaven gentlemen
(including Spedding), 16 Dec 1745.
60 'Clerk', p. 312.
61 Lutwidge LB, Walter Lutwidge to Richard Baynes, 2 July 1748. D/Lons/W
Housekeeping accounts 1737-55.
62 J. R. Wordie, 'A Great Landed Estate in the Eighteenth Century, 1691-1833'
(unpublished University of Reading PhD thesis, 1967), pp. 51-66. J. Wake
and D. C. Webster (eds), *The Letters of Daniel Eaton, 1725-32,* Northamptonshire
Record Society (1971).
63 LS 29 Nov 1739. D/Lons/W Sir John Lowther to Thomas Tickell, 27 Sept
1687. JLLB Sir John Lowther to Mr Bird, 6 Nov 1698.
64 D/Lons/W William Gilpin to Sir John Lowther, 27 May 1696.
65 LG 14 Oct 1707. LS 18 Mar 1733, 11 Oct 1744, 25 Nov 1749. SL 20 Oct, 17
Nov 1736.
66 D/Lons/W Sir John Lowther to Thomas Tickell, 27 July 1680, 6 Feb 1683.
67 SL 8 Mar 1723. LS 16 Mar 1723. D/Lons/W William Gilpin to Sir John
Lowther, 8 July 1696; Estate Rental 1754.
68 LS 30 Nov 1727.
69 LS 6 Dec 1729.
70 SL 26 Oct 1726.
71 SL 26 Feb 1729. LS 4 Mar 1729, 3 June 1746, 22 May 1749, 27 Mar 1753.
72 LS 17 Nov 1730, 17 Jan 1736. D/Lons/W Estate Memoranda Papers, bundles 2,
23; Estate Ledger 1692-8, f. 1.
73 D/Lons/W Estate Memoranda Books, book containing copies of leases, f. 185.
74 D/Lons/W Unlisted Whitehaven papers, stray letters 1705-25; Cash Book
1692-9; Box 'Various Accounts' 1705-77. JLLB, Sir John Lowther to William
Gilpin, 15 Jan, 12, 19 Apr 1698. SL 16 Nov 1718, 20, 27 Jan, 3 Mar 1720,
26 May 1731, 25 June 1732. CRO D/Lons/Le Fleming MSS, Thomas Denton's
History 1687-8, f. 29.
75 D/Lons/L Survey Lists, Barony of Kendal Box 3/14. D/Lons/W Thomas Tickell
to Sir John Lowther, 29 Dec 1687, Lowther to Tickell, 18 Feb, 9 Sept 1688,
Lowther to William Gilpin, 11 Apr 1696, Gilpin to Lowther, 10 June, 19 Sept
1696; Estate Memoranda Papers, bundle 21. JLLB 'A Short Account of the
state of the gardens at Whitehaven in Cumberland'. LS 21 Jan, 15 Apr 1731,

16 Oct 1732, 20 Nov 1733. 1 Feb 1735. SL 18 Oct 1732. D/Lons/W Whitehaven Harbour unlisted papers, lease of February 1714.

[76] D/Lons/W 'Dictionaries and General Notebooks'; William Gilpin to Sir John Lowther, 29 Dec 1697; Cash Books 1701-3, 1704-6, 1708-11; Household Accounts 1746-50, 1750-55; Estate Memoranda Books, Maxwell's report is included in a book containing copies of leases. It is also to be found published in R. Maxwell, *The Practical Husbandman* (Edinburgh, 1757). 'Various Accounts 1705-77', loose sheet dated 1754. LS 2 Mar 1723, 24 Dec 1747, 5 May, 27 Oct 1748. SL 16 Jan 1709, 20 Jan 1712.

[77] LS 13 Oct, 6 Dec 1722. SL 15, 18 Oct, 30 Nov 1722. D/Lons/W Cash Book 1726-8; Colliery Account book, Mich. 1723; Estate Memoranda Papers, bundle 23.

[78] W. G. Hoskins, 'Harvest Fluctuations in English Economic History, 1620-1759', *Agricultural History Review*, xvi (1968), pp. 15-31. G. E. Mingay, 'The Agricultural Depression, 1730-50', *EcHR*, 2nd series, viii (1956), pp. 323-38. D/Lons/W Estate Rentals 1682-1754; Estate Ledger 1706-22, f. 44, 1737-58, fos. 104, 126-38, 157-8, 160, 168, 172-3, 187; William Gilpin to Sir John Lowther, 8 July 1696.

[79] D/Lons/W Misc. Corresp. bundle 29, valuation of 1696; Box 'Various deeds relating to the Sockbridge estate'; Cash Book (Mr Bird). D/Lons/L Survey Lists, Sockbridge and Hartsop, bundle 23. D/Lons/Laleham, 4/12, 16. LS 11 Apr 1751. CRO D/Sen Corresp. box 2, Sir William Fleming to Humphrey Senhouse, 16 Jan 1755.

[80] D/Lons/W St Bees misc.; Cash Books 1701-3, 1708-11, 1692-3; Estate Memoranda Papers, bundle 11; Deeds, Dearham 32/1/11-13; Deeds Register 1709-59; Estate Ledger 1737-58 (loose sheets inside front cover). D/Lons/L Survey Lists, Sockbridge and Hartsop, bundle 22. D/Lons/Laleham 4/16. LS 12 Nov 1706.

[81] D/Lons/W Cash Books 1704-6, 1708-11, 1717-20. D/Lons/L Survey lists, Sockbridge and Hartsop, bundle 22. D/Lons/Laleham, unnumbered bundles. LS 5 Mar 1730, 14 Oct 1738, 26 Mar, 5 Apr 1748. LG 9, 20 Oct 1715. SL 11 Mar 1730.

[82] See, for example, E. Laurence, *The Duty of a Steward to his Lord* (1727), J. Richards, *The Gentleman's Steward and Tenants of Manors Instructed* (1730), G. Jacob, *The Complete Court-Keeper or Land Steward's Assistant* (1713), J. Mordaunt, *The Complete Steward* (2 vols., 1761).

CHAPTER 2   COAL: MONOPOLY AND COMPETITION

[1] See the recent debate in the *EcHR*, 2nd series, xxx (1977), pp. 340-5.

[2] L. A. Clarkson, *The Pre-Industrial Economy of England, 1500-1750* (1971), p. 122.

[3] J. U. Nef, *The Rise of the British Coal Industry* (1932), i, 70. PRO E/134/31 & 32 Charles II, Hilary no. 26.

[4] L. M. Cullen, *Anglo-Irish Trade 1660-1800* (Manchester, 1968), p. 82.

[5] E. McCracken, *The Irish Woods since Tudor Times* (Newton Abbot, 1971), p. 98.

[6] L. M. Cullen and T. C. Smout (eds), *Comparative Aspects of Scottish and Irish Economic and Social History 1600-1900* (Edinburgh, 1976), pp. 4, 6, 199-200.

[7] G. O'Brien, *The Economic History of Ireland in the Eighteenth Century* (1918), p. 215. D/Lons/L Check List 16/16, John Spedding to James Lowther, 9 July 1722. SL 31 May 1724. LS 10 Jan 1730, 30 Mar 1749.

[8] LS 15 Aug, 19 Dec 1723, 9, 28 Apr, 7, 21 May 1724, 24 Apr, 1, 4 May, 5, 28

Oct 1725, 11, 20 Jan 1726. SL 22 Mar, 3, 19 Apr 1724, 12 May 1725. D/Lons/W Colliery Papers, bundles 21–24. Cullen, *Anglo-Irish Trade*, pp. 83–4.

[9] T. H. Bainbridge, 'The West Cumberland Coalfield', *Economic Geography*, xii (1936), pp. 167–74. VCH *Cumberland*, ii, 348.

[10] Phillips, 'The Gentry in Cumberland and Westmorland', pp. 199–200.

[11] VCH *Cumberland*, ii, 366. SL 14 July 1725.

[12] D/Lons/W Sir John Lowther to Thomas Tickell, 29 Nov 1681, 27 May 1682; Tickell to Lowther, 5 Jan 1682, 13 Oct 1684; William Gilpin to Lowther, 5 Mar 1694.

[13] D/Lons/W Estate Memoranda Papers, bundle 9. SL 9 Nov 1729.

[14] CRO D/MBS Rentals.

[15] LS 1 Nov 1722, 11 Dec 1729, 11 Apr 1730. SL 19 May 1728.

[16] CRO DL/1/1 Rental 1723.

[17] LS 2 Nov 1725. E. Hughes, *North Country Life in the Eighteenth Century: Cumberland and Westmorland 1700–1830* (Oxford, 1965), pp. 134–8. CRO D/Sen Day Book 1726–36.

[18] Beckett, 'English Landownership', p. 571.

[19] CRO D/Lec leases in box 17.

[20] D/Lons/W Colliery Papers, bundle 18, John Spedding's notebook.

[21] W. H. Makey, 'The Place of Whitehaven in the Irish Coal Trade 1600–1750' (unpublished University of London MA thesis, 1952), p. 219.

[22] LS 24 May 1707 (in Spedding letter book).

[23] SL 7 Dec 1712.

[24] LG 19 Dec 1719. *Reasons for Building a Pier and making a Harbour at Elnefoot in Cumberland* (n.d. but *c*.1719).

[25] JLLB Sir John Lowther to Lord Lonsdale, 3 July 1699.

[26] SL 14 Jan 1719. For Saltcoats see note 8 above.

[27] D/Lons/W William Gilpin to Sir John Lowther, 16 Jan 1698. SL 10 May 1706. Cullen, *Anglo-Irish Trade*, p. 85.

[28] Custom House Library 82/47 Collector to Customs Commissioners, 9 Sept 1720.

[29] LG 19 Dec 1719.

[30] Custom House Library 82/47 Collector to Customs Commissioners, 8 July 1719.

[31] *Reasons for Building.*

[32] *Calculations Relating to the Coal Trade* (1721), p. 15.

[33] LS 14 July 1719, 6 July 1723. SL 30 July, 4 Aug 1723.

[34] LS 29 Jan 1723.

[35] LG 17 Nov 1719. SL 23 Feb, 10 Apr 1721.

[36] Paul M. Sweezy, *Monopoly and Competition in the English Coal Trade 1550–1850* (Harvard, 1938), pp. 140–3. P. Cromar, 'The Coal Industry on Tyneside 1715–50', *Northern History*, xiv (1978), pp. 194 ff. T. W. Beastall, *A North Country Estate* (Chichester, 1975), p. 20.

[37] LS 22 July 1725.

[38] LS 8, 13 Dec 1722, 20 July 1725.

[39] LS 23 Sept 1721, 11 May 1723, 6 June 1730.

[40] Lutwidge LB, Walter Lutwidge to Mr Gates, 23 Oct 1740.

[41] LS 10 Sept 1723, 21 Oct 1727 (and subsequent letters to 14 Dec), 19 Apr 1729, 4 Nov 1732, 19 Dec 1734. SL 10 Nov 1723, 29 Dec 1727.

[42] SL 29 Dec 1723.

[43] LS 1 June, 20 July, 21 Aug 1725, 2 Apr, 19 May, 10, 15 June 1726. SL 14, 23 July, 1, 29 Aug, 1 Sept 1725.

[44] SL 26 Mar 1735.

[45] SL 24 Dec 1727, 14, 16, 25 Feb, 13, 31 Mar, 14 Apr 1728, 28 Jan, 8 Mar 1729,

6 Feb, 10 May 1730, 11 Feb 1736. LS 19 Nov, 14 Dec 1728, 31 Jan, 3, 11 Dec 1730, 30 Jan 1731, 24 Feb, 9 Mar 1736. The draft of an agreement with Curwen, dated 1 Feb 1728, is amongst a bundle of LG letters for 1717.

[46] D/Lons/W Estate Ledger 1723–37, f. 213.

[47] D/Lons/W Deeds, Dearham 32/1/13.

[48] D/Lons/W Colliery Papers, bundle 30. SL 26 Mar 1735.

[49] D/Lons/W Deeds, Dearham 32/1/11–13. SL 11 Mar 1737. LS 22 Mar 1737.

[50] SL 17 Dec 1738. LS 23 Dec 1738. D/Lons/W Estate Ledger 1737–58, f. 219.

[51] LS 13 Aug, 20 Dec 1737, 7, 28 Jan, 9 May 1738.

[52] LS 28 Nov 1738, 20 May, 1 June 1742, 20 Mar 1750, 14 Feb, 31 Dec 1751, 20 Apr 1753. SL 7, 21 Dec 1740, 1 May 1741, 26 May 1742, 4 June 1744.

[53] LS 18 June 1751.

[54] D/Lons/L William Brownrigg to Sir James Lowther, 19 Aug 1765.

[55] LS 6 Aug 1737, 19, 22, 24 Apr, 3 May, 9 Dec 1740, 24, 28 July 1744, 18 Jan, 9 May 1752, 3 May 1753, 17 Oct 1754. SL 27 Apr 1740. D/Lons/W Deeds, Seaton 34/3/31a; Memoranda Books.

[56] LS 3 Dec 1730. SL 10 Nov 1734.

[57] SL 9 May 1736, 27 Apr 1744. LS 28 Dec 1751.

[58] D/Lons/W Estate Memoranda Papers, bundle 22. LS 14 Feb 1751, 21 Apr 1753.

[59] LS 23 Oct 1753, 29 Oct 1754.

[60] CRO D/Lec/16/87. Oliver Wood, 'The Collieries of J. C. Curwen', CW2, lxxi (1971), pp. 199–236.

[61] Custom House Library 82/49 Collector to Customs Commissioners. 27 Oct 1736.

[62] Port book entries (for details see bibliography).

[63] Pennant, Scotland, ii, 48. Cullen, Anglo-Irish Trade, pp. 84–5.

[64] Custom House Library 82/49 Collector to Customs Commissioners, 22 Dec 1736, 28 Apr 1737, 12 June 1741. SL 2, 12, 26 Oct 1743. D/Lons/L Misc. Estate books, petition dated Jan 1756. D/Lons/W Unlisted Whitehaven papers, bundle of misc. harbour papers 1674–1762. B. G. Hutton, 'A Lakeland Journey, 1759', CW2, lxi (1961), p. 292. Pennant, Scotland, ii, 51.

[65] VCH Cumberland, ii, 374. LS 14 Oct 1736.

[66] SL 30 Jan 1723. LS 2 Feb, 19 June 1725. D/Lons/W Estate Memoranda Papers, 'Abstract of Dearham Colliery'. VCH Cumberland, ii, 376.

[67] Custom House Library 82/52 Collector to Customs Commissioners, 23 Oct 1751. LS 21 Apr, 3 May 1753. CRO D/Ben/3481 Maryport Census 1765. Bouch and Jones, p. 318. J. Nicolson and R. Burn, Antiquities and History of the Counties of Westmorland and Cumberland (1777), ii, 161–2.

[68] D/Lons/W Parton Harbour Box. LS 4 Mar 1725.

[69] Custom House Library 82/49 Collector to Customs Commissioners, 22 Dec 1736.

CHAPTER 3 COAL: THE STRUCTURE OF TRADE AND INDUSTRY

[1] D/Lons/L William Brownrigg to Sir James Lowther, 29 Aug 1765.

[2] Footnote to Dr John Dalton, A Descriptive Poem Addressed to Two Young Ladies (1755).

[3] D/Lons/W Estate Memoranda Books.

[4] T. S. Ashton and J. Sykes, The Coal Industry in the Eighteenth Century (2nd edn, Manchester, 1964), pp. 16, 22.

[5] Ibid., p. 93. Binding was still not firmly established in the early nineteenth century.

[6] J. D. Kendall, 'Notes on the History of Mining in Cumberland and North Lancashire', Trans. of the North of England Institute of Mining Engineers, xxiv

(1884–5), p. 102. D/Lons/W Colliery Account Books, Mich. 1716, Lady Day 1722, Mids. 1732. SL 29 June 1743. LS 5 July 1743.

7 D/Lons/W Colliery Ledger 1, 1714–17; Estate Memoranda Papers 2; MSS History of Whitehaven Collieries, fos. 106 ff. Colliery Ledger 3, 1727–32. SL 21 June 1706, 9 Nov 1720. JLLB Sir John Lowther to William Gilpin, 15 Mar 1698.

8 SL 5 May, 27 June 1714.

9 SPCK Misc. Letters vol. 4, Henry Newman to Sir James Lowther, 7 Jan 1738; CR1/19/14392, Lowther to Newman, 10 Jan 1738.

10 SL 14, 28 May 1710, 13 Jan 1712, 10 Feb 1727. LS 30 Jan, 13 Feb 1729.

11 D/Lons/W MSS History of Whitehaven Collieries, f. 106ff; Colliery Ledger 3, 1727–32. LS 28 Dec 1727. SL 5 Aug 1737, 25 Feb 1728, 19 Dec 1739, 24 Apr 1740. Brown LB, Carlisle Spedding to William Brown, 28 Oct 1753.

12 D/Lons/W Colliery Account Books, Mich. 1716. LS 3 June 1732. SL 25 Jan 1736, 13 Oct 1738.

13 D/Lons/W Colliery Papers, bundle 20. SL 13 Dec 1732, 28 May 1738. LS 21 Dec 1732, 8 May 1733, 21 Mar 1734, 11 Jan, 13 Mar 1739. Lutwidge LB, Walter Lutwidge to Charles Pelham, 25 Sept 1739, to Sir James Lowther, 21 Dec 1740, to James Gorton, 1 Jan 1741, to John Spedding, 23 Dec 1746.

14 SL 25 Feb 1728, 26 Dec 1730.

15 Lutwidge LB, Walter Lutwidge to Sir James Lowther, 16 Feb, 30 Mar, 2 Sept 1748. LS 31 Jan 1747. D/Lons/W Colliery Papers, bundle 30. M. J. T. Lewis, *Early Wooden Railways* (1970), p. 217.

16 D/Lons/W Colliery Papers, bundle 17. Ashton and Sykes, p. 15.

17 SL 12 Oct 1712.

18 D/Lons/W Colliery Ledger 1, 1714–17. SL 30 Mar 1718, 22 Nov 1719, 5, 21 Feb, 14 Dec 1720, 11 Aug 1723, 20 Mar, 8 May 1726, 19 Jan 1733, 15 Dec 1734, 29 Nov 1738. LS 25 Jan 1733, 10, 14, 17 Dec 1734.

19 J. S. Allen, 'The 1715 and other Newcomen Engines at Whitehaven, Cumberland', *Trans Newcomen Society*, xlv (1972–3), pp. 237–68. J. V. Beckett, 'Newcomen Engines at Whitehaven, Cumberland, 1727–40', *ibid.*, xlix (1977–8), pp. 149–52.

20 L. T. C. Rolt, *Thomas Newcomen* (Dawlish, 1963), p. 113. D/Lons/W Estate Memoranda Papers, bundle 19. SL 31 Jan, 9, 16 Feb 1724, 15 Apr 1730. LS 11 Feb, 14 May, 2 July 1724, 1 Jan, 31 Mar 1726, 5 Dec 1736.

21 SL 8 May 1730, 25 Oct 1732. D/Lons/W Misc. Corresp. bundle 36, Sir Thomas Lowther to Sir James Lowther, 27 July 1732.

22 LS 17, 19 Nov 1730, 19, 21 Jan, 5 June 1731, 22, 26 Feb, 2 July 1732, 14 Dec 1734, 3 Mar, 26 Apr 1739. SL 8 Feb 1736, 8 July 1737, 13 Jan 1740. D/Lons/W Misc. Corresp. bundle 38, draft agreement; MSS History of Whitehaven Collieries, f. 101; Misc. Estate Books, 'James Spedding's Description of the Mines *c.*1756'. Brown LB, Carlisle Spedding to William Brown, 3 Mar 1751. 'Clerk', p. 308. W. Hutchinson, *History of Cumberland* (1794), ii, 62.

23 VCH *Cumberland*, ii, 366. SL 14 Apr 1742. Wood, 'Collieries of J. C. Curwen', p. 215. C. R. Hudleston, 'An 18th Century Squire's Possessions', *CW2*, lvii (1957), pp. 127–57. CRO D/Lec/16/87. R. L. Galloway, *Annals of Coal Mining and the Coal Trade* (Newton Abbot, 1970 edn), i, 261.

24 SL 24 Apr 1730, 25 Jan, 4 Feb 1736, 10 Aug 1737. LS 18, 19 Aug 1737, 28 Dec 1727. D/Lons/W MSS History of Whitehaven Collieries, f. 106ff; Colliery Ledger 3, 1727–32.

25 *Newcastle Journal*, 16 Aug 1755 (copy in D/Lons/W MSS History of Whitehaven Collieries).

[26] Dalton, *Descriptive Poem*, pp. 5–6.

[27] SL 12 Dec 1729. D/Lons/W Colliery Account Book, 1727–32.

[28] J. J. Cartwright (ed), *The Travels Through England of Dr Richard Pococke*, vol. 1 (Camden Society, 1888), pp. 16–17.

[29] J. V. Beckett, 'Dr William Brownrigg, FRS: Physician, Chemist and Country Gentleman', *Notes and Records of the Royal Society of London*, xxxi (1977), pp. 257–8. Galloway, *Annals*, ii, 346. 'An account of the damp air in a Coal-Pit of Sir James Lowther Bart', *Philosophical Transactions*, xxxviii (1733–4), pp. 109–13. SL 27 Mar, 18 May 1743. D/Lons/W MSS History of Whitehaven Collieries, f. 117; Misc. Estate Books, 'James Spedding's Description . . .'. Ashton and Sykes, p. 47. Pennant, *Scotland*, ii, 49–50. Curnock, *Wesley's Journal*, iv, 314.

[30] HMC *Egmont Diary*, ii, 262. Beckett, 'Dr William Brownrigg', p. 257. *Phil Trans* xxxviii (1733–4).

[31] SL 27 Nov 1741, 24 Aug 1743. Beckett, 'Dr William Brownrigg', p. 257.

[32] Ashton and Sykes, p. 49. VCH *Cumberland*, ii, 366.

[33] VCH *Cumberland*, ii, 360. D/Lons/W Misc. Colliery Papers, account of coal leaders, July 1706; Colliery Ledger 2, 1717–22, 3 1727–32; Colliery Account Book, Lady Day 1721. JLLB 'Queries concerning the quays and wharfs, 1677'. SL 5 June, 21 Sept 1715, 30 Mar 1716.

[34] SL 20 June, 22 Aug, 3 Nov 1725. D/Lons/W Misc. Estate Books, 'James Spedding's Description . . .'. Lewis, *Early Wooden Railways*, p. 127.

[35] D/Lons/W Colliery Papers, bundle 30. LS 31 Jan 1747. Lutwidge LB, Walter Lutwidge to Sir James Lowther, 16 Feb, 30 Mar, 2 Sept 1748.

[36] D/Lons/W Misc. Colliery Papers, 'Extract of the charge of the wagonway from Swinburn and Corporal pits'; Harbour Trustees' Minutes, meeting of 31 Sept 1732; Colliery Abstracts. SL 11 May 1743. Custom House Library 82/49 Collector to Customs Commissioners, 18 Jan 1738. Pennant, *Scotland*, ii, 48. Joseph Fisher, 'Observations and Inquiries made upon and concerning the coal works at Whitehaven in the County of Cumberland in the year 1793', *Trans Royal Irish Academy*, v (1793), p. 272.

[37] SL 2 June, 10 Nov, 3 Dec 1732, 1 Dec 1734. LS 29 Mar 1733. Custom House Library 82/49 Collector to Customs Commissioners, 18 Jan 1738.

[38] SL 17 Jan 1739.

[39] LS 5 Jan 1738, 12 Feb 1754. SL 11 Jan 1738. Lewis, *Early Wooden Railways*, pp. 127, 158, 200. VCH *Cumberland*, ii, 362.

[40] Lewis, *Early Wooden Railways*, p. 129. Custom House Library 82/49 Collector to the Customs Commissioners, 18 Jan 1738.

[41] Figures derived from D/Lons/W Colliery Abstracts; Misc. Colliery Papers and Misc. Corresp. bundle 24.

[42] Langton, 'Landowners and the development of coal mining'.

[43] LS 24 Aug 1725.

[44] Lutwidge LB, Walter Lutwidge to Jeremiah Smith, 18 Jan 1747.

[45] D/Lons/W Colliery Account Books, Seaton Colliery Account 1727–32. SL 11 Mar, 10 July 1737, 27 Jan, 20 July 1744. Lutwidge LB, Walter Lutwidge to Jeremiah Smith, 4 Dec 1739.

[46] D/Lons/W Misc. Colliery Papers, 'Profit of Scalegill Colliery'.

[47] CRO D/Cu Compartment 10. SL 9 May 1736. LS 28 Dec 1751. VCH *Cumberland*, ii, 366. Hudleston, 'An 18th Century Squire', pp. 127–37.

[48] SL 5 Mar 1721, 12, 15 Mar 1727, 6 June 1729, 5 Apr 1730, 16 Mar 1735, 15 Feb 1738.

[49] PRO E/134/31 Charles II, Mich. no. 28. D/Lons/W box of misc. estate papers; MSS History of Whitehaven Collieries, note between fos. 74 and 75.

[50] D/Lons/W Sir John Lowther's Commonplace Book, f. 96. D/Lons/L Misc. Estate Books. SL 14 Feb 1728.

[51] PRO E/134/31 and 32 Charles II, Hilary no. 26. D/Lons/W Colliery Accounts, abstracts 1702. Custom House Library 82/49 Collector to Customs Commissioners, 27 Oct 1736. A. Eaglesham, 'The Growth and Influence of the West Cumberland Shipping Industry, 1660–1800' (unpublished University of Lancaster PhD thesis, 1977), p. 45.

[52] *Calculations Relating to the Coal Trade* (1721).

[53] D/Lons/W Estate Ledger 1737–58.

[54] Cullen, *Anglo-Irish Trade*, p. 122.

[55] SL 30 Nov 1739.

[56] SL 24 Apr 1745. D/Lons/W Estate Ledger 1737–58, f. 205.

[57] E. Hughes, *North Country Life in the Eighteenth Century: The North-East 1700–1750* (Oxford, 1952), p. 202. M. M. Schofield, 'The Statutory Register of British Merchant Ships for North Lancashire', *Trans Historic Society of Lancashire and Cheshire*, cx (1958), pp. 107–25.

[58] LS 22 Nov 1744.

[59] Hainsworth, *Commercial Papers*, p. 68.

[60] R. Davis, *The Rise of the English Shipping Industry* (1962), p. 208. D/Lons/W Unlisted Whitehaven papers, bundle 1674–1762.

[61] PRO E/190/1449/1.

[62] LS 28 Oct 1725.

[63] D/Lons/L William Brownrigg to Sir James Lowther, 29 Aug 1765.

[64] *Calculations.* SL 15 May 1720.

[65] JLLB Whitehaven Customs Commissioners to Sir John Lowther, 1 Dec 1684. SL 10, 13, 22 Apr 1716, 13 Apr 1720, 6 Oct 1725. LS 12 May 1724, 30 Sept 1725. D/Lons/W Unlisted Whitehaven papers, bundle of miscellaneous papers re-Whitehaven 1698–1724; Misc. Estate Memoranda Papers, 'An Exhortation to the Coal Owners'.

[66] LS 26 Feb 1726, 14 Apr 1736.

[67] D/Lons/L Brownrigg to Lowther, 29 Aug 1765.

[68] JLLB Sir John Lowther to Mr Calledon, May 1699.

[69] SL 7 Aug 1714, 8, 11, 18, 27 Jan, 26 Feb 1721. Lowther to the Owners and Masters of Vessels, 28 Jan 1721 (in a bundle of letters to Spedding, 1711–21). Whitehaven Public Library, MS Token Book vol. 1. *Calculations.*

[70] SL 24 May, 6, 17 Oct, 25, 27, 29 Nov 1723. LS 9, 19, 21, 23 Nov 1723, 13 Apr 1725.

[71] R. E. Tickell, *Thomas Tickell and the Eighteenth-Century Poets (1685–1740)* (1931), pp. 148–9, 153. SL 4 May 1729. This account is based on the letters between Lowther and Spedding, November 1728–January 1729.

[72] SL 7, 9 Feb, 4 May 1729. LS 13 Mar 1729, 4 Feb 1731.

[73] L. M. Cullen, *An Economic History of Ireland since 1660* (1972), pp. 49, 89.

[74] SL 24 Mar 1736, 8 Apr 1737.

[75] LS 22 Apr 1736, 3 Feb, 21 Apr 1737.

[76] D/Lons/W Estate Ledger 1737–58, fos. 202–3. SL 21 Jan, 17 Mar, 25 Apr 1736, 17 Apr 1737. LS 27, 29 Jan, 21 Apr 1737, 4 Dec 1735.

[77] LS 23 Dec 1735, 3 Jan, 22 Apr 1736. D/Lons/W Estate Ledger 1737–58.

[78] SL 10 Dec 1736, 9 Mar, 22 Apr 1737. CRO D/Cu Compartment 10, Account Book 1745–52. CRO D/Sen Cash Book 1749–62.

[79] SL 18 Mar 1743, 30 Sept 1744.

[80] LS 10, 12 Jan, 2 Feb 1749. Lutwidge LB, Walter Lutwidge to Sir James Lowther, 21 Jan 1749.

[81] D/Lons/W Estate Ledger 1737–58, fos. 202, 207–9.

[82] *Ibid.*, f. 200.

[83] JLLB Sir John Lowther to William Gilpin, 23 Jan, 29 Sept 1694, to Lord Carlisle, Jan 1701, to Lord Godolphin, n.d. *Cal Treas Bks.* iv (1672–5), p. 843. D/Lons/W Whitehaven papers, bundle 16; Estate Ledger 1706–22, f. 148; Cash Book 1720–22. SL 7 Dec 1726, 8 Nov 1727. LS 22 Dec 1726, 26, 28 Jan, 22 Apr, 25 May, 2 Nov 1727, 23 May 1728, 7 June 1737, 21 Nov 1742. Whitehaven Public Library MS 31, Account Book of Sir James Lowther.

[84] SL 12 Feb 1735.

[85] SL 29 Mar 1745.

[86] D/Lons/W Unlisted harbour papers, draft lease of 28 Dec 1752; Estate Ledger 1737–58, fos. 39–40.

[87] SL 30 Sept 1744.

[88] D/Lons/W Misc. Estate Memoranda Papers, James Lowther to Mr Burchett, 17 Feb 1726. LS 17 Feb 1726.

[89] LG 8 Dec 1711.

[90] LG 10, 14 Apr, 3 May 1711. LS 5, 10 Mar, 30 Apr, 7, 10, 14 May 1726, 21 Feb 1727. SL 1 Mar 1727.

[91] LS 27 Dec 1733, 26 Feb, 7, 12 Mar 1734.

[92] LS 5 Mar 1726, 5 Feb, 15 Mar 1740, 17 Feb 1741, 30 June 1743, 7 May 1747. SL 26 Feb, 14 Mar 1742, 30 Nov 1743. D/Lons/W Misc. Corresp. bundle 19, Sir James Lowther to Thomas Corbet, 11 Aug, 14 Sept 1746.

[93] D/Lons/W John Gale to Sir John Lowther, 25 Feb 1694, 9 May 1697. SL 1 May, 2 Aug 1706, 20 Aug 1710, 30 Mar 1712. PRO E/190/1450/15.

[94] SL 5 Mar 1718, 28 Mar, 4, 8, 27, 29 Apr, 6 June 1744, 9, 12 June 1745. LS 23 Mar 1727, 3, 10 Apr, 12 June 1744. D/Lons/W Estate Memoranda Papers, bundle 19.

[95] SL 15 Dec 1725. LS 21, 23 Dec 1725.

[96] Information courtesy of David Hayton.

[97] LG 13 July 1710. LS 22 Sept 1719. Lowther to the Masters, 19 Apr 1720 (copy in LS bundle).

[98] LS 19 Feb, 13, 15 Mar 1740, 3 Mar 1741, 5 Apr 1744, 19 May, 15 June 1749. Lutwidge LB, Walter Lutwidge to Sir James Lowther, 16 Mar 1740. *CJ* xxiii, 390, 468, 498, 399, 409. 13 Geo. II c.3, c.17.

[99] LG 30 Nov 1706, 27 July 1707, 5 Feb, 9 June 1713, 3 June 1719. D/Lons/W MSS History of Whitehaven Collieries, u.n. fos; Estate Memoranda Papers box 2, Lowther to Spedding, 6 Oct 1719. SL 6 Jan, 10 Apr 1720, 10 Mar 1721.

[100] LS 15 July 1725, 9 Jan, 15, 22 Feb, 3 Apr 1729, 10, 12, 26 Mar, 9 Apr 1730. SL 12 Feb, 7 Mar, 19, 28 Dec 1729, 1 Apr 1730. 3 Geo. II c. 34. *The Case of the Masters and Owners of Ships belonging to Whitehaven* (n.d.)

[101] Cullen, *Anglo-Irish Trade*, pp. 124–5. PRO CO 388/86 D15. 11 Anne c.4, 6 Geo. I c. 2. LS 29 Aug, 1 Sept, 19 Dec 1719, 26 Nov 1723, 2 Apr 1724. SL 22 Nov 1723. Lowther to the Masters, 19 Apr 1720 (copy in LS bundle).

[102] T. Bacon, *Some Reflections on the Coal Trade Humbly Addressed to Sir James Lowther* (1738).

[103] LS 11, 13 Mar 1729, 1 May 1740. 11 Geo. II c. 17.

[104] SL 12 Oct 1712. PRO E/190/1452/16.

[105] PRO E/190/1452/10, 1453/1.

[106] SL 18 Jan 1719, 13 Nov 1720, 18 Aug 1725. LS 4 Aug 1719, 14 Sept 1721, 9 Apr 1752.

[107] LS 7, 9 May, 4, 18 June 1723.

[108] SL 16 Nov 1744. LS 25 Oct, 5, 24 Nov, 1, 6 Dec 1748, 21 Feb, 2 Dec 1749, 9 Jan 1752, 5 May 1753, 7 Feb 1754. D/Lons/W Misc. Corresp. bundle 44, Sir James Lowther to M. Murphy, 25 Dec 1749.

[109] LS 7 Nov 1738, 13 Jan 1741. John Rylands Library, Bradshaigh MSS 47/2/467, 469, 470, Alexander Leigh to Sir Roger Bradshaigh, 5 Dec 1738, 6, 20 Apr 1739. Ashton and Sykes, p. 228.

[110] D/Lons/L Brownrigg to Lowther, 29 Aug 1765.

CHAPTER 4   THE EXPANSION OF TRADE

[1] W. Parson and W. White, *History, Directory and Gazeteer of the Counties of Cumberland and Westmorland* (Leeds, 1829), p. 246. Custom House Library, Whitehaven letter books, 19 July 1820, cited in J. E. Williams, 'Whitehaven in the Eighteenth Century', *EcHR*, 2nd series, viii (1956), pp. 402–3.

[2] JLLB Sir John Lowther to William Gilpin, 8 Mar 1698.

[3] T. S. Willan, *The English Coasting Trade 1600–1750* (Manchester, 1938), pp. 68ff, 197ff.

[4] CRO D/Lons/Le Fleming MSS, Thomas Denton's *History* 1687–8, p. 29. Except where indicated otherwise, statistical information used in this chapter relating to trade is taken from the Port Books (for full details of which see the bibliography).

[5] R. Davis, *A Commercial Revolution* (1967).

[6] P. G. E. Clemens, 'The Rise of Liverpool, 1665–1750', *EcHR*, 2nd series, xxix (1976), pp. 211–25.

[7] D/Lons/W William Gilpin to Sir John Lowther, 1 Nov 1697. *Cal Treas Bks*, xxiv (1710), 151, 179. Custom House Library 82/47 Collector to Customs Commissioners, 18 July 1718, 82/49 27 Oct 1736. LG 10 May, 2 June 1711. LS 29 Sept 1743.

[8] *Cal State Papers Colonial* (America and West Indies), 1685–8, pp. 175–7. D. C. Coleman, *The Economy of England 1450–1750* (Oxford, 1977), pp. 144–5.

[9] T. C. Smout, *Scottish Trade on the Eve of the Union, 1660–1707* (1963), pp. 175–7. J. M. Price, *France and the Chesapeake* (Ann Arbor, 1973), p. 595.

[10] JLLB Whitehaven Customs Officials to the Customs Commissioners, 20 Jan 1691. PRO E/190/1448/8. Davis, *Shipping Industry*, p. 38. D/Lons/W Sir John Lowther's Commonplace Book, fos. 1, 50.

[11] *Cal Treas Bks*, xxv (1711), p. 268; xxiv (1710), p. 179.

[12] D/Lons/W Unlisted Whitehaven papers, bundle 1698–1724. The average import between 1698 and 1702 was 1,510,047 lbs, and not 1·4m as Price, *France*, p. 595, states.

[13] Custom House Library 82/47 Collector to Customs Commissioners, 13 May 1721. SL 11 June 1721.

[14] *The Case of the Merchants Trading in Tobacco at Whitehaven in the County of Cumberland* (1720). *Cal Treas Papers* (1720–8), p. 116. LS 5 Feb 1723, 29 Dec 1724. SL 5 Jan, 16 Feb 1724, 18 Aug, 22 Oct 1725, 31 Mar 1727. Price, *France*, p. 590.

[15] J. M. Price, 'The Economic Growth of the Chesapeake and the European Market, 1697–1775', *Journal of Economic History*, xxiv (1964), pp. 496–516. SL 30 Apr 1740). Custom House Library 82/49 Collector to Customs Commissioners, 1 Oct 1740.

[16] The best account is Price, *France*.

[17] LS 27 Jan, 16 June 1743. SL 10 Apr 1745.

[18] Hutton, 'A Lakeland Journey', p. 292. LS 21 Feb 1751. Pennant, *Scotland*, ii, 47.

[19] CRO D/Lons/Le Fleming MSS, Thomas Denton's *History* 1687–8.

[20] D/Lons/W William Gilpin to Sir John Lowther, 17 Jan 1694.

[21] JLLB Sir John Lowther to Mr Serjeson, 29 Apr 1700, Feb 1703, to Mr Lyddal, Feb 1703, to Sir Ben Ayloff, Feb 1703. *CJ* xxiii, 460. SL 25 Mar 1744. LS 24 June 1721. D/Lons/W Misc. Estate Books, 'James Spedding's Description . . .'.

[22] SL 4, 29 Mar 1724, 11 June 1721, 8 Mar, 5 Apr 1730. LS 4 May 1732, 26 Jan 1749.

[23] LS 23 Oct, 1 Dec 1753.

[24] D/Lons/W James Lowther to Sir John Lowther, 16 Oct 1703. LG 29 Apr 1707.

[25] D/Lons/W James Lowther to Sir John Lowther, 2 May 1699. LG 10 May, 2 June 1711, 9 June 1713. LS 23 Mar 1745, 28 Dec 1748, 27 Apr 1749. D/Lons/W Misc. Corresp. bundle 44, Sir James Lowther to Peter How, 18 May 1751.

[26] JLLB Sir John Lowther to James Lowther, 21 Aug 1701. LS 16 Dec 1731, 12 May 1753, 14 Mar 1745. SL 1, 29 May 1745.

[27] LS 24 June, 15 July 1725, 24 May 1733.

[28] D/Lons/W Estate Ledger 1737–58, fos. 197, 220.

[29] D/Lons/W Cash Book 1726–8, entries of 12, 31 Oct 1726; Estate Ledger 1723–37 f. 129, 1737–58, f. 211; Estate Memoranda Papers box 2, 'A List of Securities . . .'. LS 2 Apr 1748. SL 4 Oct 1723, 3 Apr 1745.

[30] D/Lons/W Whitehaven Papers, bundle 88. SL 2 Oct 1741, 20 Jan, 1 Feb 1738. LS 24 May, 23 July 1737, 22 Sept 1738, 12 Mar 1741. Lutwidge LB, Walter Lutwidge to Robert Herries, 18 Jan 1741. Hughes, *Cumberland and Westmorland*, p. 29.

[31] LS 15 Jan, 5 Nov 1742. *London Daily Advertizer*, 6 Oct 1772, cited in Price, *France*, p. 602.

[32] CRO D/Ben/624/4.

[33] Carlisle Library, Gale Family Wills.

[34] LS 19 Oct 1754.

[35] SL 23 Feb 1735, 28 Apr, 2 May 1736, 28 Jan 1739, 28 Dec 1744, 3 Apr 1745. LS 23, 27 Mar 1736, 12 May 1747. D/Lons/W Estate Ledger 1723–37, f. 137.

[36] LS 28 May, 16 July 1751, 13 Mar 1753.

[37] PRO E/134/31 Geo. II Hilary no. 7. Price, *France*, pp. 601–2.

[38] G. Jackson, *Hull in the Eighteenth Century* (Hull, 1972), pp. 111–12. T. Devine, *The Tobacco Lords* (Edinburgh, 1975), chapter 5a.

[39] PRO B1/43/272.

[40] SL 26 June 1737, 25 May 1739, 9 Nov 1740, 11 Jan 1741. LS 24 Jan 1741. Lutwidge LB, Walter Lutwidge to John Thomson, 10 Aug 1740, to Col. Earle, 12 Nov 1740.

[41] D/Lons/W Estate Ledger 1737–58, f. 210. LS 2, 13, 16 Oct 1750, 24 Jan 1751.

[42] D/Lons/W Misc. Estate Books, 'James Spedding's Description . . .'. Price, *France*, p. 602.

[43] LS 6 Apr 1749. *Cal Treas Bks*, xvi (1702), p. 158. Custom House Library 82/47 Collector to Customs Commissioners, 7 Aug 1719, 2 Jan 1723, 82/42, 4 Dec 1730. 82/49, 28 Dec 1734, 6 Dec 1735, 23 Sept 1737.

[44] LG 12 Jan 1716, 21 Dec 1717, 13 Jan 1719. LS 13 Jan 1726, 10 Jan 1727, 7, 11 Jan 1729, 31 Jan 1734. SL 16 Jan 1729.

[45] W. R. Ward, *The English Land Tax in the Eighteenth Century* (Oxford, 1953), p. 108. LS 29 Jan 1740, 19 Jan, 26 May, 26, 29 Nov 1743, 5 Dec 1730.

[46] SL 13 Nov 1726. LS 8 Nov 1726. Lutwidge LB, Walter Lutwidge to Sir James Lowther, 12 Nov 1739. Price, *France*, p. 598.

[47] SL 4 Jan 1745, 2 Feb 1743. LS 8 Feb, 2 Apr, 2 June 1743. Whitehaven Public Library MS 31, Account Book of John Spedding. Hoare's Bank, ledger T, f. 214.

CHAPTER 5   THE DEVELOPMENT OF INDUSTRY

[1] Parson and White, p. 246.
[2] LS 3 June 1721. *Considerations Relating to the Coal Trade* (1721).
[3] D. J. Rowe, 'The Chronology of the Onset of Industrialization in North-East England', in M. Palmer (ed), *The Onset of Industrialization* (Nottingham, 1977). B. Trinder, *The Industrial Revolution in Shropshire* (Chichester, 1977).
[4] *Cumberland Pacquet*, 26 Aug 1851. D/Lons/W Estate Memoranda Books, 'Register', Inhabitants of Whitehaven 1702. 1762 Census (copy in CRO). CRO D/Ben/3481 Maryport Census. Bouch and Jones, pp. 217, 318.
[5] F. E. Hyde, *Liverpool and the Mersey 1700–1970* (Newton Abbot, 1971), p. 21. C. Northcote Parkinson, *The Rise of Liverpool* (Liverpool, 1952), p. 109. W. E. Minchinton (ed), *The Trade of Bristol in the Eighteenth Century* (Bristol, 1957), p. ix.
[6] Jones, 'Some Population Problems', p. 127.
[7] Dickinson MSS.
[8] P. Clark, 'Migration in England during the late seventeenth and early eighteenth centuries', *Past and Present*, 83 (1979), p. 72. P. Deane and W. A. Cole, *British Economic Growth 1688–1959* (2nd edn, Cambridge, 1967), pp. 120–2.
[9] Tickell, *Thomas Tickell*, pp. 148–9.
[10] SL 10 Apr 1726.
[11] Rowe, 'The Chronology', p. 63. Joyce M. Ellis, 'A Study of the Business Fortunes of William Cotesworth, 1668–1726' (unpublished University of Oxford PhD thesis, 1976), pp. 12–13, 139ff. Devine, *Tobacco Lords*, pp. 34ff.
[12] D/Lons/W John Gale to Sir John Lowther, 21 Mar 1697. LS 12 Apr 1735, 21 Jan 1720.
[13] PRO E/190/1449/1.
[14] JLLB Sir John Lowther to William Gilpin, 10 Aug 1697, 29 Sept 1694. D/Lons/W William Gilpin to Sir John Lowther, 27 June, 27 Oct 1694.
[15] SL 14 July 1725. LS 20 July 1725.
[16] J. V. Beckett, 'The Eighteenth-Century Origins of the Factory System: a Case Study from the 1740s', *Business History*, xix (1977), pp. 55–67.
[17] T. C. Barker, 'Lancashire Coal, Cheshire Salt and the Rise of Liverpool', *Trans Historic Society of Lancashire and Cheshire*, ciii (1951), p. 92. SL 3 Mar, 21 Nov 1736.
[18] *Cal State Papers Dom* (1693), p. 114. *The Case of Sir John Lowther* (1705).
[19] LS 2 Apr 1737, 11 Feb, 20 Apr 1738.
[20] LS 28 Sept 1736, 27 Sept 1738, 2 Jan 1739.
[21] T. M. Devine, 'Colonial Commerce and the Scottish Economy, c.1730–1815', in Cullen and Smout, pp. 177–90. Clemens, 'Rise of Liverpool', p. 217. Jackson, *Hull*, chapter 2.
[22] LS 26 Feb 1737.
[23] CRO D/Lec/17/126; Box 170, Thomas Simpson to Thomas Elder, 26 Nov 1747. D/Lons/W Sir John Lowther's Commonplace Book, f. 139; Cash Book 1692–3. JLLB Sir John Lowther to William Gilpin, 2 Apr 1698. SL 1 Oct 1708. Kendall, 'Notes on the History', p. 87. H. A. Fletcher, 'The Archaeology of the West Cumberland Iron Trade', *CWI*, v (1879–80), pp. 18–19. For Furness see Marshall, *Furness*.

24 Fletcher, 'Iron Trade', pp. 10, 19–20. CRO D/Lec/170, Thomas Simpson to Thomas Elder, 26 Nov 1747.
25 C. B. Phillips, 'The Cumbrian Iron Industry in the Seventeenth Century', in W. H. Chaloner and B. M. Ratcliffe (eds), *Trade and Transport* (Manchester, 1977), p. 4. H. R. Schubert, *History of the British Iron and Steel Industry* (1957), p. 371. D/Lons/W Sir John Lowther to Thomas Tickell, 15 Oct 1681, 21 Apr 1685, 18 Aug, 3 Nov 1688; William Gilpin to Lowther, 2 Nov 1694, 16 June 1697; John Gale to Lowther, 21 Mar 1697. JLLB Sir John Lowther to Dr Lister, 29 Sept 1698. Bouch and Jones, p. 130.
26 Fletcher, 'Iron Trade', p. 5. See also John MacKellar Main's article on the iron industry in VCH *Cumberland*, ii, 385, for the dismissive view.
27 SL 7 Apr 1736. W. H. Chaloner, 'Isaac Wilkinson, Potfounder', in L. S. Pressnell (ed), *Studies in the Industrial Revolution* (1960), pp. 23–51. Bouch and Jones, pp. 252–4.
28 L. B. Namier, 'Anthony Bacon MP, an Eighteenth-Century Merchant', *Journal of Economic and Business History*, ii (1929–30), pp. 20–70. C. K. Hyde, *Technological Change and the British Iron Industry 1700–1970* (Princeton, 1977), p. 77.
29 D/Lons/W Colliery Papers, bundle 30, agreement of 20 May 1734. SL 30 Aug 1723, 24 Nov 1728, 18 Apr 1736, 9 Jan 1737. LS 13 Apr, 22 Sept 1736, 7 Mar 1752. Lutwidge LB, Walter Lutwidge to James Kilhouse, 25 Nov 1739.
30 SL 8 Feb 1738.
31 PRO PC1/4/106, f. 50.
32 This account of the Woods' project is based on J. M. Treadwell, 'William Wood and the Company of Ironmasters of Great Britain', *Business History*, xvi (1974), the Lowther/Spedding correspondence (not used by Treadwell), and PRO PC1/4/106.
33 *A Letter from a Merchant at Whitehaven to his Friend in London* (c.1730).
34 D/Lons/W Colliery Abstracts.
35 SL 1 Nov 1728.
36 LS 28 Dec 1727.
37 LS 29, 31 Jan 1730, 11 May 1731. D/Lons/W Estate Ledger 1723–37, f. 136. SPCK CR1/15/10899, 10918, 10934, James Lowther to Henry Newman, 26 Aug, 9, 27 Sept 1730.
38 CRO D/Ben/596/4; D/Lec/16A, Box 240, 'Peter How's Accounts'. LS 1 Nov 1750, 23 Nov, 24 Dec 1751, 22 Feb 1752.
39 CRO D/Lec/16A; D/Ben/624/4. D/Lons/W Misc. Corresp. bundle 44, Sir James Lowther to Peter How, 2 June 1753, (another letter, of 22 Nov 1750, with the LS correspondence). LS 13 Nov 1750, 1, 19, 23 Nov, 12 Dec 1751, 22, 25 Feb 1752, 3 Mar, 2, 16, 26 June 1753, 2, 19 Mar, 7, 17 Dec 1754. Hyde, *Technological Change*, p. 54.
40 Fletcher, 'Iron Trade', pp. 11–13. LS 21 May 1752. H. R. Schubert, 'The Old Blast Furnace at Maryport, Cumberland', *Journal of the Iron and Steel Institute*, 172 (1953), p. 162.
41 LS 4, 23 Mar 1738.
42 Hyde, *Technological Change*, p. 19. LS 20 July 1725, 3, 24 Dec 1734, 22 Sept, 25 Nov 1736, 4 Jan 1737, 2, 13 Jan, 19 May 1739, 30 Mar 1742, 30 Dec 1742. SL 14 July, 22 Oct 1725, 19 Feb 1738, 13 May, 5, 14 Oct 1739, 18 Oct 1741, 9 Apr 1742.
43 CRO D/Pen/Agents' Correspondence, Sir William Pennington to Sir William Fleming, 14 Aug 1718, Pennington to Joseph Pennington, 14 Aug 1718.
44 LS 12 Apr 1735, 14, 18 Nov, 12 Dec 1738, 26 Jan 1748. SL 6 Dec 1738.

D/Lons/W MSS History of Whitehaven Collieries, fos. 106ff. See also appendix 3, section 6.

[45] W. R. Scott, *The Constitution and Finance of English, Scottish and Irish Joint-Stock Companies to 1720* (1912), ii, 437. H. Hamilton, *The English Brass and Copper Industries* (2nd edn, 1967), pp. 20–31, 54–5, 101–5. J. R. Harris, *The Copper King* (Liverpool, 1964), p. 5. D/Lons/W William Gilpin to Sir John Lowther, 16 June, 24 July, 2, 4 Sept 1697. JLLB Sir John Lowther to Dr Lister, 29 Sept 1698, to the Duke of Somerset, 5 Oct 1699.

[46] LS 20 June 1721.

[47] SL 29 Oct 1740, 19 May 1742.

[48] LS 21 Apr 1737, 15 May, 1 Dec 1739, 17, 19 Apr, 1 May 1740, 3, 9 June 1742, 14 June, 9, 28 July, 10 Dec 1743, 19 Apr, 23 Aug 1744, 22 May, 12 June 1746. SL 19 May 1742, 5 June 1745. W. J. Lewis, *Lead Mining in Wales* (Cardiff, 1967), p. 100.

[49] W. Brownrigg, *The Art of Making Common Salt* (1748).

[50] Phillips, 'The Gentry in Cumberland and Westmorland', p. 203. LS 23 Dec 1749. CRO D/Lec/113, 115. D/Lons/W Sir John Lowther to Thomas Tickell, 17 Dec 1689, Tickell to Lowther, 29 July 1691; Estate Ledger 1692–8, f. 20; William Gilpin to Sir John Lowther, 31 Oct 1696, 25 Jan, 3, 24 Feb, 21 Apr, 12, 19 May 1697. JLLB Sir John Lowther to Mr Beech, 14 Oct 1700. Barker, 'Lancashire Coal', pp. 88–9.

[51] *Cal Treas Bks*, xxix (1714–15), p. 107. SL 22 Dec 1725, 20 Apr 1729. CRO D/Ben/549h; D/Lec/16A.

[52] E. Hughes, *Studies in Administration and Finance 1558–1825* (Manchester, 1934), p. 409n. SL 11 Nov 1722, 15 Dec 1725.

[53] LS 16 Nov 1734, 20 Mar 1736. SL 20 Nov 1734, 5 Mar, 6, 18 Apr, 7, 14, 16 May 1735, 3 Mar, 21 Nov 1736. D/Lons/W Estate Rental 1754.

[54] LS 9 Mar 1736, 3 Apr 1740. SL 8 Feb 1738. 'Clerk', p. 313.

[55] D/Lons/W Estate Ledger 1737–58, f. 203; Colliery Account Books, Mich. 1748. *Gentleman's Magazine*, xviii (1748), p. 5.

[56] D/Lons/W William Gilpin to Sir John Lowther, 4, 23 Sept, 27 Oct 1697, 14 Mar 1698; Misc. Corresp. bundle 14, Lowther to Gilpin, 2 Nov 1697. JLLB Lowther to Gilpin, 18 Jan, 22 Mar, 12, 16 Apr, 7, 28 May 1698.

[57] D/Lons/W Misc. Estate Papers, 'Copperas work at Gins'; Estate Ledger 1723–37, f. 142, 1737–58 f. 153. LG 16 May 1719. LS 9, 12 Mar, 11 May 1723. SL 1 Mar 1724. LS 11 Jan 1743.

[58] Cartwright, *Pococke*, p. 17.

[59] JLLB Sir John Lowther to William Gilpin, 29 Sept 1694, 5, 12 Apr 1698. LS 24 Aug 1706 (in Spedding letter books).

[60] LG 14 Apr 1713, 10 Sept, 29 Oct 1715, 16 Dec 1718, 21 Feb, 21 Mar 1719. SL 8 Mar, 21 May, 3 Dec 1721. D/Lons/W Colliery Account Books, Lady Day 1722/3.

[61] LS 12 Sept 1723, 15 Aug, 6 Oct 1725, 1 Jan, 21 May 1729. D/Lons/W Misc. Estate Papers, James Lowther to John Brougham, 29 July 1725.

[62] LS 19 Dec 1730, 25 Nov 1732, 29 Apr, 16 Dec 1735, 23 Mar 1736. SL 13 Dec 1734, 4 May, 18 Nov, 10 Dec 1735, 20 Mar 1737.

[63] LS 26 Mar 1734, 14 Feb, 20 Apr 1736, 21, 23 Nov, 30 Dec 1738, 30 Jan, 19 Apr, 3 May, 18 Oct 1739. SL 8, 15 Feb, 11 Apr 1736, 20, 22 Dec 1738, 3 Jan 1739. Whitehaven Public Library MS 31, Account Book of Sir James Lowther, entry of 7 Apr 1739.

[64] LS 4 Dec 1740, 28 Apr, 26 May, 9 June 1745. SL 28 Nov 1740. D/Lons/W Colliery Papers, bundle 21, 'Memorandums concerning the Glass House';

Estate Rentals 1741, 1754. Lutwidge LB, Walter Lutwidge to Jeremiah Smith, 18 Jan 1747.
65 CRO D/Sen Day Book, 1726–36.
66 CRO D/Lec/16A.
67 D/Lons/W Colliery Papers, bundle 30.
68 LS 5 Feb 1732, 4 Jan 1737.
69 W. E. Minchinton, 'Bristol – Metropolis of the West in the Eighteenth Century', *Trans Royal Hist. Soc.* 5th series, iv (1954), pp. 69–89. Jackson, *Hull*, chapter 2. Clemens, 'Rise of Liverpool', p. 217.
70 A. Slaven, *The development of the west of Scotland, 1750–1960* (1975), pp. 5, 36–8. A. J. Durie, *The Scottish Linen Industry in the Eighteenth Century* (Edinburgh, 1979), p. 145.
71 D/Lons/W William Gilpin to Sir John Lowther, 14 Nov 1696. Hughes, *Cumberland and Westmorland*, pp. 31–2.
72 CRO Lawson MSS, Journal of a Cockermouth Merchant
73 Marshall, 'Kendal', p. 221. T. Pennant, *A Tour in Scotland 1769* (Chester 1771), p. 219. Bouch and Jones, pp. 137, 263.
74 JLLB Sir John Lowther to Thomas Addison, 25 Sept 1686, to Thomas Tickell, 7 Dec 1686, 19 Nov 1687, to William Gilpin, 14 June 1698. D/Lons/W Sir John Lowther's Commonplace Book, f. 109. *Reasons for Opening the Port of Whitehaven for Importing Irish Wool* (n.d.).
75 18 & 19 Car. II c. 2. 7 & 8 William III c. 28.
76 JLLB Sir John Lowther to Richard Stainton, 11 Sept 1697.
77 *Ibid.*, 11 Jan 1698, to William Gilpin 19 Mar, 2 Apr 1698. D/Lons/W Cash Book 1693–9; Misc. Corresp. bundle 44a, Richard Stainton to Sir John Lowther, 26 June 1698.
78 D/Lons/W James Lowther to Sir John Lowther, 8, 15 Apr, 2 May 1699; Cash Books, Thomas Benn's account 1699–1700. JLLB Sir John Lowther to Lady Lonsdale, 27 June 1701, to Mr Addison, 1701, to William Gilpin, 14, 25 June, 5 July 1698.
79 D/Lons/W Housekeeping accounts, 1729–39. SL 16 Feb 1724, 20 Feb 1737. LS 29 Feb 1724, 26 Feb 1737.
80 *Reasons for Opening the Port.*
81 D/Lons/W Misc. Corresp. bundle 44, 'Sir James Lowther's Paper for exciting the Lords and Gentlemen to Encourage Manufactures'. LS 20 Feb 1752.
82 *To the Author of a Scheme for improving and extending the Woolen Manufactures of the County of Cumberland* (1752).
83 D/Lons/W Misc. Corresp. bundle 44, Sir James Lowther to Humphrey Senhouse, 21 May 1752. LS 14, 21 May 1752, 24, 27 Feb 1753. 26 Geo. II c. 11.
84 LG 29 Nov, 16 Dec 1712, 1 Jan 1713. LS 30 Apr 1726. SL 21 Apr 1728, 27 July 1743. D/Lons/W Colliery Ledger 3, 1727–32, various entries. PRO E/190/1460/4, 8.
85 Custom House Library 82/47 Collector to Customs Commissioners, 18 July 1718, 82/42, 28 Dec 1733. D/Lons/W Estate Memoranda Books, green-covered book with articles of agreement, 15 Oct 1735. Price, *France*, pp. 601–2.
86 D/Lons/W Misc. Estate Books, 'James Spedding's Description . . .'.
87 D/Lons/W Whitehaven Papers, bundles 14 and 15; Misc. Corresp. bundle 40, memoranda to Thomas Tickell 1682; Estate Ledger 1692–8 f. 125; William Gilpin to Sir John Lowther, 25 June 1693; John Gale to Sir John Lowther, 3, 31 Jan, 21 Mar 1697. JLLB Sir John Lowther to William Gilpin, 11 Jan 1698. D/Lons/W Misc. Estate Memoranda Books, 'E.H.'
88 SL 9 Apr 1740. LS 22 Nov, 16 Dec 1746, 6 Jan, 10 Nov 1747. Lutwidge LB,

Walter Lutwidge to Sir James Lowther, 2 Jan 1747, to Jeremiah Smith, 12 Jan 1747, 12 July 1749. D/Lons/W Estate Ledger 1737–58, f. 37. CRO DX/448/14 Millbeck Estate Accounts.

89 Coleman, *Economy of England*, p. 165. JLLB Book of Notes, Letters &c 1675–86, f. 5. D/Lons/W John Gale to Sir John Lowther, 26 Dec 1697. SL 7 Sept 1712, 1 Feb 1713, 20 Sept 1721. LS 2 Nov 1723, 14 Dec 1736.

90 Davis, *Shipping Industry*, p. 35.

91 D/Lons/W William Gilpin to Sir John Lowther, 13 Sept 1696. SL 7 Sept 1712, 1 Feb 1713, 20 Sept 1721.

92 D/Lons/W Estate Ledger 1737–58, f. 219. SL 25 Jan 1740. PRO E/190/1460/4, 8.

93 D/Lons/W Estate Ledger 1737–58, f. 60. LS 9 Dec 1736, 19 May 1739, 19 Mar 1741. PRO Adm. 66/106, letters 1737–41, fos. 416, 417, 421, 430, 449. Eaglesham, 'The Growth and Influence', p. 210.

94 LS 14 July 1744, 3 Apr, 19 June, 20 Nov, 11 Dec 1746, 7 Jan, 2 Mar 1749, 30 Apr, 15 Sept, 18 Dec 1750, 7 Dec 1754. D/Lons/W Estate Ledger 1737–58, fos. 59–60; Estate Memoranda Books, green-covered book fos. 190–1. Brown LB, Carlisle Spedding to William Brown, 3 Mar 1751.

95 LS 7 Dec 1754. Hutchinson, *Cumberland*, ii, 83. Davis, *Shipping Industry*, p. 70.

96 D/Lons/W Estate Ledger 1737–58, fos. 36, 50–9; 1723–37, fos. 61–2, 67; Accounts, Sir John Lowther 1700; Cash Book 4 (1714–17), 5 (1717–20); Estate Rental 1754; Various Accounts 1705–77, 'Buildings'. LS 14 Feb 1738, 14 Oct 1739.

97 D/Lons/W William Gilpin to Sir John Lowther, 14 Feb 1698.

98 JLLB Sir John Lowther to William Gilpin, 25 Jan 1698. D/Lons/W Estate Ledger 1723–37, fos. 73–4; 1737–58, f. 154; Estate Rental 1754. LS 30 Jan 1735. SL 5 Feb 1735. Brown LB, Carlisle Spedding to William Brown, 18 Sept 1751.

99 JLLB Sir John Lowther to John Gale, 28 July 1688, to Thomas Tickell, 18 Aug 1688, to William Gilpin, 10 Aug 1697, to Mr Stainton, 11 Sept 1697. D/Lons/W William Gilpin to Sir John Lowther, 12, 23 June, 25 Aug 1697, 17 Feb 1698.

100 LS 21 Feb 1734.

101 A. M. Samuel, *The Herring* (1918), pp. 129–33. LS 10, 12 Apr, 1 May, 13 Dec 1750, 21 Dec 1751.

102 LS 31 Dec 1751, 28 May, 9, 14, 25 Nov 1752, 5 May 1753, 18 Apr, 31 Dec 1754. Brown LB, Carlisle Spedding to William Brown, 20 Mar 1752. W. Serjeant, 'A Whitehaven–Isle of Man fishing dispute in 1753', *CW2*, lvii (1957), pp. 173–84.

103 JLLB Sir John Lowther to William Gilpin, 21 Aug 1697, 25 Jan, 8 Mar 1698. D/Lons/W William Gilpin to Sir John Lowther, 2 Mar 1698; Misc. Corresp. bundle 44, licence to Abel Robinson, 6 Dec 1698; Various Accounts 1705–77, 'Buildings'; Estate Ledger 1706–22, f. 62; Cash Books, 1693–9 (entry of 6 Jan 1699), 3 (1711–13), 4 (1714–17), various entries; Estate Ledger 1737–58, f. 86; Colliery Abstracts, coal sales to the pot house.

104 SL 24 Sept 1714, 11 Mar 1730, 4 Nov 1741. LS 5 Mar 1730, 3 Apr 1736, 5, 15 Mar 1743. D/Lons/W Estate Ledger 1737–58, fos. 36, 219; Housekeeping Accounts 1750–55.

CHAPTER 6 COMMUNICATIONS

1 A. H. Dodd, *The Industrial Revolution in North Wales* (3rd edn, Cardiff, 1971), p. ix. Trinder, *Industrial Revolution in Shropshire*, p. 150. Barker, 'Lancashire Coal' p. 93.

2 LS 13 Oct 1744.

3 D. Swann, 'The Pace and Progress of Port Development in England, 1660–1830', *Yorkshire Bulletin*, xii (1960), pp. 35–6.

4 *Reasons for Opening the Port of Whitehaven*. . . .

5 Nef, *Rise of the British Coal Industry*, i, p. 70.

6 *Cal State Papers Irish* (1633–47), p. 12. PRO E/134/31 & 32 Charles II, Hilary, no. 26. D/Lons/W Whitehaven Papers, bundles 5, 6a, 7, 19, 20.

7 PRO E/134/31 & 32 Charles II, Hilary no. 26. R. C. Jarvis, 'The Appointment of Ports in Cumberland, Westmorland and Lancashire north-of-the-Sands', *CW2*, xlvii (1947), pp. 128–65.

8 D/Lons/W Whitehaven Papers, bundles 6a, 7, 20.

9 *Ibid.*, bundle 19; John Gale to Sir John Lowther, 3 Jan 1697.

10 D/Lons/W William Gilpin to Sir John Lowther, 29 Nov 1696, 5 Jan 1698; John Gale to Sir John Lowther, 16 Jan 1698.

11 D/Lons/W William Gilpin to Sir John Lowther, 17 Aug 1693, 21 Nov 1695, 6 June 1696, 25 Jan 1697; John Gale to Sir John Lowther, 8 Sept 1695; James Lowther's 'Advice to his Heirs'.

12 *The Case of Sir John Lowther*.

13 D/Lons/W James Lowther to Sir John Lowther, 2, 4, 16 Nov 1704, 7 July, 22 Sept 1705 and subsequent letters; Misc. Corresp. bundle 44, Thomas Lamplugh and Thomas Fletcher to Sir John Lowther, 23 June 1705. HMC *House of Lords MSS*, vi (N.S.), pp. 398–402. 4 Anne, c. 18.

14 LS 10 June 1707.

15 LS 24 Apr 1707 (in Spedding letter book). *CJ* xvi. 28, 38, 153, 170. 7 Anne, c. 9.

16 10 Anne, c. 17.

17 D/Lons/W Harbour Trustees Minutes, elections of 3 Aug 1722 and 7 Aug 1752.

18 D/Lons/W Estate Ledger 1723–37, f. 127; 1737–58, fos. 213, 220; Harbour Trustees Minutes, meetings of 10 June 1740, 26 Aug 1741, 19 Mar, 4 Aug 1743, 5 Apr 1753; Whitehaven Papers, bundle 24.

19 Lutwidge LB, Walter Lutwidge to Sir James Lowther, 12 Apr 1740.

20 SL 18 Feb 1711, 23 Apr, 6 July 1712, 18 May 1718, LG 3 Apr 1712.

21 SL 2 Nov 1707.

22 LG 6 Sept 1707, 24 Jan 1708, 14 June, 3 Sept 1715, 17 Jan 1716. LS 18 Apr, 6 Aug 1717. SL 28 Aug, 7 Sept 1715, 11 Jan 1716, 1 Sept 1717, 3 Dec 1718. D/Lons/W James Lowther's 'Advice to his Heirs'.

23 LG 2 Feb, 6, 13 Mar 1716. LS 18 Apr, 6 Aug 1717, 9, 20 July 1719. SL 7, 14 Mar 1716. *The Miserable Case of the poor Inhabitants of Parton* . . . (1716).

24 LG 17 Nov, 29 Dec 1719, 23 Jan 1720. LS 3 Aug, 17 Sept, 10 Dec 1723, 8, 13, Dec 1722. SL 10 Apr 1721, 23 Feb 1723. Custom House Library 82/47 Collector to Customs Commissioners, 9 Sept 1720.

25 D/Lons/L Check List 16/11 Lord Lonsdale to James Lowther, 20 Oct 1721.

26 LS 6 July 1721, 22 Aug 1723.

27 LS 1 Nov, 6, 18 Dec 1722, 12, 26 Jan, 26 Feb, 16 Mar, 21 May, 23 Nov 1723, 30 Jan 1725. SL 23 Jan 1723. D/Lons/W Parton Harbour Papers, Thomas Lutwidge to James Lowther, 23 Jan 1722; 'Lamplugh v Lowther', William Gilpin to ?, 27 Jan 1722.

28 SL 16 Apr, 11 Aug 1721, 9 Aug, 6, 8, 13, 15 Sept, 25 Dec 1723, 4 Aug, 1 Oct 1725, 4, 6, 8, 28 May, 2, 11 Dec 1726. LS 21 Apr 1721, 7 Mar, 7, 9 May, 3 Sept 1723, 6, 19 Nov 1724, 28 Jan, 25 Feb, 2, 11, 13, 16, 23, 25, 30 Mar, 6, 13 Apr 1725. D/Lons/W Misc. Estate Papers, Parton Trustees, 13 Mar 1725, James Lowther to John Brougham, 29 July, 10 Aug 1725.

29 LS 30 Apr 1726, 30 Dec 1727, 30 Jan, 9, 18 Feb 1731, 15 Jan, 3 Feb, 21 Dec

1732, 10 May 1733, 21 Mar 1734. SL 4 May 1726, 24 Jan 1733. D/Lons/W Misc. Estate Papers, Sir James Lowther to Henry Curwen, 27 July 1725.

[30] LS 31 Dec 1726, 9 Feb 1727, 27 Feb 1731. SL 13, 16, 18 Dec 1726, 23 Apr 1727. *CJ* xxi, 789, 866, 890, 939. 5 Geo. II c. 13.

[31] LS 15 May 1733, 1 May 1735. D/Lons/W Estate Ledger 1723–37, f. 127. *CJ*, xxiii, 433, 460–1, 475, 508, 530. 13 Geo. II c. 14.

[32] LS 30 Dec 1742, 22 Oct, 19 Nov 1747. SL 10 Dec 1740, 24 Oct, 17, 22, 24 Dec 1742, 2, 5 Jan, 20, 25 Feb, 6, 25 Mar, 17 Aug 1743.

[33] LS 1 June 1749, 24 Oct 1754. Brown LB, Carlisle Spedding to William Brown, 3 Mar 1751, 22 Nov 1752, 5 Apr 1753.

[34] D/Lons/W Harbour Trustees' Minutes, meetings of 20 Dec 1750, 18 Sept 1752. LS 10 Jan, 2 Feb, 4, 11 June, 22, 24, 29 Oct 1751, 9 June 1752.

[35] Lutwidge LB, Walter Lutwidge to Sir James Lowther, 24 May 1747. Fletcher, 'Iron Trade', p. 20. D/Lons/W Estate Ledger 1737–58, f. 214.

[36] LS 17 Jan, 14 Feb, 4 Apr 1751. Brown LB, Carlisle Spedding to William Brown, 3 Mar 1751. Pennant, *Scotland*, ii, 51. Nicolson and Burn, ii, 49. W. Whellan, *The History and Topography of the Counties of Cumberland and Westmorland* (Pontefract, 1860), p. 422.

[37] D/Lons/W Misc. Corresp. bundle 44, John Christian to Sir James Lowther, 2 May 1748, Lowther to Christian, 7 May 1748. LS 11 Mar, 6 May 1749, 16 Feb, 3 Dec 1754. *CJ* xxv, 709, 766, 785, 807. 22 Geo. II c. 6. E. Hughes, 'The Founding of Maryport', *CW2*, lxiv (1964), pp. 306–18.

[38] LS 10, 12 Jan, 2 Feb 1749, 3 Jan 1751. Lutwidge LB, Walter Lutwidge to Sir James Lowther, 21 Jan 1749. CRO D/Cu/6/118, 119. Eaglesham, 'The Growth and Influence', pp. 206–8.

[39] Bouch and Jones, pp. 262, 272. Cullen, *Anglo-Irish Trade*, pp. 84–5.

[40] LS 6, 15 June, 16 Nov 1721. D/Lons/L bundle '5 letters to Whitehaven branch of family 1698–1706', Lord Lonsdale to James Lowther, 7 Dec 1721; Check List 16/12, James Lowther to Lord Lonsdale, 14 Dec 1721.

[41] LS 28 Jan 1735. L. A. Williams, *Road Transport in Cumbria in the Nineteenth Century* (1975), p. 19.

[42] Morris, *Celia Fiennes*, p. 197. HMC *Various Collections*, viii, 232.

[43] Williams, *Road Transport*, p. 27. LS 12 Dec 1734. 'Clerk', p. 306. *CJ* xxiii, 460–1.

[44] *CJ* xxiii, 433.

[45] LS 22 Dec 1733, 18 Feb, 18 Dec 1735, 1 Jan 1736. SL 3 Jan, 9 Feb 1735.

[46] SL 5 Mar 1742, 17 Aug 1744. *Gentleman's Magazine* xviii (1748), p. 5. D/Lons/W Estate Rental 1754.

[47] LS 31 May, 30 Aug 1750. 23 Geo. II c. 40

[48] Lutwidge LB, Walter Lutwidge to Col. Mordaunt, 30 Aug 1740.

[49] SL 14 Oct 1744, 15 Feb 1745, LS 20 Oct 1744, 12, 21 Feb, 3 Nov, 15 Dec 1747, 2 June 1748, 17, 20 Feb 1750.

[50] D/Lons/W Misc. Corresp. bundle 44, John Peile *et al* to Sir James Lowther, 18 Mar 1749, Lowther to Peile, 25 Mar 1749. LS 18 Apr 1749, 16 Feb, 6 Apr 1751.

[51] LS 12 June 1753.

[52] LS 16 Dec 1742, 19 Mar 1745, 8 Oct 1747, 10 May 1748, 15 Feb 1750, 20 Jan 24, 27 Feb, 3, 6 Mar 1753. Lowther to Peter How, 31 Jan 1745 (copy with LS 29 Jan 1745).

[53] Lowther to How, 31 Jan 1745.

[54] D/Lons/W Harbour Trustees' Minutes, meetings of 6 June 1751, 18 Sept 1752. Eaglesham, 'The Growth and Influence', p. 242.

1 C. W. Chalklin, *The Provincial Towns of Georgian England* (1974), p. 19. Peter Clark and Paul Slack, *English Towns in Transition* (Oxford, 1976), pp. 39ff.

2 D/Lons/W James Lowther to Sir John Lowther, 27 Nov 1703. LS 9 Jan 1735, 30 Mar 1723, 25 May 1751.

3 Dalton, *A Descriptive Poem*, p. 15. D/Lons/W Misc. Corresp. bundle 37, Sir Thomas Lowther to Sir James Lowther, 19 Sept 1735; MSS History of Whitehaven Collieries, f. 118. Hutchinson, *Cumberland*, ii, 49.

4 W. G. Hoskins, *The Making of the English Landscape* (Harmondsworth, 1970), pp. 274–8.

5 Custom House Library 82/49 Collector to Customs Commissioners, 30 May 1737.

6 C. A. Edie, 'New Buildings, New Taxes and Old Interests: an Urban Problem of the 1670s', *Journal of British Studies*, vi (1966–7), pp. 35–63. JLLB Sir John Lowther to John Gale, 7 Apr 1685. D/Lons/W Sir John Lowther's Commonplace Book, f. 206.

7 JLLB Sir John Lowther to William Gilpin, 19 Apr 1698.

8 D/Lons/W Sir John Lowther to Thomas Tickell, 8 June 1686, 28 July 1688; William Gilpin to Sir John Lowther, 29 Jan 1696. Christopher Chalklin, 'The Making of Some New Towns, *c*.1600–1720', in C. W. Chalklin and M. A. Havinden (eds), *Rural Change and Urban Growth 1500–1800* (1974), pp. 239–40. *Whitehaven: A Structure for a Restoration Town* (Whitehaven, n.d.). J. V. Beckett, 'Andrew Pellin of Whitehaven', *CW2*, lxxvii (1977), pp. 181–2.

9 LS 14 Mar 1751. D/Lons/W Misc. Estate Papers, extract from the Harbour Trustees' Minutes, 4 Dec 1755.

10 LS 12 Feb 1734. SL 19 Feb 1744.

11 LS 23 Aug 1750. Pennant, *Scotland*, ii, 46. James Eyre Weeks, *A Poetical Prospect of Workington and Whitehaven* (Whitehaven, 1752), p. 14.

12 JLLB Sir John Lowther to John Gale, 7 Apr 1685, to Thomas Tickell, 6 Dec 1685, 9 Nov 1689, to William Gilpin, 5 Feb 1698. D/Lons/W Gilpin to Lowther, 14 Feb 1698; Register of Deeds and Grants Relating to Whitehaven; Estate Ledger 1706–22, fos. 56–64. *The Case of Sir John Lowther . . .*

13 JLLB 29 Whitehaven inhabitants to Sir John Lowther, 19 Feb 1677. D/Lons/W Misc. Corresp. bundle 13, T. Addison to Sir John Lowther, 7 Oct 1678. PRO E/134/31 & 32 Charles II, Hilary no. 26. D/Lons/W Whitehaven Papers, bundle 20; Lawsuits, 'Lowther v Addison'.

14 D/Lons/W William Gilpin to Sir John Lowther, 13 Mar 1695, 22 June 1696, 3 Apr 1697; Cash Books 1708–11, 1714–17, 1717–20. LS 26 Feb 1726, 7 Mar 1727.

15 D/Lons/W Whitehaven Papers, bundle 63; Street Books; Estate Ledgers 1723–37, fos. 200–4; 1737–58, fos. 147–9. LS 5 Nov 1726, 19, 23 Dec 1727, 22 Jan 1730, 2 Jan 1748, SL 9 Nov 1726.

16 JLLB Sir John Lowther to Mr Atkinson, 23 Oct 1686.

17 D/Lons/W Whitehaven Papers, bundle 20; Misc. Estate Papers, petition to Sir James Lowther dated Nov 1723. LS 10 Nov 1722, 25, 29 June 1723. SL 16 Nov 1722, 23 Jan, 5 June, 16 Aug, 20 Dec 1723.

18 D/Lons/W Estate Ledgers 1723–37, fos. 61–2; 1737–58, fos. 37ff; Estate Rental 1754. LS 2 May, 14 Oct 1738. SL 12 Apr 1745. WTB, court of 6 May 1720.

19 D/Lons/W Whitehaven Papers, bundle 85; Estate Ledgers 1723–37, f. 117; 1737–58, f. 152.

20 D/Lons/W Cash Book 1726–28; William Gilpin to Sir John Lowther, 5, 10 Mar

1694; John Gale to Lowther, 14 Feb 1697. JLLB Lowther to Dr Lancaster, 24 Apr, 1 May 1686. SL 26 July 1721. SPCK CR2/2, James Lowther to Henry Newman, 6 June 1716. F. J. G. Robinson and P. J. Wallis, 'Some early mathematical schools in Whitehaven', *CW2*, lxxv (1975), pp. 265–6.

21 D/Lons/W Addnl Listed Acc. 528, papers relating to the old chapel; John Gale to Sir John Lowther, 13 Jan 1695; William Gilpin to Lowther, 9, 19 Jan 1695. JLLB Lowther to Lady Lonsdale, 27 June 1701. SL 26 July 1721, 26 Jan, 29 Mar 1724, 22 Aug, 5 Sept, 17 Oct 1725. LS 2 Apr, 21 May 1724, 6 May 1737.

22 D/Lons/W Whitehaven Papers, bundle 20; Cash Book 1692–9; William Gilpin to Sir John Lowther, 19 July 1693; 'Lowther v Gale'. JLLB 33 Whitehaven people to Sir John Lowther, 3 May 1678. D. Hay, *Whitehaven: A Short History* (Whitehaven, 1968), p. 101. W. Jackson, *Papers and Pedigrees* (1892), i, 234. R. Hopkinson, 'The Appointment of the first minister of St Nicholas's Church, Whitehaven', *CW2*, lxxii (1972), pp. 283–302.

23 D/Lons/W Whitehaven Papers, bundle 29. SL 17 May 1714, 18 Sept 1715, 4 Apr 1716, 13 Nov 1728, 3 Jan 1739, 11 Jan 1744, 16 Jan 1745. LS 17 Apr 1729, 21 Dec 1738. Whitehaven Public Library MS 41 Minute Book, Holy Trinity Church.

24 LS 13 Nov 1750, 21, 30 May, 9, 11 Apr 1751, 11 Feb 1752. D/Lons/W Estate Ledger 1737–58, f. 195. D. P. Sewell, *History Notes on St James' Church, Whitehaven* (Whitehaven, 1972).

25 SPCK CR1/20/15034, 15062, 15070, 15091, 15119; Misc. Letters vol. 6, Henry Newman to Sir James Lowther, 26 July 1739, Lowther to Newman, 9 Aug 1739.

26 LS 26 Dec 1728, 17 Apr 1729.

27 D/Lons/W John Gale to Sir John Lowther, 13 Aug 1693, 28 Jan 1694; William Gilpin to Lowther, 1 Jan, 26 Mar, 22 Sept 1694; Lowther to Gilpin, 18 Sept 1694; MSS History of Whitehaven Collieries, f. 65; Whitehaven Papers, bundle 65. LS 29 May 1725. HMC *Lonsdale MSS*, p. 246.

28 LS 24 July 1725, 28 Feb, 24 Oct 1751. SL 14 Apr 1736. D/Lons/W Misc. Corresp. bundle 44, Sir James Lowther to the Whitehaven ministers, 21 May 1751. Curnock, *Wesley's Journal*, iv, 430–1. Hay, *Whitehaven*, p. 108. Pennant, *Scotland*, ii, 47. Hutchinson, *Cumberland*, ii, 44.

29 JLLB 12 Whitehaven men to Sir John Lowther, Sept 1703. SL 1 Sept 1706, LS 29 May 1753, 30 Mar 1754.

30 SL 2 Apr 1736, 12 Jan 1737. LS 8 Apr 1736. Hay, *Whitehaven*, p. 113.

31 SL 6 Oct, 17 Dec 1736, 12 Jan, 1 July 1737. Carlisle Library, *Whitehaven Weekly Courant*, 20 Jan 1736/7. F. Barnes and J. L. Hobbs, 'Handlist of Newspapers published in Cumberland, Westmorland and North Lancashire', *CW2* Tract Series, xiv (1951), p. 13. G. A. Cranfield, *The Development of the Provincial Newspaper 1700–60* (Oxford, 1962), pp. 202–3.

32 Clark and Slack, pp. 43, 126.

33 PRO E/134/31 & 32 Charles II, Hilary no. 26.

34 *The Case of the Inhabitants of the Town and Port of Whitehaven* (1695).

35 D/Lons/W Whitehaven Papers, bundles 19, 41; Unlisted Whitehaven papers, bundle of misc. harbour papers.

36 D/Lons/W Misc. Corresp. bundle 21, Richard Jackson to James Lowther, 30 July 1708. Hay, *Whitehaven*, p. 101.

37 WTB, court of 4 Oct 1717. LG 4 July 1719. D/Lons/W Harbour Trustees' Minutes, memorandum dated 25 Aug 1719.

38 LS 8 Sept 1719. SL 22 Nov 1719, 25 May, 21, 23 Dec 1720, 8, 11 Jan 1721. LS 24 Dec 1720. D/Lons/W Estate Memoranda Papers box 2, 'Mr Lowther's Advertizement', 2 Mar 1721.

[39] SL 10 Mar 1721.

[40] LS 10 Nov 1721, 10 Nov 1722, 12 Jan, 1 Mar 1723, 5 Mar 1724.

[41] D/Lons/W Addnl List Acc. 528 Gale Papers. SL 6 Aug 1725. Hopkinson, 'The Appointment'.

[42] D/Lons/W Harbour Trustees' Minutes, meeting of 6 Aug 1722. SL 12 Dec 1722.

[43] SL 9 Dec 1743, 9, 15 Mar, 1 Apr 1744. LS 27 Mar 1744. D/Lons/W Harbour Trustees' Minutes, meeting of 8 Mar 1744. WTB court of 6 Apr 1744.

[44] LS 8 Feb 1743, 22 Sept, 2, 6, 9 Oct 1750. Galloway, *Annals*, i, 349.

[45] LS 23 Oct, 3 Nov 1750. *Jollie's Cumberland Guide and Directory Part Two* (Carlisle, 1811), p. 28. D. Hay, *Whitehaven: An Illustrated History* (Whitehaven, 1979), pp. 82–4.

[46] D/Lons/W William Gilpin to Sir John Lowther, 13 Sept 1696; Various Accounts 1705–77. LS 10 Jan, 5, 9 Feb 1740. SL 30 Jan 1740.

[47] SL 2, 4 Oct 1741, 12 Jan 1742. LS 6, 15, 27 Dec 1748, 25 Mar, 13 Apr 1749. D/Lons/W Estate Ledger 1737–58, f. 147. Hutchinson, *Cumberland*, ii, 82. J. Britton and E. W. Brayley, *Topographical, Historical and Descriptive Delineations of Cumberland* (1803), p. 223.

[48] D/Lons/W William Gilpin to Sir John Lowther, 4 June 1693. SL 29 Apr, 1, 6 May 1743. J. Dixon, *A General State of the Whitehaven Dispensary* (Whitehaven, 1800).

[49] SL 11 Mar 1733, 2 Nov 1740. LS 8 Nov 1740.

[50] J. Stevenson, *Popular Disturbances in England 1700–1870* (1979), p. 96. SL 23, 26 Apr 1728.

[51] SL 14 Feb 1742. LS 23, 25 Apr 1751. CRO D/Pen Agents' Correspondence, J. Herbert to Sir John Pennington, 19 Apr, 8 May 1751.

[52] WTB courts of 17 Oct 1755 and 21 Apr 1758.

[53] Clark and Slack, p. 90. PRO E/190/1449/4. D/Lons/W William Gilpin to Sir John Lowther, 3 Feb 1697; Housekeeping Account 1713–17. SL 3 July 1715.

[54] SL 23 Apr, 8, 22 Nov, 25 Dec 1728, 8, 12 Jan, 2, 4 Apr, 31 Dec 1729, 17 Apr 1730, 25 Mar, 24 July 1737, 5, 12 Apr 1741, 28 Oct 1744, 15 Feb, 24 Mar, 3 May 1745. LS 31 Dec 1728, 10 Oct 1740, 22 Feb 1752, 14 Feb 1754. D/Lons/W Colliery Ledger 3, 1727–32; Estate Ledger 1723–37, f. 141, 1737–58, f. 203; Various Accounts 1705–77; Housekeeping Accounts 1737–55.

[55] D/Lons/W Estate Ledger 1723–37, f. 141, 1737–58, f. 203. SL 25 Mar, 24 July 1737.

[56] SL 5, 12 Apr 1741, 28 Oct 1744.

[57] LS 22 Feb 1752.

[58] D/Lons/W Housekeeping Accounts 1737–42. SL 9 Sept 1744. Pennant, *Scotland*, ii, 50.

[59] D. Hay, 'The Fortifications at Whitehaven', *CW2*, lxv (1965), p. 291.

[60] JLLB Sir John Lowther to William Gilpin, 29 Sept 1694. D/Lons/W James Lowther to Sir John Lowther, 25 June, 15 Aug 1702. LS 10 Nov, 22, 27 Dec 1739, 27 Mar, 17 May 1740, 17 Mar 1741. SL 16 Nov, 28 Dec 1739, 1, 11 Feb, 5, 15 Apr 1741, 4 Apr, 11 May 1744. D/Lons/W Harbour Trustees' Minutes, meeting of 26 Aug 1741; Estate Ledger 1737–58, f. 213.

[61] Custom House Library 82/51 Collector to Customs Commissioners, 20 Oct, 14, 30 Nov 1745, 1, 17 Jan 1746. R. C. Jarvis, *The Jacobite Risings of 1715 and 1745* (Carlisle, 1954), p. 325. SL 16 Nov 1715. LS 20, 29 May 1746.

[62] *Jollie's Cumberland Guide*, p. 29.

CONCLUSION

[1] Hyde, *Technological Change*, pp. 181, 183.
[2] Devine, 'Colonial Commerce', pp. 177–90.
[3] J. M. Price, 'The Rise of Glasgow in the Chesapeake Tobacco Trade 1707–75', in P. L. Payne (ed), *Studies in Scottish Business History* (1967), pp. 299–318.
[4] Clemens, 'Rise of Liverpool', p. 215.
[5] SL 27 July, 14 Aug 1743. LS 30 June 1744.
[6] LS 5 Dec 1747, 9 Jan, 9, 16 Feb 1748, 9 May 1749, 9 Jan 1752.
[7] LS 16, 18 Nov, 2 Dec 1749, 23 May 1751. D/Lons/W Misc. Corresp. bundle 44, Sir James Lowther to Peter How, 18 May 1751. *CJ*, xxvi 241.
[8] LS 2 June 1742.
[9] LS 4 Jan 1724, 9 Mar 1736, 7 Nov 1751. SL 24 May 1732.
[10] C. M. L. Bouch, 'Jonathan Boucher', *CW2*, xxvii (1927), pp. 148–9.

APPENDIX 2   SIR JAMES LOWTHER'S INVESTMENTS

[1] P. G. M. Dickson, *The Financial Revolution in England 1688–1756* (1967), p. 294.
[2] Lord Edmond Fitzmaurice, *Life of William, Earl of Shelburne 1737–66*, i (1875), pp. 34–5.
[3] LS 25, 28, 30 Mar, 8, 22 Apr 1732. HMC *Egmont Diary*, i, 263. British Library, Additional MSS, fos. 98, 100–1.
[4] British Library, Additional MSS 25545, fos. 1, 4, 6, 17; 25506, fos. 10, 54, 72–3, 76, 92. LS 3, 6 Feb, 8 Mar, 26 Apr, 9, 12 June 1733. *Gentleman's Magazine*, iii (1733), p. 97. *CJ*, xxii, 129, 164–5. Dickson, *Financial Revolution*, p. 208.
[5] LS 11 Apr 1734, 1 Feb, 17 Apr 1735.
[6] Levens Hall MSS 13/73.
[7] D/Lons/W Cash Trans. Book 1703–54, fos. 1, 5, 112, 115.
[8] W. A. Speck, *Stability and Strife* (1977), pp. 79, 228. D/Lons/W Cash Trans. Book 1703–54, fos. 64, 85, 86. LS 30 Nov 1731. HMC *Egmont Diary*, i, 275.
[9] British Library Harleian MSS 7497, f. 4. D/Lons/W Misc. Corresp. bundle 33, James Lowther to William Gilpin, 4 Feb 1720.
[10] LG 10 Apr 1711. LS 6 Jan, 3 Feb 1732, 28 Dec 1725.
[11] LS 21 May 1726.
[12] D/Lons/W James Lowther to Sir John Lowther, 28 Nov, 2 Dec 1704. LS 4 Jan 1752.
[13] D/Lons/W Cash Trans. Book 1703–54, fos. 57, 67–9, 92, 104, 106, 110, 111, 113, 119–21. India Office Records, L/AG/14/5/4–12.
[14] Christopher Clay, 'The Price of Freehold Land in the later Seventeenth and Eighteenth Centuries', *EcHR*, 2nd series, xxvii (1974), p. 174.
[15] D/Lons/W Deeds Seaton 34/3/31a.

APPENDIX 4   COLLIERY FIGURES

[1] D/Lons/W Misc. Colliery Papers, 'Observations about the measures of coals'.
[2] D/Lons/W Colliery Papers, bundle 42.
[3] D/Lons/W William Gilpin to Sir John Lowther, 30 May 1697.

Bibliography

MANUSCRIPT SOURCES

PUBLIC RECORD OFFICE

B/1/42–44, 4/17 Papers relating to Peter How's bankruptcy
CO/388/86 D15 Board of Trade Petition
E/112/381 no. 75 Sir John Lowther's bill in the Exchequer
E/134/31 Charles II, Mich.28 Cumberland
E/134/31 & 32 Charles II, Hilary No. 26 Cumberland
E/190/1448/6, 8, 11; 1449/1, 4, 6, 12; 1450/15, 20; 1452/10, 16; 1453/1; 1456/5,
    6, 8, 10; 1460/4, 6, 8; 1461/2, 3, 6, 8, 10 Port Books
PC1/4/106 Mar 1728 Evidence taken in the case of William Wood

BRITISH LIBRARY

Additional MSS 25544–45, 25506 South Sea Company Minutes
    32688 f. 34, 32724 f. 182 Newcastle Correspondence
Stowe MSS 747 fos. 101, 102, 131

CARLISLE RECORD OFFICE, CARLISLE

Lonsdale MSS (D/Lons/W, Whitehaven, D/Lons/L Lowther). These have not
    yet been fully catalogued, and any attempt to describe the records in detail is
    attended with considerable difficulty. Since many of the records are referred
    to in the footnotes, the reader is advised to consult these for specific class-marks.
Leconfield MSS
Curwen MSS
Senhouse MSS
Lawson MSS
Pennington MSS
Benson MSS
Lutwidge Letter Books

WHITEHAVEN PUBLIC LIBRARY

MS 30 Token Book
MS 31 Account Book of Sir James Lowther
MS 41 Minute Book, Holy Trinity Church
MS 42 Book of Copy Deeds
MS 43 'Memorials of the Several Collieries'

BIBLIOGRAPHY

CARLISLE PUBLIC LIBRARY

Whitehaven Town Book 1706–82

NORTH OF ENGLAND INSTITUTE OF MINING AND MECHANICAL ENGINEERS, NEVILLE STREET, NEWCASTLE UPON TYNE

William Brown's letter book no. 1, 1749–56
Watson Collection 3093

LEVENS HALL, NR KENDAL, CUMBRIA

Box 13/73 Wills of Sir James Lowther of Whitehaven and Sir William Lowther of Holker (copies)
Correspondence

RED HOW, LAMPLUGH, WORKINGTON, CUMBRIA

Family papers of the Dickinson family

JOHN RYLANDS LIBRARY, MANCHESTER

Bradshaigh MSS 47/2/467, 469, 470, 472, 480, 481, 482

GREATER LONDON RECORD OFFICE

HI/ST/A1/6, 7, A6/5, E2, E13/2 Records of St Thomas' Hospital
A/FH Records of the Foundling Hospital

ST BARTHOLOMEW'S HOSPITAL, LONDON

Ha 1/11, 12 Hospital Records

CUSTOMS HOUSE, LOWER THAMES STREET, LONDON

Customs Letter Books, Whitehaven, 82/42, 47, 49–52, 55

SOCIETY FOR THE PROMOTION OF CHRISTIAN KNOWLEDGE, HOLY TRINITY CHURCH, MARYLEBONE ROAD, LONDON

CR1/9–24, CR2/2
Society's Letters, vols. 12, 26, 28
Miscellaneous Letters, vols. 1, 2, 4, 6, 7

HOARE'S BANK, FLEET STREET, LONDON

Ledgers G–X, 32, 60

BANK OF ENGLAND RECORD OFFICE, ROEHAMPTON

Bank Stock Ledger n. 41, 1753–61, f. 935
Bank Stock Register, no. 11 (Death Book) no. 8272
Private Drawing Office, ledger K–M ledger 119 f. 3575, ledger 189 f. 3241, ledger 196 f. 3221

BIBLIOGRAPHY

3% Annuities 1726, ledger B f. 607, ledger C f. 587.
Reduced Threes Ledger E, f. 3416, Second Subscription ledger B, f. 854
Consols ledger 1, f. 2809
South Sea Old Annuities 1st Subscription ledger 58, f. 139, 2nd subscription ledger 58, f. 348
New South Sea Annuities 1st Subscription ledger 135, f. 142, 2nd Subscription ledger 139, f. 374.

INDIA OFFICE, FOREIGN AND COMMONWEALTH OFFICE, LONDON

L/AG/14/5/4–12, 257, 329, 253

OFFICIAL PUBLICATIONS

Calendars of State Papers Domestic, 1664–1703
Calendars of Treasury Papers, 1556–1734
Calendars of Treasury Books, vols. 4–31, 1672–1717
Calendars of Treasury Books and Papers, 1735–38
Commons Journals
Statues of the Realm
Statues at Large
Historical Manuscripts Commission Reports, *Lonsdale MSS, Downshire MSS, Portland MSS, Egmont Diary*

CONTEMPORARY PRINTED PAMPHLETS

All that have votes at the ensuing election at Whitehaven. n.d.
Bacon, T. *Some Reflections on the Coal Trade.* 1738
The Case of the Inhabitants of the Town and Port of Whitehaven. 1695
The Case of the Masters and Owners of Ships belonging to Whitehaven. n.d.
The Case of the Merchants trading in Tobacco at Whitehaven. 1720
The Case of Sir John Lowther Bart. 1705.
The Case of Some Particular Merchants at Whitehaven. 1715
The Case of Thomas Coates. n.d.
Calculations Relating to the Coal Trade. 1721
Considerations Relating to the Coal Trade. 1720
Dalton, J. *A Descriptive Poem Addressed to Two Young Ladies.* 1755
Harris, W. *Remarks on the Affairs and Trade of England and Ireland.* 1691
A Letter from a Merchant at Whitehaven to his Friend in London. 1730
A Letter from a Merchant in Whitehaven to an Iron Master in the South of England. 1730
The Miserable Case of the Poor Inhabitants of Parton. 1716
Parton is Ruined and Whitehaven in danger. n.d.
The Pulverizing Ironmasters or An Unfair Trial no Trial. 1730
Queries about Parton. n.d.
Queries Relating to the Coal Trade and Harbour of Whitehaven. n.d.
Reasons for Building a Pier, and Making a Harbour at Elnefoot in Cumberland. n.d.
Reasons for Opening the Port of Whitehaven for Importing Irish Wool. n.d.
Reflections on the Coal Trade. n.d.
To the Author of a Scheme for improving and extending the Woolen Manufactures of the County of Cumberland. 1752
Weeks, J. E. *A Poetical Prospect of Workington and Whitehaven.* Whitehaven, 1752
Wood's Pit-Coal Iron. n.d.

265

SECONDARY SOURCES

(Place of publication for books is London unless otherwise indicated. Only items with material specifically relating to west Cumberland are included here. Comparative and other works are cited in the notes.)

Allen, J. S. 'The 1715 and other Newcomen Engines at Whitehaven, Cumberland', *Transactions of the Newcomen Society*, xlv (1972–3).

Ashton, T. S. and Sykes, J. *The Coal Industry of the Eighteenth Century*. Manchester, 1929

Bainbridge, T. H. 'The West Cumberland Coalfield', *Economic Geography*, xii (1936).

Beckett, J. V. 'Landownership in Cumbria 1680–1750'. Unpublished University of Lancaster PhD thesis, 1975.

Beckett, J. V. 'English Landownership in the later Seventeenth and Eighteenth Centuries: the Debate and the Problems', *Economic History Review*, 2nd series, xxx (1977).

Beckett, J. V. 'The Eighteenth-Century Origins of the Factory System: a Case Study from the 1740s', *Business History*, xix (1977).

Beckett, J. V. 'Dr William Brownrigg, FRS: Physician, Chemist and Country Gentleman', *Notes and Records of the Royal Society of London*, xxxi (1977).

Beckett, J. V. 'Andrew Pellin of Whitehaven', *Transactions of the Cumberland and Westmorland Antiquarian and Archaeological Society*, new series (*CW2*), lxxvii (1977).

Beckett, J. V. 'Newcomen Engines at Whitehaven, Cumberland, 1727–40', *Transactions of the Newcomen Society*, xlix (1977–8).

Beckett, J. V. 'Illness and Amputation in the Eighteenth Century: the Case of Sir James Lowther (1673–1755)', *Medical History*, xxiv (1980).

Beckett, J. V. 'The Disinheritance of Sir Christopher Lowther in 1701', *CW2* forthcoming.

Beckett, J. V. 'The Making of a Pocket Borough: Cockermouth 1727–1756', *Journal of British Studies*, forthcoming.

Bouch, C. M. L. *Prelates and People of the Lake Counties*, Kendal, 1948.

Bouch, C. M. L. and Jones, G. P. *A Short Economic and Social History of the Lake Counties, 1500–1830*. Manchester, 1961.

Chalkin, C. 'The Making of some New Towns *c.*1600–1720', in C. W. Chalklin and M. A. Havinden (eds), *Rural Change and Urban Growth 1500–1800*. 1974.

Cullen, L. M. *Anglo-Irish Trade 1660–1800*. Manchester, 1968.

Curnock, N. (ed). *The Journals of the Rev. John Wesley A.M.* 8 vols. 1909ff.

Davis, R. *The Rise of the English Shipping Industry*. 1962.

Eaglesham, A. 'The Growth and Influence of the West Cumberland Shipping Industry, 1660–1800'. Unpublished University of Lancaster PhD thesis, 1977.

Fell, A. *The Early Iron Industry in Furness and District*. Ulverston, 1908.

Fletcher, H. A. 'The Archaeology of the West Cumberland Iron Trade', *Transactions of the Cumberland and Westmorland Antiquarian and Archaeological Society*, old series (*CW1*), v (1881).

Fletcher, I. 'The Archaeology of the West Cumberland Coal Trade', *CW1*, iii (1878).

Ford, P. 'Tobacco and Coal: A Note on the Economic History of Whitehaven', *Economica*, ix (1929).

Galloway, R. L. *Annals of Coal Mining and the Coal Trade*. 2 vols. Newton Abbot, 1970 reprint.

Hainsworth, D. R. 'Christopher Lowther's Canary Adventure: A Merchant Venturer in Dublin, 1632–3', *Irish Economic and Social History*, ii (1975).

Hainsworth, D. R. *Commercial Papers of Sir Christopher Lowther 1611–44*. Surtees Society, vol. clxxxix, 1977.

Hay, D. 'The Fortifications at Whitehaven', *CW2*, lxv (1965).

Hay, D. *Whitehaven: A Short History*. Whitehaven, 1968.

Hay, D. *Whitehaven: An Illustrated History*. Whitehaven, 1979.

Hopkinson, R. 'The Appointment of the first minister of St Nicholas's Church, Whitehaven', *CW2*, lxxii (1972).

Hudleston, C. R. 'An 18th Century Squire's Possessions', *CW2*, lvii (1957).

Hughes, E. 'The Founding of Maryport', *CW2*, lxiv (1964).

Hughes, E. *North Country Life in the Eighteenth Century: Cumberland and Westmorland 1700–1830*. Oxford, 1965.

Hutchinson, W. *History of Cumberland*. 2 vols. 1794.

Hyde, C. K. *Technological Change and the British Iron Industry 1700–1970*. Princeton, 1977.

Jackson, W. *Papers and Pedigrees*. 2 vols. 1892.

Jarvis, R. C. 'The Appointment of Ports in Cumberland, Westmorland and Lancashire north-of-the-sands', *CW2*, xlvii (1947).

Jarvis, R. C. 'Cumberland Shipping in the Eighteenth Century', *CW2*, liv (1954).

Jones, G. P. 'Some Population Problems relating to Cumberland and Westmorland in the Eighteenth Century', *CW2*, lviii (1958).

Jones, G. P. 'The Commercial Interests of Wilfrid Hudleston', *CW2*, lxvii (1967).

Kendall, J. D. 'Notes on the History of Mining in Cumberland and north Lancashire', *Transactions of the North of England Institute of Mining Engineers*, xxxiv (1884–5).

Langton, J. 'Landowners and the development of coal mining in south-west Lancashire, 1590–1799', in H. S. A. Fox and R. A. Butlin (eds). *Change in the Countryside*. 1979.

Lewis, M. J. T. *Early Wooden Railways*. 1970.

Makey, W. H. 'The Place of Whitehaven in the Irish Coal Trade 1600–1750'. Unpublished University of London MA thesis, 1952.

Marshall, J. D. *Furness and the Industrial Revolution*. Barrow in Furness, 1958.

Marshall, J. D. 'Kendal in the late Seventeenth and Eighteenth Centuries', *CW2*, lxxv (1975).

Namier, L. B. 'Anthony Bacon MP, an Eighteenth-Century Merchant', *Journal of Economic and Business History*, ii (1929–30).

Nef, J. U. *The Rise of the British Coal Industry*. 2 vols. 1932.

Nicolson, J. and Burn, R. *Antiquities and History of the Counties of Cumberland and Westmorland*. 2 vols. 1777.

'Northern England: Cumberland and Westmorland', forthcoming in Thirsk, J. (ed), *The Agrarian History of England and Wales*, vol. v, *1640–1750*.

Parson, W. and White, W. *History, Directory and Gazeteer of the Counties of Cumberland and Westmorland*. Leeds, 1829.

Pennant, T. *A Tour in Scotland 1772*. 4th edn. Dublin, 1775.

Phillips, C. B. 'The Gentry in Cumberland and Westmorland 1600–65'. Lancaster PhD thesis, 1973.

Phillips, C. B. 'The Cumbrian Iron Industry in the Seventeenth Century', in W. H. Chaloner and B. M. Ratcliffe (eds), *Trade and Transport*. Manchester, 1977.

Prevost, W. A. J. 'A Journie to Carlyle and Penrith in 1731', *CW2*, lxi (1961).

Prevost, W. A. J. ' "A Trip to Whitehaven to visite the coal works there in 1739" by Sir John Clerk', *CW2*, lxv (1965).

Price, J. M. *France and the Chesapeake*. 2 vols. Ann Arbor, 1973.

Robinson, F. J. G. and Wallis, P. J. 'Some Early Mathematical Schools in Whitehaven', *CW2*, lxxv (1975).

Schubert, H. R. 'The Old Blast-Furnace at Maryport, Cumberland', *Journal of the Iron and Steel Institute*, 172 (1953).

Serjeant, W. 'A Whitehaven–Isle of Man fishing dispute in 1753', *CW2*, lvii (1957).

Sewell, D. P. *History Notes on St James' Church, Whitehaven*. Whitehaven, 1972.

Tickell, R. E. *Thomas Tickell and the Eighteenth-Century Poets 1685–1740*. 1931.

Treadwell, J. M. 'William Wood and the Company of Ironmasters of Great Britain', *Business History*, xvi (1974).

Victoria County History, *Cumberland*. 2 vols. 1905.

Willan, T. S. *The English Coasting Trade 1660–1750*. Manchester, 1938.

Williams, J. E. 'The Growth and Decline of the Port of Whitehaven, Cumberland, 1650–1900'. Unpublished University of Leeds MA thesis, 1951.

William, J. E. 'Whitehaven in the Eighteenth Century', *Economic History Review*, 2nd series, viii (1956).

Williams, L. A. *Road Transport in Cumbria in the Nineteenth Century*. 1975.

Wood, O. 'The Development of the Coal, Iron and Shipbuilding Industries of West Cumberland 1750–1914'. Unpublished University of London PhD thesis, 1952.

Wood, O. 'The Collieries of J. C. Curwen', *CW2*, lxxi (1971).

Index

industries at, 114, 125, 131, 133, 141, 146, 148
legislation for, 70
Lowther purchases at, 20, 49, 52–3, 56
Lowther role in improvements, 158, 170, 171, 206
new town, 58
planned town, 180, 201
population of, 120, 179
wagonway to, 76
mentioned, 54, 157, 161, 167, 177, 203, 208
Maxwell, Robert, 33, 34
merchants
bills of exchange, 115–17
cargoes, 142–5
coal trade, 110
communications, 118, 172, 173
community, 102–3, 112–13, 179–80
customs, 181, 205
enfranchisement, 184
Glasgow, 104, 106, 108, 204
import grain, 197–9
industry, 114–15, 125, 130–1, 154, 208
land purchase, 114
Lowther and, 30, 111, 191–2
origins, 113
store system, 204
tobacco, 7–8
wealth, 113
Whitehaven harbour, 157–8, 168–9, 177
Workington harbour, 159
'Merchants' Quay', Whitehaven, 168
'Merchants' Quay', Workington, 171
Metcalf, John, 67
Milham, James, 112
Millom, 125, 133, 174, 175, 176
Mines Royal Company, 2, 3, 128–9, 132
Molesworth, Robert, 172
Montagu, Duke of, 126
Moor, John, 67
Moor, Thomas, 151
Moore, R. W., 70
Moorside Park, 21
Moresby
coal mining, 50, 77, 81, 142, 160, 166, 167, 170, 230–4, 235–6
industries, 132, 138, 152
Lowther acquisitions, 21–2, 24, 27, 35, 41, 165, 220–6
manor of, 159
wagonway, 76
Morgan, Mr (lighthouse owner), 97
Musgrave, Sir Christopher, 17

nails, 119, 122, 123, 131–2, 142, 154
Navigation Laws, 103–4, 106
Navy Board, 93, 95
Nef, J. U., 38

Netherhall, 49, 134
Newcastle
bills of exchange, 115
coal trade, 38, 61n, 203
coal vend, 52
coal-fuel industries, 121
comparison with Whitehaven, 210
convoys, 95
goods from, 108, 142, 147
iron sales to, 127
road to, 172, 174, 175
tobacco sales at, 109
see also under Tyneside
Newcastle Journal, 171, 188
Newcomen, Thomas, see under steam engines
Newman, Henry, 18
Newry, 89, 98, 100
Nicholson, Timothy, 112
Nicolson, J., 170
non-ferrous metals, 123, 132
Northumberland, 44, 64, 85, 93, 94
Norway, 92, 106, 108, 109, 115, 133, 139
Nowell, John, 5–6

Ogilby, John, 172

Palmer, William, 150
Parliament
Irish, 62, 89, 95–6
Lowthers in, 9, 10, 13, 15, 95–7, 177
merchant petitions to, 205
South Sea Company, 211, 212
turnpike road schemes, 174–7
Workington legislation, 166
mentioned, 160, 190
Parson, W., (Directory author), 119, 154
Partis, Fletcher, 56
Parton
coal exports, 1605, 39
coal mining in sixteenth century, 3
destruction of pier, in 1718, 50, 83, 164; in 1795, 170
establishment of harbour, 15, 46, 158–61, 189
glass made at, 137–8
land at bought by Lowthers, 223–4
legislation for, 177–8
little use post-1737, 169, 171
Lowther control of collieries, 41, 59, 61
'Lowther v Lamplugh', 164–6, 192, 193
Newcomen engine at, 70
rebuilding of pier, 166–9
salt made at, 134
shipbuilding at, 148
size of, 179
wagonway to, 70
mentioned, 24, 156, 157